Wig's Secret War
The Biography of an
SOE Air Operations Expert

To Marie,

Please enjoy the journey.

love

Gavin

Other Bomber Command books from Mention the War

Striking Through Clouds – The War Diary of 514 Squadron RAF
(Simon Hepworth and Andrew Porrelli)
Nothing Can Stop Us – The Definitive History of 514 Squadron RAF
(Simon Hepworth, Andrew Porrelli and Harry Dison)
Lancasters at Waterbeach – Some of the Story of 514 Squadron
(Harry Dison)

A Short War – The History of 623 Squadron RAF
(Steve Smith)
A Stirling Effort – Short Stirling Operations at RAF Downham Market 1942-1944
(Steve Smith)

RAF Bomber Command Profiles by Chris Ward:
83 Squadron
103 Squadron (with David Fell)
106 Squadron (with Herman Bijlard)
300 (Masovian) Squadron (with Grzegorz Korcz)
617 Squadron

'…and in the morning…' Bomber Command Compendiums by Barry Hope:
57 Squadron RAF
630 Squadron RAF
514 Squadron RAF

A Special Duty – A Crew's Secret War with 148 (SD) Squadron
(Jennifer Elkin)
Wig's Secret War – The Biography of an SOE Air Operations Expert
(Gavin Wigginton)
Skid Row to Buckingham Palace
(Ed Greenburgh)
The Boy and the Bomber
(Francois Ydier)
The Pendulum and the Scythe
(Ken Marshall)

The above books are available through Amazon worldwide, as well as from the publisher. For further details or to purchase a signed and dedicated copy, please contact *bombercommandbooks@gmail.com* or visit
www.bombercommandbooks.com

Wig's Secret War
The Biography of an
SOE Air Operations Expert

Gavin Wigginton

Bomber Command Books

from

MENTION
THE WAR
PUBLICATIONS

This edition first published 2017 by Mention the War Ltd., 32 Croft Street, Farsley, Yorkshire, LS28 5HA.

Copyright 2017 © Gavin Wigginton.

The right of Gavin Wigginton to be identified as Author of this work is asserted by him in accordance with the Copyright, Designs and Patents Act 1988.

A CIP catalogue reference for this book is available from the British Library.

ISBN 978-1-911255-19-2

Cover design: Topics - The Creative Partnership www.topicsdesign.co.uk

Cover image: Des Knock www.desknock.co.uk

All photos are attributed to the author unless otherwise stated.

Contents

Sydney Wigginton 1940

Dedication

This book is dedicated to my mother Eunice Wigginton (Mrs Wig, Grand-mamma, or Mummy as she was variously known) who, although at times it must have been sad and even painful, kept the memory of my father alive. There is a brief biography of her life in Appendix 1, and I only wish I could have shared with her the story about her husband which I have uncovered.

Apart from its wider appeal, this record of Sydney Wigginton's ("Wig's") life has been written for all those who count themselves as members of the Wigginton clan.[1] We should celebrate the story, the character, and the achievements of our father, grand-father, great-grand-father, and otherwise family member. He was one of England's finest.

At the time of writing, the only member of our family still alive who knew Wig is his first son Michael, and his contact was fleeting including the memory of a young man pushing him around on his bicycle when he was a child in the 1940s. However, having researched Wig's life, I feel that I have come to know him by his deeds, and by what was said of him. And I am the richer and wiser for it.

Thinking of the man in the troubled times of the Second World War, one quote comes to mind. Edmund Burke is reported to have said *"The only thing for the triumph of evil is for good men to do nothing".*[2] Wig was one of many who confronted the evil that faced the world in 1939, took responsibility, and tried to do the right thing to the best of their ability. In many respects, I believe that his story defines who the Wigginton family are, and should be. And we must never forget him.

---

[1] Throughout this book, for convenience, I will refer to Sydney Wigginton as "Wig", although he often referred to and signed himself as "Wigs" which was I think a diminutive of "Wiggers". As a matter of interest, and in keeping with the military custom, his war-time contemporaries mainly referred to him as Wigginton.

[2] Edmund Burke PC was an 18th Century Irish statesman who, after moving to live in England, served for many years in the House of Commons as a member of the Whig Party. The quote, from around 1770, is apocryphal.

Acknowledgements

Although only one name appears as the author on the title page of this book, no biography of a deceased person can be constructed without the help and co-operation of a huge number of people to all of whom I extend a warm thanks.

My first acknowledgement is of course to my late mother, Eunice Wigginton. As I discovered after her death, she kept some important papers which turned out to be vital source material during the re-construction of Wig's life. And, from interviewing her before she died, I had the benefit of her personal memories of him and their life together.

For information about the ancestral home of North Luffenham, I would like to thank the Church Warden of St John the Baptist Church, Mrs Janet Whittaker, who not only shared her local knowledge with me, but was kind enough to provide a cup of tea to an unannounced visitor from a foreign land one warm summer afternoon in 2015.

Noel Gubbins, President of the High Pavement Society, Jane Parker who is Operations Manager of New College Nottingham, and Colin Salsbury provided valuable information on Wig's school days. Robert Bartlett, local Surrey historian, provided interesting material on the village of Brockham and Brockham Park where Wig and Eunice lived for part of the War. On Wig's early life, I would also like to thank the staff of the Nottinghamshire County and Leicestershire County Archives for their help in pursuing the needles in the haystacks.

I am greatly indebted to Jennifer Brookman, archivist at the Mercian Regiment Archives, who was most helpful in tracing the history of the Sherwood Foresters Regiment during the time when Wig joined the regular army through to his transfer to SOE. I am also grateful to Dr Anthony Morton of the Sandhurst Collection for his assistance in piecing together an account of life at Sandhurst College in the 1940s.

I would like to thank all the authors with whom I have spoken and corresponded on SOE matters. In particular, Roderick Bailey, who has written several books on SOE, provided a wealth of background information on the organisation as well as a number direct references to Wig which he had encountered in his own research. I am also indebted to all the other authors listed in the bibliography, for the wealth of information provided on war time history and SOE activities, and particularly Jennifer Elkin for her encouragement and contacts.

I am especially grateful to all the people who helped in locating my father's final resting place in Mewaing, and the site of the crash of the Dakota Flight KN 584 in Myanmar. My friend Dick Gupwell gave me an important lead, by introducing me to Sally Maclean of H4FA and the Royal Commonwealth Ex-Services League.[3] Sally, and her associate Lt Colonel Sam Pope, provided helpful advice and introductions to local Karen people, including Naw Jercy and her son Ephraim who made the epic journeys on my behalf to the burial site at Mewaing in 2014 and 2016. My friend Robert Agnew and his son Toby introduced me to the journalist, Tom Kean, who provided important exposure about the crash in Burma, through his story in the Myanmar Times and subsequent article in Frontier Myanmar magazine, and introduced me to Khaing Tun who did some field work for me in Myanmar.[4] [5] I must also mention the Rt Hon the Viscount Slim who is the son of General William Slim, British Defence Attaché in Yangon Colonel Tony Stern, Sue Raftree at the MOD, and Nic Andrews and Thet Mon who helped me to achieve official recognition by the CWGC of the burial site in Mewaing.[6]

---

[3] H4FA is an organisation called "Help for the Forgotten Allies" which provides aid to veterans in Myanmar.

[4] Tom Kean is an award winning Journalist based in Yangon.

[5] The government changed the name of the country from Burma to Myanmar in 1989, and at the same time changed the names of many cities, towns and geographical features. In this book, I use the name Myanmar for all references to the country post that date. Similarly, for all references to the city of Rangoon post 1989, I use the name Yangon.

[6] I met with Lord Slim at the House of Lords in July 2015. He provided helpful information and advice on a range of matters.

On the details of the work of SOE Force 136 in the Far East thanks are due to Matt Poole, who provided maps and other material on Allied air operations in the Far East including the work of 357 Squadron and 358 Squadron, Duncan Gilmour who is the grandson of Lt Colonel Edgar Peacock who was the commander of the *Otter* zone of *Operation Character* in war time Burma, and various veterans of the Karen Hill Tribes who provided eye witness accounts of SOE exploits.

I would also like to thank Ian Wigginton, the grandson of Wig's brother James, who provided some insights into the wider Wigginton family history.

I wish to note and acknowledge that some general information about the history and events of the war in Europe, North Africa, and the Far East are modified versions of what is available on the public record through Wikipedia and other similar sources.

Finally, I would like to thank a number of people who have assisted me in bringing this book to completion. In particular, Martin Alexander, John Atkin, Roderick Bailey, Roderick Burgess, Patrick Coghlan, and Tom Kean were generous with their time in reading and giving feedback on the text. And I am indebted to Simon Hepworth of Mention the War Publications for his gracious and diligent work in achieving publication.

Introduction

This book was written over a period of three years between 2013 and 2016, and provides the story of the author's voyage of discovery about his father. First and foremost it is a biography of Sydney Wigginton ("Wig"), including his origins, early adult life, and war time experience before his untimely death in 1945. In particular, because Wig was an air operations expert with Britain's undercover organisation the Special Operations Executive ("SOE"), this includes an account of that organisation's part in the Second World War operating from Cairo, Italy and the Far East. There is also extensive contextual material about the world in which he lived, including the events and conduct of the Second World War from political, military and covert points of view. Wherever possible, I have sought to provide references to identify the origins of the material presented.

As I commenced research, I quickly came to realise that my enterprise was a far from straightforward matter. Apart from the fact that Wig died some 70 years before I started the journey, most of his formative years were completely unknown, either to me, or to any other living members of the family. I was also confronted with the fact that, whilst apparently being a member of the regular armed forces, during the final years of his short adult life he lived under cover and did not survive to tell the tale.

In the course of my investigations, two major areas of mystery about his personal life emerged. From when I was quite young, I distinctly remember my mother telling me that Wig had had a difficult childhood, with the death of his parents and a period of living with a "guardian". According to my mother, it was something about which he didn't like to talk. Over time, although I remember various explanations for the death of his parents, the version that stuck with me was that they had both been killed in a road accident in the 1920s. The eventual truth of the matter, which was revealed through lengthy research using the British Census data and records of Births, Deaths and Marriages, is that the identity of Wig's father is actually unknown and that he was for all intents and purposes an orphan.

The second mystery of Wig's early life was something I just stumbled on when looking at the Marriage Certificate for his wedding to my mother Eunice in 1939. There, boldly presented on the Certificate, was the name of a witness to the marriage, James Edward Wigginton. And later, when I got records from the MOD, the name James Edward Wigginton popped up again. This time, James was identified as Wig's brother and immediate next of kin (prior to his marriage). None of the living members of the family known to me at the time had ever heard of James, and the absence of any recognition of his existence was immediately the source of speculation. Again, this matter was resolved by lengthy research. The truth is that Wig did indeed have a younger brother, who survived him by more than 60 years. And, before and during the war, it would seem that there was a close bond and normal family relationship between them. But, after the war, for some reason there was a falling out between surviving family members. As a result, the two parts of the family ceased communication and went their separate ways. The children of Wig and James, and their successors, lived in blissful ignorance of each other until I tracked down James' grandson Ian Wigginton in 2015.

The material particular to Wig's war time activities is drawn from official records at the British Ministry of Defence ("MOD"), material from the Mercian Regiment Archives, the Sandhurst Collection, references in various books about SOE, letters from his colleagues and friends, the SOE papers held by the British National Archives in Kew, and some anecdotal material arising from interviews of retired combatants available from the records held by the Imperial War Museum.[7][8] The number of references to him, in official and anecdotal records, is quite extraordinary, and it is amazing to me that I spent 68 years of my life blissfully unaware of this information waiting to be

---

[7] The Mercian Regiment Archives, which are held at the Chetwynd Barracks in Toton, Nottinghamshire, incorporate material for a number of regiments including the Sherwood Foresters who have been consolidated into the Mercian Regiment.

[8] The Sandhurst Collection is based in the vaults of old Sandhurst College, Sandhurst, Camberley, Surrey which I visited in July 2015.

discovered in so many places.

Obtaining access to all this personal data was quite a challenge. In particular, undertaking research of the non-electronic hard copy SOE files and other records at the British National Archives and Imperial War Museum requires patience and fortitude. The search for relevant information is almost literally like "looking for a needle in a haystack". One cannot, as we have become accustomed in the electronic age, just start browsing. The hard copy system requires structured requests for information, and diligent pursuit of trails through a labyrinth of documentation.

In presenting the material about SOE, I have chosen to present a fairly extensive picture of the history, activities, and character of the organisation which so dominated Wig's existence in the latter part of his young life. I have done this because, although this interrupts the flow of the biography, this book is designed to be read by a public (as opposed to scholars of the subject) for whom SOE and their air operations may be a mystery. I have also sought to provide information about the individuals and places involved in the momentous events which were unfolding. This extends to providing insight into the lives of both agents in the field (British Liaison Officers, or BLOs), the air crews that delivered and collected the people and goods used by the resistance forces, and the physical and social environment in which SOE staff lived "in foreign parts". As a reference for the more than 80 missions and operations mentioned in this book, in Appendix 2, I have provided a summary of the Code Names used for the various units and activities. Apart from being relevant context, when reading the source material it was difficult not to be intrigued and excited by the activities and places of work of such an amazing group of men and women. And I have endeavoured to pass this on to the reader.

In compiling this information, I have relied on the contents of more than 40 books written by people who either worked for SOE in the 1940s or are current scholars of the organisation, and on material gathered from visits in 2015 to the British National Archives and the Imperial War Museum. Most of the books which provide first-hand accounts were written in the 30 years following the end of the war, by people who are sadly now long deceased, and relatively few were current publications. A number made direct references to Wig's work, and it is one of my regrets that I did not start this venture 25 years ago!

In the search for personal information, the names of certain people known to Wig cropped up repeatedly. Just as an example, one of Wig's SOE associates was a man named Sir John Anstey who, after the war, became a Director of Imperial Tobacco in Nottingham, a company for whom my mother worked in the 1930s[9]. After Wig's death, he was a good friend to the family and, in the late 1940s, Eunice worked with him at the University of Nottingham in establishing the Convocation department.[10] After two years working with Rolls Royce Aero-engines, I was then myself an employee of Imperial between 1970 and 1985.[11]

The book also includes some broader contextual material relating to the war. That's because one simply cannot understand the work and achievements of SOE without appreciating the related strategies, places, events, and circumstances. In trying to set this context, I was drawn into reading an immense amount of background information available in a large number of books on the history of World War Two, and a range of other material sourced via internet searches. Based on this material, I have endeavoured in particular to provide appropriate accounts of national histories, and war time events in North Africa, Southern Europe and the Far East which are the main areas where Wig worked. In this respect, the book is therefore not only a biography but also an account of four wars of national liberation involving resistance movements, specifically in Greece, Yugoslavia, Italy, and Burma. Importantly, in chronological order, Wig had a significant role in the Balkans in 1943, in Yugoslavia, Italy and Eastern Europe in 1944, and in Burma in 1945.

---

[9] Eunice worked for John Player & Son.

[10] Sir John Anstey was a long-time member of the Nottingham University Council.

[11] I worked variously for the Food, Brewing and Packaging Divisions, and the Group Head Office, of Imperial Group of which Imperial Tobacco was a major Division.

The writing of this book has been a cathartic experience. Before I started my research, I knew very little about my father. I now have a real understanding of who he was, what he was like, and what he did both before and during the war. And, after all the research, I have to say that in many respects I feel that I have a great deal in common with him. This is not least because of the career he chose in what today would be called logistics. In the 1960s, I studied for a degree in Operations Research (itself a methodology developed in war time which involved the development of systems for making optimal use of military resources), and then spent nearly ten years of my life in developing logistical systems for a variety of commercial operations.[12]

Having obtained a sense of Wig's character and personality, I feel that I share many traits with him including his commitment to physical fitness, his tendency to over-commit himself, his generosity of spirit, and his good-humoured nature. Writing as someone in late middle age, it is also worth mentioning that this is a book about a young person. Thus, I selected the words *"Forever Young"* as the title. We will only ever know him as a young man, because that's all he had a chance to be. Having completed my research, I have no hesitation in saying that he was someone I would have been privileged to know and happy to call a friend. And I am proud to be his son.

Finally, I need to comment on the structure of the book. A chronology for Wig's life is provided in Appendix 3, and the early and final Parts (One to Four, and Nine to Eleven) fit naturally into a chronological order. However, the chapters on the war in Europe were less easy to present. Between November 1942 and February 1945, Wig spent nearly all his time in two places, Cairo in Egypt, and Bari in the south eastern Puglian region of Italy. Cairo is a special case as far as

---

[12] The first Operations Research ("OR") Centre was established by the Ministry of War in 1941. Interestingly for our story, OR units were subsequently established in Cairo, Italy, and India. Amongst other things, OR Analysts developed systems and methodology to optimise the use of radar for aerial search, prepare flight plans to minimise fuel usage, and simulate the impact of alternative tank movements.

SOE activity is concerned. It was always a relatively independent centre for SOE operations into a wide range of Mediterranean countries, and is therefore the subject of a fairly lengthy section (Part Six). During his time there, whilst he was learning his air operations area of expertise, Wig spent a good deal of his time working on missions to Greece, and this Part therefore includes a chapter (Chapter 17) on the war and SOE activities in that country. In reading this material, it will be evident that there are few direct references to activities in which Wig had a hand. More than anything, this is because more than 80% of SOE files have been destroyed either by accident or design and the evidence has been lost.

Part Seven of the book, which relates to Wig's time in Italy, covers the period when SOE was supporting covert operations throughout the south and east of Europe. The material presented covers the war in Italy in 1944 (Chapters 18 and 19), operations organised out of Bari in southern Italy (Chapters 20 and 21), and a brief account of SOE activities in other countries where Wig was involved (Chapter 22). Because of its importance, in Part Eight of the book, I have presented separate chapters on the war in Yugoslavia. An account of his final years, which were spent in the Far East, is presented in Parts Nine and Ten.

In Part Eleven, the book concludes with an account of how the author was able to locate the site of Wig's air crash and burial, and secure a lasting memorial to his exploits.

Now read on!

Gavin Wigginton

1 March 2017

Part One: Origins

1: Some Unexpected Revelations

When I was at prep school in the 1950s, a friend of mine said to me *"So your Dad was a war hero?! I heard he was one of the Dam Busters."* Somewhat taken aback, but instantly proud, I didn't deny it. I never found out how he came by his information, but when I got home I asked my mother about my father's role in the war. She showed me his OBE medal, and said that he wasn't one of the *Dam Busters* but had done other heroic things.

A few days passed, and then I asked some other questions about my father. My mother dug out some pictures, and reinforced the view that he was someone of whom I should be proud. Around the same time, I also asked about how I came to have so many Christian names – Gavin Sydney Stewart (or "Guss" as I used to be known at school). My mother gave me what seemed to be a very straight forward explanation, into which I read nothing in particular at the time. She told me that I was named after my father ("Sydney") and one of his friends, Gavin Stewart, with whom he worked in the latter years of the war. In the course of writing this book, I found out that this man was a great deal more than my father's friend. In 1945, Lt Colonel Gavin Stewart CBE was the deputy head of the Special Operations Executive ("SOE") mission in the Far East.

A few years later, I was rummaging through some papers in the attic at our home in Nottingham, as teenagers do, and I found a heavily worn brief case inside of which were some papers, including a letter signed by an American General named Twining.[13] I showed them to my mother, and she swept them up and said they must go to the government. I don't know why she did that, except that it was probably in keeping with how my mother generally dealt with anything to do with the war – better not discussed. But perhaps she was also staying true to what Wig must have always told her, that he did secret work which was not for prying eyes. Anyway, there I left it - for quite a few years.

In the 1980s, I emigrated to Australia and, in 1995, my mother who was then aged 78, joined me in the Antipodes, moving to a bungalow a few kilometres from where I then lived in Melbourne. Seven years later, in 2002, she contracted bowel cancer and, not knowing how long she would live, I interviewed her about her life. In the course of several conversations, of

---

[13] I subsequently found this same letter in Wig's SOE Personnel File in 2015. The full transcript is provided in Chapter 33.

which I made an extensive written record, she talked at length about Wig, and a picture of my father emerged which was quite intriguing.

In particular, although she was unable to provide details about any of the missions, she revealed quite a bit about my father's wartime activities. She began with the period before he went overseas, when they had lived for a time in a lodge within a military installation near a small village close to Dorking in Surrey. Subsequently, he been a member of the 8th Army in North Africa during the crucial period of the two battles at El Alamein. Then there was a time when he was parachuting into occupied Europe, and returning to England via Lisbon to meet up with her at the Rembrandt Hotel in London. She went to tell me that he had "been involved" with Marshal Tito in Yugoslavia, and that he been very busy in Egypt, Italy and the Far East.[14] And she added that more about all of this could be found in a set of letters sent from Cairo, Calcutta, and other locations which she kept in a safe place. Even more intriguing, my mother also indicated that he had died in a plane crash in Burma, although the circumstances were not known.

On a more personal note, she divulged that, according to his close friend Leonard Ward with whom he had worked during peace time, Wig was a daring man whose work involved taking considerable risks. And she tentatively divulged that Wig had had an unhappy childhood, and that after his death she never remarried because she could not find another man good enough to replace my father as a parent to my brother and me.

Arising from these revelations, in 2003, my mother agreed that we should contact the UK Ministry of Defence, with the aim of obtaining further details about my father's war time activities including the circumstances of the plane crash in Burma. Eventually, we received a reply which included a brief and largely unrevealing history of his military record, and some details about the date (7 September 1945) and place (Mewaing – pronounced "may-why") of his plane crash.[15] At the time, I investigated the possibility of visiting Burma (now called Myanmar) but, languishing under a military dictatorship, that country did not welcome visitors. And there the matter lay.

---

[14] The Rembrandt Hotel still operates as a hotel, located in Thurloe Place (opposite the Victoria and Albert Museum in Kensington, London). I visited this establishment in 2015. It is much changed, with no memorabilia from earlier days. However, the main Dining Room is still in the same place, with large mirrors at either end which according to staff were there in the 1940s.

[15] My mother also recalled that, in 1946, the Ministry of Defence had offered to arrange a visit to this burial site – an opportunity she declined because circumstances dictated other priorities.

On 20 May 2009, my mother died, and I inherited all the materials relating to my father. As often happens following a death, whilst I was conscious that there was unfinished business, my first instinct was to file things away for another day and the papers went into storage. In fact, 2009 was not a good year for me. Apart from the death of my mother, my son Andrew and I were caught up in the devastating fires which swept through Victoria in February of that year, and we narrowly escaped death as my home in Callignee burnt to the ground. Fortunately, important family papers survived with us where we sheltered in the shed.[16]

In 2012, I completed the rebuilding of the house at Callignee and started to consolidate the remnants of my records. In the course of sorting through various papers inherited from my mother, I came across the stuff relating to my father most of which was in an old tin box, including his wallet engraved with the oak leaves of his regiment the Sherwood Foresters, a military pass from 1940 when he was at Sandhurst Military College, his compass, a dagger, the OBE medal and related citation, some letters, and some photos of the place where he was buried. A latent curiosity about my father was aroused, and I decided that it was time to find out more.

On a trip to the UK in 2013, I visited the British National Archives in Kew to discover what had led to his receiving the OBE, and I started to uncover an amazing story about his life in the Special Operations Executive ("SOE"). Suddenly, there was so much more to know and an amazing journey had begun.

---

[16] I am not Andrew's biological father, but he is in every other respect my son.

2: Meet the Ancestors

Searching for the ancestors has become quite a preoccupation for many people in recent times. Before getting into this project, and apart from finding out about my father, I wasn't particularly enamoured with the idea. In the event, I found the work quite compulsive. A full account of this exercise is provided in Appendix 4, and an important outcome which is the family tree is found in Appendix 5.

My research eventually revealed that Wig's ancestors lived in the village of North Luffenham in the English County of Rutland. This is an ancient centre of population whose history stretches back to Saxon times.[17] By the 18th Century (when the last Stuart monarch Queen Anne was on the throne, and there is factual evidence of Wiggintons living in the village), the population was around 500, and local activity was dominated by farming. Today, North Luffenham is a village of 2,034 acres with a population of 700 people, including the farming community, workers in the neighbouring water industry (the adjacent Rutland Water is a major wetland feature) and commuters travelling to neighbouring industrial centres.[18] Not surprisingly, when I visited the village in 2015, I felt a strange affinity for the place. And when I found the graves of my ancestors buried in the graveyard of St John the Baptist Church, I could sense their presence and my connection going back more than 300 years.

In tracing the family back to these roots, the earliest member of the family that I was able to find was a John Wigginton who was born in the village around 1710. He, and the next two generations (son William was born in 1745, and grandson James was born in 1780) were all farm workers.[19] [20]

The first member of the family for whom we have some material evidence, in that his gravestone sits leaning against a wall in the graveyard of St John the Baptist church, is James Wigginton who was born in January 1813. He died aged 75 on 16 August 1888. James was married to Elizabeth Beale (named as Betsy on his gravestone) who came from the neighbouring

---

[17] Excavations in 1900 revealed a Saxon Cemetery to the north of the village, and artefacts dated back to the 5th Century.

[18] The estimate of 2,034 acres and other data comes from "British History On-line".

[19] John Wigginton was married to Elizabeth.

[20] William's date of birth, 29 May 1745, and his parentage were recorded in the North Luffenham Register.

village of Edith Weston.

James and Elizabeth had a son called Isaac (also Wig's middle name), who was born on 17 March 1847. Isaac lived his early years in North Luffenham and married a local girl with the same name as his mother, Elizabeth. In the 1870s, no doubt in search of work and a better life, this family moved to Toton in Nottinghamshire which at the time was a booming centre of the railway industry. The Census of 1881 shows that Isaac was a Rail Guard and the records of the local Parish Council also show that, in his later years from 1895 until 1907, he was a Parish Constable for which he was paid 10 shillings per annum.[21] [22] This was a respected position in the community, with some status including responsibility for maintaining order and even resolving local disputes. Isaac died at the age of 69 in 1916, and his wife Elizabeth died in 1917. Isaac and Elizabeth had at least ten children including a girl called Annie born in 1879 who had a daughter named Hilda (Wig's mother).

Establishing the connection of Wig to this family line was far from straight forward. What follows is the story of how I came to make the link. Before undertaking my research, the main source of information about Wig's parents was his Ministry of Defence ("MOD") record of 1939 in which it was stated that his parents were Arthur and Alice. This parentage was subsequently repeated in a number of places including Wig's Wedding Certificate, a newspaper article published when he died, and the CWGC citation for his memorial at Taukkyan cemetery in Yangon, Myanmar.

Consistent with this information, the family story which I had been given by my mother was that Arthur and Alice were killed when Wig was young, and that he was raised for some years in Lenton (an inner suburb of Nottingham) by guardians whom we know to be a Mr and Mrs James Sandell who lived at 6 Kennington Road, Old Radford.[23] [24] Interestingly, given what I now know about the family, Mr Sandell was a Railway worker. Based on this evidence, when I commenced my research at the National Archives in 2015, I sought to identify Arthur and Alice in the Census and Births/Deaths/Marriages records. Whilst I found an Arthur and an Alice of

---

[21] From 1894, Toton was administered by Stapleford District Council. Currently, it sits in a district administered by Broxtowe Borough Council within the City of Nottingham.

[22] Isaac's pay is recorded in the Minutes of the Toton Parish Council held in the vestry of the Church on 21 February 1895. The Minute Book is held in the Nottinghamshire Archives.

[23] According to the Wedding Certificate, Arthur Wigginton was a lace manufacturer.

[24] The house in Kennington Road no longer exists and is currently the site of a car park.

the right age in the Nottingham area, I could not find any information which suggested that they were married, died in an accident, or which linked them to the village of Toton. I couldn't make sense of it.

Then I uncovered another official record which took me by surprise. In his confidential SOE Personnel File, whilst confirming that he was born in the village of Toton, Wig stated that his father was John Wigginton and that his mother was Hilda Bestwick.[25] He also recorded what I had discovered from his Wedding Certificate - that he had a younger brother named James Edward who was born in 1916 (he lived happily until 2006).[26] I now set out on a hunt for the identity of John Wigginton and Hilda Bestwick. According to my examination of Birth, Death and Marriage records for the period, and the Census returns for 1901 and 1911, the only persons who fitted the location and age profile were two teenagers.[27] If this was correct, then John would only have been 16 years old when Wig was born, and Hilda would have been 17. Despite the plausibility of this data, I felt some discomfort with the line of enquiry. In particular, I could not find any reference to the marriage of John and Hilda.

However, I then found a reference to the same Hilda getting married to someone called Longdon in September 1913 and this did not square with the birth of Wig in December 1913 or James Wigginton in 1916. Furthermore, I was unable to find a record of the death of either of the Longdons during the 1920s when Wig's parents were supposed to have been killed.

Stumped by all this uncertainty, and after several days of further archival search and a good deal of reflection, there was only one way to proceed. Indeed, with the benefit of hind-sight, I should have done this earlier. I applied for a copy of Wig's Birth Certificate. This took a few days to arrive from the General Register Office, and the evidence it provided was a turning point. The Certificate stated that Wig's mother was a Hilda *Wigginton* and that the father was unknown. There was no mention of a John Wigginton, and no mention of the mother's surname as being "Bestwick". Tellingly, the official record stated that "Wigginton" was Hilda's **maiden** name. As further corroborative evidence, the birth was recorded in the presence of a

---

[25] SOE Record HS 9/1589/8 which I accessed in May 2015

[26] I first discovered the existence of James Edward Wigginton when looking at Wig and Eunice's Wedding Certificate in 2013 where James is identified as a witness. The full story about verifying his existence, and discovering his family including living members is given in Appendix 6.

[27] These records are kept at the National Archives in Kew.

grandmother named Elizabeth (wife of Isaac as I was to identify later which was Wig's middle name).

It didn't take me long to realise what this meant, and I immediately wondered about Wig's brother. So I sent for his Birth Certificate, which was similar to Wig's. Hilda Wigginton was again stated as the mother and there was no information about a father. Needless to say, by now I was in a state of surprise and, initially, even shock. It is one thing to find that there was no corroborative evidence for the story one had been told by one's family about the death of one's grand-parents. But to find that Wig had given two different answers about parentage in official records was even more startling. Of course, one has to realise that, in those days, illegitimacy was a matter of some shame, and a cover-up was entirely plausible.

So now I began a completely new search for Hilda Wigginton. And, in the family records at the National Archives, a woman immediately presented herself. There was only one Hilda Wigginton in Toton in 1913 and 1916. As I found out from her Birth Certificate, she was born in 1895 and was the daughter of another unmarried Toton girl called Annie Wigginton who was the daughter of Isaac and Elizabeth (the grandmother Elizabeth mentioned on Wig's Birth Certificate). It was all adding up.

Annie's occupation was stated as being a Lace Worker, and Hilda was a Dress Maker. The reference to lace was interesting as, on his Wedding Certificate, Wig's father was said to have been a lace manufacturer. It is hard not to speculate as to how Hilda became pregnant. The occupation of Dress Maker would have involved visiting the homes of wealthy people to make clothing for the lady folk, and one can only guess about the people that Hilda may have met through this work. However, it is intriguing that, although his mother and guardians were of modest means, Wig went to a fee paying school. He was also admitted as an Officer Cadet at Sandhurst College which usually required some social status and, until 1940, was the subject of a significant entry fee and living costs. One wonders therefore whether there was a person of means fulfilling a parental responsibility from behind the scenes.

The plot thickens when you bring Wig's brother James into the picture. Given that there is no name given as a father on the Birth Certificate of either boy, it is by no means a certainty that their father was the same man. Indeed, given that James was sent to a state school and served in the ranks during the war, it seems likely that they had different fathers and that James' father was a man of lesser means than Wig's. Whatever the truth, it would seem that no

27

father assumed a direct role in their early life. In Wig's early years, it is reasonable to assume that he was living with Hilda and her mother and even her grandparents (who were alive until 1916/17) with James joining them in 1916. And the boys were kept together when they transferred to their guardians.

The process and means of guardianship is also of interest. In the early 20th Century adoption law was in a state of flux. The old "Court of Wards", which had been the vehicle for adoption for centuries, was wound up in 1898. And a new system for adoption was not established until 1927 with the introduction of the Adoption Act. In the critical intervening period, adoptions were managed by local charitable institutions, and often on an informal basis. I researched adoptions recorded in Nottingham in the period 1910-1920, but could turn up no reference to the name Wigginton. I am therefore inclined to conclude that the boys were adopted through a relatively informal arrangement with people known to the Wigginton family who certainly had no children of their own.

And there are some final thoughts. My research shows that Annie Wigginton (Wig's grand-mother) died in 1940 in her 60s, and that Hilda (Wig's mother) died in January 1946 aged 53. One wonders, despite the adoption arrangement, whether the grand-mother and/or mother had any contact with Wig and/or James in the years that followed their adoption. If the Sandells were indeed family friends, then maybe they did keep in touch. But, we have no evidence for this. In any event, it is worth noting that this kind of arrangement was not that uncommon in the first half of the 20th Century. One does wonder though whether Hilda knew what happened to hers sons and, in particular, whether the shock of Wig's sudden death had anything to do with her own premature demise so soon afterwards. And then there is the question of a secret benefactor, if indeed there was one. Did that man, a father that would not own his own son, know of what happened to him? Again, probably, we will never know.

Given all the above information, Wig's early childhood is a matter of guess-work. When the Census taken in 1921 becomes available, it will probably be possible to pin-point the whereabouts of both Wig (then aged 7) and James (then aged 5) during their critical early years. Until then, we can only speculate about what may have happened. For want of an explanation, and until better information comes to hand, I believe that the circumstances of Wig's early years are probably something like the account in the next Chapter.

3: Childhood

Sydney Isaac Wigginton was born in Toton on 10 December 1913. With the First World War looming (war was declared on 28 July 1914), it was a turbulent time. Apart from the outbreak of hostilities, during the first year of Wig's life the first sedan type car came into existence, Woodrow Wilson was inaugurated as US President, the foundation stone of the Australian capital in Canberra was laid, suffragette Emily Pankhurst's fight for women's emancipation led to a three years' jail sentence, the first performance of Stravinsky's Rite of Spring provoked riots in New York, and the UK Parliament approved Home Rule for Ireland.

Sydney Wigginton aged 3, 1916

Wig was initially taken care of by his mother (Hilda), with the help of his grand-mother (Annie) and great-grandmother (Elizabeth). In 1916, James was born. Sadly, his great grandfather Isaac died in 1916, and his great grandmother Elizabeth died in 1917. For a time, Wig and James lived with their mother and grand-mother. But eventually, with the absence of a father, and challenged by financial circumstances, Hilda decided to transfer them to guardians.

In those days, and with no legal framework, this was probably concluded informally, with friends of the family taking on responsibility for the children in good faith and perhaps with access arrangements for Hilda. Indeed, the guardian James Sandell may well have been a family friend through the work he had undertaken on the railways with grand-father Isaac who did work of a similar nature. However, it is possible that the children were in some way abandoned, or that their mother was seen by the authorities to be incapable of caring for them. In that case, they would almost certainly have been taken into care by a charity who would have found foster parents and/or guardians.

29

Whatever the truth of the matter, given the location of their Primary School in Radford, it would seem that the Sandells took over responsibility for the children sometime before Wig was eligible for school, which would put the date at around 1918/19 when he was around 5/6 years old. It may well be possible to verify this when the Census data for 1921 are released in 2021.

The official Nottinghamshire school records show that Wig attended two schools in Nottingham.[28] He started at Radford Boulevard Primary School at the age 6 in 1920 and continued there until 1925. This facility was run by the local Council, and the location is revealing. Significantly, the school, which no longer exists, was in Radford not Toton. Indeed, Radford Boulevard is just round the corner from Kennington Road where the boys' eventual guardians, the Sandells, lived. I think it is therefore safe to say that Wig did not live with his mother beyond the age of 5. How this would have affected him, not to mention his younger brother who would have been only 2 or 3 when parted from his mother, is hard to say. The words of my mother *"... your father had an unhappy childhood ...."* ring in my ears.

On 14 September 1925, at the age of 11, Wig gained admission to High Pavement School which was a fee paying establishment financed in part by the local authority, Nottingham City Council.[29] To gain entry, he would have had to pass an entrance exam. He was a day scholar and, as an "orphan", it is possible that he was exempt from tuition fees. Unfortunately, there are no records from the time of fees paid to the school. However, the enrolment records show that in his first term he was a member of Class Lower 1B.

High Pavement was a relatively traditional school. Founded in 1788 by the members of High Pavement Chapel, it was the first non-sectarian *("unsectarian")* school in England, and was a pioneer in providing "education in practical science" which was introduced into the curriculum in 1880. Although co-educational, it was modelled on the structure and operations of the classic English Public School. In the 1920s, there were just under 500 students at the school which offered a wide range of subjects for study, and there was formal external assessment of student performance through the University of London Board of Education.

The School Motto was Virtus Sola Nobilitas ("Virtue (or Truth) alone is Noble"), and there was a House system with just four houses in the 1920s,

---

[28] Information provided by Nottinghamshire Archives at Nottinghamshire County Council.
[29] High Pavement School, subsequently became a Grammar School in 1955, then a Sixth Form College in 1975, and is now part of a secondary school called New College Nottingham.

Basford House (of which Wig was a member), Sherwood House, Wollaton House, and School House. As the school prospectus said, this system ensures that " ... *the character and needs of the particular pupil receive full attention, and his or her individuality is not lost sight of.*"

The school uniform recommended for boys was a flannel shirt, Norfolk jacket, grey flannel trousers or shorts, and brown boots. Girls wore boaters with a ribbon in school colours. Every boy was required to wear a tie in the school colours ("Art" Green and Red), although boys who had received their House Colours could wear special House ties.

High Pavement School, Stanley St, Nottingham – The Pavior

According to the school prospectus, discipline was maintained through corporal punishment or "written imposition". The prospectus goes on to indicate that the system for administering discipline involved a **Black Book** for serious "offences" *(examples being gross impertinence, bullying, lying, playing truant, molesting girls, and assault!)*, an **Appearing Book** for minor offences *(such as insubordination, destroying school property, cutting games, riding a bicycle in the playground, and "tiresome folly" which included things like breaking a window)*, and a **Task Book** used to deal with pupils who were late for school or whose work was "defective". Discipline was maintained by Prefects and Monitors.

In terms of performance, the school put emphasis on both effort and ability. At the Annual Prize Giving in the 1922, a guest speaker Dr Scott spoke of the values of the school.[30] *"School prizes are a symbol"* he said.

---

[30] These events were held in November at the Albert Hall in Nottingham, a centre for non-conformist religious activity as well as all manner of other cultural events. It was also used for the Annual Prize Giving by other schools including Nottingham High School, of which Wig's children are alumni.

"They stand for unadulterated merit for successful effort – effort that has been mixed as in the larger world with natural ability and with a certain amount of luck ....they are the first steps on the road to success." And he made reference to the students at the school with the following words. *"This school is composed of keen, intelligent, responsive, wholesome, and lovable pupils. The golden rule for success is to treat others as you would have them treat you."* I suspect that these sentiments say a great deal about the values and culture with which Wig would have been imbued.

As regards extramural activity, the school offered a range of sports and other activities. In keeping with a number of Public Schools, the school had changed from playing soccer to rugby following an appeal from the headmaster to embrace "the Public School spirit", but the syllabus still included soccer. The school also offered cricket, swimming, hockey, boxing, rowing and badminton.[31] [32] There was a Scientific Society, a Dramatic Society, and a French Dramatic Society.

Although the school was keen to promote athletic performance, it was not particularly well endowed with sporting facilities. Before the switch to rugby, both soccer and cricket matches were played on "The Forest", and that's also where the annual sports day was held.[33] However, in the late 1920s, the school did gain access to a large field off Hucknall Road at Bagthorpe for rugby matches, although there were no changing facilities. As H J Derry, who was at the school from 1922-27 during Wig's time, records *"We changed in a barn. Water was heated in a copper (this refers to a large copper drum) in a corner and ladled into tin baths for a wash-down afterwards."* Later, the school gained access to another field in Bobbers Mill. This time the boys had to change in the cloak-room at the school, and then run a mile to the ground including a scramble over a railway track. However, when there was a visiting team, the boys changed at the neighbouring Whitemoor Inn, which apparently led to a little illicit drinking after the game

---

[31] The records show that there were cricket matches against other local public schools in the area including the King's School Grantham, the Minster School in Southwell, Newark Magnus School, and Queen Elizabeth School in Mansfield.

[32] There was an inter-schools trophy for rowing, called the Spenser Cup, which seems to have been won a great deal of the time during Wig's day by Nottingham High School, the school later attended by his sons.

[33] Anyone acquainted with Nottingham will know that "The Forest" is a big public open space directly to the north of Nottingham High School where, amongst other things in current times, the City's Goose Fair is held in the autumn.

was over!

Finally, towards the end of Wig's time, the school's sporting activities moved to Daybrook where, according to one student, High Pavement finally matched its status with other fine schools (including the one attended by both of Wig's children, Nottingham High School). It was here that the school's joinery department eventually built a pavilion with changing rooms and showers.

For most of the time that Wig was at High Pavement, the Head Master was Dr H J Spenser.[34] When he came to High Pavement in 1921, he already had a considerable reputation as a reforming educationalist, through his time as headmaster of University College in Cambridge. By now he was the President of the Incorporated Association of Heads of Secondary Schools and, amongst other things, he introduced self-government at the school. He was a controversial figure in the Nottingham education community, and was noted for a hard hitting assessment of what he saw as the old fashioned approach to education of the Nottingham City Council Education Committee. Indeed, at the school's Annual Prize Giving in November 1926, he delivered a strident critique of the Council's Education Committee policy which made quite a stir through publication in the local papers. He also made a significant contribution to the national Hadow Review of Adolescent Education.[35] A report with significant proposals for changes to curriculum and teaching methods was published by the national Board of Education in 1927.

In his annual report of 1927, Dr Spenser pronounced on the objects of education, which were, in rank order, *"Character, physique, intelligence, manners, and scholarship."* Whatever one may think of his public pronouncements, from all accounts he was much loved by teachers and students alike. Given Wig's home background, I also suspect that he was a dominant figure in the young boy's development during the 1920s. Writing in the *Pavior* School magazine about Dr Spenser after his departure, a pupil recalled his *"ringing voice, his challenging manner, the flaring moustache, and the oratorical wit."* He was very keen on sports and, apart from establishing the Spenser Cup for rowing, he instituted a practice whereby two

---

[34] Dr HJ Spenser served from 1920 until 1928, and was succeeded by Gilbert JR Potter who served from 1929 to 1947.
[35] Named after Sir W H Hadow CBE who was the national Chairman of the Consultative Committee responsible for the Report.

boys with a grievance could have two private rounds with the gloves to work it off! Rowing and boxing were Wig's main sports.

Dr Spenser's assemblies were remembered in the Pavior magazine by several boys including the following unattributed account. *"From 1927, an essential prop was the gong which had been brought back from the East by Mrs Spenser's first husband and presented to the school. According to the 1927 edition of Pavior, the gong had been taken by Mr Melton Prior from a wrecked temple in Burma (an interesting detail given the events 18 years' later and Wig's final resting place!). It is hundreds of years old and was used to summon the people to prayer. It serves the same purpose at High Pavement School."*

An indication of the experience which Wig would have had in the second half of the 1920s is reflected in the following extract from the Pavior school magazine of the time. A student called AH Atkins who was three years ahead of Wig wrote of life at the school in the late 1920s in the following terms.

"Coming to the school in 1921, from the nearby preparatory school by way of the 11-Plus exam and a small scholarship, I was bowled over by the style, energy, and momentum of the place and everybody in it. House meetings, clubs and societies, packed notice boards, crowd movements, masters and mistresses swishing about in black gowns – it left a boy of 11 at first stunned and bewildered. House prefects were snapping out projects and sports programmes for the term; we hurried from room to room for different lesson periods; we were ducked under the pump as first year "fags", we bought colours, house football shirts and football boots; we met Tunnaley for Art and were introduced to science in the separate wing. I quickly immersed it all. Bright boys had two promotions a year and I was soon out of Lower IB and into Lower IIB, a delightful form in the Music Room where Crosslar was the master and we mixed with the girls. This was pleasant as they were good looking. It was a sunny life, the Great War was over, and the cheerful Twenties were just beginning. From this point, you chose Arts, Science or General. House football and cricket were played on Forest pitches and there was rugby at Bobbers Mill and Bagthorpe."

Given my own background, it is of interest that, for a week in April 1925, there was a visit to the school by a group of 140 Australian schoolboys who were cadets.[36] According to the school magazine, the object of their visit to England was *"to broaden the conception of Empire by visiting historical sites, and meeting people in the Mother Country."* To honour this event, a poem written by "Touchwood" appeared in the school magazine. It has some resonance for me, living as I do in Australia, and reads as follows:

"You come to us from a happy land
From a place in the land down under
Likes sons to a mother whose life was planned
Leagues and leagues asunder
You come from the land of the kangaroo
The wallaby and the possum
From the land of the gum and the wattle too
To the land of the apple blossom.

It's a long long cry to the Thames and the Trent
From the Yarra's yellow flowing [37]
And Sydney boy's thoughts are homeward sent
Where the harbour lights are glowing
But England holds to eternity
A place in each heart I wager
So here's to you all, with a one, two, three
And here's to the little Drum Major.

From all accounts, Wig was both happy and successful at school. He studied a broad curriculum, excelling at science, maths and languages. The official records show that he completed his studies at the school on 5 July 1929 in his 16th year. He officially "graduated" from the school at the Annual Prize Giving conducted at the Nottingham Albert Hall on 22 November 1929 when, according to the records he officially received his School Certificate.[38] In the equivalent of the current British system of "GCSE" exams (Australian Year 10), Wig achieved passes in 8 subjects with credits in Arithmetic, Elementary Mathematics, Written and Oral French, and Heat Light and

[36] The visit was between 21 and 24 April 1925.
[37] The River Trent is the main river flowing through Nottingham. The Yarra flows through Melbourne, and the colour of the water is attributed to the fact that it flows upside down.
[38] A copy of the Programme for the Annual Prize Giving of 1929 lists Wig.

Sound (i.e. Physics).

In addition to being a better than average student academically speaking, Wig was also athletic and participated in a number of sports. He rowed for the school, played for the first XV at rugby, and learnt to box at the tender age of 12.[39] Indeed, he reached the semi-final of the Middleweight Division in 1928. He was therefore a well-rounded student, and the school provided an important grounding for the rest of his life in terms of values, attitudes and behaviours, given his disadvantaged beginnings and what may have been a relatively narrow home life living with guardians who had probably not had the benefit of an enlightened and extended secondary education.

On leaving High Pavement, Wig got a job with Nottingham City Transport, but he continued his studies, attending night classes. As a result, in 1931, at the age of 18, the records show that he sat the equivalent of what are known in the current British system as "A" Levels, in examinations conducted by the East Midlands Educational Union.[40] His achievements included First Class passes in Practical Mathematics and Mechanics and Heat. According to his SOE Personnel record, after starting full time employment, he also studied at night school a subject that we would nowadays call Business Administration, and obtained a Diploma in "Organisation and Control of Business Services".

---

[39] There is a record of him competing in the Lightweight Division in April 1926.
[40] There is a Certificate in family archives.

4: What Kind of Man?

Before telling the rest of Wig's story, I'd like to share with the reader what I know about this man from all the evidence. It is difficult to describe a person that you have never met. Yet, through the material available to me, I have been able to piece together a picture of a quite remarkable person. What follows is based on what my mother told me, what people actually said in letters and other written and official documents, and just a little speculation based on the circumstances of his birth and childhood.

Beginning with the physical man, as an adult Wig was of average height for his time – 5 feet nine inches tall. According to his army record, he had blue eyes and light brown hair. In his late 20s, and in keeping with the times, he grew a moustache. He was slim and athletic, and was known for keeping fit by going for runs regularly wherever he was living during peacetime and throughout the war.

Wig's parental background was challenging, and would have left a lasting impression. Whilst the concepts of being "born out of wedlock" or being "illegitimate" are no longer in common usage, in the early 20th Century these conditions were the subject of public opprobrium. In most cases, an unmarried woman who bore a child would either find a husband or surrender the child to the State. In a few cases, grand-parents or family friends might step in to assume a parenting role. For children surrendered to the State, they would have been the subject of the Poor Law, with many cast into work houses and only a relatively small number adopted by foster parents into families. For many children born into these circumstances, there would have been a sense of shame and even denial, and it is hard not to conclude that this would have been the case for Wig and his brother James. However, there were some redeeming aspects. They **were** "adopted" by a guardian, albeit probably on an informal basis in the absence of a formal legal structure for adoption. And Wig **was** the beneficiary of financial support from some "guardian angel" who may well have been an otherwise absent wealthy male parent.

One can only imagine the impact of this unfortunate start in life on the character of both children. In the case of Wig, he had the benefit of a quality education at an institution which would have instilled traditional qualities consistent with middle class values. The secondary school that he attended included tuition designed to remove the "regional accent", as it was called by the school, and one can envisage that Wig may have created for himself a background that very adequately covered up the actual circumstances. The invention in adult life of a legitimate parentage which would avoid embarrassing explanations is therefore entirely understandable, although he took quite a risk in changing his story between the time he joined the regular army and his admission to the SOE.

Given this background, one is bound to wonder about the impact on personality. Like all orphans, one of the most important things he would have had to learn is that it wasn't his fault. And, assuming that he was ignorant of the fact, he would have speculated about the identity of his father. At the very least, one imagines that he would have been someone who was relatively private, self-contained, and inclined to keep his own counsel. And the ability to hold a secret and maintain an identity of one's choosing would have been second nature. It is not difficult to see that someone with such a background would be ideal material for employment in a security agency like the undercover SOE where secrets and confidences were *de rigueur*.

Apart from these speculations, it is clear from a range of evidence, that Wig was a charming man, and a thoroughly decent human being. Apparently, he had an excellent sense of humour, and an unflappable approach to life. My mother indicated that whilst he was politically conservative, he had no time for Fascists whom he despised. Most importantly, he espoused what might nowadays be regarded as old-fashioned values in that he believed that people with the benefit of his relatively privileged background (in terms of education at least) had a duty to help those less well off.

According to his friend Leonard Ward, who worked with Wig at Nottingham City Transport and was my brother Michael's godfather, Wig was a risk-taker and a bit of a dare-devil. But when it came to his job in the army, he never asked anyone to do anything he wouldn't do himself. However, he wasn't a handy-man (in terms of what we would nowadays call DIY), and didn't enjoy that kind of thing. He had what would be regarded in modern times as somewhat eccentric views on such matters (although I probably share them). As my mother told me, he would always say that it was important to employ other folk to do jobs around the house. That's what kept the economy going.

At his pre-war workplace as a Scheduling Clerk in the Nottingham City Council Transport Department, his responsibilities included negotiating with the workforce and he was respected for his reasonable and fair minded approach. Outside of work, he was well-liked amongst his sporting friends.

As the Honorary Secretary of Nottingham Britannia Rowing Club said, in a letter to my mother after it was revealed that Wig was "Missing in Action" in October 1945,

> *"We are extremely proud to have had the honour of knowing him, and have watched his meteoric rise with great admiration feeling that we could share in his triumphs. He was always very popular with Club Members".*

Letters from his work colleagues in the army reveal that he was an incredibly hard working and well regarded human being, who probably had the common Wigginton failing of over-committing himself. Extracts from some of the material in my archives follow.

Speaking of Wig when they were working in Cairo in 1943, a member of his staff Captain Basil Irwin said of him during a recorded interview in the 1960s " *...he was a frightfully nice chap, hard-working and supportive .....".* His personal secretary while he was in Bari in Italy in 1944, Barbara Sampson, wrote to my mother in November 1945 from HQ Allied Commission Central Mediterranean Force in the following vein:

> *"I admired him more than any other person I have ever met. He had absolutely no enemies, and I have never heard an adverse criticism of his work. He did a wonderful job during the war in Europe, and all of the people he looked after had such faith in him that their difficult job was made far easier. I would like you to know what a very very fine man he was even in the office and how very kind he always was to me."*

Another colleague from the Italy period, Geoffrey Meredith, wrote in June 1944 *"Wig is doing a wonderful job in Italy and has made a good name for himself. Sometimes in the evenings we run together."*

In June 1945, in a poignant and unsolicited letter to my mother, a friend and colleague Dugald Macphail of HQ Group B of Force 136 in Colombo, wrote:

> *"He's one of those thorough, conscientious chaps who never farms out his work to subordinates when he can do it himself. The result is that he has hardly any time to do anything but work, eat and sleep. He's doing*

more than his share to finish this nonsense, so that we can all get home and put our bowler hats on. In his few leisure moments, his topics of conversation are in this order: Yourself (Eunice), Wig junior (my brother Michael), the Wigs that are not yet (my good self), Post-War, and finally rowing, boxing and other sports which are a poor last.

He'll be a very tired man by the time his work is finished, but he's got amazing reserves of energy, fitness, and adaptability. A short spell at home will set him up soon enough. And, as some sort of recompense for your years of separation, you'll have the satisfaction of knowing that he's done more than half a dozen average Lt Colonels to win the war. I wish there were more like him."[41]

The Head of SOE Force 136, Colin Hercules Mackenzie (later Sir Colin), wrote on 12 October 1945:

"Wig was not only a particularly capable and hardworking officer but was extremely popular with everyone. We all feel we have lost a friend whom we admired as well as liked. He was always a gay companion and I am sure he was happy in his work. The more problems he had to wrestle with, the better he seemed to be placed."

When Wig went missing, his Commanding Officer Colonel Stephen Cumming of HQ Group A Force 136 South East Asia Command wrote:

"Wig arrived here at a time (February 1945) when we were very heavily involved in the campaign in Burma, and his knowledge and experience were of the greatest possible assistance to us. He tackled the many problems involved with his usual keenness. He was liked and admired by everyone."

In a letter written to Eunice in 1946, one of his closest friends wrote:

"To you he was a dear husband; to me he was a dear friend. He was

---

[41] While Wig was in Calcutta running the air operations into Burma from Group A, Dugald Macphail with Group B was based in Colombo and involved in operations into Thailand and Malaya. He was a medical officer and was previously with Wig in both Cairo and Bari. See Appendix 19.

40

without doubt the finest, cleanest, best all round fellow I've ever met anywhere.[42]

In summary, a fair assessment would be to say that Wig was a decent and likeable human being who loved his family, his work and his sport. If he had a failing, it was his inclination to work too hard. Given his origins, and the need to maintain a family identity which was not entirely in accordance with the truth, I think he was someone who would have understood that people were not always what they might seem. He was a person you could trust, and with whom you could share a confidence. He was intelligent, hard-working, a good organiser, and diligent. He was brave, and he was not frightened to take risks. He was also a man of social conscience who clearly had some understanding of what makes a civil society. And he was proud to be British.

---

[42] The letter from which this is extracted was sent to my mother in March 1946. The letter was from an American friend living in Detroit Michigan who served with him in the Far East. Unfortunately, only the first page survives and the name of the sender is unknown.

Part Two: Halcyon Days

5: Making His Mark

Our current use of the expression 'halcyon days' tends to invoke a sense of nostalgia, and perhaps the memory of the seemingly endless sunny days of youth. Its origin is from Greek times, and refers to a temporary period of calm between two periods of conflict in which the Halcyon bird was able to build its nest and breed its young. This makes it a most appropriate expression to describe the years between the First and Second World War when Wig was in the prime of his young life. Indeed, for those who had a job and a reasonable education, living in England between the World Wars was in many ways just like the classic halcyon period.

Having said that, life in the early 1920s in England must have been quite daunting for many, not least the young. There was of course a palpable sense of relief that the "war to end all wars" was over. But the legacy of the slaughter of the First World War hung over the country like a wet blanket, with the impact of losing half a generation of young men reaching into most families. "Armistice Day", as it was then called, on 11 November, was a very important day even at schools. Then, as memories of war started to fade, Bolshevism stalked the continent of Europe, and Britain was hit by a series of shocks with the General Strike in 1926, the Stock Market Crash in 1929, and the years of the Depression which extended well into the early 1930s. Concerns about the difficult prospects for getting work must have been on the minds of most people in the community, from whatever their background.

For Wig, who completed his further education in 1932, he was better off than most. Once he finished at High Pavement School, he got a job as a Scheduling Clerk with the Department of Transport of the Nottingham City Council.[43] Starting at a junior level, over the next ten years he gradually advanced to positions with more responsibility. According to my mother, much of his work involved developing schedules for the movement of passenger vehicles and negotiating with the drivers and conductors over rosters for implementation of those timetables. The City's transport network included a substantial fleet of petrol buses, and electric trolley buses which ran around the city powered through rods which connected to overhead wires (which lasted until the 1950s).

---

[43] Information about his employment commencing in 1929 is to be found in the Minute book of the Passenger Transport Management Sub-Committee of the Nottingham City Council held at the Nottinghamshire Archives in Nottingham.

Nottingham City Transport Scheduling Department 1935

Wig reported to a man called Ben England who spoke well of him. By the time he left the Transport Department in 1939, he was on an annual salary of £195.[44] Apparently, Wig showed a particular talent for organising both men and vehicles, and he was highly respected. This record foreshadowed his highly successful career in logistics during the war.[45] At the Transport Department, which was a fairly large organisation employing over 1,000 people in the mid-1930s, he met a man named Leonard Ward who was to become a great friend (Leonard is the second man from the left on the back row of the picture). Leonard was also a Schedule Clerk and a rower. Details of Wig's career can be traced through the archives of Council Committee meetings in the 1930s.[46] According to these records, Wig was promoted on several occasions, including a final promotion on 28 December 1938 which was nine months before departure for military service. Interestingly, the last entry to Wig and Leonard in those same records shows that they both resigned from employment on 2 September 1939 (a day before war was declared) because they had volunteered to join the armed forces.

For most of the 1930s, Wig lived with his guardians and his brother James at 6 Kennington Road in the suburb of Lenton in Nottingham. The house where they lived has been demolished and is now a car park. However, there

---

[44] For reference and interest, the same records show that the General Manager of the whole Department, Mr J L Gunn, who was appointed in 1934 was on a salary of £1,500 per annum.
[45] In an interview Mr England gave to the Nottingham Evening Post in June 1945, when contemplating Wig's return after the war, he spoke with pride about Wig's outstanding wartime record.
[46] Minutes of Meetings of the Passenger Transport Sub-Committee of Nottingham City Council, in which there are several references to Wig relating to various activities, are held at the Nottinghamshire Archives.

Left: Old Paviors Rugby First XV 1934. Right: NBRC Club House, River Trent, Nottingham

is one building left from the street which existed in the 1930s. No 6 was a substantial three storey house in a modest part of town fairly adjacent to the Players Tobacco warehouses across Ilkeston Road Nottingham. It would have been a short trip on the trolley bus into his office in the city.

Outside work, Wig spent most of his time in simple pleasures including sport. After leaving school, he continued his interest in boxing, rowing and rugby. He played rugby for the Old Paviors, the High Pavement old boys club, and was in the County second team. He was a fly-half, but also played on the wing. This picture (he's on the left) was taken in 1934 when he was twenty years old and a member of the Old Paviors First XV.

He was also a member of the Nottingham Britannia Rowing Club ("NBRC"), and was ranked as a *"Provincial senior oarsman"*. He took part in a number of regattas on the River Trent and elsewhere. In 2015, I visited the premises of the NBRC which, amazingly to me, were right next door to the entrance to the Nottingham Forest Football Club.[47] As a schoolboy, I had walked past that Club House on my way into the ground on more than 50 occasions in the 1950s without realising its significance. The NBRC colours were, and still are, a combination of light and dark blue as still proudly emblazoned on the outside of the Club House. When I visited the Club, it

---

[47] Nottingham Forest play at the City Ground, even though this is technically outside the city, with the adjacent River Trent as the boundary between City and County.

was locked up; but I talked with local rowing club members who were cleaning the boats in a neighbouring shed, and they told me that the NBRC had now been amalgamated with the Nottingham Rowing Club. Then a young man approached me and, seeing that I was trying to get access to the Club, asked if he could help. He turned out to be a member of the Nottingham University Boat Club who currently use the NBRC premises. He offered to let me in, and I was able to walk along a short corridor and up the stairs to the main body of the Club. There, in the lobby, and to my astonishment, I found a memorial to Wig. And, in the Club, which included a strange "cave

The Berrey Cup, 1935

like" area which was the bar, there were other interesting pictures and, in an ante room, a cabinet full of ancient trophies all of which Wig would have known.

Amongst other things, in 1935 and at the age of 21, Wig won the Berrey Cup Pairs competition at the Nottingham Regatta – a feat which his son Michael emulated 25 years later in the same place. The cup that Wig won is still in family possession and is shown here. As he got older, Wig was also active in managing regattas, and served on the Nottingham Regatta Committee as a representative of the NBRC for the 1939 Annual Head of the Trent Regatta.[48]

---

[48] The programme for this event, in the family archive, records that the regatta took place on 24 June 1939. It makes interesting reading and includes annotation in Wig's handwriting of the results of all the main events.

6: Life With Eunice

Edith (left) and Harry Smith (right), 1935

In 1936, when he was 22 years old, Wig met Eunice who was then aged 19. She too had avoided the worst of the inter-war depression. Partly of Scottish heritage (her maiden name was Piper and her mother's maiden name was Carlisle), she had been born in London in January 1917 and lived her early years in Dulwich and then Camberwell. In the early 1920s, the family of which she was one of the younger members (two parents and five children) moved to Oshawa in Canada. But the young men in the family did not like the cold, and Eunice's mother missed home. So, in the late 20s, they all returned to England.

In the early 1930s, Eunice's sister Edith moved to Nottingham and married Harry Smith who worked with John Player & Son.[49] When Eunice had finished her schooling in 1935, her brother-in-law helped her to get a job as a junior secretary with the same company, and she moved to live with Edith and Harry at 9 Orston Drive, Wollaton Park. This was a new house built in what used to be the grounds of Wollaton Hall which was an adjacent 16th Century house.

---

[49] Born in 1896, Edith passed away in 1974.

Left: 9 Orston Drive, Wollaton Park, Nottingham 2015. Right: NBRC Rowing Four c. 1935

In those days, the new estate of Wollaton Park was a lovely place to live with walks in the extensive grounds of the adjacent Hall.[50] It still is. Although Eunice used to cycle to work at John Player & Son in Lenton Boulevard, she sometimes went on the trolley bus and that's where she and Wig met one fateful day in 1936. As was usual at that time, they courted for a couple of years before getting engaged in 1938. The location of their respective homes must have been pretty convenient. Eunice's home was but 2.5 kms from Kennington Road in Lenton, and her place of work was even closer to his home.

Eunice related the many happy times they had together in those days. In particular, she actively supported Wig in his sporting activity and attended countless rowing contests, as well as his rugby matches for Old Paviors. They also played tennis together at the courts owned by John Player & Son off Western Boulevard, went dancing, visited the "Flicks", walked in the country via mystery trips on the train, and went to local events like the Goose Fair at Nottingham Forest.[51] They visited pubs in the city and out in the country including the Plough at Normanton, which was a bit of haunt for the rowing set.[52] Wig and Eunice also did cryptic crosswords together, an inherited family past-time.

In the inter-war years, Nottingham was a relatively prosperous city. The lace industry was in decline, but there was a range of thriving economic

---

[50] Wollaton Hall was taken over by Nottingham City Council in the 1930s.

[51] The "Flicks" is a term used at the time for the cinema.

[52] It is still a functioning pub today, and Eunice and I visited it on a number of occasions for lunch during the 1960s and 1970s.

activity including Boots the chemists, Raleigh bicycles, as well as John Players tobacco. There was also an excellent University College which eventually became Nottingham University. In 1929, the new domed Nottingham Council House had been completed, with the current "Slab Square" established in its current form, an important formal and informal meeting place. Significant buildings in the city also included the renowned department store of Griffin and Spalding which, in the 1950s, was well known to the younger Wigginton family. "Griffins" Corner was a famous meeting point. And there was the Black Boy Inn which was an up market hotel built in the 19th Century on a site where there had been a hostelry since earlier times. It was not only known to the Wiggintons of the 1930s, but also to younger post-war generations being used by current members of the Wiggintons as a place for family gatherings. Sadly, it was demolished in the 1960s.

On the sporting front, cricket grabbed the local headlines. Eunice was a cricket player when she was at school and followed the sport, as did Wig.[53] In the 1930s, Trent Bridge was a ground which was used on a regular basis for Test Matches including those against Australia, and I imagine that Wig and Eunice would have attended the matches in 1930, 1934, and 1938.

Before the outbreak of war, Wig and Eunice had a number of holidays, which included a visit to the Giant's Causeway in Northern Ireland, a trip to the sea-side in Newquay Cornwall, and several trips sailing around the Norfolk Broads.

Despite enjoying happy days, there was also a dark side. According to Eunice, in the mid-1930s, people in England followed what was happening in Germany with growing concern. In 1935, her sister Edith went to Germany on holiday and provided a first-hand account of local events and tensions. As a result, they and their friends began to expect the worst, and saw the Nazis in Germany as a threat not only to neighbouring countries on the continent but also to the British Empire.

---

[53] When I was a lad, I remember Eunice at the Trent Bridge ground, sitting with her knitting in the Ladies Stand which was to the right of the main stand.

Left: Wig and Eunice in Northern Ireland, 1938. Right: Sailing in the Norfolk Broads, 1938.

Reflecting their concerns, in late 1938 Wig decided to get some military training and, whilst still retaining his regular job, he joined the local branch of the Territorial Army ("TA") as a volunteer. Initially, he tried to join the Royal Navy, but he wasn't admitted because he lived too far from the sea! So he was enrolled in one of the many TA units in Nottingham. Immediately prior to the declaration of war, on 2 September 1939, he resigned his job and joined up as a full time member of the armed forces. We return to this phase in his life in the Chapter 8.

With the war looming, on 21 October 1939, 25 year old Wig (as he was already enlisted, he is dressed in the uniform of a Gunner with the Royal Artillery) and 22 year old Eunice got married, and Wig moved out of the house he shared with his brother in Lenton. He joined Eunice to live with her sister Edith, her husband Harry, and a dog named Ruff, at 9 Orston Drive, Wollaton Park. The witnesses at their wedding at Lenton Parish church were Wig's younger brother James Edward Wigginton, and a family friend and neighbour from Orston Drive, William James Field. Interestingly, on the Wedding Certificate, Wig stated that his father was Arthur Wigginton, a lace manufacturer. In the war time circumstances, they did not have a honeymoon.

A final point of interest from this period is Wig's membership in the 1930s of the Nottingham Ancient Imperial United Order of Oddfellows. When I first came across this in his MOD personnel record, I wondered whether it was some sort of secret society of the Masonic variety. However, the explanation was more banal. On investigation, I discovered that it was an organisation registered under the National Health Insurance Act 1924 which provided medical insurance for the families of members. In the 1930s, meetings of the organisation were held at the wonderfully named Generous Briton Hotel, in Alfreton Road Nottingham which today is a Chinese Restaurant! The organisation was run by a Committee of 12 elected at the AGM, and chaired by someone called the *Grand Imperial*. Members made contributions which varied according to the age of entry. In the 1930s, Wig paid £1.4.0 per annum (0.5% of his income).[54] Verified claims involved payments over three years according to the following schedule: 10s per week for 13 weeks, 8s per week for the next 13 weeks, 5s per week for the next 26 weeks, and 2s6d for a final 104 weeks. The Oddfellows employed a "steward" who monitored the sick, a "warden" who managed the assets and a surgeon. This was Britain before the National Health system!

Wedding Day, 21 October 1939

---

[54] The British currency was pounds (£), shillings (s) and pence (d) represented as £1.4.0.

7: The World Beyond in the 1930s

Although Wig's life in England in the 1930s was relatively prosperous and care-free, there was a lot happening in the outside world. This was a turbulent period in British and World history. Following the stock market crash in 1929, unemployment in the UK soared to over 3 million, and was still at 1.5 million in 1937. At the beginning of the decade, Prime Minister Ramsay McDonald was eagerly pursuing his peace agenda through the League of Nations, but hopes of any serious progress in building an effective international body for world peace and co-operation were dashed when Japan invaded Manchuria and left the League. In 1930, there were huge demonstrations in India, led by Mahatma Ghandi demanding independence, and there were lengthy discussions with the British government which eventually resulted in a new Government of India Act (in 1935) granting India free elections and self-government for internal affairs. Meanwhile, the British economy was in dire straits, and Ramsay McDonald proposed drastic public expenditure cuts which were voted down in Parliament. He tried to resign, but in 1931 King George V persuaded him to form a National Coalition Government of Liberals, Conservatives, and just three Labour ministers. This government won a General Election on 27 October 1931.

In early 1932 Eamon De Valera won a General Election in Ireland and started to dismantle the Irish Free State, ahead of full Irish independence. By the end of 1937, the country had a new constitution which made it a republic in all but name. On the mainland of Europe, fascism was on the march. In 1933, Adolf Hitler came to power through elections in Germany and he soon left the League of Nations, to enable rearmament. Despite the support of the public for disarmament, the British government started to talk with other European powers about how to respond to this aggressive German policy. Meanwhile, in England, Sir Oswald Mosley established the British Union of Fascists who were active for several years until they were banned in 1940.

On 27 June 1935, there was another General Election. All parties were opposed to re-armament, and Stanley Baldwin became Conservative Prime Minister for the third time.[55]

1936 was to see a major constitutional crisis in Britain. On 20 January

---

[55] He first became Prime Minister in 1923 and, after a brief period out of office during Ramsay Macdonald's tenure, won an election in 1924. He was defeated in the 1929 election. He joined the 1931 National government, and succeeded Macdonald when he fell ill.

1936, King George V died, and was succeeded by his eldest son the Prince of Wales who became King Edward VIII. Edward had formed a relationship with an American divorcee, Mrs Wallace Simpson, and was determined to marry her despite constitutional barriers. After many months of national debate, on 10 December Edward abdicated, and he broadcast his decision to the nation on the following day. Within six months he married Mrs Simpson in France and they became the Duke and Duchess of Windsor. He was succeeded by his brother who was crowned as King George VI on 12 May 1937. Prime Minister Stanley Baldwin was widely credited with saving the monarchy, and on 28 May 1937, he retired to be succeeded by Neville Chamberlain.

Meanwhile, there was a major development in Egypt. On 20 August 1936, the British Protectorate of Egypt was terminated and a new security treaty was negotiated. This included provisions for Britain to maintain control of the Suez Canal for twenty years, and to occupy Egypt in the event of a threat to its independence. The significance of this treaty will be very evident later in this book as Cairo became a centre for British operations in the war following the attempted invasion by Italy. The subsequent crisis of 1956 when Nasser reclaimed the Canal will not be lost on the reader!

In early 1938, the first refugee children started to arrive in Britain, from Germany and neighbouring countries, including a number of people who were to become friends of the Wigginton family in post-war years, such as Mrs Felicity Rose.[56] A total of 10,000 Jewish children between the ages of five and 17 were sent from Germany, Austria and Czechoslovakia to Britain between December 1938 and the outbreak of war in September 1939. Many were given homes by British families, or lived in hostels. Very few of them saw their parents again.

On 20 February 1938, Foreign Secretary Anthony Eden resigned in opposition to Chamberlain's acquiescent approach to dealing with Germany and Italy. On 12 March Germany occupied Austria and declared "Anschluss".[57] Chamberlain then visited Hitler and negotiated the Munich Agreement allowing German occupation of the Sudetenland. He returned with an announcement that there would be "Peace in Our Time". In the

---

[56] Felicity Rose, born in February 1926 and married to Harry, played bridge with Eunice for many years. She is a great friend of the Wigginton family, and I have stayed with her on a number of occasions on recent trips to the UK.

[57] Anschluss, meaning "connection" or "joining", was Hitler's term for the annexation of Austria.

meantime, British rearmament was well under way. In March 1939, Hitler invaded Czechoslovakia. Then everything hinged on what would happen to Poland, a country to which Britain and France had given guarantees of defence against any aggressive moves from Germany. Believing that Britain would never honour this commitment, on 23 August, Hitler signed a pact with Joseph Stalin to divide Poland with the Soviet Union. The scene was set for the conclusion of Halcyon Days.

Finally, in preparing the ground for what is considered in the rest of this book, it is worth saying just a little about the foreign policy of Britain and its allies during this period. The apologists for the failure to prepare for war have written about the well intentioned commitment of British leaders to peace through the League of Nations. Others have asserted that, once Hitler came to power in 1933, there was a failure of British foreign policy in the face of the "bleeding" obvious. Interestingly, one person who wrote about this at the time was the man who was later to become the 35th President of the United States, John F Kennedy. In 1940, he was a senior at Harvard University, and he wrote a thesis which was turned into a book entitled *"Why England Slept."*[58] His father was the US Ambassador in London, which gave the young Kennedy access to much of the inner workings of British foreign policy as seen through American eyes. In this book, Kennedy published some very interesting data on the *defence expenditure* of the eight main Allies and Axis powers during the fateful years between 1932 and 1939, as shown below. The figures tell their own story. All figures are in $US million. The percentage and bold figures are explained in the footnote. I think the English were not the *only* ones sleeping.

---

[58] *"Why England Slept"* by John F Kennedy was published in New York by Wilfred Funk Inc in 1940. As Henry R Luce said when the book was re-published in 1961 ahead of Kennedy's run for the US Presidency *"It is an electrifying account of England's unpreparedness for war, and a sober and serious study of the shortcomings of democracy when confronted by the menace of totalitarianism."*

Nation	1932	1933	1934	1935	1936	1937	1938	1939
Britain	426	456	481	596	847	1263	1693	1817
	16%[*]	16%	13%	8%	7%	9%	15%	16%
France	509	**679**	583	624	834	909	731	1800
USA	**668**	540	710	912	964	992	1066	1163
	25%	19%	19%	12%	8%	7%	9%	9%
Germany	254	300	382	**2600**	**3600**	**4000**	**4400**	**4500**
	9%	10%	10%	35%	28%	29%	38%	34%
Italy	271	241	263	778	916	573	526	873
USSR	283	310	**1000**	**1640**	**4002**	**5026**	1352	1500
	10%	11%	26%	22%	31%	36%	12%	11%
Japan	199	253	271	296	305	1121	1755	1600
	7%	9%	7%	4%	2%	8%	15%	12%
China	93	108	112	93	95	95	95	95
GRAND TOTAL	**2703**	**2887**	**3802**	**7539**	**12779**	**13979**	**11618**	**13348**

By way of example, British expenditure of US$426m in 1932 represented 16% of the total spent (US$2,703m) by all eight countries in 1932. Figures in bold show where the expenditure of one country is 20% or more of all eight countries.

Part Three: Gathering Storm

8: Black Over Bill's Mother's [59]

On 1 September 1939, Germany invaded Poland. On 2 September, at the age of 25, Wig resigned from his job with the Nottingham City Transport Department and enlisted in the army.[60] The following day, Britain declared war on Germany and, three days later, Wig was admitted to the Royal Regiment of Artillery ("Royal Artillery"). For the Wigginton family, as for everyone else in Britain, the world had changed for ever. Initially, Wig was a gunner based in Nottingham with the 276th Anti-Aircraft ("AA") section of the 68th Regiment. After six months, in March 1940, he was promoted to Lance Bombardier, and three months later he became a full Bombardier. During this time, he did a range of training at a Royal Artillery base in Alfreton Road Nottingham and elsewhere around the county.[61] Whilst attending various training courses, he continued to live in Wollaton Park and it was during this period that my brother Michael was conceived and born. This period was called the "Phoney War", when Britain was still gearing up for military operations, after the relative lack of preparation by the pre-war government led by Neville Chamberlain. Like many others, Wig and his wife found this period pretty frustrating.

However, in the late spring of 1940, things started to warm up. On 10 May, the Germans invaded France and, on the same day, Winston Churchill became Prime Minister. The French eventually surrendered on 22 June. At the time, Hitler hoped for a negotiated settlement with Britain, but Churchill had a different view and daggers were drawn! On 16 July, Hitler ordered the preparation of invasion plans and, knowing that the Wehrmacht would not be able to cross the English Channel without air superiority, he decided to begin with an all-out attack on Britain with the Luftwaffe. War was engaged in earnest on what the Germans called *Eagle Day*, 13 August 1940, with attacks on British airfields. This was the beginning of what has been called the "Battle of Britain". On 7 September, there were attacks on the London

---

[59] This is a saying, local to the Nottingham area, in which reference is made to dark clouds on the horizon as an omen of a gathering storm. I have no idea who Bill was, but my mother often used the expression as a more general foreboding regardless of the weather.

[60] There is a record of this resignation in the Minutes of a Meeting of the Passenger Transport Sub-Committee of Nottingham City Council held on 17 November 1939, which are held at the Nottinghamshire Archives.

[61] This remained a military base until recent times, and I recall my mother pointing it out to me in the 1970s.

docks. On 15 September, two massive waves of German attacks were decisively repulsed by the RAF. Shortly thereafter, lack of progress resulted in Hitler deferring the land invasion until the spring of 1941. Subsequently, in October 1940, the aerial attacks were called off. For the British, Fighter Command had achieved a great victory in successfully preventing the Germans from knocking Britain out of the war, and enabling the country to survive until reinforced by allies. The performance of Fighter Command was so well regarded that the conclusion to Churchill's famous speech to Parliament, on 20 August 1940, is remembered by his reference to their ongoing efforts - *"Never in the field of human conflict was so much owed by so many to so few."*

The successful British defence also signalled a significant shift in American opinion. Prior to and during the *Battle of Britain*, when the country stood alone against the German war machine, many people in the US accepted the view promoted by Joseph Kennedy, the American ambassador in London, who believed that Great Britain could not withstand the German war machine. However, President Franklin D Roosevelt, whose personal sympathies were certainly with Britain, wanted a second opinion. To this end, he sent "Wild Bill" Donovan on a brief visit to Britain in the autumn of 1940. Donovan became convinced that Britain would survive, and advised Roosevelt that the country should be supported in every possible way. Donovan was later to become a leader of the American Office of Strategic Service ("OSS") which worked closely with the British *Special Operations Executive*.

Sandhurst College – Sandhurst Collection.

All of this was the backcloth to the next phase of Wig's life. As the Germans were preparing to attack Britain, like many young men, Wig determined to play his part in defending the country to the best of his ability. For him, this meant becoming an army officer and, with the support of his Commanding Officer at the Royal Artillery, he applied for officer training at the Royal Military College. This institution had recently moved from buildings at Woolwich to Sandhurst College which is located near Camberley in Surrey.

Wig was successful in his application, and was admitted as a "Gentleman Cadet" to the Officer Cadet Training Unit on 12 July 1940, a few weeks before the Battle of Britain began. As he joined the course, one can only imagine the deep sense of urgency and foreboding in his mind. In those days, the training process was accelerated, and he completed the course at the end of October. He was formally appointed to a Commission on 1 November 1940 (aged 26).

In search of details of Wig's time at Sandhurst College, I visited the establishment on 8 July 2015 where I met with the curator of the Sandhurst Collection, Dr Anthony Morton. In particular, the purpose of my visit was to find out how Wig came to be admitted, what he did during his time there, and what life was like in what would have been quite an elitist organisation in the early 1940s.

Dr Morton kindly furnished a range of files relating to Sandhurst College training in those days. We also tried to trace specific references to Wig. However, there was a problem. Unfortunately, the detailed administrative records for 1940 and 1941 were inadvertently destroyed in 1942 to make way for the accommodation of more staff! In the absence of detailed records, we could only surmise the circumstances of Wig's admission. Dr Morton explained that, prior to 1940, there was a complex system, including provisions for the gentry to purchase entry, an "Orphan" class for the sons of officers who were financially embarrassed, bursaries for men of outstanding ability, and "Nomination" by the War Office. However, in 1940, faced with the need for an increased supply of officers, the War Department determined to admit civilians by examination whose fees would be paid by the government. Given Wig's background, Dr Morton thought that the most likely route of entry would have been that he was recommended to sit the entry examination by the Commanding Officer of his military unit (the Royal Artillery). On passing the examination, his fees would then have been paid by the government. This does leave the not insubstantial costs of living, and this must have been paid by a well-wisher. With the records destroyed, we will never know who that was.

Given the lack of a military background prior to 1939, and Wig's subsequent role in the regular army and *Special Operations Executive*, it is of interest to note some of the content of the training at Sandhurst in 1940. There was of course the usual physical training, weapons training, and parade drill. But the programme of formal education in a range of military topics was substantial. There was also plenty of extramural activity, of which more anon. In the first term, the cadets studied a range of subjects including the following: The Principles of War, Preparing for Battle, Battle Tasks, March Discipline, Vanguard, Attack in Depth, Consolidation, Infantry-Tank Co-operation, Night Operations, Defence, Infantry Action Against Tanks, Artillery, German Tactics, Message Writing, Sentries, and Street Fighting. In reading the 1939 Syllabus, I was especially struck by the section on The Principles of War which provided a rationale for going to war that was specifically geared to contemporary circumstances. The Syllabus stated that:

"A Nation must protect interests vital to its security, and a Nation must uphold the international covenants to which it is a party. When either of these great principles is endangered, we endeavour to persuade our would-be opponent to abandon his policy, by all the means in our power – i.e. by imposing our will on him. The means employed are: Diplomacy, Economic Influence, and War. In particular, the armed forces are only one means of overcoming the will of the opposing nation. Diplomacy and economic warfare continue to play an important part in the struggle for supremacy, by assisting our Allies and embarrassing our opponents."

The summary in the Syllabus of how to approach war is also of note. It reads as follows:

"Victory can only be won by offensive action. Defensive action may ward off defeat for the time being; but if he wishes to achieve victory sooner or later the defender must change over to the offensive. This is easily explained by taking as an example any field game. (!)[62] *You must choose wisely an aim within the means available. Concentrate all possible forces*

---

[62] This is the author's exclamation mark and underlining. Reference to war as being analogous to a game provides an insight into the contemporary mind set.

on its attainment by skilful economy in providing for the security of your force; thus making available the maximum force for offensive action. Seek always to surprise your enemy by secrecy and mobility; then, by the co-operation of all your forces towards the common aim, victory will be attained."

At the end of the cadetship, students sat a Final Term Examination which covered the following: Military Law, Imperial and International Affairs, British Military History, Strategy and Tactics, Organisation and Administration, Artillery, and Mathematics. Interestingly, candidates were passed the papers the evening prior to the exam to assist preparation.[63]

The absence of records on Wig's performance is disappointing. However, there is a register that records that Wig was in "C" Company and that he obtained a B in the academic Order of Merit. And anecdotally, according to my mother Eunice who was present at the time, he did also receive the "Sword of Honour" in recognition of his outstanding all-round performance. Amongst other things, this entitled the winner to ride up the steps of the College on horse-back during the "Passing Out" parade. Prior to the War, it also involved the actual receipt of a sword. However, this practice was suspended during the war and no swords were subsequently ever issued.

Apart from learning his military craft, at Sandhurst Wig played rugby for the College and, according to Eunice, he lost his wedding ring, never to be found, during a match on the College rugby field. During this period, he also trialled to play for the Three Counties rugby team although one wonders why they were having "trials" at such a difficult time.

Within the College, life was not unlike the boarding schools which most of the cadets would have attended. They shared a dormitory, and got up to the sounds of Reveille played on a bugle. They washed and shaved in cold water because no-one kept the boiler going overnight. They were fed in a canteen during the day, but dined in an oak panelled dining room with considerably more formality at night.

Apart from the training, life at the College also involved a range of other activities. In the College Library which I visited on 8 July 2015, I found copies of what was called the *OCTUPLE* Magazine which was produced by

---

[63] All this material is drawn from the Syllabus for 1939 and 1942, the papers for 1940 and 1941 having been destroyed. It should also be noted that, in modern times, there is a minimum of two years basic training followed by at least a third year of specialist training.

Left: Cricket on the Sandhurst Oval 1940 - Sandhurst Collection.

Cadets during their time at the College. The 1940 editions were available. These magazines revealed that the sports played in those days included cricket, rowing, rugby, soccer, hockey, athletics, and swimming.[64] There was also a theatre company.

The Octuple magazine included essays, poetry, and cartoons. I re-produce a couple of items which Wig must surely have seen.

In examining files in the Sandhurst Collection, I was particularly interested to see information on the rates of pay and the conditions of Officers in those days. In 1938, the most junior rank of 2nd Lieutenant received £200.75 per annum, a Captain was paid £301.15, a Major was paid £520.15, and a Lt Colonel received £784.75 per annum. As a rule, in peace time, an officer might expect to reach the rank of Captain after 8 years' service and a Major in 17 years. Clearly, war time changed the pace of promotion, but Wig's rise to a Lt Colonel by 1944 (after 4 years) was pretty good going!

---

[64] To this we may add Polo in the current era.

On being commissiomned as an officer in 1940, Wig was transferred from the Royal Artillery to the Sherwood Foresters, which was the natural regiment for someone born in Nottingham.

"But Harold it may only be a coincidence"- Sandhurst Collection

The Life of an Octurion

C Company *(to which Wig belonged)* undergoes the same system of training as others. We take it for granted that we are not the only ones who are compelled to shave with uncertain hand by electric light and to slope arms in depressing stygian gloom comparable only to night travel on the Southern Railway. ...... Socially, we are quite convinced that we set a standard entirely unsurpassed - post prandial orgies were never more convincingly performed. We can recall many amusing episodes – the tying of "clove 'itches" for kapok bridging, almost culminating in tragedy when the Company proceeded to cross the local stream (in spite of some wit's remark of "Fall in Officers", there were no casualties), the joys of bog-wheel inspection, the pleasures of digging trenches solidly for a week .....

9: Preparing For War

Following his appointment to the Sherwood Foresters regiment in 1940, Wig spent the next two years in the regular army, 18 months of which involved an extended period of preparation and training. He was deployed to active service in the Middle East in July 1942.

The term "Sherwood Foresters" is said to date back to the 15th Century. It was a name used to describe archers who hailed from Nottingham and fought as part of the English army at the Battle of Agincourt in 1415. In later times these soldiers became known as the 45th (Nottinghamshire) Regiment of Foot. The secondary title of "Sherwood Foresters" was formally granted to the Regiment by Queen Victoria in 1866. In 1881, the 45th was amalgamated with the 95th Derbyshire Regiment, and in 1902 the Sherwood Foresters (Notts and Derbys) came into being. This name continued in use through the 1914-18 and 1939-45 wars of the 20th Century and was the name in use when Wig was alive.

Army records show that Wig joined this Regiment on 8 November 1940 when he received his commission as a 2nd Lieutenant. He would eventually be deployed to the 14th Battalion (proudly and fondly called the "14th Foresters" by the members of the Battalion). It is fortunate that a history of this specific military grouping has been written and was released in 1980. The contents of this chapter draw heavily on this history, entitled *Preparing for War* and *Going to War*, which was obtained from the Mercian Regiment Archives.[65] The document was based on war diaries written by members of the 14th Foresters which are available at the British National Archives.

The document has a moving dedication from the Rt Reverend Eric Mercer, the one-time Lord Bishop of Exeter who, as Captain Mercer, served in the 14th Foresters from March 1941 until the end of the War. It reads as follows:

"The 14th Foresters consisted of a collection of one thousand of the most ordinary individual men – men of differing gifts, and from different backgrounds – who learned from each other perhaps the most difficult

---

[65] The source document is called "A Family of Fighting Men - A brief outline of the activities of the *14th Battalion the Sherwood Foresters* from 1940-1944" by Godfrey Walker MC. Written in 1980, this is an official history maintained within the Mercian Regiment Archives and permission to publish a modified version has been granted by them.

lesson that a man must ever master. They learnt that this life is not all about grabbing and keeping, not all about trampling on others in order to get to the top of the pile. Rather, it is about learning how to give, and to contribute to the greater good of the rest of the family. We learned that lesson the hard way, and the learning of it took us four years and many tens of thousands of miles. It was in the learning of it that we became a family of fighting men ....."

In the remainder of this chapter, an account is provided of how the 14th Foresters were formed, were prepared for war, and were eventually deployed to North Africa. The story covers an important eighteen months of Wig's life when expectation and anticipation were palpable for many waiting to enter the fray.

The 14th Foresters came into existence as an infantry battalion at Markeaton Park, Derby, on 9 October 1940. Membership was drawn from what was called the 50th Holding Battalion, which had been established on 1 June 1940 under the command of Major Andrews MC. In its first few months of existence, the new Battalion was short of both officers and NCOs. Indeed, on the first day following its establishment, and just a month before Wig joined the Unit, there were only 22 officers under the command of the newly promoted Lt Colonel Andrews and his second in command Major A H Gardner.

On 20 October 1940, an advance party under the command of Major Gardner was despatched to Burton Pidsea in Yorkshire which for a time became the headquarters. Two days later the whole Battalion travelled from Nottingham by train to relieve the 1st Cameron Highlanders. Their job was to defend the coastline from Withernsea, a few kms north of Spurn Point, to Great Cowden north of Hornsea. Living conditions were tough, as the men were under canvas during some unseasonal cold and wet weather, and duties involved long patrols along the much extended seaside front. Fortunately for those involved, this deployment was short-lived. Towards the end of November, orders were received for the Battalion to move to Keighley in Yorkshire, and an advance party left on 26 November 1940. The Battalion left for Keighley by train on 29 November.

Wig's MOD record shows that he joined the 14th Foresters in Keighley on 4 December 1940. He would have travelled up by train from Nottingham. As a newly graduated 2nd Lieutenant, he was urgently needed and more than welcome. Almost immediately after he joined the Battalion, the unit was told that it was to become part of the Support Group of the newly formed 8th Armoured Division (ie involving tanks). The inclusion of the 14th Foresters into this new Division was to have a considerable impact on the destiny of the Battalion and Wig. It transformed the Unit from the normal and more limited role of an infantry battalion into being an integral part of a relatively complex structure of armoured formations supported by motor and lorried infantry battalions. Many of these armoured divisions had evolved from former cavalry regiments, and the Support Group deployment carried with it a certain élan.

During the early months of 1941, the unit slowly accumulated vehicles and equipment. There was some frustration with the rate of progress, but in reality there was little opportunity for training with the new equipment because much of the country was covered in snow and ice. Indeed, at that time, many of the troops were employed in clearing snow from blocked roads and villages in the area, while in off-duty hours everyone was welcomed by the communities of Keighley and Baildon.

As the weather improved, training resumed. This was both an exciting and an anxious time for the Wigginton family as Eunice was pregnant with their first child, Michael, who was born in Nottingham on 26 March 1941. In March, the whole Battalion was on the move. The billets in Keighley and Baildon were handed over to the Royal Ulster Regiment, and the 14th Foresters Headquarters was now established in Lambourn (a large village between Swindon and Newbury in Berkshire), with the various companies disbursed in the surrounding area. Wig was located 20kms away in Chippenham. Lambourn was a centre of the horse-racing industry, and most of the billets were converted stables.

In April and May 1941, the 14th Foresters took part in several brigade and divisional training exercises. In its support group role, the unit had relatively little to do in these exercises, but their participation provided good experience of moving in convoy, and occupying defensive positions. In April, Wig was appointed as the Liaison Officer for the 8th Armoured Division ("the Division") with the rank of Captain. At the end of May, the Division was moved to the Dorking area in the English county of Surrey, and effected a complete exchange of billets with the various units of the 1st Armoured Division. The Battalion was settled in and around the village of Ockley, mainly in the buildings and outhouses of large country houses which had been requisitioned for military use.

At this time, Eunice was allowed to join Wig on the move down to Surrey,

Above left: Christ Church, Brockham, Surrey. Above right: The Lodge, Brockham Park, Surrey. Below: Box Hill White Cliffs, Surrey

and for a while they lived at a property called Brockham Park, a few kilometres from the village of Brockham which is six kms from Ockley. This substantial property had been requisitioned by the Army in 1939 from the then owner a Mr Paul Rykens who was a Dutch Wine Merchant. Between June 1941 and May 1942, when the 14th Foresters left for North Africa, Wig, Eunice, and Michael lived at "The Lodge" *(see picture)* which was, and still is, situated at the entrance to the park.

The nearby village of Brockham is a pretty place. It has the classic village green and cricket oval, with the church of Christ Church at one end and the Royal Oak pub at the other. There is little doubt that Wig and Eunice frequented both places. And just to the north are the white cliffs of Box Hill which the Germans are reported to have used for lining up on their bombing raids over London.[66] There was heavy bombing of London on 19 and 21 May 1941. I dare say that the droning noises of those aircraft often woke up the inhabitants of Brockham Park and its environs during the early 1940s.

Once settled into Surrey, the Division went through a series of major training exercises, including inter-brigade combat which involved the forces of Southern Command. As a gentle relief from these manoeuvres, when local farmers called for assistance in gathering the harvest in August 1941, the Battalion was deployed to a range of individual farms to help in the harvest.

At the end of September, a number of the officers and NCOs were redeployed and new people joined the Division and, on 15 October 1941, Major-General Charles Norman was appointed as General Commanding Officer (a position he held until 24 August 1942). In mid-October, the Battalion moved to the Chiddingfold area which is just south of Godalming in Surrey, and there was doubtless speculation about where the 14th Foresters might be sent to fight.[67]

As context for their eventual deployment of the regiment to North Africa, it should be appreciated that in late 1941 the war was not going well. In early October the Germans, who had swept across Eastern Europe, were rumoured to be advancing on Moscow. On 13 November the British aircraft carrier Ark Royal was sunk by U Boats off Gibraltar. And, throughout this period, Field

---

[66] This information is based on a contribution by local historian Robert Bartlett with whom I met in 2013.

[67] Note the location of Shere, a place which might well have been frequented by members of the 14th Foresters in 1942, and is well known by current members of the Wigginton family. An eerie thought.

Marshall Erwin Rommel was continuing to put huge pressure on British forces in North Africa. Then, on 7 December 1941, the Japanese bombed Pearl Harbor. This fateful attack on the Americans brought the Americans into hostilities, and on 11 December 1941 Hitler declared war on the United States. This succession of setbacks triggered a huge debate amongst the Allies about where the battle should be fought to turn the tide. The Russians were pushing for a second front in Western Europe, but Churchill preferred an advance from the south, with the war in North Africa assuming strategic importance. This would involve Allied landings in the West to complement an expansion of existing forces in the east. His view prevailed, and the die was cast for the 14th Foresters.

The reader should appreciate that ahead of any physical deployment, a military force would receive an order to mobilise which could take many weeks. In early 1942, rumours about such mobilisation were rife. Eventually, on 1 February, the 8th Armoured Division received its orders. Then, a few weeks later, and to the frustration of all, this decision was put on hold. Finally, on 19 March, further orders to mobilise were received for deployment to a "tropical" climate by the end of April. This was accompanied by large scale "Embarkation Leave" allowing the troops to spend a final period with their family and friends before departure. Clearly, this was "it".

At this time, the strength of the Battalion was 822 including officers, which was well down on the establishment of just over 900. In April, there was feverish activity to reinforce the existing complement with the arrival of additional transport and a new draft of 115 men. Now at full strength and awaiting orders to move, on 25 April there was an inspection by General Officer Commanding Home Forces accompanied by the Secretary of State for War Viscount Cranbourne. Prior to departure, on 1 May 1942, the Battalion was also honoured by a royal visit. King George VI inspected the whole Division drawn up on the village Green at Cranleigh in Surrey.

Three days later, the Battalion's baggage was loaded onto a train at Godalming and the baggage party left for the port of embarkation in Scotland. Wig spent his last few days with Eunice and then, on 6 May 1942, he and the remainder of the Battalion boarded a train which travelled overnight to Gourock. On 7 May 1942, the entire Battalion, with 40 Officers and 922 other ranks boarded the USS Orizaba. On the same ship travelled the HQ of 8th Armoured Division Support Group which included Wig and the personnel of the 56th Light Anti-Aircraft Regiment.

The convoy including the USS Orizaba set sail for the Middle East on 10 May 1942, on what was to be a long ten week journey around the Cape of Good Hope because the Mediterranean was not secure for Allied shipping. For many, it was the first time that they had been at sea for any length of time and they found the monotonous routine, cramped living conditions and unaccustomed American food challenging. As the ship sailed down to Portugal, and then to Africa, the heat added to other discomforts. But it wasn't all bad.

For Wig at least, he had shore leave on the Costa do Sol in Portugal. In May, he sent a post card to Eunice from Estoril in which he wrote *"One step further. I have just enjoyed a warm sunny day. Lovely sea – blue. Houses, white and red, set in brilliant green. I hope you are well. How are Michael and Edie; give them my love. Had marvellous lunch which would make you green with envy. Wine isn't much cheaper. All my love, Wig x"*

By 19 May, all ranks were dressed in the khaki drill uniform with which they had been issued before departure. Sun helmets, reminiscent of Kitchener's army in the Sudan, were much in evidence, although these were discarded on arrival in the Middle East. In an effort to break the monotony and to provide some exercise in the confined conditions, there were compulsory parades for physical training, weapons training, and signals. And at 10.30 am every day, everyone paraded to practise the drill for abandoning ship, leaving the sleeping cabins empty for inspection by the ship's officers.

Two weeks into the journey, on 22 May 1942, the convoy arrived off Freetown in Sierra Leone, but no shore leave was permitted. After a stay of four days for re-fuelling, the voyage was resumed. In early June, the convoy reached South Africa, with some ships weighing anchor at Cape Town and the remainder including the USS Orizaba travelling on to Durban. On 9 June, the 14th Foresters marched through the city of Durban to a bivouac area known as the Wool Sheds. Here, the entire personnel of the Battalion as well as other parts of the 8th Armoured Division including the 56th Anti-Aircraft Regiment were accommodated on one huge floor.

The party stayed in South Africa for five days, during which time one third of the Battalion was granted daily leave from 2.00 pm until midnight. They were warmly welcomed by the locals, including the staff of the local Dunlop factory which adjoined the camp. These kindly folk sent in lorry loads of fruit and confectionery, as well as offering the use of their playing fields for sporting activity.

The voyage resumed on 19 June, with the convoy steaming north towards the Arabian Gulf. As they approached the Gulf, the main flotilla continued towards the Suez Canal. However, the USS Orizaba accompanied and protected by HMS Devonshire, diverted to India to pick up supplies. Both ships berthed at Bombay on 1 July 1942 and, for five days, the men were allowed shore leave. On 8 July, the ship then left for Aden where it anchored for 8 hours before proceeding up the Red Sea. It arrived at the Port of Suez on 18 July. For Wig and the 14th Foresters, they were now about to enter the fray.

Part Four: North Africa

10: The Desert War

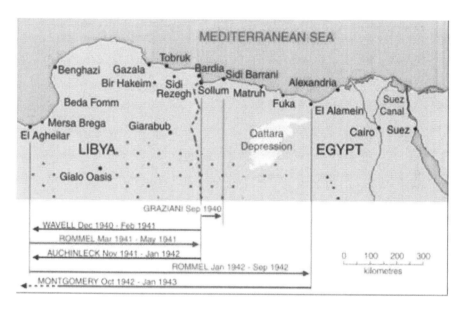

War in North Africa, 1940-43 - Dept of Pub Inf, US Army

The war in North Africa raged from December 1940 until May 1943, and the aim of this chapter is to provide the context for the account of Wig's involvement in the second half of 1942. The main ebb and flow of hostilities in this theatre is shown in the accompanying map, and much of the action centred on Tobruk. When Allied reinforcements such as Wig's unit arrived in mid-July 1942, Rommel was engaged in a concerted advance to take Egypt, the Suez Canal, and the oil fields beyond. The outcome was in the balance and things were not going at all well for the Allied cause.

To some extent, this was due to the fact that, through his Unit 621 team, Rommel was able to access Allied intelligence. Unknown to the Allies, in 1941 an American diplomat had inadvertently leaked vital codes to the Germans through the US embassy in Berlin and, as a result, Rommel always seemed to know the Allied strategy and was able to out-manoeuvre Allied troops. So the Allies suffered a succession of losses, at Gazala, Tobruk (which was lost in late June), and Matruh. Eventually, in July 1942, the Allied troops stood their ground at El Alamein only 100 kms from the port of Alexandria, and there was a stale-mate for several months despite two attempts by Rommel to break through.

The principal form of land force in the desert war in 1942 was tanks, the use of which had commenced during the First World War. In the early 20th Century, strategies and tactics for deployment of what were still called "cavalry" units were initially based on the traditional use of equine forces. But, in the course of hostilities on the western front, there was much learning about the potential and limitations of these vehicles. By the beginning of World War Two, the deployment of "armoured" divisions had become quite a complex matter combining the use of the tanks, artillery batteries, motorised units in support, and ground troops. And, by 1942, an Armoured Division consisted of a Headquarters team *(of which Wig was a member)*, Armoured Brigades, a Support unit, and Engineer Units including Signals. The Armoured Brigades consisted of a number of Armoured Regiments (i.e. tanks) which were the primary form of attack. The significantly vulnerable Support unit included motorised infantry battalions *(such as the 14th Foresters)* and artillery, and their role was to ensure that the tanks were maintained as fully operational.

On 31 July, the Allied Commander General Claude Auchinlek ceased offensive activity to allow the 8th Army to regroup with vital reinforcements arriving including the Foresters. In Cairo, there was deep concern that the Allies were about to be overwhelmed, and many units were either moved to other locations in the Middle East or were preparing to evacuate. The *Special Operations Executive* in Cairo for one had a full evacuation plan about which we will hear in a later chapter. Frustrated with the failure of first Field Marshall Archibald Wavell and then Auchinlek, on 13 August 1942, Churchill appointed General Bernard Montgomery as Commander of the 8th Army reporting to General Harold Alexander who was Commander-in-Chief for the whole Middle East.[68] Montgomery was almost immediately confronted with a major assault from the Germans. On 30 August 1942, Rommel launched an attack on Alam el Halfa, and the battle lasted until 5

---

[68] After his dismissal, Auchinlek returned to India and, in June 1943, he was appointed as Commander-in-Chief of the Indian Army. When Mountbatten was appointed Commander-in-Chief of South East Asia Command in November 1943, Auchinlek became responsible for the internal security of India, the defence of the NW Frontier, and the consolidation of India as a military base for subsequent Allied military offences. He made the training and supply of the XIVth Army a high priority ahead of its advance into Burma in 1944/45, and was commended for this work by General William Slim. He was eventually knighted.

September when the Allies succeeded in driving him back. This was followed by the 1st battle of Himeimat where the Germans were again unsuccessful in gaining ground.

Montgomery now applied all his energies to devising new strategies to defeat the Axis forces including a variety of deceptive and diversionary moves.[69] And he determined that one of the key dimensions to enabling success on the ground was to achieve air superiority. The Allies were also able to turning the tables on the Germans regarding access to intelligence. Thanks to the successful breaking of the *Enigma Code* at Bletchley, the Allies obtained access to German signals. And, by chance, Allied troops over-ran the German Unit 621 and discovered that the Germans had access to British codes. Thereafter, they began to feed false information to the enemy through their own channels. The German position was not helped by the temporary absence of Rommel for medical reasons in October 1942.

The turning point came in late October 1942, with the second Battle of El Alamein around 250kms to the west of Cairo. On 23 October, in *Operation Lightfoot*, Allied bombers launched a huge air attack on Axis front line positions which lasted for four days until 28 October. This significantly weakened the Axis forces on the ground. With air superiority, the Allies ground forces engaged the Axis troops in a series of tank and infantry battles resulting in a major penetration of Axis lines to the south. Between 23 and 28 October, these attacks included the battles of the Oxalic Line, Ruweisat Ridge, Kidney Ridge, Tell el Eisa, and Point 29. In response, the Axis formations retreated but then on 26-28 October, they launched a major counter-attack, with significant advances in the battles at Position Snipe and Thompson's Point.

On 1 November, the Allies launched *Operation Supercharge* with a major attack on Axis lines. The Axis forces were confronted with an overwhelming Allied force, and were defeated at the battles of Tell el Aqqaqir, Sidi Abdel Rahman, and Himeimat on 2 November. By 5 November, Axis lines had been broken on a wide front. Rommel sought Hitler's permission to retreat and this was refused. But Rommel retreated anyway. The news of Allied success, after such a torrid year, quickly fed back to Cairo and London. The people in Britain were jubilant and the church bells literally rang out. On 8

---

[69] It should be noted that, whilst the Axis forces were led by Rommel, the majority of the troops consisted of Italian Divisions. Use of the term "Axis" reflects the joint German/Italian nature of the forces.

November 1942, in a speech at the Mansion House in London, Prime Minister Churchill said: *"This is not the end. It is not even the beginning of the end. But it is, perhaps, the end of the beginning."*

However, the war in North Africa was far from finished and, at this point, US forces joined the fray together with a further British force. On 8 November, *Operation Torch* was launched with mass landings in Morocco and Algeria to the west. The Americans and British troops made rapid progress, travelling east, and were soon entering Tunisia. On 17 November, the US 1st Army met with German troops at the battle of Djebel Abiod and there was fierce fighting until 26 November. Meanwhile, in the east, the British 8th Army continued its offensive westward from Egypt, soon to be reinforced by additional fighter planes deployed by the Americans. The advance was relentless, with a series of battles resulting in the re-taking of Tobruk on 13 November, the airfield at Derna on 15 November, and then Benghazi and the Tocra airfield on 20 November.[70] This was followed by further battles, with the main Allied force attacking through Libya from the east and the recently arrived British and Americans advancing through Tunisia from the west. Finally, the siege of Malta was lifted and by Christmas Day 1942, the 8th Army was in Sirte in western Libya.

By April 1943, Rommel had left North Africa leaving General Hans-Jürgen von Arnim to handle a last-ditch defence around Tunis and Bizerte. His surrender, with 230,000 Axis troops, on 7 May 1943, meant the war in North Africa was over, and a new phase would soon begin -- the attack on southern Europe.

---

[70] The airfields at Derna and Tocra were significant as bases south of Italy for SOE air operations.

11: Wig and the Eighth Army

Wig and the 14th Foresters arrived in North Africa at what was one of the turning points of the war, which culminated in the victory of the 8th Army at the 2nd Battle of El Alamein in November. The precise role played by Wig is difficult to specify as the various accounts on record make no specific mention of him. However, as a Captain and a Liaison Officer with the 8th Armoured Division, he was "in the thick of it" with responsibility which included communications.

At this critical point in the Regular Army, there is some doubt about Wig's physical location. According to his MOD record, he was based in Cyrenaica which is the eastern coastal region of Libya running up to the Egyptian border and including significant places such as Tobruk and the airfield at Derna. However, at the time of his arrival, the Allies did not occupy this territory, and it is likely that this entry in his file reflected either a commitment to regaining lost ground or even possibly a difference in the boundaries between then and the current day. In any event, it would be correct to say that he spent most of his time in western Egypt and eastern Libya as the 8th Army engaged and defeated Rommel.

MOD records show that he personally arrived in the Middle East on 5 July 1942. This is a couple of weeks ahead of the arrival at Port Said of the USS Orizaba carrying the main force of the 14th Foresters (which had been diverted to Bombay), and suggests that for the voyage from South Africa he transferred to one of the other ships in the convoy. It is therefore likely that he was involved as a Liaison Officer in the first action involving the 8th Armoured Division under the command of Major-General Charles Norman. They went into battle in the second week of July and suffered heavy casualties in a minefield. As a result, thereafter they were never able to operate as a complete formation. By the end of the year the men had been allocated to other divisions, and Wig himself had moved on to the Special Operations Executive.

The main body of the 14th Foresters (still a unit of the 8th Armoured Division) disembarked at Port Said on 19 July 1942 and were immediately located to what was called Camp 23 at the village of Tahag near the town of Qassasin. This was close to the Suez Canal and about 30kms to the west of Ismailia lying between Port Said and Cairo. There they "dug in" with other units, preparing for action, and Churchill is reported to have visited them as they prepared for battle.

On 5 August 1942, the 8th Armoured Division, which at this point consisted of 13,325 men and 130+ tanks, staged a three day exercise wearing the Divisional emblem "GO" on their uniforms. This was their first real experience of desert conditions, with much learning. According to records, this was to be the last time that the 14th Foresters operated as part of the 8th Armoured Division. Later that month, the 14th were redeployed to the 9th Armoured Brigade.[71]

For the next three months, there is no record of what happened to Wig apart from the fact that he was one of many directly involved in the military manoeuvres that culminated in the second battle of El Alamein commencing 23 October.[72] During this period, the depleted 8th Armoured Division was involved in a variety of support activities including the dangerous business of clearing mines ahead of and during *Operation Supercharge*. So this is one possible explanation of how he spent his time. However, it *is* possible that he was deployed to 8th Army headquarters which were at Burj al Arab near Alexandria. Or he may have remained with the 14th Foresters, in which case he would have transferred to the 9th Armoured Brigade although this does not appear on his MOD record.

Given the importance of the battle of El Alamein, and clear evidence of Wig's presence, what follows is one account of the battle. Since Wig had a close association with the 14th Foresters, and in the absence of any other record, I have chosen to draw on the available material on the battle from their perspective which is provided in the history by Godfrey Walker.[73]

On 12 August, the 14th Foresters were moved to a new camp at Fayid and, within ten days, all heavy baggage was deposited at the Infantry Base Depot at Genefa. On 22 August, the Battalion moved in two trains to Amiriya near Alexandria, and then camped about eight kms into the desert. At this point the Battalion was split into a number of teams working in support of other military units. One became part of a composite Regiment of tanks and infantry commanded by the Officer Commanding the Royal Wiltshire

---

[71] Following the second and decisive Battle of El Alamein, the 8th Armoured Division was broken up, and eventually disbanded in Egypt on 1 January 1943. In the meantime, the name of the division continued in use for the purpose of military deception.

[72] Wig's wife Eunice provided first hand corroboration of this.

[73] The following material draws on the previously mentioned history of the 14th Foresters history written by Godfrey Walker MC made available by the Mercian Regiment archive.

Yeomanry. A second group moved six kms east to become part of a composite force named CALFORCE based on the 151 Infantry Brigade. Another company was placed with the 3rd Hussars, and yet another with the Warwickshire Yeomanry. The remaining troops moved to the 8th Army rest camp at El Gami outside Alexandria.

On 30 August reports were received of what was to be the unsuccessful German counter offensive on Alam el Halfa and, on 9 September, after some re-organisation and re-equipment, the 9th Armoured Brigade came under the command of the 2nd New Zealand Division led by Lt General Freyburg VC. In mid-October, the Battalion moved 60 kms westward to an area south of

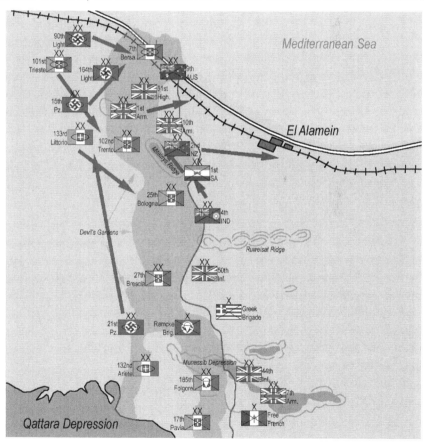

2nd Battle of El Alamein, October 1942 - Wikipedia

83

the El Hammam station, and on 22 October, they moved further west. This was all part of the build-up which culminated with the major 8th Army offensive on 23 October known as the second and decisive *Battle of El Alamein* as described below.[74]

According to the Regimental war diaries, following an extensive exercise to remove minefields undertaken by Wig's 8th Armoured Division, the 8th Army attacked on a front consisting of four Armoured Divisions. On the right was the Australian 9th Division, at right centre was the 51st Highland Division, at left centre was the 2nd New Zealand Division supported by the 14th Foresters, and on the left was the 1st South African Division. The HQ, where Wig was probably located, was on the coast to the north of El Alamein.

The task of the 9th Armoured Brigade was to fight in its tank role. Each of the armoured units had with it a Motor Company of 14th Foresters moving in what were called "soft skinned" vehicles such as jeeps, and 15 cwt and 30 cwt trucks which had no armoured protection. The task of the Motor Company was to provide infantry support to the tanks whenever they needed it and this meant being up behind the tanks at all times. Not surprisingly, the Motor Company units suffered heavy casualties from enemy fire.

A major battle ensued on the Miteiriya ridge, in which the 2nd New Zealand Division achieved its objective and ventured further ahead, clearing minefields as they went, and driving back and destroying German tanks. Enemy shelling of the ridge continued all day, causing heavy casualties. After considerable confusion, some regrouping, and a few hours respite during the night, the 9th Armoured Brigade moved forward again but met with considerable resistance. In the meantime, the 14th Foresters dug in to defend themselves against sustained enemy shelling. At 4.00 pm, the Brigade was ordered to withdraw behind the ridge to occupy the positions held the previous evening. On 26 October, there was regrouping behind the ridge and, at last light, the whole of 2nd New Zealand Division was relieved by the South Africans.

On 30th October, the 9th Armoured Brigade moved to a new assembly area at El Alamein to prepare for the next offensive which was *Operation Supercharge*. The plan for this operation was that, on 1st November, the 2nd New Zealand Division with the 151 and 152 Infantry Brigades would put in

---

[74] An account of the contribution of the 9th Armoured Brigade and the 14th Foresters to the Battle of El Alamein, prepared by Brigadier C E Lucas Phillips, can be found in a book he wrote entitled *"Alamein"* (William Heinemann, London, 1962).

8th Army troops at Great Pyramid, Giza 1942

a night attack to continue an earlier attack by the Australian Infantry Division. Then, during the night, the 9th Armoured Brigade would follow up with a forward surge of 2 kms. Finally, at first light, the 1st Armoured Division would advance through the 9th Armoured Division.

This plan was implemented at 01.05 hours on 1 November and the infantry attacks went well behind a very heavy barrage. For a while, the Armoured Divisions were held up due to congestion on the approach tracks and trouble with mines. However, at 05.45 hours, all the armoured regiments with their 14th Forester motor units were moving forwards as planned, and at dawn they met fierce resistance. The Royal Wiltshire yeomanry and their support units were fought to a standstill and lost nearly all their tanks. Across the front, there were similar stories for the other armoured divisions and support units. The 14th Foresters were under extreme pressure with heavy losses. But they performed gallantly under continuous heavy fire and, by the end of the day, the Germans began a major withdrawal. The Armoured Brigades went in hot pursuit for several days.

By 5th November, the army reached Fuka Airfield and the next target was

Sidi Hameish. At this point, torrential rain rendered the desert impassable for tanks and vehicles alike. Supply lines were cut, and the motor units could not keep up with the tanks. Everything ground to a halt. Four days later, on 9th November, conditions improved and the leading units of the Brigade passed through the Mersa Matruh minefield and turned north onto the Sidi Barrani Road.

With the main battle won, the troops were elated but also hugely exhausted. There must have been great relief when orders were received that the Brigade including the 14th Foresters was to withdraw and return to Cairo to reform and refit. For a few days, the troops rested, and then the move back to Cairo commenced on 21 November 1942. This involved a journey of 250 kms along the coast, via a staging area at El Onayid. The following day, the unit covered 220 kms and they reached what was called Cowley camp in the shadow of the Pyramids outside Cairo at 8.15 pm that evening. This picture, taken in a spot next to the Cowley camp, shows Wig (He stands in the centre of the back row with a folder under his arm) with troops of his unit. This may well have been the last picture taken of him whilst he was genuinely an active member of the Regular Army.

Finally, it is interesting to note that, during this period of his life (five months July to November 1942), there is evidence that Wig was able to communicate with people back in England. Indeed, Eunice tells of post cards, telegrams, and letters which she received providing fairly innocuous information about everyday life, including the heat, the squalor, and the infiltration into everything of sand. Like many of his comrades, he also shared with those at home the joy of the victory of the 8th Army in North Africa.

I end this part of Wig's story with pictures of a couple of personal items. The first is a belonging which was clearly dear to him. Somewhere along the part of the journey that involved the Sherwood Foresters, he had a wallet made which he then carried with him to the end of the war. For some reason, he did not have it with him when he made his last trip in the Far East and it survived at his home in Calcutta in 1945. It was returned to the family in 1946. Interestingly, when I came to examine the wallet, it contained a pass for Sandhurst dated 1940 and a map of the West of Scotland, probably from when he did training at Arisaig.[75] The second picture shows Wig's personal army compass, which is dated 1940 and which is also in the Family archive.

---

[75] As we will see later, this was an SOE training centre in Scotland north-west of Fort William.

The next stage of Wig's life, commencing on 29 November 1942, was to take him in a very different direction. To understand what he was doing, we must now consider a totally different approach to war that Britain, and eventually its Allies, undertook to overcome the forces of darkness.

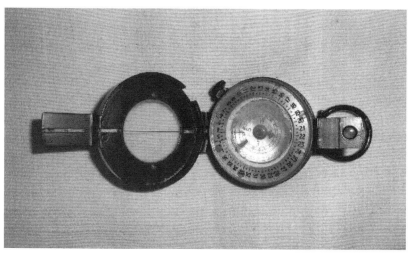

Two treasured possessions. Above: Wig's Wallet with initials and Sherwood Foresters emblem. Below: Wig's Sighting compass

Part Five: Irregular Warfare

12: The Special Operations Executive

During his period of respite at Cowley camp, in the shadow of the Great Pyramid at Giza, Wig was recruited to join the *Special Operations of Executive* ("SOE"). To those he knew outside the organisation, probably including his wife Eunice, he continued to be a member of the Sherwood Foresters with a military rank. The reality was very different. For nearly three years, from November 1942, Wig was to become pre-occupied with SOE air operations.

Since the end of the war, many books have been written about SOE and its work in theatres of war which stretched from Europe to the Far East. What follows in this chapter is a brief history of the organisation, with information sufficient for the reader to understand the nature and scope of its activities relevant to Wig's life. As a kind of pre-history, the story begins in the late 1930s when, with the prospect of war, a number of undercover bodies were established in Britain to exploit

SOE wartime emblem - Pinterest

opportunities to undermine Germany and its allies. In 1938, the *Secret Intelligence Service* of the British Foreign Office (the "SIS"), which was mostly involved in collecting intelligence, created a unit called *Section D* to specialise in subversion and sabotage in Germany. The Foreign Office also established a propaganda unit most frequently referred to as *EH* (named after the office in which it was based, Electra House in London). Meanwhile, the War Office established a small research unit called *Military Intelligence Research* ("MIR") to assist in its intelligence gathering. As will be evident, these and similar activities attracted a plethora of acronyms designed to confuse and confound outsiders.

During the summer of 1940, following a review undertaken by Sir Maurice Hanky, it was decided to place all the *"irregular"* activities under a unified command, independent of the normal processes of Parliamentary scrutiny, which became known as the *Special Operations Executive* ("SOE"). This was a name to which reference was never actually made during the war, with the organisation being identified by a range of other names to hide its true identity. SOE was actually founded on 19 July by Neville Chamberlain who was still a member of the Cabinet. Initially, the organisation was responsible to a left-leaning Labour Party politician named Hugh Dalton who was appointed Minister of the Department of Economic Warfare ("MEW"). This was considered to be an adept front for the *"irregular"* activities and the Prime Minister, Winston Churchill, gave Dalton the mission to *"set Europe ablaze"*.

To understand the true nature of Wig's activities as described in the rest of this book, it is worth noting the mission of SOE bearing in mind the United Nation's post-war charter for "Irregular Warfare". Under Article 51 of the Charter, there is provision for "self-defence" that may be interpreted to encompass political, economic and strategic elements.[76] Foreshadowing this in its own terms of reference, SOE's political aim was to undermine the morale of the enemy and their collaborators, and to raise the spirits of resistance movements. Economically, the aim was to damage the enemy's materiel, and infiltrate weapons, explosives, and sabotage equipment to sympathetic forces. Strategically, the aim was to damage the enemy's man-power and communications and improve those of the Allies and their supporters. Consistent with these objectives, SOE was conceived as a world-wide secret organisation despatching trained agents by land, sea and air to carry out specific missions working where possible with resistance movements.

Initially, the national leadership team of the new organisation consisted of Dalton as Minister, Sir Frank Nelson (known as "CD" and equivalent to Executive Chairman in modern organisational parlance), and Gladwyn Jebb as CEO and leader of operational activity. This team established three branches covering the delivery of propaganda, the conduct of operations in the field, and a planning capability. The new organisation was slow to recruit staff, and inherited most of its first employees from the Foreign Office's SIS. Initially, most of the new people were drawn from the English public school system and the ranks of merchant bankers, stock brokers, and business

---

[76] The United Nations Charter was signed in San Francisco on 26 June 1945 and came into force on 24 October 1945.

executives based in the City (ie the financial sector of London). Later, from late 1942, there was a significant influx of people with a military background such as Wig.

Apart from the recruitment and training of new people, during the establishment phase there were significant challenges. To start with, the existing covert organisations (e.g. the SIS) were not well disposed to assisting what they saw as a "bunch of amateurs". Secondly, for SOE to become operationally effective, there was a need for specialist training. The facilities and staff for this were not readily available, and a range of training units had to be established from scratch. Also, the resistance movements in occupied countries that SOE was designed to assist (in setting Europe ablaze) did not materialise out of thin air. 1940/41 were bleak years, when the population of Europe was left reeling by the advance of the Axis powers, and resistance was barely evident.

In the early stages of the war, the two arms of "special" or covert operations (SIS and SOE) worked reasonably well together. Indeed, SOE terms of reference provided that all of its cypher communications would run through SIS, that intelligence collected by SOE would be passed to SIS, and that SIS approval would be sought when engaging agents. However, the two operations were occasionally at odds and, with the reputation of the SIS severely under pressure because of perceived failure to provide intelligence in the face of mounting set backs on all fronts of the war, SOE had the opportunity to grow. And, as the size and scope of SOE expanded, so did the tensions between the two organisations, particularly at a senior level. Relationships were not helped by the fact that SOE was not a direct party to the deliberations and determinations of either the Foreign Office or the military Joint Chiefs of Staff. Eventually, as a result of a major dispute between the two bodies, in August 1941, responsibility for propaganda was wrested away by the Foreign Office and, at the same time, SOE took over responsibility for its own communications activity.

Following a Cabinet reshuffle on 19 February 1942, Hugh Dalton moved from the MEW to the Department of Trade and was succeeded as the Minister responsible for SOE by Lord Selborne.[77] Shortly after, Nelson (CD) retired, and CEO Gladwyn Jebb left. In May 1942, Nelson was succeeded by Sir Charles Hambro who became Executive Head. Effectively, this meant that the three heads had been reduced to two. At first, Selborne and Hambro

---

[77] A summary of the succession of SOE leadership is provided in Appendix 7.

SOE HQ, 64 Baker Street, London

worked well together. However, during 1943, they had a falling out and, in September 1943, Hambro resigned and was succeeded as Executive Head by Major General Sir Colin Gubbins. Selborne and Gubbins then proceeded to see out the war, and Gubbins eventually turned out the lights in Baker Street in January 1946.

Initially, SOE had its headquarters at 2 Caxton Street in London's West End. However, the organisation soon outgrew these premises and, on 31 October 1940, moved to its own separate headquarters at 64 Baker Street, London W1 which, amongst other things, was used for induction briefings.[78] Eventually, adjacent buildings were also commandeered. Outside London, SOE established a large number of training centres including a lodge at Arisaig in western Scotland and Inchmery House, Beaulieu in Hampshire.[79]

For implementation of its operational activity, which in the first two years was focussed on Western Europe, the organisation initially used RAF bases. However, it eventually established its own airfield at RAF Tempsford which was north of London in Bedfordshire. This secret airfield became the home to what were called the *"Special Duties"* Squadrons.[80] No. 138 Squadron dropped SOE agents and their supplies into occupied Europe, and No. 161 Squadron specialised in delivery and retrieval of virtually anyone by actually

---

[78] I visited this building in May 2015. It has not changed, and has a plaque on the outside wall commemorating its function in the 1940s.

[79] Arisaig is another place that I visited in 2015. See Chapter 13 which covers Wig's recruitment and training.

[80] The term "Special Duties" refers to aircraft made available by various Allied air forces to undertake SOE operations. They were crewed by members of the regular air forces and deployed by SOE on covert missions.

landing in enemy occupied Europe.[81] Adjacent to the airfield was *Gibraltar Farm Barn*, where agents were kitted out before leaving for occupied territory. This structure was designed to look like a normal farm building to fool German air-reconnaissance. Supplies for entering the field included a parachute, foreign currency, Benzedrine tablets to combat tiredness, some purification tablets to render stream water drinkable, and the L (lethal) pill containing cyanide.

Apart from training facilities, SOE established a number of specific purpose "Stations" in the UK which specialised in various types of activity designed to support the under-cover operations. These stations included **Station X** which was a scientific research centre, **Station XII** which focussed on the invention, testing, and manufacture of devices for undercover warfare, and **Station XV** which involved the provision of a multitude of "irregular" products. This station created all the things required to maintain a false identity including identity cards, birth certificates, ration cards, and travel permits. They also converted items of English clothing and footwear to continental specification and appearance.[82] And perhaps the most interesting section of the unit was the "Dirty Tricks" Department which was responsible for inventing exploding rats, animal-dung tyre-bursters, explosive bicycle pumps, incendiary cigarettes, wireless transmitters disguised as vacuum cleaners, explosive sewing machines and musical instruments, explosive coal, a fountain pen which shot tear gas, and double-edged commando knives.

SOE eventually set up offices abroad in all theatres of war. In Western Europe, there were bases in the capital cities of three neutral countries, Portugal (Lisbon), Sweden (Stockholm), and Switzerland (Berne) to which was added a number of bases in Italy after the invasion of that country in 1943.[83] In the early years, these missions were centres for SOE's activities in sabotage of infrastructure - destroying railways, power stations, factories and canals in western and Eastern Europe. SOE would arrange to parachute agents into occupied territory and "extract" them afterwards. However, by late 1942 when Wig was recruited, the main focus switched to instigating,

---

[81] Over 80 aircraft were lost from Tempsford during the war, with many of their crews being killed.

[82] This account is taken from *"A Pictorial Record of the SOE"* by Juliette Pattinson (Caxton Editions, London, 2001).

[83] An "official" history of the Berne mission, written by Malcom Munthe, is provided in SOE File HS 7-199.

assisting, leading, and supplying insurgents in occupied territories, in support of Allied military activity where appropriate.

Of passing interest for Wig's story is the base in Lisbon which, in the early years of the war, was a stop-over for what were regular flights between Africa and London. Like many SOE staff, he passed through the city on a number of occasions. And we have in family possession some earrings which he brought from that city as a present for his wife. Eunice used to speculate that they had been used to transport messages, because they have a secret compartment accessed by unscrewing the lower section.

In the early years of the War, SOE established a base in Cairo with a very wide remit to cover the Middle East, North Africa and the Balkans. It was semi-independent of London and became a great hub for SOE activity in the middle years of the war, with a variety of Code names including MO4 and Force 133. The status of the mission was at times precarious, with the possibility in 1942 of the Germans and Italians launching a successful invasion of Egypt. To cover this eventuality, there were well advanced evacuation plans and, when Rommel was making his last big push at El Alamein, staff began to destroy files and transfer some staff to Jerusalem.[84] However, by the time that Wig joined this mission in November 1942, the *"Flap"* as it was called was over and things had settled down. Operations out of Cairo were also not without their difficulties, including tensions with SOE headquarters in London, the Foreign Office and associated governments in exile, and the military, not to mention conflict between internal factions. There will be periodic references to these tensions in later chapters of this book, and they would at times have made the work of operational people like Wig quite difficult. A full account of life in that office is provided in Part Six of this book.

With the entry of the Americans into the War, following the Japanese attack on Pearl Harbor in December 1941, Churchill persuaded Roosevelt to establish a presence in the western part of North Africa. Consequently, in 1942, SOE set up a major centre called *"Massingham"* under the leadership of Colonel Douglas Dodds-Parker and later Brigadier John Anstey.[85] The unit operated out of the *Club des Pins* at a place called Guyotville which was 24

---

[84] Details of these plans are provided in SOE File HS 3-123.

[85] As will be related later, John Anstey (who was later to become Sir John Anstey) was a friend of Wig's and of Eunice. In peace time, he was a Director of Imperial Tobacco based in Nottingham. He was also to work with Wig in South East Asia.

kms from Algiers. It was deliberately located adjacent to the then Allied Force Headquarters of General Dwight D Eisenhower. Initially established to support Allied efforts on North Africa, for a time this became the main base for major operations right across southern Europe including into Italy.

In early 1943, with the end of the war in North Africa and the establishment of an Allied foothold in Italy, there was a major redeployment of SOE resources to that country, with bases in the south eastern Puglia region which became the main centre of support to resistance movements across the whole of southern and Eastern Europe apart from Greece (which continued to be serviced from Cairo).

The build-up in Italy came from several sources. Massingham established No 1 Special Force with responsibility for Italian operations and, following various preliminary deployments, this was consolidated into what became the *Maryland Mission* at a town called Monopoli under the leadership of Commander Gerald Holdsworth. Consequently, the level of resources based at Massingham was wound back, with residual forces supporting resistance in the south of France until the war was concluded. As hostilities advanced up the leg of Italy, in February 1945, Holdsworth eventually transferred the *Maryland Mission* to Siena.

SOE in Cairo also wished to take advantage of the geographical position of southern Italy, with their focus on the Balkans and other European theatres. In September 1943, they sent a small advance team to support the exiled King of Italy and his provisional government who moved across from Cairo to Brindisi to establish a forward base. Shortly after, Wig and a few others were deployed to Caserta in south west Italy in order to liaise with what became the forward base for AFHQ. As will be indicated in Chapter 20 of this book, SOE eventually established the overarching Special Operations Mediterranean ("SOM") in Bari, with Major General William Stawell taking up residence in Mola di Bari in April 1944. This new unit was created to co-ordinate operations across the whole of southern and eastern Europe including No 1 Special Force.[86]

Finally, from early on, SOE had a presence in the Far East, which eventually became known as Force 136.[87] The main theatres of covert

---

[86] The SOE facilities in southern Italy were based in a number of locations north of Brindisi, of which the main centres were Bari (where Wig was based in 1944), Torre a Mare (10kms south of Bari), Mola di Bari (20kms south of Bari) and Monopoli (45kms south of Bari).

[87] An account of Far East operations, particularly during Wig's time, is provided in Chapter

activity were Burma, Thailand, Malaya, and Singapore. The scope of operations was restricted by a firm understanding with the Americans that SOE would not work in certain parts of the region. In particular, this applied to China, Indo-China, and Japan itself which were the province of American military activity and where the main vehicle for covert operations was the American Office of Strategic Services ("OSS"). This effectively left the British to focus on territories bordering the Indian Ocean.

Reflecting the focus on defending India, in 1941 SOE operations were initially based in the city of Meerut near Delhi under the leadership of Sir Colin Mackenzie. However, when Mountbatten established the headquarters of South East Asia Command in Kandy in modern day Sri Lanka in 1944, he persuaded Mackenzie to relocate SOE headquarters to adjacent offices on the island. As the war in Europe moved to its final stages, with the invasion of France in June 1944, and the advance on eastern and western fronts of large allied armies, SOE forces were gradually redeployed to the Far East. And this is what took Wig to India in early 1945.

Beyond the headquarters, SOE had a range of operational bases in India and what is now known as Bangla Desh. Throughout the war, Calcutta was a major centre with an airport at Jessore, and it was to Calcutta that Wig was deployed in 1945. Interestingly, there was close co-operation with an SOE off-shoot based in Melbourne called SOA (Special Operations Australia).[88] This unit undertook operations in New Guinea, Indonesia and Singapore, with some notable under cover attacks on the Japanese navy.

Despite its wide reach, the actual number of people employed by SOE, across the globe, was quite modest. By the end of the war, SOE employed just under 10,000 men and 3,200 women. However, it was by far the biggest organisation of its kind. And there were hundreds of thousands of resistance fighters operating under its command or influence, not to mention the 32,000 men working as the crews of Special Duties aircraft.

Although, in the early years, SOE mostly operated through agents in plain clothes, a principal form of engagement was the deployment of uniformed British Liaison Officers ("BLOs") who were inserted behind enemy lines to support the resistance. These were called *Jedburgh* teams, the first of whom operated in northern and Western Europe.[89] They were the first SOE units to

---

[88] SOA was also known as IASD – the Inter Allied Service Department.

[89] The expression took its name, probably selected at random from a list of pre-approved code names, from the town of Jedburgh in the Scottish Borders.

co-operate directly with the American OSS, whose involvement in late 1943 was warmly welcomed as they quickly deployed a fleet of B-24 Liberator aircraft operating from RAF Harrington in England in what was called *Operation Carpetbagger*.[90]

No account of SOE activity would be complete without a reference to the FANYs on whom Wig would have relied for much of the administrative work in the offices were he was stationed.[91] Women in the British military services were precluded from combatant action by the Geneva Convention. Accordingly, female agents were recruited from civilian life. However, SOE required competent administrative staff to undertake a wide range of confidential work. Apart from administrative duties, the FANYs were also trained to encode and decode messages and to act as wireless operators. In the course of the War, they were despatched to bases in the UK, North Africa, Italy and the Far East working alongside operators from the Royal Corps of Signals.

Also, we must not forget the all-important system of secret communication which would have been the daily "bread and butter" for SOE staff. Every SOE agent had a personal code that was specific to them, and a copy was held at home base. Initially, agents used a single word but, as the organisation expanded, the coding became more complex and agents used phrases or even poems called *"Work-Out Keys"* or WOKs which were lines from published works.[92] The system was refined by Leo Marks who was the head of Coding at SOE's F section involving operations into France. He required that agents made up their own poems which the Germans would never be able to fathom. One such is the famous poem which he wrote in memory of a loved one for use by the redoubtable SOE agent Violette Szabo in sending signals which reads as follows:[93]

---

[90] *Operation Carpetbagger* was a term used for a number of missions involving the aerial supply of weapons and other materiel to the resistance in France, the Low Countries, Denmark and Norway by the US Army Air Force that began on 4 January 1944. They also picked up airman who had bailed out of aircraft.

[91] Much of this material is drawn from the book by Juliette Pattinson entitled *"Secret War – A Pictorial Record of the SOE"*.

[92] Again, material taken from the book by Juliette Pattinson, entitled *"Secret War – A Pictorial Record of the SOE"*.

[93] Violette Szabo's story is told in the book and film of the same name entitled *"Carve Her Name with Pride"* by RJ Minney (1958), and these words figure prominently in that film.

The life that I have
Is all that I have
And the life that I have is yours.

The love that I have
Of the life that I have
Is yours and yours and yours.

A sleep I shall have
A rest I shall have
Yet death will be but a pause.

For the peace of my years
In the long green grass
Will be yours and yours and yours.

SOE Commemorative Relief, 'Spirit of Resistance'

Later, Marks invented a system of what were called One Time Pads ("OTPs"). With this system, both the agent and the coding office had identical pads which were pages of randomly selected groups of five letters.

Finally, with the end of the war in Asia in mid-1945, the authorities in London began to wind back SOE operations. In July 1945, there was a General Election in the UK and the Labour Party came to power. They inherited a decision already made by outgoing Foreign Minister Sir Anthony Eden to liquidate the organisation. The final act was implemented on 15 January 1946 by the new Foreign Minister Ernest Bevin.

During the period 1946-48, a history of the organisation was prepared by William Mackenzie although it was not published until much later.[94] Another notable history, which was prepared for a BBC TV series, was written by M R D Foot.[95] SOE Files at the British National Archives also contain a large number of unpublished histories covering various theatres of the war.

---

[94] William Mackenzie's book is entitled "The Secret History of the Special Operations Executive 1940-45" (St Ermin's Press, London, 2000).
[95] MRD Foot's book is entitled "An Outline History of the Special Operations Executive 1940-46" (BBC, London, 1984).

However, around 80% of SOE papers have been destroyed, partly as a result of a fire in 1948 but also as a result of deliberate and periodic weeding.

Although well and truly gone, the SOE is not forgotten, and lives on in the memory of many through what is known as the Special Forces Club. This institution was established in 1945 with premises in a discretely identified building in a pleasant part of London near Hyde Park. The current Patron is the Princess Royal, and includes amongst its members those retired from the SOE, MI6, and the Special Air Service. Interestingly, membership is open not only to SOE people but also their offspring.

I had lunch there with SOE contacts in May 2015. It's a delightful place, in the style of the classic "English gentleman's club", with many portraits of notable SOE personalities on the walls. There are a lot of special touches. Even the coffee was served with a special flourish as can be seen in this picture.

Parachute in coffee, Special Forces Club

13: Wig's SOE Recruitment and Training

There is no written account of the process by which Wig came to be recruited to SOE, nor are there any detailed records about his training apart from his attendance at a course on parachute jumping. However, from the experience of contemporaries, one can make an educated guess about both his recruitment and training. As we have seen, towards the end of November 1942, the war in North Africa was drawing to a close. Having brought together a formidable range of resources, the commanders of the Middle East and North African forces (Generals Alexander and Montgomery) and their political masters convened to consider the redeployment of the troops after a period of rest and recovery. Pending a decision, many of the forces were camped in and around Cairo, with Wig at the Cowley camp near Giza. Others were despatched to other parts of the Middle East for recovery, before being prepared for their part in the next stage of the war which involved the attack on Sicily and then Italy.

As a Liaison Officer with the headquarters of one of the Armoured Divisions within the British 8th Army, in November 1942 Wig was put into a "Holding Group" of personnel ahead of redeployment. In his case, the 8th Armoured Division was about to be wound up and the 9th Armoured Division deployed to Europe.[96] At this time, SOE was already established at Rustum Building in Cairo and was gradually expanding its operations. In particular, newly appointed Chief of Staff Brigadier Keble was keen to see an expansion of air operations, and he and Head of Mission Lord Glenconner were lobbying strongly for the deployment of additional Special Duties aircraft to improve SOE effectiveness in the Balkans. To this end, it was decided to establish an Air Operations section at Rustum Building and the search was on for a suitable officer to run the show.

If the recruitment of other SOE officers is anything to go by, Keble would have had access to information on officers who were available pending redeployment, and Wig's background in logistics, his inter-personal skills, and his organising ability would have come to his attention. One imagines that Wig would have been called to a meeting for a relatively casual discussion about his aspirations, and that Keble would have decided that he was the kind of fellow who would get on with the job without too much fuss.

---

[96] The 8th Armoured Division was disbanded in Egypt on 1 January 1943. Thereafter, the name was used for military deception.

Arisaig House

And, from all accounts, Wig was a pretty charming kind of guy which might have helped. From Wig's perspective, I think he would have jumped at the idea of joining SOE, providing an opportunity for adventure and excitement not to mention the covert nature of activities.

Almost immediately after his transfer to what was called MO4 (otherwise known as SOE Force 133), Wig was sent on the parachute course which he attended at an airfield near Cairo in December 1942. The training included jumps from Dakota, Liberator, Hudson, Wellington and Halifax aircraft. However, since he was at various stages involved in the full range of "Irregular Warfare" activities, although he was never an agent or British Liaison Officer ("BLO"), he was involved in field work such as reconnaissance. It is therefore probably correct to say that, in preparation, he would have gone to one or more of the places which provided the standard modules for training SOE staff.

Training for SOE people working in the field was conducted in two phases, Group A and Group B.[97] The preliminary Group A course lasted about two to four weeks and, for this, most people attended an Elizabethan house called Wanborough Manor near Guildford in Surrey. Assuming that the individual successfully passed this first hurdle, they then went on to a para-military Group B course which lasted between three and five weeks.

One of the first of the Group B training schools to be established was in Arisaig which is a relatively remote village to the west of Fort William in Scotland. The training was run out of a local country mansion called Arisaig House, as shown in the picture. I visited this place in June 2015. It is set in some pretty wild and beautiful country, with a river flowing along the southern boundary of the grounds. The house is fairly extensive, and is still used as a conference and training centre.

Access to this remote area is either by road or rail, and the village still has

Wig's Sleeve Dagger

a railway station. These days, it is served by a steam railway which runs through to the nearby coastal town and harbour of Mallaig which is a port giving access to the Hebridean island of Skye. The surrounding terrain would have been excellent for survival training.

As Juliette Pattinson records: *"The Group B course focussed on survival skills, such as field-craft and map work, as well as being taught unarmed combat and silent killing. The agents also underwent sabotage training, learning how to blow up railway bridges and locomotives with plastic explosives. A poacher taught them how to live off the land and they were shown how to load, aim and fire a range of weapons."* The training in armed and unarmed combat skills at Arisaig was provided by William E.

---

[97] These descriptions of the training centres are taken from the book by Juliette Pattinson *"Secret War - A Pictorial Record of the SOE"*.

Fairbairn and Eric A. Sykes, former Inspectors in the Shanghai Municipal Police.

I have reason to think that Wig may have attended this place because, in his wallet which was returned from his office to the family after his death in 1945, was a map of that part of Scotland. In any event, one thing that Wig acquired in these days was a "sleeve" dagger, as shown in the picture. This is still in family possession, and is a pretty lethal weapon which I keep in a drawer close to the front door at my house in Kew (robbers beware!). When visiting the exhibition on SOE at the Imperial War Museum in London in June 2015, I found an exact replica on display.

Interestingly, although recruited in 1942, Wig was not *"Put Through the Cards"*, or PTC as it says in his SOE Personnel Records, until November 1943.[98] One suspects that they just didn't get around to it. The records show that he eventually signed the Official Secrets Act on 13 November 1943.

---

[98] This refers to a review of all personal information to ensure that the person is trustworthy, loyal, and not a security risk.

14: SOE Air Operations

Given the mission of SOE, to infiltrate and extract people, and drop equipment and other supplies behind enemy lines, the availability and deployment of aircraft became an essential element of the organisation's operations. At its peak, there were some 32 squadrons and 32,000 men involved operating out of UK, Middle East, Italian, and Far East bases.[99] As we will see in the following chapters, Wig became an acknowledged *"air operations expert"* at deploying Special Duties planes, and the purpose of this chapter is to provide some insight into the nature of this vital aspect of SOE work.

UK Bases

Initially, SOE in England made use of a variety of planes allocated to it on an ad hoc basis by Bomber Command. This arrangement proved to be quite frustrating, since Bomber Command often considered that they had better uses for the planes. However, in August 1941, the organisation acquired its own fleet of aircraft and pilots called the Special Duties 138 Squadron. This Squadron had had a previous life in the First World War, between May and August 1918, and was reconstituted for Special Duties after a lapse of nearly 24 years with the motto "Liberate".

In their time, the Special Duties squadrons operating out of England used quite a range of aircraft types.[100] The primary means of infiltrating agents and dropping supplies *by parachute* were the Armstrong Whitworth Whitley V (February 1942 – December 1942), the Handley Page Halifax B Mk II (September 1942 - December 1942), and the Handley Page Halifax B Mk V (November 1942 to November 1944). At various times, SOE also used the Havoc I (February 1942 - December 1943), the Lockheed Hudson III / V (October 1943-June 1945) and, during the September 1944 – June 1945 period including the D Day landings, the Short Stirling III and IV.

However, SOE also undertook many missions in which a plane would *land*. For this purpose, the main aircraft used was the beloved Westland

---

[99] Data in SOE File HS7-13 shows that there were 10 squadrons based in the UK, 14 in the Middle East and 8 in the Far East.
[100] As we will see below, 161 Squadron was established as a second Special Duties unit covering Western Europe in 1942.

Westland Lysander - Pinterest

Lysander Mk III (known as a Lizzie). In particular, the Lysander specialised in landing and removing agents, and retrieving Allied aircrew who had been shot down over occupied territory and had evaded capture. The plane was capable of landing and taking off within 300-400 metres, usually in a field lit up at night with beacons.

For its Special Duties role, the Lysander Mk III was modified to give it a longer range. It was originally designed to carry one passenger in the rear cockpit. However, for SOE use, the rear cockpit was reconfigured to carry two passengers, albeit in extreme discomfort. All unnecessary equipment, such as guns, armour protection, and excess radio equipment, was removed leaving just the radio telephone for communication with the ground. The pilot would find his way by map, using a reading light and the all-important glow of a full moon. In France, where there were many missions at the start of the war, landing strips were marked out by four or five torches, lit at the last minute and doused as soon as possible. In order to slip in unobtrusively, the Lysanders were painted *matte* black. The aircraft were fitted with a fixed ladder over the port side to hasten access to the rear cockpit and a large drop tank below the undercarriage. The aircraft was a major vehicle for SOE

107

activity until the liberation of France in November 1944.

Although the main English airfield was eventually established at Tempsford north of London, SOE was initially based at Newmarket (during February and March 1942), and Graveley (during March and April). In addition, they used regular RAF stations to fuel-up for crossing the English Channel, particularly RAF Tangmere near Chichester in West Sussex. In February 1942, this latter airfield became the home of Special Duties 161 Squadron which also had a secondary role as the King's Flight.

As the war progressed, the pilots of 138 and 161 squadrons provided a service not only to the resistance movements in France, but also to agents in the Low Countries, Denmark and Poland. There were also occasional longer sorties to Czechoslovakia and Austria. From early 1942, they transported 101 agents to and recovered 128 agents from Nazi-occupied Western Europe. Interestingly, the Germans knew little about the British aircraft and wished to study one. In March 1942, German soldiers captured an intact Lysander when its pilot was unable to destroy it after a crash, but fortunately it was destroyed when a truck carrying the aircraft to an airfield was struck by a train.

Middle East Bases

As will be appreciated, given the distance and hostile air space, it was infeasible to supply the Balkans, the Adriatic, and Eastern Europe from airfields in England. Accordingly, to reach other parts of Europe, SOE established air operations based in the Middle East, North Africa, and eventually in southern Europe.[101] As in other spheres of operation, a typical mission would involve dropping British Liaison Officers behind enemy lines with the aim of contacting and training local insurgents, and undertaking specific missions such as sabotage. The drops would also include the delivery of equipment for communications, medical supplies, and a wide range of munitions. From time to time, SOE also organised the extraction of key Allied personnel and local political and military leaders. These activities required the allocation of a growing number of Special Duty aircraft which

---

[101] A full history of SOE Air Operations from the Mediterranean are available in SOE files HS 7-11 – Special Duties Air Operations Mediterranean, and HS 7-12 – Balkan Air Force. Here, and later in the book, I also draw on information contained in a number of other HS 7 files.

Consolidated B-24 Liberator - Pinterest

would otherwise have been used for bombing.

Initially, SOE in the Middle East operated out of an airfield at Derna in eastern Libya. This was used for flights into the Balkans, and was managed out of the SOE office in Cairo. Later, a second airfield was requisitioned at a place in the west called Blida near Algiers, which was managed by the SOE unit at Massingham and focussed on southern Europe. Once the war in North Africa had been concluded in early 1943, Cairo operated out of a new airfield at Tocra in western Libya which was more convenient for access to southern Europe.[102]

The delivery of supplies to the Balkans from North Africa started in May 1942, when a Flight of 4 Consolidated B-24 Liberator aircraft was made

_____

[102] Details of the Ringlet project to establish the Tocra airfield are provided in SOE File HS 7-238.

Handley-Page Halifax - Pinterest

available from 108 Squadron of Bomber Command. These long-range aircraft had the capacity to carry people and supplies to the whole of the eastern Mediterranean. For the rest of 1942, this was the extent of the fleet because of other pressing military priorities, and was the capability available to Wig when he started his job in late November 1942. However, in May 1943, 148 Squadron was established with the addition of 14 of the shorter range Halifaxes, and by July this number had increased to 36.

Italian Bases

With the establishment of a foothold in Italy in September 1943, there was a radical change in logistics and, over the next nine months, a rapid change in capability. Brindisi became the main airfield for SOE operations into Italy, the Balkans and Eastern Europe, with a number of other smaller Italian airfields being used as required. As the operations in Italy were expanded, the bases in North Africa were wound back, but Tocra continued to be a base for the Middle East and Greece, and a small fleet of aircraft (624 Squadron) was retained at Blida for operations into southern France (together with a fleet of Liberators of the US 885 Squadron which was deployed in February 1944).

As the number of squadrons operating out of Italy proliferated, a new unit for co-ordinating activity was eventually established called No 334 Wing. The new squadrons which became part of this unit included the following:

- In November 1943, the 2 Liberators and 4 Halifaxes of Flight 1586 (Polish Air Force)
- In February 1944, the 50 Dakotas of the US 62nd Troop Carrier Division

and the 36 aircraft of No 1 and No 88 Squadron of the Italian Air Force.[103]

- In March 1944, the Hudsons and Dakotas of 267 Squadron Transport Command, and
- In July 1944, 24 aircraft of a Russian Air Force Group.

In summary, the deployment of aircraft in the Puglia region for which Wig had responsibility in 1943/44 encompassed the following:

Airfield	Squadron	Aircraft
Brindisi	148 (RAF), 1586 (Polish), 62 (USAAF)	Halifax, Liberator, Dakota, C47
Bari	267 (RAF), Russian Air Force	Hudson, C47
Lecce[104]	1 and 88 (Italian Air Force)	Cants, SM 82
Foggia[105]	205 (Back-up group)	Liberator, Wellington

Given their ability to provide a serious challenge to German forces, the main target for No 334 Wing operations throughout this period was Yugoslavia and Italy. However, the original 148 Squadron had substantial commitments to agents and resistance movements in Greece, Albania, Bulgaria, Rumania, and Hungary, the Polish Air Force obviously focussed on Poland, and support was also provided to the resistance in Austria, Czechoslovakia, and Southern France.

In June 1944, AFHQ ("Allied Forces Headquarters') established the Balkan Air Force ("BAF"). Although the name suggests a body involved in air operations to the Balkans, this entity was actually established as an integrated command structure for the deployment of all military and covert operations. A more detailed account of the creation and scope of this body is given in Chapter 20. From an SOE perspective, the creation of this integrated military unit was potentially a threat to its ability to act independently. Indeed, in some circles which were hostile to or critical of SOE, the establishment of the BAF was seen as an opportunity to establish control over their operations. However, SOE resisted this pressure, and retained freedom to act in supporting the network of agents and resistance forces across many theatres according to local priorities rather than the conduct of the principal

---

[103] The Italian Air Force had transferred its loyalty to the provisional government formed after the dismissal of Mussolini.

[104] Lecce is a town 25kms south of Brindisi.

[105] A location about 120kms NW of Bari.

military operations.[106] In particular, this authority included the control of air operations co-ordinated by Wig, who had by now been promoted to Lt Colonel with an overarching responsibility for deploying Special Duties aircraft across the whole of southern and Eastern Europe.

Finally, following the invasion of northern France in June 1944, and southern France in August, the supply of materiel to southern France from a remote location was no longer necessary and both 624 Squadron and the US 885 Squadron at Blida near Algeria switched their operations to supplying the resistance in Northern Italy. Then, in September 1944, 624 Squadron was disbanded and 885 Squadron transferred to Brindisi.

The impact of all this activity, in supporting the BLOs and the resistance movements operating in Southern and Eastern Europe, and engaging significant Axis troops which might otherwise have been available on the Russian and eventually on the Western fronts, was enormous. According to Wig's OBE citation which relates to his time in Italy *during the single year of 1944*, the results achieved by the air operations for which he was responsible encompassed 15,000 sorties, and the supply of 20,000 tons of stores to over 200 missions operating in the field. This activity was undertaken by over 200 aircraft of 5 different nationalities (British, American, Russian, Polish, and Italian) from 7 different airfields to pinpoints in a total of eleven different countries. From a wider perspective, the equivalent statistics for all Special Duties operations flown out of the Mediterranean *for the whole period of the war*, encompassed 21,513 sorties, delivering 31,677 tons of supplies, and delivery of approximately 1,900 agents by parachute.[107] In total, during the war, some 20,000 people of all nationalities were sent in by air and 4,000 were picked up.

Far East Bases

Finally, we come to the Far East. In the later years of the war, SOE Force 136 established two teams for Special Duties operations called 357 Squadron and 358 Squadron.[108] Wig was directly involved in the deployment of aircraft

---

[106] In SOE File HS 5-147, there is a record of correspondence on 24 May 1944 from Brigadier Miles to Lt General James Gammell at AFHQ. He writes at length in opposition to the integration because the current operations were running smoothly.

[107] This data is taken from SOE series 7 history files.

[108] The material for this section is derived from SOE file HS 7-13 – Clandestine Air Operations South East Asia.

from both squadrons in 1945, although his main focus was 357 Squadron.

357 Squadron was formed at Digri (a town which is 70kms to the SE of the modern city of Hyderbad in Pakistan) on 1 February 1944. Their motto was "Mortem Hostibus" ("We bring death to the enemy"), and their badge was a crocodile. Initially, there were two Flights. The "A" flight, had three Liberators IIIs and seven Hudson IIIAs. The Liberator IIIs were eventually superseded by Liberator VIs and the Hudsons were replaced by Dakota IVs in January 1945. The "B" flight was equipped with Catalina IVs. A third "C" Flight using Lysanders was added in January 1945.

Over its history, 357 Squadron operated out of several bases. Initially (from February 1944 to September 1944), although based at Digri, there were detachments at Redhills Lake in Madras and Dum Dum in Calcutta. However, in September 1944, the main base moved to Jessore which was 100kms to the north east of Calcutta.[109] Later, there were detachments at Cox's Bar (a coastal town in modern day Bangladesh on the border with Burma), Minneriya and China Bay in Sri Lanka, Rangoon (Mingaladon), Meiktela in central Burma, Toungoo north of Rangoon, and at Drigh Road in Karachi in modern day Pakistan. In September 1945, the headquarters was moved to Mingaladon Airport in Rangoon with a detachment at Don Muang in Bangkok.

Initially the Squadron used the Hudsons for supply drops to guerrilla forces in Burma, while the Liberators and Catalinas undertook long-range flights dropping supplies and agents into Malaya and Sumatra. On 21 March 1944, the Catalinas became 628 Squadron, but the Liberators continued their supply flights until the end of the war. The Lysanders were mainly used for landing and picking-up agents, and for supplying Force 136 operatives working behind the Japanese lines. In this respect, 357 Squadron had a comparable role to 138 and 161 Squadrons working out of the UK. As will be evident, Dakota KN 584 of 357 Squadron, which carried Wig on his last journey in September 1945, was based at Jessore. Subsequently, the whole Squadron was disbanded on 15 November 1945, with "C" Flight becoming the Burma Communications Squadron.

358 Squadron was formed on 8 November 1944, with crews taken from the "Heavy Conversion Unit". Their Motto was "Alere Flammam" ("Feed the Flame") and their emblem was a torch. They flew Liberator VI aircraft and, initially, the squadron was based in Calcutta. But on January 1945 it

---

[109] Jessore is now in Bangladesh, and Calcutta is now known as Kolkata.

113

moved to Digri, and on 10 February it moved to the SOE base at Jessore. The squadron's main activity was to drop supplies and agents behind enemy lines and, in the later stages, to supply Prisoner of War camps. For its final days, it operated out of Bishnupur which is 100kms from Calcutta and it was disbanded on 21 November, 1945.

Finally, it is worth noting the scope of Far East operations. During his six months in Calcutta, Wig was responsible for over 1,000 sorties undertaken by 357 Squadron alone, with more than 500 people dropped behind enemy lines. A detailed analysis is provided in Appendix 8. As in other theatres, the impact of this work was enormous. And, in the case of the Far East, SOE had the management of requirements off to a fine art, albeit in an extremely hostile terrain. The successful deployment of these aircraft required a huge amount of information, including data on intelligence, the availability and capability of aircraft, suitability of particular crews, knowledge of enemy defensive positions, landing opportunities, refuelling, communication systems, and weather conditions. A more detailed account will be provided later in the book.

Part Six: In and Out of Cairo

15: SOE Mission in Cairo[110]

For twelve months of his life Wig was based in SOE's Cairo office. There is extensive evidence of his time there, details of which are provided in the next chapter. However, to understand the nature of his responsibilities, we need to examine the organisation in which he worked and the scope and content of its operations which is the subject of this chapter.

Although there are a number of memoirs and files about the Cairo office, the availability of formal documentary evidence is quite limited. This is because, during what was called "the Flap" in 1942, when there was a great fear that Rommel might take Egypt and Cairo, a great number of records about the early years were destroyed. Then, when the British wound back their activities in 1945, a further destruction of SOE files was authorised for security reasons.[111]

At the beginning of the war, SOE's presence in the Middle East consisted of a mission based in Istanbul under the command of a man named Colonel Bill Bailey.[112] At that stage, there was no SOE mission in Egypt.[113] The Cairo office was established in January 1941, and was initially located in what was known as the *"Grey Pillars"* building which housed the military headquarters. During its existence, it had a number of names, including MO4 and Force 133. Although the initial focus of its work was Greece, for a time it became a major centre of operations covering the whole of the Middle East, Turkey and the Balkans. But in early 1944, responsibility for most of its operational work transferred to Special Operations Mediterranean ("SOM") based in southern Italy, and the role of the Cairo office was then much diminished with activity again centred on Greece.

When it was established in 1941, the Cairo mission appears to have been given the following initial remit: *Subversive Propaganda, Political Subversion, Raiding, and Sabotage*.[114] This reflected the full range of covert

---

[110] Some material for this chapter is drawn from SOE Files HS 7-268, 7-269, and 7-270 which are Middle East War Time Diaries.

[111] This assertion, is based on p262 of the book by Artemis Cooper called *"Cairo in the War – 1939-1945"* (H Hamilton, London, 1989).

[112] Col Bailey would eventually lead an SOE mission to the Chetniks in Yugoslavia.

[113] This material is based on a number of sources including the book entitled *"The Secret History of SOE 1940-45"* by William Mackenzie.

[114] This is taken from a letter from Hugh Dalton to General Wavell dated 5 January 1941 in War Office records.

operations. In the first year of its existence the leadership of the mission was in an almost continuous state of flux. At the beginning, the mission had two arms, SO1 (Propaganda) lead by Colonel Thornhill and SO2 (Operational Activity) lead by Lt Colonel George Pollock. Pollock had a nominal overall leading role. However, after only a few months, Pollock was replaced by Brigadier Taverner, who in turn was succeeded in July by a civilian named Terence Maxwell. In August 1941, the Foreign Office's SIS then took back control of propaganda, leaving SOE with responsibility for covert operations. From that point, Maxwell was in charge of the Cairo mission, and he set about establishing a unified structure. This went through several manifestations creating much uncertainty and anxiety for the staff.

Maxwell did however institute one significant change that lasted. He moved SOE headquarters from the military controlled "Grey Pillars" building to the Rustum Buildings (known as "Red Pillars") which was previously a block of flats converted to offices for the purpose. This gave the organisation an actual physical separation, to reflect what SOE intended to

Rustum Building, 1943 – Michael Ward

be a degree of operational independence from the military.

In October 1941, an important new player joined the Cairo office. Lord Glenconner was appointed as head of the Balkans and Middle East section, and it didn't take him long to form a view about the deficiencies not only of his own team, but also the rest of the SOE Cairo mission which now encompassed over 1,100 staff. In particular, he thought that the structure, and "command and control" culture, did not adequately provide for liaison with people in the field and their intelligence, and failed to take account of the importance of operational capability which required close liaison with the military. This view about the management of a covert organisation was held by a number of people in SOE senior ranks, and Glenconner did not keep his opinions to himself. He voiced them at meetings, and they are recorded in a Minute from 3 April 1942 in the Middle East Establishment File.

"Directing SOE activities, whether they be in occupied countries or making preparations against invasion, is not an affair which can be conducted either on big business or still less on military lines. The success of SOE operations depends on their secrecy, the most laborious and closest attention to detail, and on the most intimate knowledge of the countries concerned. If this is not present, the patient work of months can be thrown away by one mistake or ill-judged action. Moreover, each country constitutes a different problem requiring its own treatment and solution. We should look therefore to what I may call the 'handcraft principle' as opposed to that of mass production, and to throwing responsibility as much as possible on to the officer responsible for each country section."

Aware that this view was a direct attack on his management style, Maxwell attempted to deflect the criticism. In the meantime, events in the field reached a major turning point with the advance of Rommel to El Alamein on 1 July 1942 and the decision to evacuate many staff at short notice to Palestine. With the office in turmoil, in late July and early August, the consequences of poor leadership came to a head. In July, the newly appointed Minister for Economic Warfare and head of SOE in London, Lord Selborne, decided to remove Maxwell from the position as overall head of SOE in Cairo and appointed Lord Glenconner in his place.[115]

---

[115] Based on material in "*The Secret History of SOE*", pp 178-190, by William Mackenzie.

The overall organisation of British operations in the Middle East at this point is worth noting because it would have a profound effect on Wig's role and work environment when he joined the office in November. Within the Ministry of Economic Warfare with a Minister reporting directly to Churchill, Glenconner had control of all covert operations deployed out of Cairo. Control of *military* operations in Greece, Yugoslavia, and Albania continued to lie with the respective Commanders in Chief based in London. And responsibility for activities which were deemed to have a *political* dimension was firmly in the hands of the Foreign Office in London and their agents in the field the SIS. Therein lay the seeds of much of the discord and controversy which epitomised the work of SOE in Cairo for the remainder of the War. In the account which follows, which traces some of the more significant events in the Cairo office during Wig's time in 1943, the tension between these three seats of power and the impact on effective operational decision making, was significant. It affected the work of everyone involved.

Following his appointment, Glenconner immediately sought to make major changes to both the style of leadership and the culture at the Cairo office. In terms of style, he operated on the basis that *"those to whom he had delegated authority were expected to get on with their work, without constantly referring to him."*[116] And, as the level of covert activity across the Balkans and elsewhere expanded, he became an increasingly remote figure with many of his subordinates in Rustum Buildings referring to him by the nickname "God". As regards the culture, and true to his previously expressed views, he made considerable effort to establish effective working relations with the military, on whom SOE depended for much of its operational activity, and to strengthen liaison with agents in the field.

To lead the implementation of these changes, on 25 September 1942, Glenconner appointed Brigadier Mervyn Keble as his Chief of Staff with two assistants – Group Captain Domville responsible for operations in the Arab world, and Colonel Tamplin responsible for the Balkans. He also maintained a small Special Propaganda unit which was directly responsible to him alone.

As his immediate boss, Keble was to become a major influence in Wig's life. He came from a military background via GHQ in the Middle East. Latterly, he had been the head of the military intelligence section with responsibility for monitoring communications and supplies to Rommel. After

---

[116] This statement and the characterisations which follow are taken from p262 of the book by Artemis Cooper, *"Cairo in the War 1939-1945"*.

only a month, and following the second and decisive battle of El Alamein in October 1942, his SOE job was expanded as he was appointed to be the Director of Military Operations.

Much has been written about this man. "Bolo" as he was known, was an energetic fellow and, from all accounts, highly effective at his work. In the heat of Cairo, he sweated profusely and fronted for work wearing shorts and a vest. He was reputed to be strategic in his thinking, had an excellent head for detail, and was single minded in pursuing his own plans. However, he probably wasn't the most popular man in Rustum Building. For one thing, he was inclined to be a bully. Moreover, he was ambitious, and his new role gave him great scope for advancement given Glenconner's inclination to delegate. As circumstances would have it, this freedom to act was eventually the source of his own destruction.[117] How this came about is a long story, but some elements of the history are worth recounting here because it was the direct backdrop to Wig's time and work in the Cairo office during 1943.[118] The story begins with SOE's support for the resistance movements in Yugoslavia.

In the early stages of the war, the main beneficiaries of SOE support within the Yugoslav resistance were the Chetniks led by Colonel Dragoljob Mihailović who would eventually become a General and Minister of War in the Yugoslav Government in Exile. But there were other players about whom relatively little was known. And, a few months before Keble's appointment, the military Chiefs of Staff in London asked SOE to find out more about the Partisans, who appeared to be fairly active in resisting the occupation. In response to this request, SOE recruited some Croats in Canada in what became known as the *Typical Mission*.[119] These individuals happened to be communists, but this was kept a secret as it would not have been well received by the Yugoslav Government in Exile and Mihailović. Glenconner seemed to have the confidence to operate in this covert manner because, at the time, the reputation of the SOE Cairo office was riding high. Not least

---

[117] This characterisation of Keble is taken from page 262 of the book by Artemis Cooper entitled *"Cairo in the War 1939-45"*, and is corroborated on page 170 of the book by Bickham Sweet-Escott entitled *"Baker Street Irregular"* (Methuen, London, 1965). A detailed account of many other events.

[118] A full account of the dramatic events in the Cairo office in 1943 are provided in a Chapter entitled "Behind Closed Doors (SOE Cairo) in the book by Artemis Cooper.

[119] A detailed account is provided in the book by David Stafford entitled *"Camp X: Canada's School for Secret Agents"* Lester & Orpen Dennys, 1986, and is also covered in Chapter 24.

this was because, on 25 November 1942, just as Wig joined the office, SOE agents had pulled off a most successful operation in Greece, in which the Gorgapotamos viaduct had been destroyed. This cut a vital line of supply to Rommel and was a major factor in the eventual failure of his campaign in North Africa. The success was widely celebrated, and a detailed account of this and similar operations is given in Chapter 17 which covers the war in Greece.

Whilst the *Typical Mission* was being organised, Keble established a project to analyse information on German military movements within Yugoslavia.[120] In particular, his aim was to optimise the placement of new British Liaison Officers ("BLOs") and other support personnel. As it happened, he was still receiving intelligence from sources available to him through his previous role at the military GHQ in the Grey Pillars building in Cairo. Through this source, he had obtained access to German signals which revealed that the German army were spending a good deal of time fighting with the Partisans. He directed a couple of men to research and analyse this material – a Basil Davidson who was the head of the Yugoslav section in Cairo, and a Captain Bill Deakin (later to become Sir William) who had joined the Cairo office in late 1942 having previously been an academic and then a research assistant to Churchill (both Deakin and Davidson were later to become BLOs). The results of the analysis revealed that, in the areas controlled by Mihailović (largely in Serbia) the resistance was holding down nine German Divisions. However, in the rest of the country, "other" resistance activity was engaging nearly 30 Divisions, constituting just over half a million men! Assessing all the material, during the Christmas and New Year period (1942/43), Keble formed the view that the Partisans (who were currently receiving *no* support from SOE) were at least as worthy of support as were the Chetniks (who were at that time receiving all the available support).

At this point, fate would play a hand. On 28 January 1943, Churchill came through Cairo en route from Casablanca to Moscow and had lunch with Deakin. Deakin told him about the results of his latest project and, intrigued, Churchill arranged to have a meeting with Keble. That evening, Keble provided a full analysis of the resistance activity. He also tabled a proposal for additional aircraft, which would facilitate the expansion of Balkan

---

[120] This account is based on pages 263 and 264 of the book by Artemis Cooper *"Cairo in the War 1939-45"*.

operations including support for both the Chetniks and the Partisans. Churchill was impressed and insisted on the immediate supply of a written report. Keble complied, and Churchill left Cairo with documents that had not been screened by Keble's superiors. Filliped by his meeting with Churchill, Keble extended his research project to monitor the movement of resistance forces.

A few days later, Churchill arrived back in London, carrying with him both Keble's proposal requesting more aircraft, *and* his evidence about the relative effectiveness of the Chetniks and Partisans. He pursued the latter point with his ministerial colleagues. Somewhat blind-sided, the response of the Minister of Economic Warfare, SOE boss Lord Selborne, was to resist any move to support the Partisans because of their communist leadership. And he was supported by the Foreign Office who were determined to maintain good faith with the King and Yugoslav Government in Exile. The Chiefs of Staff were also opposed to supporting both the Chetniks and the Partisans, because this would require more aircraft which they were reluctant to release. Notwithstanding all this opposition, based in large part on his personal briefings by Deakin and Keble, Churchill became convinced of the need to support the Partisans, and *also* decided that SOE should have more aircraft.

By mid-year 1943, the Cairo mission received ten Halifaxes to join the existing fleet of four Liberators. This was a god-send as far as Wig was concerned, but sadly it didn't entirely measure up to requirements, because there was a significant logistical issue which seemed to have been lost on the higher ranks.[121] Keble had asked for the longer range Liberators rather than Halifaxes for a good reason. The fact was that, from North Africa, the Liberator was capable of reaching not only Serbia, but also Croatia and Slovenia. On the other hand, even when modified for SOE work, the Halifax struggled to reach further north because of fuel consumption. The additional Halifax aircraft were only really suitable for trips to Greece rather than Yugoslavia. The SOE history files of the time provide a very clear picture of the problem. An estimate of the volume of *monthly* sorties required to meet all Yugoslav and Greek needs in early 1943 is shown in the following table:

---

[121] To be fair, the evidence is that in February 1943 Churchill understood this performance issue and was pressing the military for the release of 8 more Liberators, but apparently they were either unavailable and/or not released by the military because of other priorities.

Destination	No of Monthly Sorties		Destination	No of Monthly Sorties
Mainland Greece	24		Serbia (Chetniks)	28
Crete	4		Slovenia (Partisans)	6
			Croatia (Partisans)	14
Total Greece	**28**		**Total Yugoslavia**	**48**

To meet this demand, SOE actually needed 12 Liberators for Yugoslavia, and 6 Halifaxes for Greece and Crete. And, given the current small fleet of 4 Liberators, SOE estimated that they would only be able to undertake the following sorties to Greece, and Yugoslavia.

1943	Greece	Chetniks in Serbia
February	8	8
March	16	12
April	20	16
June	24	16

The tensions arising from this logistical issue were significant. Wig's unit did not have the capability to meet the policy objectives of expanding the supply to the Chetniks and/or begin a service to the Partisans. And in the meantime, Mihailović was increasingly unco-operative because he said that supplies were insufficient and inconsistent. Indeed, there was a real concern that his dissatisfaction would drive him into the arms of the German supported Nedic government in Serbia.

Whilst the debate over aircraft continued, in February 1943, the 12 Canadian Croats recruited for the *Typical Mission* to establish contact with the Partisans arrived in Cairo, and were installed under-cover. They were briefed by Deakin, Davidson, and a Captain Klugmann who was an Intelligence Officer in the Yugoslav section of the Cairo office with a special understanding of the Balkans. Klugmann was an avowed communist and had been appointed to this important SOE position with the help of an old school friend, Lt Colonel Terence Airey. Despite being a communist, Klugmann had slipped through the screening system because security files which might have incriminated him had been destroyed in a bombing raid on London. An assessment of how Klugmann was recruited and succeeded in being retained as an SOE officer, despite his political views, is given in an article by

124

Roderick Bailey.[122] Since the war, there have been allegations that he was a Soviet mole, but these have been not been proven. In any event, he was in favour of supporting the Partisans and, after their briefing and other preparation, on the night of 20/21 April 1943, Wig arranged for a small team of the Canadian Croats to be parachuted into Yugoslavi with the aim of identifying resistance groups in Croatia to which BLOs might be sent, and their drop was well targeted as they found themselves very close to Tito's headquarters. Almost immediately, after engaging with Partisan leaders, they signalled that Tito would be willing to receive a more formal British mission.

Back in Cairo, Keble was delighted and he lined up Deakin to command an official SOE mission to the Partisans. At this stage, this was of course still something of a secret from the British military and the Foreign Office. Deakin's mission was to check out the advice provided by the Croats, and to ask Tito whether he would be prepared to receive a more senior mission and allocation of other support. A full account of his remit and mission is provided in Chapter 24 on SOE Operations in Yugoslavia. Deakin was despatched in May 1943 and was well received by Tito. On 31 May, he signalled that Tito was indeed willing to receive a senior British mission.[123] This had now become a major operation which could no longer be kept under wraps. News of the development quickly reached London, and Churchill soon took matters into his own hands deciding to proceed with the despatch to Tito of a senior officer and team.

Against the better judgement of both Lord Selborne, Foreign Minister Sir Anthony Eden, and Brigadier Keble, Churchill decided to make a personal appointment and selected Captain Fitzroy Maclean.[124] Keble in particular opposed this choice because, in his view, Maclean had little military experience and would not command Tito's respect. However, Maclean had the kind of pedigree that appealed to Churchill. He had excellent references

---

[122] Roderick Bailey (2005): Communist in SOE: Explaining James Klugmann's Recruitment and Retention, Intelligence and National Security, 20:1, 72-97.

[123] Some of the following material is based on the account provided on pages 268-272 in the book by Artemis Cooper entitled *"Cairo in the War 1939-45"*.

[124] Sir Fitzroy Maclean is the author of several books about World War Two, including *Josip Broz Tito – A Pictorial Biography, Tito: The man who defied Hitler and Stalin,* and *Eastern Approaches.* He is credited with being the inspiration for the fictional character James Bond created by Ian Fleming, and also wrote many books about Scotland.

and was immediately available.[125]

The original terms of reference for Maclean, as reflected in a note within the SOE Balkans history file dated 23 July 1943, are of interest given what followed. In summary, he was to act as political adviser to a military head of mission, and provide both a status report and ongoing advice. He was also alerted to the fact that it was British policy to reconcile all resistance parties and get them to work together, with the objective that actions in the field should facilitate the return of King Peter ahead of the re-establishment of a constitutional monarchy.

Ahead of deployment, Churchill invited Maclean to a meeting at Chequers, and briefed him on the mission. He also told him that he would carry the rank of Brigadier. Maclean must have been delighted, but his enjoyment would have been tempered by the news from Churchill that there was some opposition to his appointment. In particular, he was told that General Henry Maitland Wilson had raised an objection. Maclean found this intervention difficult to understand, because he had worked closely with Wilson on secret operations in Persia in 1942-43 and considered him a friend and ally. Churchill reassured Maclean and indicated that he would reprimand Wilson for his interference. He then fired off a cable to Wilson telling him to mind his own business.

Soon after these events, in a cable date 3 August 1943, Churchill changed his view about Maclean's remit, deciding that, instead of being a military adviser, Maclean would be responsible for both military and political matters. On 11 August, new Terms of Reference were issued encompassing the same scope of activity as on 23 July but putting Maclean in the position of Head of Mission, supported by a military adviser yet to be appointed. Political matters were to be referred to the Foreign Office and operational matters to SOE who would facilitate the allocation of appropriate resources to the Partisans with military assistance.

With these revised terms of reference, a few days later Maclean flew to Cairo. His first stop was military HQ where he met with Wilson. Wilson was quick to deny ever sending any cable to Churchill on Maclean's suitability,

---

[125] Before the war, Maclean had been a diplomat at the British embassy in Moscow. In 1940 he resigned this position, stood for Parliament, and was elected as the MP for Lancaster in northern England. He then enlisted and ended up in the Special Air Service. His referees were the ambassador to the Greek Government in Exile Rex Leeper, Sir Orme Sargent from the Foreign Office, and Churchill's son Randolph!

and suggested that this communication was probably a "dirty trick" perpetrated by SOE in Cairo. Armed with this information, and with some apprehension, Maclean then took himself to SOE headquarters at Rustum Buildings. Apparently, on arrival, the smartly dressed Maclean found Keble sitting in his office, wearing his usual T shirt and shorts with his feet on the desk. Maclean explained his remit from Churchill but apparently Keble showed little enthusiasm. Indeed, after some heated discussion, he reprimanded Maclean for visiting Wilson, told him that he would not be sent to Yugoslavia, and denied him access to any SOE files on the Balkans. Given his credentials, Maclean was understandably outraged and said that he would certainly be going to Yugoslavia and, if necessary, he would make arrangements for his deployment directly with GHQ. As his senior SOE officer, Keble forbade him to do this. One can only imagine what kind of tension this generated in the office, with Wig and his team sitting in an open plan area on the other side of the door to Keble's office.

Maclean went straight back to General Wilson at the Grey Pillars GHQ office. At this second meeting, he was introduced to the Director of Political Warfare in the Middle East, Colonel P C Vellacott who said that he was indeed the target of an SOE whispering campaign designed to undermine his appointment. Apparently, it was being said that he was a hopeless drunk, a homosexual, and a coward who had jeopardised SAS operations in North Africa. After ordering Vellacott to scotch any such rumours, Wilson promised Maclean he would "utterly destroy" SOE in Cairo.

Wilson then convened a meeting with SOE Head of Mission Lord Glenconner, Maclean and others at which he severely criticised SOE and indicated that a very strong complaint would be sent to London. Aware of the danger to his organisation, Glenconner tried to mollify Maclean over dinner. But Maclean would have none of it and, apparently, Wilson proceeded to send a damning report to London. In response, Churchill was furious, and SOE head Lord Selborne soon heard about it. For this and perceived other "misdemeanours" some of which are recounted below, Glenconner and Keble would eventually pay with their jobs, although for a time they were protected by the excellent results of the air and other support operations.[126]

---

[126] For example, Keble outraged Lord Selborne when he tried to block the appointment of Julian Amery as a BLO in Yugoslavia on the grounds that his brother was a traitor, working as he did for the Nazis for which he was eventually executed. He was over-ruled.

After the fracas with Keble, Maclean now became directly responsible to General Wilson and the military at GHQ, and SOE reluctantly agreed to co-operate by providing a proper briefing and organising transport to Yugoslavia. In *Operation Pikestaff*, Wig arranged the infiltration of Maclean and his team into the Podrasnica district of Yugoslavia on the night of 17 September 1943. That evening Maclean dined with Tito, and he had a further meeting with him on 19 September. In a subsequent message to his superiors, Maclean indicated that Tito had been most communicative and had assured him of complete co-operation on military matters. It was not long before it became British policy to support the Partisans as well as the Chetniks.

Whilst *Operation Pikestaff* was a success, Keble in particular had made a bad choice of enemies. Maclean would eventually assume responsibility for the direction of what would turn out to be a most important and successful mission working closely with Tito, and he would not forget how Keble had tried to block him. And, from this point, Keble effectively lost overall control of Yugoslav operations, and his reputation was now under a cloud.

In the meantime, the ordinary business of SOE in Cairo proceeded relentlessly. In August 1943, Wig's unit dropped 243 tons of arms, ammunition and other military equipment to a wide range of resistance groups in Yugoslavia and Greece, as well as 79 individuals, 37 tons of propaganda leaflets and 26 wireless sets. And there would soon be a growing imperative to provide a similar service to Italy. The rapid growth in this activity stretched the Cairo operation to breaking point. Signal facilities were a particular challenge with information vital to military operations often delayed. Sometimes, this led to the wrong materiel being sent to operatives in the field, and in an untimely manner. And the despatch airfield in Derna in Libya (which had become available in late 1942 following the retreat of Rommel) was a long way from the Cairo office.[127] Finally, some of the agents sent into the field were insufficiently briefed on political matters.

In the face of this rising tide of work, Keble did not sit idly by. Apart from his direct communication with Churchill in January 1943, when he had requested more aircraft, he was highly vocal in making other demands for more resources and GHQ began to complain. However, at the same time as the debacle over the appointment of Maclean, another crisis developed at the SOE Cairo office, this time involving Greece. In mid-1943, the Foreign

---

[127] Note that, because of this logistical issue, in the autumn of 1943, operations moved to Tocra which was north of Benghazi.

Office learned that the two guerrilla groups which SOE were assisting, EAM/ELAS, and EDES, had republican leanings. This policy was consistent with Churchill's instructions to support resistance groups capable of fighting the Germans even if they were opposed to the Greek King and Government in Exile ("GGE"). Although frequently at odds, the leaders of the two groups had been persuaded to work together and, in an attempt to consolidate this co-operation, the chief BLO in Greece, Brigadier Edmund Myers, organised a mission to meet with the Anglo-Greek Committee in Cairo.

The *"Andarte"* delegation arrived on 10 August 1943.[128] [129] As it turned out, SOE in Cairo were quite unprepared for what turned to be the wide scope of the delegation's representations. It was expected that the conference would involve a discussion about the involvement of the resistance in implementing military plans, but the guerrilla leaders raised political issues including the future of the monarchy which exposed a deep division in the GGE. Their representations were rebuffed and, on 17 September 1943, they returned to Greece, the same day by coincidence that Fitzroy Maclean was parachuted into Yugoslavia. It must have been a busy day for Wig's team! Within a month, and once the immediate military intentions of the Allies became evident, civil war broke out in Greece. Blind-sided by the political demands of the resistance delegation, SOE in Cairo were condemned for their political naivety and blamed for the ensuing civil war which threatened to undermine the resistance to the Germans. The political and military leaders in London were especially displeased because they saw SOE as meddling in politics which was deemed to be beyond their province.

In response to all these events, in late August 1943, a proposal was developed by the Middle East Defence Committee ("MEDC") to bring SOE "to heel". It was proposed to establish a new body in Cairo, the Special Operations Committee, comprising military, diplomatic, SOE, and Political Warfare Executive representatives. This body would have responsibility for covert policy and strategy, and would have direct control of all SOE work in the Balkans and Greece. Not surprisingly, SOE opposed this proposal. In policy terms, it contravened SOE's charter which was to pursue independent covert operations. And it would have been difficult to implement from an organisational point of view, given that the work of SOE's Cairo office

---

[128] A full account of this episode is given on in Chapter 17 on SOE operations in Greece, but this is a brief version for context.

[129] The word "Andarte" is taken from the Greek word "Andartiko" meaning guerrilla warfare.

encompassed a much wider sphere of activity than just the Balkans and Greece. SOE's potentially perilous position was also helped by the fact that they were well regarded by some in high places. In particular, General Eisenhower had accepted SOE as being a de facto 'Fourth Service' in the war (in addition to Army, Navy and Air Force) and he was keen to give it strategic and tactical tasks in support of his military objectives in Italy. This view was supported by other Allied military commanders.

For some days, there was a fierce debate over the future of SOE in Cairo. Finally, on 30 September 1943, Churchill presided over a special meeting of Ministers at which he decided the issue unequivocally by maintaining SOE Cairo's independent status.[130] The Minutes of that meeting reflect the following settlement.

a) The integrity of the SOE organisation would be preserved.
b) SOE policy was to be determined in London through consultation between SOE and the Foreign Office.
c) Implementation of SOE policy in the Balkans was to be the responsibility of the local military commanders with advice from a committee of local representatives.
d) SOE was to appoint senior staff in the field, with the Foreign Office to deploy a political adviser where needed.
e) Chiefs of Staff were to liaise with SOE on all operational matters.

But there was a significant fall-out as regards several careers. Following this settlement, in early October all of Wig's bosses in Cairo were removed. The head of SOE Cairo Office, Lord Glenconner, was recalled to London and replaced by Major General Stawell. Brigadier Keble and Colonel Tamplin of the Balkans section were also removed from their positions, with Brigadier Karl Barker-Benfield placed in charge of Balkan operations. Keble was shunted into a backwater role with the regular army and, shortly after the changes, Tamplin was found dead at his desk. He had apparently suffered a massive heart attack. Later in the month, a newly appointed SOE CEO, Major-General Gubbins visited Cairo in order to conclude the changes involved. In the months ahead, the organisation settled down. But the importance of the Cairo office as a centre of operational activity went into

---

[130] At this very time, there had been a reorganisation at SOE head office with Brigadier Colin Gubbins succeeding Sir Charles Hambro and Lord Selborne taking over from Hugh Dalton.

decline, with most of the Balkans staff and people like Wig switched to Italy in late 1943 and early 1944. Cairo was left with responsibility only for Greece and the less operationally active Middle East.

Despite all these changes in Cairo, back in Yugoslavia Maclean was busy liaising with the resistance, and he prepared a detailed report on both Partisan and Chetnik activities. He returned to Cairo on 25 November and discussed his findings with Sir Anthony Eden the next day. In summary, he proposed that the Partisans should be recognised as an Allied Force in Yugoslavia and indicated that Tito was likely to be the power in the country after the war. He recommended a big increase in aid to the Partisans, and the cessation of support to Mihailović because he was collaborating with the Italians and the Germans. Although there was a separate and contrary report about Mihailović presented by Brigadier Charles Armstrong who was the senior BLO based at the Chetnik's headquarters, this did not see the light of day until it was too late to have any influence.

The outcome was that, during the Teheran Conference which opened on 28 November 1943, Churchill, Roosevelt and Stalin determined to provide unequivocal support to Tito. There was no mention of Mihailović and thereafter he received very few British supplies. Indeed, in the last three months of 1943, Wig's unit delivered over 2,000 tons of supplies to the Partisans. While the Teheran Conference was in progress, Maclean again visited Yugoslavia and then returned to Cairo a few days later with Deakin and a delegation of Partisan leaders. On 8 December, he briefed Churchill on his latest visit , asserting that Mihailović was contributing little to the Allied cause. He also asserted that Tito would emerge as the main political force in post-war Yugoslavia, leading a regime that was likely to be communist.[131]

Because Wig transferred to Italy in late 1943, this is where we leave the main account of activities at the SOE mission in Cairo. Operations from there during the final 18 months of the war were largely focussed on supporting the resistance movements in Greece. The rest of the story of SOE's work in Yugoslavia, involving Wig's in Italy, will be told in Chapter 24.

---

[131] In his book *"Eastern Approaches"* (Penguin, London, 1949) Fitzroy Maclean refers to his concerns about giving this advice because of the likely consequences for Yugoslavia's post-war government. He wrote "The Prime Minister's response to my briefing resolved my doubts. *"Do you intend"* he (Churchill) asked *"to make Yugoslavia your home after the war?"* *"No, sir"* I replied. *"Neither do I."* he said. *"And that being so, the less you and I worry about the form of Government that they set up, the better."* This anecdote also appears on p 275 of Artemis Cooper's book *"Cairo in the War 1939-45"*.

16: Red Pillars (Wig's Work in Cairo)

Having provided an account of the main events associated with the SOE Cairo office before and during 1943, the aim of this chapter is to tell the story of Wig's operational contribution. As mentioned earlier, whilst maintaining cover as an officer with the Sherwood Foresters, Wig formally joined Keble's team on 29 November 1942 and was appointed to establish the new air operations function. This job involved responsibility for logistics management, and liaison with the military, SOE command, and a number of country sections. His appointment was very much in keeping with the changing nature of SOE work, involving closer ties with the military.

In the next twelve months, Wig was to establish a significant reputation. Reflecting his performance, and the turn of events, the scope of his responsibilities were expanded fairly rapidly, and he was promoted on several occasions. When he started, he held the rank of Captain and, following his induction, in March 1943 he was appointed to the SOE grade of General Staff Officer III (Air).[132] On 12 May

Wig in Maadi, Cairo, 1943

1943, he was promoted to Acting Major and given the SOE position of GSO II. In August, he was accorded the military rank of a Full Major and, by the time he left Cairo for Italy in December 1943, he was promoted to Acting Lt Colonel and GSO I.

On joining the team in late 1942, Wig soon discovered that the Cairo office was not a particularly happy workplace, for all the reasons provided in the previous chapter. Working for a man like Keble must have been quite challenging. The other key officer with whom Wig worked closely was

---

[132] Military personnel in SOE had both military ranks for external appearances, and SOE grades reflecting their position within SOE.

Colonel Guy Tamplin who was in charge of the Balkan country sections. In contrast to Keble, it appears that Tamplin was an amenable fellow, although he had some difficult subordinates in the country sections and was implicated in both the Yugoslav and Greek debacles. Beyond the rarefied environment of Rustum Building, Wig also had frequent contact with representatives of the other services some of whom did not necessarily have a high regard for SOE.

Despite these challenges, from all accounts, in 1943 Keble and Tamplin had in fact established a highly effective if somewhat stretched team at the Cairo office and Wig must have been stimulated by the company as well as the work. Amongst many who have written about the Cairo office, the words of the author Artemis Cooper probably provide a fair assessment. Commenting on the staff, Cooper has written:

"As well as Davidson and Deakin who undertook research and analysis, there was the historian Hugh Seton-Watson who specialised in Balkan languages, and Mrs Hasluck who had devoted her life to studying the languages and customs of Albania. Captain Wigginton organised air sorties which, as SOE's commitment spread, required not only administrative (ie logistical) skill but fine judgement and immense tact. Wigginton had started his career on the Nottinghamshire tramways and was <u>eventually</u> responsible for co-ordinating SOE's air sorties over the whole of Europe."[133] [134]

Cooper also comments on the frenetic nature of work in the office, stating:

"Despite the tireless dedication of the staff, SOE was growing too fast. People came and went at Rustum Buildings at a moment's notice, either to take up another appointment or to parachute into the Balkans. There was hardly time for induction, and people just had to get on with it. Signals came pouring in every day and not all of them were seen by the right people, while a huge backlog of un-coded telegrams built up due to a chronic shortage of signals staff to decipher coded messages."[135]

---

[133] The word underlined has been inserted by the author.
[134] This is an extract from page 267 of the book by Artemis Cooper entitled *"Cairo in the War 1939-45"*.
[135] This too is an extract from page 267 of the book by Artemis Cooper entitled *"Cairo in the War 1939-45"*.

From these comments, it is clear that the early days in his new job must have been quite a demanding experience for a professional army officer like Wig. Nevertheless, given his previous work in military liaison, and in logistics from his peace time job, he was certainly well suited to the role, and it appears that he quickly built up the requisite knowledge and insight. And, having satisfied himself as to Wig's competence, Keble seems to have let him get on with it, leaving him to have full responsibility for planning and implementing air operations. Accordingly, at a detailed level, Wig's role soon encompassed responsibility for liaising with individual country sections representing the whole of the Balkans, monitoring which Special Duties aircraft were available for missions on any given day, matching available aircraft to the specific requirements of current operations, organising the supplies, setting up communications in the field, and planning a rolling programme of sorties.

A key part of Wig's work involved liaison with the RAF staff of the Special Duties 148 Squadron. Equipping the airfield used for Cairo operations at Derna in Libya, which was a long distance from his office, was a complex and technically challenging matter. It required effective systems for communication with people in the field, other operating units, and supply depots. It also involved ensuring that appropriate military and other supplies, including expertly packed parachutes, were available for changing operational needs. From mid-August 1943, a vital part of each day was the preparation of the Sit Rep (MO4) Report.[136] This was compiled on the basis of incoming telegrams from sources in the field, from London and from other SOE bases. The contents included information on recent operations, strength of German, Italian and resistance forces, movement of the enemy and Allied forces, and countless other intelligence of use to military and political deliberations. Wig received these reports, together with submissions from the various country sections based at Cairo, as part of his daily briefing when planning air sorties. The reports to the country sections came from all parts of the Balkans and beyond including Yugoslavia, Slovenia, Albania, Greece, Crete, the Dodecanese (ie Greek Islands), Rumania, and Hungary.

During the early part of 1943, when SOE resources were small, the main

---

[136] There are a large number of these daily *"Sit Rep"* reports in the SOE Files, with details of current operations, and requests for support. Not surprisingly, Wig is included on the circulation list as a Major. From November 1943, the collating centre changes from MO4 to Force 133, as that name became operative within SOE circles.

focus of air operations was very much on supporting the establishment and development of the various resistance movements. Given the significance of this activity, there are separate accounts on the work in Greece and Yugoslavia in later chapters of this book. However, during the middle of 1943, as the Allies were preparing for an invasion of Sicily and then the Italian mainland, the focus changed. In particular, during the crucial months of July and August, it became the objective of SOE Cairo to tie down as many German divisions as possible in Greece, Yugoslavia and Albania. Consistent

SOE Team in Cairo 1943

with this objective, in September, the number of aircraft made available to SOE Cairo was doubled. Needless to say, whilst a welcome recognition of the importance of the activity, this increased Wig's work load by a huge amount, with virtually no increase in his own staff.

Given the success of his work, it is not surprising that Wig's unit survived the major organisational upheaval in the Cairo office in October 1943. Following the removal of Keble and Tamplin, the new leaders were Head of Mission Major General William Stawell and Head of the Balkans section Brigadier Karl Barker-Benfield and, from all reports, the change in personnel must have been a relief. In any event, the special air operations work only intensified with the landings in Italy. And, in London and Massingham, plans were afoot to deploy SOE staff to Italy as soon as conditions made it possible to establish a local base. Wig would soon be moved to mainland Europe.

To complement the above account, we do have some more personal material which reflects on Wig's life in those days. First, by way of a tribute, a colleague, Bickham Sweet-Escott, says of Wig *"In a few months, Wigginton had built up a well-deserved reputation for running special air operations. He ended up in Europe by being responsible for operations of this kind throughout the European theatre of war, and then went on to do the same thing in South East Asia."*[137]

At a more detailed level, there is a quite lengthy oral account of Wig's work. When I visited the Imperial War Museum in June 2015, I had access to a number of recordings made in the 1980s of interviews of SOE personnel who had worked in the Rustum Building in Cairo. One such interview involved Captain Basil Irwin who joined Wig's Air Operations team in May 1943.[138]

In his interview, Irwin states that he was introduced to working for SOE through a man named GPS McPherson who was a fellow officer in the London Irish Rifles and had an administrative job in Rustum Building. As evident from the recording, Irwin clearly had a high regard for Wig who was his direct boss. When questioned as to how Wig came to be doing this air operations work, he states in very laid back tones: *"Oh, well, before the war Wigginton worked out bus timetables for Nottingham City Council. It seemed to have been a good preparation for this kind of work."* He then goes on to describe the work of Wig's team as well as commenting on the office politics of the time. As regards the work, he states that the role of the Air Operations section was to organise all air operations into the eastern Mediterranean. And he indicates that in the first half of 1943 Wig had a team of four staff including a liaison officer at the airfield at Tocra in Libya (to the north east of Benghazi and known by the code name Snood).

According to Irwin, Wig's team were the only people in Rustum building who knew *"where everything was and who was where"*. This referred in particular to the location and current needs of BLOs in the field, the number and status of aircraft, and the status of supplies held in Cairo. Irwin goes on

---

[137] Colonel Bickham Sweet-Escott worked with SOE throughout the War and knew Wig whilst he was in Cairo and the Far East. Material here is an extract from his book entitled *"Baker Street Irregular"*, page 171.

[138] This material is taken from the recording of an interview conducted in 1987 and filed as Item 9772 in IWM Archives.

to describe the daily flow of bids from the country sections, and the setting of priorities for allocation of resources according to the priorities set by a small Operations Committee consisting of Keble, Tamplin, Wig and others. Wig's team would then set about implementing the Committee's decisions which involved liaison with members of the country sections whose bids had been successful, the RAF, quartermasters to organise the provision of supplies, the signals team, and wireless operators in the field. Apparently, they did not organise the actual loading of aircraft which was the role of a separate aircraft loading section.

In Irwin's view, in the early months of 1943 the Liberators (long range) and Halifaxes (short range) deployed by Wig's unit were adequate for purpose in terms of capacity and fuel capacity for the various Balkan destinations. Trips to the middle of Yugoslavia, including the search for the Dropping Zone, typically took eight hours. The main problems were aircraft serviceability, changes to weather conditions, and pilot availability. For each sortie, the team were responsible for preparing a Mission Form which identified the plane, the pilot, the date of mission, the Dropping Zone, communication arrangements, and the mission objectives. The day after the mission returned, the Form would be completed with an indication of the outcome. All this material was systematically filed to provide the basis for regular summary reports which were reviewed by the Operations Committee.

Irwin also describes the frustration arising from the vagaries of the weather and the cycles of the moon. When there was no moon, flights were infrequent and, in the absence of flights, the staff apparently amused themselves by playing *Liar Dice*. Irwin also refers to the working environment. He confirms that Wig and his team were in an open plan General Office, immediately adjacent to the offices occupied by Keble and Mission Head Glenconner. His comment on Keble was that he seemed to be quite a grumpy fellow, and he states that Glenconner was always coming and going because he was forever in meetings.

Research at the Imperial War Museum uncovered another recorded interview, with a charming reference to Wig from a friend of his, Captain Robert Wade, who eventually became a BLO in Yugoslavia.[139] According to his account, in the latter part of 1942, he had been *"in the desert"* as an ADC to General Gardner. Like many survivors of the North Africa campaign, in

---

[139] Robert Wade was interviewed in 1991, and the recording is kept as Item 12142 at the Imperial War Museum.

December 1942 he was in Egypt awaiting redeployment. He reports of a conversation with the General in which he asked what had happened to his friend Wig after El Alamein. The General told him that *"Oh, he's gone to a place in Cairo. You can look him up there, no doubt."*

Wade then describes how, being at a bit of a loose end, he went up to Cairo and *"looked him up"* in Rustum Building. As he reports *"When I got to the building and asked for Wigginton, he arrived to meet me in the most awful state and said **"How did you know I was here?"**. I was able to tell him that everyone knew about Rustum Buildings, including all the Arabs and everybody else in Cairo, I think. And then I said **"Well, the General told me you were here, and I thought I'd look you up."***

As regards his own story, Wade continues *"Then, one thing led to another, and I spoke to several other people. Eventually, someone said "Would you like to join us?" So I joined, and that's how I got started in the SOE."* Thereafter, he had a job in the Cairo office before being appointed as a BLO in Yugoslavia in what was known as *Operation Huggate*. We will hear of him again in Part Eight of this book.

Although Wig had a busy job in the Cairo office, he was on occasions drawn into field operations. According to his wife Eunice he was involved in a number of sorties into German occupied territory in Europe to reconnoitre drop areas, and there is corroborative evidence from the newspapers, in which it was reported that he parachuted into the Balkans to establish communications between the USAAF and the Partisans, to collect information, and to help crashed airmen back to safety.[140] However, in the absence of many operational files, I have been unable to uncover a detailed account of any of his exploits.

Finally, to round off this account of Wig's time in Cairo, it is worth noting that there are a number of other records which provide insight into the organisation, including an interview recorded in April 1989 made by Ian Macpherson who tells of how he was recruited into SOE and what it was like working and living in Cairo. In particular, he talks about everyday life for the average British person. Apparently, for most of the staff, the working hours were 8.00 am to 1.00 pm and 5.00 pm to 8.00 pm or later. For him a typical day would include lunch at the Gezira Sporting Club which was on an island in the Nile accessed by a houseboat, and in the afternoon he might choose to swim, sun-bake, watch cricket, or play golf. In the evening, he would either

---

[140] Report in an edition of the Nottingham Evening Post dated 29 July 1945.

dine at his flat in a *pensione* in the suburb of Mailika or visit local restaurants such as Groppi's or the Ferida Tea Room. According to Macpherson, there was little contact with the local Egyptians. Finally, he adds as an afterthought that, in November 1943, *"Wigginton and Harcourt went off to Italy with Wigginton replaced by Julian Dobrski whose code name was Dolbey"*.[141]

A more colourful picture of life in Cairo for SOE staff in 1943 is provided by a FANY named Margaret Pawley who is sadly now deceased.[142] In her book on the period, she refers to *"the people and buildings in the hot and dusty streets which reflected a multitude of humanity and the culture of several centuries"*. One feature of interest is her reference to the mode of transport for SOE staff. Apparently, at certain times of day there was a "bus" service between Rustum Building and the various residential units. The buses were modified trucks, *"with a row of benches fixed down each side of the back and one bench down the middle."* Pawley also states that Cairo was not the healthiest of places for any of the inhabitants. The water and air were polluted, and the absence of sanitation among the poor was a major issue. Insect bites and scratches could become infected very quickly and might end up with temporary hospitalisation. The weather was also very trying. Apart from having to endure the high temperatures in days before air conditioning, Pawley refers to the hot desert wind called the *khamsin* which blew with tremendous speed bending over palm trees, and the all-pervasive nature of the dust which was up in the air like a thick yellow cloud so that it was dark in the middle of the day and in your eyes, ears, noises, throats, and teeth. (In a brief letter home, Wig refers to the same problem. There was sand in everything.)

Finally, in reflecting on the operations managed out of Cairo, we should not forget the operational people who "delivered the goods". In writing this book, I have frequently reflected on the fact that at the "sharp end" were the agents and resistance fighters in the field and the air crews who implemented Wig's plans. As regards the agents, the scale of activity can be seen in the number of BLOs located in the Balkans. By September 1943, there were over 300 of them. Details are provided in Appendix 9. As regards the level of air traffic, a summary for mid 1943 is provided in Appendix 10. On a typical

---

[141] Initially, they moved to Caserta where AFHQ had relocated from Massingham. They moved to Bari in the spring of 1944. Harcourt is Lt Col (Viscount) Harcourt.

[142] This is a precis of an account provided on pages 57 and 58 of the book by Margaret Pawley entitled *"In Obedience to Instructions"*, Leo Cooper, (Barnsley 1999).

flying day there were 5 to 10 sorties and, as is evident in the data, as the number of longer range Liberators became available there was a significant change in the balance of flights to Greece and Yugoslavia.

There are a number of accounts of intrepid flights over the Balkans during 1943 by members of Cairo's 148 Squadron. In a memoir about her father Tom Storey, who was a Halifax pilot, Jennifer Elkin recalls the tough, adventurous, and sometimes tragic life of a typical air crew.[143] Flight JN 888 was based at Tocra in Libya, which as previously noted had replaced Derna as the main base for operations deployed by Wig's office in Cairo following the retreat of Rommel. When the crew arrived from England in late 1943, the operations room at the airfield was just a tent on the south side of the runway. The air crews were also billeted in tents, surrounded by trenches which the men had to dig for themselves to avoid flooding. In the event, the weather was atrocious and the crews were stomping around in mud. And there was sand in everything. Despite these conditions, the men involved were mostly young and resilient, and they just got on with it. In due course, the engineers established a more permanent building as the Mess, and Nissen huts were established as personal space for the operations team which included Wig's Liaison Officer. The place was pretty remote, so the men had to amuse themselves with card games and improvised soccer. And there was a fair amount of sickness with Hepatitis A, desert sores, skin infections, stomach upsets and tired eyes.

Whilst based at Torca, Storey's crew were responsible for flights to a wide range of dropping zones. The crew knew that their missions were essential to maintain BLOs and the resistance movements in Greece, Albania and Yugoslavia, and they became briefly acquainted with many people who were being dropped into the field. But they never knew what was in the bags and containers that were being tossed through the hole in the floor of the plane. After each flight, the crew was debriefed and completed post mission documentation for Wig's unit which, amongst other things, was used to compile a league table on air crew performance. This acted as some form of motivation although success was largely dependent on factors outside the crew's control. And many of the crews like Tom Storey's rightly earned great praise and recognition for their bravery and resilience in operating under extremely difficult conditions.

---

[143] Jennifer Elkin's book about her father Tom Storey is entitled *"A Special Duty"* (Mention the War Publications, 2015). Life in Tocra is described in Chapter 2, pages 19-35.

During this period Wig was accorded very significant recognition for his efforts. On 12 May 1943, he was mentioned in despatches for his work in co-ordinating air operations.[144] Then, on 2 September 1943 he was recommended for an MBE, the citation for which read as follows:[145]

"Major Wigginton has been the Staff Officer responsible for the detailed planning and organisation of air transport sorties to the Balkans since early 1943. He has daily to arrange, with between 5 and 14 different agents or British officers in the Balkans, for reception of stores, arms etc., dropped from transport aircraft. These arrangements require the most painstaking, meticulous, and accurate staff work.

During the five months, April to August, he has arranged for the successful reception throughout the Balkans, from Trieste to the Peloponnese, of 500 sorties. The failures other than for "met" conditions and mechanical troubles have been few and in no case could they have been prevented by Major Wigginton. During these months, rapid expansion of the air transport side of MO4 operations has taken place. In April, only 28 successful sorties were flown, whereas in August there were 145.

That these successful sorties have been possible has only been as a result of long hours, much hard work, and excellent liaison with the RAF by Major Wigginton, and it is only by his excellent organisation that this large increase in number of sorties has been possible. He has only just received the staff necessary to continually deal with such a large number, and he deserves the highest praise and recognition for the manner in which he has handled these operations at the same time as attempting to train his new and inexperienced staff."

The Award was gazetted on 4 April 1944, but not published in the London Gazette for security reasons. Although there is a record of this in SOE files, there is also some mystery about it because Wig himself does not make reference to it at any point and there is no medal to hand. This may reflect the secrecy of the times. Wig was again mentioned in despatches on 15 December 1943.

---

[144] In the British National Archives there is a microfiche section which provides details of "Mentioned in Despatches" citations, but I was unable to find those relating to Wig.
[145] This is taken from Wig's SOE Personnel File, HS 9-1589-8.

17: Nearly a Greek Tragedy

During 1943, Wig spent much of his time organising air operations into Greece although, as the year advanced and additional aircraft were allocated, there was a growing number of sorties into Yugoslavia. The reader should note that the number of references in SOE papers which specifically link Wig to individual Greek operations is limited, but he did have a detailed involvement in all the missions that involved air operations into the country in that year and he played a vital if unrecorded part in the associated events. This involvement in Greek affairs terminated when he moved to Italy in late 1943.

Greek Historical Perspective

At the outbreak of war in 1939, Greece was a traditional ally of the British but relations were not particularly cordial. The country was governed by an authoritarian regime under a Prime Minister named General Ioannis Metaxas. By the summer of 1940, it was becoming clear to the Greeks that the Italians had designs on their country. In August the Italians torpedoed a Greek cruiser, and in October they launched a surprise attack from the north. This was repulsed by Greek forces after which there was a stand-off.

However, by the beginning of 1941, the Greeks were increasingly apprehensive. There were potentially hostile powers coming from all directions, and allies like Britain were under siege elsewhere. To make matters worse, on 29 January 1941, Metaxas died suddenly. He was succeeded by a right wing associate named Alexandros Koryzis who had been the governor of the Bank of Greece. Then, on 25 March 1941, the Yugoslav government decided to join their neighbours to the north and east by signing the Axis Pact with Germany and Italy and, two days later, there was a coup in Belgrade by forces opposed to this action. This triggered a German invasion of Yugoslavia in early April 1941. Unprepared, the Yugoslavs surrendered in just ten days and suddenly there were German troops on the Greek border. The Germans hardly paused for breath before proceeding with their Italian allies to invade Greece with a massive and overwhelming force. On 18 April 1941, as the city of Athens was placed under martial law, Prime Minister Koryzis committed suicide. As the Germans were advancing on Athens, the King (George II) appointed a new government with the centrist Emmanouil Tsouderos as Prime Minister. The Greeks endeavoured to defend their country, aided by a small and insufficient British military force. But, with the occupation of Athens imminent, on 29 April Tsouderos and the King removed to Crete. The Royal Navy rescued the British troops and some civilians, but many of the Greek troops were either captured or escaped into the hills.

It did not take long for the Germans to complete their conquest of Greece, and they then set about carving up the country. Control of much of the territory was handed over to the Italians, and Bulgarians, but the Germans retained control of Thessaly in the north, and some other strategically significant areas relating to the oil industry in Rumania.

Having consolidated their hold over the mainland, on 20 May 1941, the Germans and Italians invaded Crete with a massive *airborne* attack called *Operation Mercury*. The battle for Crete lasted ten days with fierce resistance from the locals. As defeat loomed, the Greek government along with many thousands of troops were hurriedly evacuated to Cairo, leaving behind 500 Allied soldiers and a number of SOE agents on the run.[146] [147] The island was then partitioned between the Germans and Italians. This was a major setback for the Allies who had failed to recognise the strategic importance of the ports and airfields on the island situated as it was in the Eastern Mediterranean.

In Cairo, what was now the Greek Government in Exile ("GGE") quickly settled into a relatively friendly environment where there was a large and mostly welcoming Greek community. After lengthy consultations with the British, they started to formulate plans to organise resistance to the German occupation, and to prepare the ground for the eventual return of the King and the GGE. As the dust settled, in September 1941, the GGE then removed to London, with its interests maintained in Cairo through an embassy.

Back in Greece, with extended lines of communication, the Germans were experiencing serious logistical challenges. And they were finding the Greeks far from amenable. With British encouragement and assistance, a number of resistance groups were established with the potential to cause disruption including the left-leaning EAM with its military wing ELAS, EDES, and EKKA. The formation of these groups was strongly facilitated by SOE and,

---

[146] One such renegade was a New Zealander who was hidden in a loft for two years by the grand-father of an Australian Greek friend of mine, Ross Tzannes.
[147] A detailed account of these events is provided in the book entitled *"The Fall of Crete"* by Alan Clark (Cassell, London, 2000).

by mid-1942, they had all become very active. In April, a general strike was called to take effect across the whole country. And, in May and July 1942, ELAS saboteurs led by SOE British Liaison Officers struck German naval interests in the port of Piraeus near Athens to undermine supplies from the north being sent to support Rommel's campaign in North Africa. This was followed by a docks strike and the destruction of a key railway bridge connecting Piraeus with the roads leading north.

Although the level of resistance activity in mid 1942 was encouraging to the Allied cause, not all was well. There was mounting internal political conflict between the various Greek factions, both between the resistance groups in Greece and within the GGE in London. After much pressure from within Greece and from the British, the GGE accommodated a broader spectrum of political views, and they appointed a republican named Panagiotis Kanellopoulos as "Vice President of the Council" with a remit to liaise with the resistance. In July 1942, he moved from Greece to Cairo where he became a member of the recently formed Anglo-Greek Committee. This body had responsibility for overall Allied policy on Greek matters including the co-ordination of military and covert activity.[148]

The latter part of 1942 marked a critical point in the war in North Africa, in which the Greek resistance played an important part. There were several major operations designed to disrupt the movement of German war materials destined for Rommel in North Africa, and this had a substantial effect on the Axis war machine. Together with other factors this eventually led to Rommel's defeat at the second battle of El Alamein. Meanwhile, there continued to be tensions in the Greek theatre of war. Members of the GGE had differences of view about resistance strategy and other political issues, and there was a serious disagreement between the Foreign Office and the British military as to whether MEHQ in Cairo (the Allied military) or the GGE were responsible for military operations.[149]

In early 1943, the Allies commenced their planning for a second front in Europe. To assist in the attack on Sicily, which eventually took place in July 1943, it was decided to create a diversion in the Balkans by launching in June what was called *Operation Animals*. This initiative was designed to convince the Germans that the Allies were in fact going to attack the western coast of

---

[148] A detailed account is provided in the book entitled "A Concise History of Greece" by Richard Clogg (CUP, Cambridge, 2002).

[149] I have based much of this account on reports filed in SOE File 7-158.

Greece, and the deception proved to be a great success.[150] The possibility of an Allied invasion boosted morale in Greece, but this was short-lived. The ability of the resistance to pursue their main aim of attacking the Germans was undermined by renewed tension between the various parties the field. In particular, ELAS initiated a series of skirmishes designed to eliminate the other groups or take them over. When news of the internecine conflict reached the King and GGE, they made fervent representations to the British that aid to the left wing ELAS should be discontinued. This request fell on deaf ears because it failed to recognise the close relationship between British agents and ELAS members in the field who were working closely together in pursuit of military objectives. Indeed, it put SOE and GHQ Middle East in Cairo (the military) in an invidious position generating conflict within the British leadership.[151]

In the third week of March 1943, with the Axis powers no longer a threat in North Africa, the King and Prime Minister Tsouderos returned to Cairo, together with a new British Ambassador Rex Leeper who took over the chair of the Anglo-Greek Committee. Mindful of the tensions between the Greek resistance movements, Tsouderos formed a new government which encompassed a more representative group of politicians including moderate republicans. In the meantime, and in the face of what he saw as a mounting tide of republican sentiments, the King was determined to maintain *his* role, including his right to return to Greece as and when liberation began. Accordingly, on 4 July 1943, he made a broadcast to the nation in which he indicated that, within six months of his return to Greece, he would institute free elections and a vote on whether to retain the monarchy. This broadcast was not well received by many local politicians in Greece, who had not forgotten what they saw as the King's support for dictatorship under Metaxas. They provided feedback that the King should not return until *after* a plebiscite on the monarchy, organised by a coalition government under a Regency.

---

[150] For more on the impact of this deception, see the Article by Klaus-Jurgen Muller in the book edited by Michael Handel on *Deception and Military Operations* Frank Cass, London (1987).

[151] See "Alex – The Life of Field Marshall Earl Alexander of Tunis" by Nigel Nicolson (Weidenfeld & Nicholson, London,1973), *"The Alanbrooke War Diaries 1939-45"* by Alanbrooke and Danchev (Wiedenfield and Nicholson, London, 2001), and *"War Diaries: Politics and War in the Mediterranean 1943-45"* by Harold MacMillan (St Martin's Press, New York, 1984).

Despite these tensions, the British managed to obtain from all the resistance groups an agreement to establish a *Joint HQ* at Pertouli for the oversight of resistance support for military operations. And, in August 1943, in an attempt to unify the resistance and ensure the continued flow of supplies to all parties, SOE organised the *Andarte* mission to meet with the Anglo-Greek Committee in Cairo. After several weeks, during which the resistance leaders made a number of political demands which exposed divisions in the GGE, they returned to Greece empty handed with major repercussions for both the Greek resistance (civil war) and the Cairo office of SOE (a major re-organisation).

On 3 September 1943, the Italians signed an armistice with the Allies, as a result of which a number of Italian garrisons in Greece were disarmed either by the Germans or the resistance and the Germans assumed complete control of the country. British attempts to recruit Italians to a local Division to fight the Germans were quickly undermined by EAM. The last months of 1943 were a period of great bitterness between ELAS and EDES and their respective BLO leaders and supporters. All the parties were on the run from the Germans but, at the same time ELAS guerrillas were attacking EDES forces. EDES appealed to the British who issued a stern warning to EAM/ELAS to desist and Wig's team briefly suspended the delivery of supplies. However, given the impact on military activity, the senior BLO in Greece made strong representations against this move, and sought to bring about an accommodation between the two sides. In an attempt to recover their reputation and supplies, EAM sent messages seeking recognition by the GGE in Cairo.

At the end of 1943, as Wig was preparing to transfer to Italy, a great deal of energy was being committed to terminating the civil war. A military proposal to consolidate all resistance forces into the Greek Army, with a promise that the King would not return to Greece until after a plebiscite on the monarchy, was not successful. Instead, in what became known as the *Plaka Agreement,* it was agreed with the resistance that they should be organised into 5 geographical areas. In theory (although not in practice), this Agreement brought an end to the civil war and committed the parties to implementing a three-phase plan designed to re-launch Greek resistance activity ahead of *Operation Overlord* in France which was scheduled for the late spring of 1944. The Agreement also envisaged the resumption of SOE supplies to EAM/ELAS. Despite having signed this agreement, with a German withdrawal on the cards, EAM continued to prepare for an all-out attempt to take power. In March, they established a Political Committee of National Liberation, including a range of non-communist allies but excluding Napoleon Zervas (EDES) and Dimitrios Psarros (EKKA). Subsequently, they started to round up opposition groups in the mountains, and in no time the country was again lurching towards civil war. Being aware of this conflict, the Germans took the opportunity to attack the mountain bases of various resistance groups, destroying the *Joint HQ*, and killing a number of guerrillas. At the same time, ELAS hunted down and killed the EKKA leader Psarros and totally eliminated his forces. Now, only EDES led by Zervas and the British Liaison Officers stood between EAM and total power inside the country following German withdrawal.

Whilst there was mayhem in the mountains, back in Cairo, in April 1944, Tsouderos was replaced as Prime Minister by George Papandreou who was brought from Athens to Cairo to form a government of national unity. He was leader of the Social Democratic Party and a republican, and his government included the previously mentioned Kanellopoulos. In May 1944, Papandreou joined with representatives of EAM at a conference in Lebanon and an agreement for military co-operation was reached in return for the expansion of military supplies. The terms were quickly repudiated by EAM leaders in the field but, with the prospect of the arrival of a British military force, on 9 September representatives of the EAM high command had second thoughts and joined the government.

In late August 1944, there was a coup in Rumania, and they pulled out of the war. It then became clear that the Germans would soon withdraw from Greece. In anticipation of liberation, the British prepared for a landing which involved a group called *Force 140*, including some 10,000 troops. On 10 September 1944, and ten days before the landing of this army, the Allies launched an operation called *Noah's Ark* designed to beleaguer the German withdrawal. The campaign of harassment and sabotage continued for six weeks until the last German forces had left the country. The main battles were fought on the only two escape roads to the east and west of the mainland, and huge damage was inflicted on the retreating Divisions to both equipment and troops.

In October 1944, the King and the GGE returned to Greece, supported by the British troops which included a significant group drawn from the Sherwood Foresters. As remnants of the German forces finally departed Greek territory in late November, EAM had one last shot at seizing control. In December 1944, they launched an uprising. This was almost a total failure with little support from the local population anywhere. Instead, the people welcomed the British troops and supporting resistance forces as they reinstated order across the country. Following the liberation, and despite some opposition from republican elements, the British ensured that King George II and the GGE were able to return to Athens and assume power. The King then fulfilled his long-stated commitment to facilitate free elections and a plebiscite about the monarchy. In the subsequent elections, George Papandreou was elected Prime Minister whilst, in the plebiscite, the people voted to retain the monarchy.

SOE Operations in Greece

The material presented here mostly refers to the period of 1943 when Wig was responsible for all the related air operations. However, we begin with an indication of the policy framework adopted for SOE operations in the Balkans.[152] For the purposes of this policy promulgated in 1941, the Balkans was defined as Albania, Bulgaria, Greece, Hungary, Rumania, and Yugoslavia, and the scope was *"to prepare a revolt of the "Balkan peoples" against the Axis powers and their "quisling" supporters, with preparations to be completed by April 1942, and to pursue such individual acts of sabotage, terrorism and other subversive activity as may be undertaken without compromising the primary aim of preparing the revolt."* The policy was to be implemented with reference to a strategic construct of which the following is a precis.

i)   The Balkans was important to Allied defence because it provided the principal base for an Axis offensive against the Middle East.
ii)   The Balkans provided the only available land route for the Allies to invade Europe from the Middle East.
iii)   The Balkans presented diversionary potential, undermining German operations in southern Russia, facilitating future Allied advances through Italy, and holding up German Divisions which might be deployed in other theatres of war.
iv)   The Balkans was a source of economic activity vital to the German war effort, including the Rumanian oil wells, the Danube River, the railway network, agriculture, minerals, and manpower.

---

[152] The following material is taken from SOE file HS 5-904 dated December 1941.

v)   There was a need to be mindful that the situation in the Balkans following the war would be influential in addressing a number of related issues: "the German problem", Anglo-Russian relations, "the Italian problem", and the balance of power in the eastern Mediterranean.[153]

Implementation of the policy to engender revolt encompassed the following:

a)   Establishment of communication with existing or potential centres of revolt, involving where appropriate, the despatch of an "Englishman" to make personal contact.[154]
b)   Supply of revolutionary centres with arms, ammunition, explosives, food, and other materials using aircraft and submarines.
c)   Co-ordination of revolutionary activity, with cells co-ordinated from Cairo, and led by individuals to be identified by the "English" Officer.

The policy statement then maintained that a primary means of engendering revolt would be the use of "Propaganda", which was conceived to consist of material from outside (broadcasts, leaflets dropped from the air, and rumours planted with travellers) and inside (local printing of leaflets), and "Action" (consisting of terrorism and spectacular revolutionary incidents). Finally, as the basis for engaging with external representatives of the people and the internal resistance, the policy document concluded with an assessment of the sociological, political, and economic conditions in each of the Balkan countries.

Despite this well-defined strategy, implementation was easier said than done. It is interesting to note the views of Colin Gubbins (to become the head of SOE in September 1943) who had undertaken a survey of "current assets" in mid-1941. In his report, he had said that SOE was not going to be in a position to deploy significant resources into the Balkans until the winter of 1942-43. This presumed a successful outcome of the war in North Africa and turned out to be an accurate assessment, with an enhanced air operations unit

---

[153] The reference to the German and Italian "problems" probably refers to the perceived political issues arising from the pre-eminence of pre-war Fascism.

[154] The use of the term "Englishman" in the SOE document is a quaint reflection of the lack of sensitivity in those days to the diverse nature of the British peoples.

under Wig emerging after the major reorganisation of the SOE Cairo office in late 1942.

In the meantime, SOE prepared the ground. In September 1942, it had been decided to despatch a significant British Military Mission to Greece to facilitate the development of effective and co-ordinated resistance activity in the field. This was led by Lt Colonel Edmund C Myers *("the Englishman")* with Captain C M Woodhouse as his deputy.[155] [156] Their initial remit, under what was called the *Operation Harling*, was to destroy one or more of three viaducts on the railway line connecting Greece with central Europe to further hinder reinforcements for Rommel through the port of Piraeus. The main resource for this mission was EDES and ELAS guerrillas. On completion, Myers was to withdraw and Woodhouse was to stay on with Zervas and the EDES forces as a permanent mission. The team was dropped into Greece in several separate sorties in early October, and Myers/Woodhouse linked up on the slopes of Mt Giona in central Greece. Woodhouse then travelled some 100kms across country to rendezvous with Zervas. In the meantime, a third British group was inserted and linked up with the ELAS guerrillas led by a man called Ares.[157] After some equivocation from their political masters EAM, the ELAS group was committed to the mission bringing the total number of guerrillas to 150.

Under the leadership of Myers, the main attack was launched by a combination of ELAS and EDES guerrillas on the evening of 26 November 1942 and they destroyed considerable infrastructure including the Gorgapotamos viaduct which was then closed for traffic for a critical 39 days. The bridge was defended by a significant Italian force. They lost at least 13 troops, although some reports mention many more casualties. Allied casualties were just two wounded. This operation gave great heart to the resistance, and reflected considerable credit on SOE who were earning a reputation for motivating and leading operations in Greece. The important role played by ELAS and EDES was also recognised and, in the aftermath, there was a hope that this would augur well for future joint resistance activity.

---

[155] Myers was a 36 year old regular Sapper officer with no Greek experience, but excellent engineering skills suitable for sabotage activity. Within a few months, he was appointed as the head of the SOE mission in the field.

[156] Monty Woodhouse was a 25 year old classical scholar who had already worked in Crete and was well versed in the Greek language and politics. He became a notable MP after the war.

[157] Ares was the *nomme de guerre* of Athanasios ("Thanasi") Klaras.

However, three days after completion of the operation, the two resistance forces parted company, with Zervas (EDES) moving with the British to the west and Ares (ELAS) moving to the east.

This was exactly the point at which Wig joined SOE, and the optimism arising from *Operation Harling* would have been all around the Cairo office as he joined the team in Rustum Building. However, the success was not met with universal acclaim. The Tsouderos government had reservations about both ELAS and EDES because of their republican leanings. As a result, there was now a bit of hiatus in Cairo as to how to proceed with support for resistance activity. After serious reflection during the Christmas/New Year holiday break, it was decided to consolidate the resistance command structure. On 8 January 1943, Myers and Woodhouse reconvened at a place called Botsi in central Greece and, following discussions with SOE in Cairo, Myers was appointed a Brigadier with responsibility for all BLOs in Greece, and Woodhouse (now appointed a Lt Colonel and his deputy) was sent to liaise with resistance leaders in Athens (known as the six Colonels). In Athens, Woodhouse met with a variety of people including representatives of both the army and EAM, and the agent known as *Apollo* (his real name was Ioannis Peltekis) who led a subversive group that had been active for some time. Meanwhile, back in Cairo, Keble was establishing his new air operations unit under Wig designed to improve air operations support. From this point, Wig was involved in all of SOE's operations involving air support.

In early 1943, there was a growing sense of optimism amongst the Allies, and in the Cairo office, with the siege of Leningrad being raised on 18 January 1943, Rommel retreating westwards into Tunisia on 29 January, and the German army surrendering at Stalingrad on 30 January. On the ground in Greece, as news of German reverses spread across Europe, EAM started to think about how they should prepare for the departure of the Axis powers, and decided that it was essential to establish themselves as the dominant resistance force so that they could become the *de facto* government in the country before the *de jure* GGE had a chance to return from Cairo.

Given these considerations, SOE made a concerted effort to extend the bands of guerrillas established through Zervas to whom they gave significant financial as well material air support. In February, a Colonel Sarafis began to promote the idea at EDES HQ of raising national bands throughout the country. The aim was to construct an organisation that would seriously rival ELAS and ultimately drive the two groups into a united resistance movement. However, before SOE could lend material support to this initiative, Sarafis was captured by ELAS and a while later he re-emerged as an ELAS military leader!

In the following months, SOE sponsored several similar attempts to proliferate resistance activity and, by April 1943, Wig's team were providing air support to a network of 10 BLO led missions in the mountains who were stationed with local bands located in Mt Olympus, Macedonia, East Roumeeli, Parnassus, West Roumeli, west Thessaly, the Peloponnese, and Epirus. Through these dispersed groups, head of mission Myers hoped to encourage a mix of autonomous teams each of which would work relatively independently under a nominated BLO. However, SOE in Cairo, supported by the GGE, preferred a centralised model. Cairo's approach prevailed, and this played into EAM's hands. As each of the 10 new SOE missions were established, they were openly attacked or undermined whenever they appeared to be gaining traction as independent operating units. In the end, almost all of them were taken over by ELAS who were skilled in exploiting the fear amongst the general population that the Allied sponsored teams would facilitate the return of the King and a Metaxas style leadership. Eventually, only a minority of groups that were independent of ELAS survived, and the main competitors, EDES led by Zervas and EKKA led by Psarros, were both intermittently under attack.

Given EAM's approach, the staff in SOE Cairo were "between a rock and hard place", and this must have had a significant impact at all levels in the organisation. For Wig's team, who had daily discussions with the Greek desk in the Cairo office and had to respond to requests for supplies from many groups in the field, it must have been exceedingly difficult to determine priorities. The reality was that, if SOE wanted EAM support in fighting the Germans, they would probably need to turn a blind eye to attacks on the rival EDES and EKKA groups.

With this backcloth, in March 1943, SOE in Cairo began to formulate *Operation Animals,* the aim of which was to create a diversion ahead of the Allied invasion of Sicily in July. This was an operation which required major air operations support and Wig would have been involved in much planning. In early June, Myers was briefed on the operation which was scheduled to take place between 20 June and 7 July 1943. It involved an attack on German communications in Greece to convince the Axis powers that the Allies were about to land troops on the Adriatic coast of Greece. It was anticipated that, in response, the Germans would allocate significant forces which would not then be available for redeployment elsewhere. Implementation of this plan

153

required the full co-operation of all resistance forces which Myers now set out to achieve.

In preparation, Myers started discussions with the central EAM team, and also attempted to negotiate a cease fire between ELAS with its 15,000 men, EDES with its 5,000 men and the smaller EKKA force. Not yet seeing themselves as strong enough to act independently of the British, EAM elected to co-operate. However, in return for their support, they sought to extract an undertaking to increase supplies. They also saw an opportunity through the contact with the EKKA teams to try and disperse them. Myers then toured British missions in the field where many BLOs had good relations with the local ELAS people, with the aim of getting *them* on side. Finally, on 14 June he successfully negotiated a military agreement between all the parties that provided for the establishment of a unified command to control all guerrilla activity under the direction of the Commander in Chief Middle East, General Wilson. Under this agreement, Ares of EAM/ELAS, Zervas of EDES and Psarros of EKKA would be represented at a *Joint HQ* which would issue orders through Myers. Whether EAM would obey these orders remained to be seen.

In any event, thanks to this preparatory work, *Operation Animals* achieved its objectives, starting with a spectacularly dangerous attack undertaken by 5 British and an Arab on the Asopus Bridge on 21 June 1943 which was subsequently out of action for several months. This was followed in the next three weeks by no less than 44 major cuts in road and rail communications, and a five day strike in Piraeus. All the guerrillas, led by BLOs, and supported tirelessly by Wig's air operations unit in Cairo, played their part diligently. As a result of these activities, the Germans became convinced of an Allied invasion and allocated substantial reinforcements from the northern Balkans. Partly as a consequence, the invasion of Sicily, *Operation Husky*, proceeded on 10 July with great success.

Whilst all this had been going on, the King and GGE had returned to Cairo, together with a new British Ambassador, Rex Leeper. He took over as chairman of the Anglo-Greek Committee which continued to co-ordinate all resistance activity despite reservations from the military.[158] Following completion of *Operations Animals*, on 18 July all the relevant resistance parties convened at the first meeting of the new *Joint HQ* which was at

---

[158] In SOE Files there is correspondence regarding an unsuccessful proposal to disband the Anglo-Greek Committee at this time.

Pertouli in the mountains. And this body almost assumed the status of a *de facto* government, an impression that was bolstered by the participation of a formal representative of the British Foreign Office and GGE, Major David Wallace who was appointed to act as a political adviser to Myers. However, there were serious undercurrents arising from the republican sympathies of both EAM/ELAS and EDES. The GGE did not trust either group, and there were tensions between the Foreign Office committed to the reinstatement of the King and the military for whom the ability to prosecute the war against the Germans was the main objective. As a result, there was talk in Wig's office of ceasing the provision of supplies to ELAS, and even to EDES as well.

Back in Greece, Myers was most concerned. Mindful of the effectiveness of the resistance movements in achieving the military aim of undermining the German occupation, he and his BLOs were keen to ensure that all the parties continued to receive supplies. He decided that the best way of addressing this issue was to send a delegation of resistance leaders to talk with the Allied leaders in Cairo. The aim of this mission would be to demonstrate that, after the success of Operation Animals, the resistance were capable of working together despite their republican leanings and were worthy of full-blooded support. In July 1943, he asked for permission to send a team of resistance leaders to meet with the Anglo-Greek Committee, and his request was granted. The delegation arrived in Cairo on 10 August.

With the benefit of hindsight, and despite the best of intentions, the *Andarte* mission was doomed because it had the potential to seriously compromise both the military and the political aims of the Allied leadership. From a military perspective, the cooperation between the resistance movements depended on the expectation that the Allies were about to launch an invasion of Greece. The reality was that the Allies had no such intention and, if this got to the ears of the resistance leaders, any unity of purpose would quickly evaporate. Unknown to Myers, the *Andarte* team were also intent on pursuing certain political objectives. As it happened, when they arrived, the GGE was debating the timing of a plebiscite on the future of the monarchy and the resistance leaders bought into this debate supporting the view that the King should not return until after the plebiscite. Fortunately for the King, the Allied leadership were adamant in supporting his position that he would return before the plebiscite but the King and his supporters were not happy. As a result SOE attracted considerable opprobrium as reflected in correspondence between Sir Orme Sargent at the Foreign Office and head of

SOE Lord Selborne in SOE File HS 5-425.[159]

Following the failure of the Andarte mission, and much debate at several meetings between all the parties, the British government produced a renewed version of its Greek policy, in beautifully expressed diplomatic language which read as follows:

"In view of the operational importance attached to subversive activities in Greece, there can be no question of SOE refusing to have dealings with a given group merely on the grounds that the political sentiments of the group are opposed to the King and Government; but, subject to special operational necessity, SOE should always veer in the direction of groups willing to support the King and Government and furthermore they should impress on such groups as may be anti-monarchical the fact that the King and Government enjoy the fullest support of His Majesty's Government. In general, nothing should be neglected which might help to promote unity among resistance groups in Greece and between the latter and the King and Government."[160]

Disappointed with the position taken by the Allied leaders in supporting the King, and no doubt having discovered the Allies true intentions regarding an invasion of Greece in the near future, on 17 September 1943 the *Andarte* mission returned to Greece. Despite his valiant attempts to bring unity and order, Myers was now discredited and made to stay in Cairo, with Lt Colonel Woodhouse promoted to take over as chief BLO in Greece.

Meanwhile, in Italy, on 25 August, Mussolini was deposed and by 3 September 1943, the Italians had signed an Armistice which significantly changed the balance of power in the Balkans. In Greece, Italian troops were in a state of chaos, some being disarmed by the Germans and others by ELAS which was now led by General Stefanos Sarafis. In Thessaly, the BLOs took charge and managed to negotiate with the Italian General Infante the transfer of the whole Pinerolo Division to British command. On 12 September 1943, Colonel Woodhouse then signed the first *Co-Belligerency Agreement* and this was endorsed by Cairo. However, seeing them as a threat, ELAS tried to undermine this force, and eventually dispersed the troops so ending the *Agreement*.

---

[159] Sir Orme Sargent was Deputy Permanent Under-Secretary at the Foreign Office.
[160] Extract from SOE Balkan diaries.

With the failure of the *Andarte* Mission, affairs at the Joint HQ in the Greek mountains deteriorated quickly. EAM now became very unco-operative. They were disillusioned by the failure of the British to invade as suggested by the *Operation Animals* activity (they were not party to the diversionary nature of the operation) and saw the British as stalwart supporters of the old order under the King. Anticipating the end of the war, they were also preparing to seize power on the back of the German withdrawal. During the final months of 1943, Civil War broke out across the whole of Greece. On 9 October, ELAS rounded up most of the EDES forces in Macedonia, Thessaly, Roumeli, and the Peloponnese and disarmed them. They then turned on the main Zervas stronghold in the south west. In the process they shot a BLO called Hubbard. Zervas escaped to Epirus in the mountains with a remnant of 5,000 men, compared with the current ELAS strength of 25,000. The Germans took advantage of this activity and attacked resistance camps, including the base of the *Joint HQ* at Pertouli which ceased to exist. They also tried to implicate Zervas in being a collaborator, although he always remained loyal to the British and followed SOE orders (unlike Mihailović in Yugoslavia). In the next four months, Civil War continued to rage between ELAS and EDES.

The last months of 1943 were a period of great bitterness for the Allied military mission. The BLOs in the field were working under huge stress, and Wig's work in the SOE air operations office must also have been very difficult, particularly in terms of determining which requests for supplies should take priority or even be sent at all. Initially, the supply of arms and materials to ELAS was largely terminated, and most of the SOE air operations were focussed on EDES and Zervas. However, given the number of BLOs working with ELAS, and the view that ELAS were the most effective group to attack the Germans, the supplies never completely dried up. This continued to concern the Greek King and Prime Minister, and there was constant friction with the Allied command. An indication of the *actual* number of SOE agents and staff in the field being supported by Wig's team at this time (November 1943) is as overleaf:[161]

---

[161] Material taken from SOE File HS 5-157 and dated 24 November 1943.

Resistance Group	BLOs	Other Ranks	Greek Personnel	Americans	Total
EAM/ELAS	56	47	34	3	140
EDES	18	19	5		42
EKKA	3	1	2		6
Others	1		12		13
TOTAL	78	67	53	3	201

Meanwhile, there were forces elsewhere trying to make life difficult. Back in the USA, an interesting article by a Drew Pearson appeared in the Washington Post.[162] His views reflected the views of many Americans that the British were bent on restoring the old monarchical order throughout Europe, and that this *"king-bowing"* policy was the reason for the outbreak of civil war in Greece. Despite Roosevelt's continued support for the King, Pearson and others advocated that the US should insist on a policy of supporting only "democratic" forces. This conveniently avoided the other American pre-occupation regarding the threat of communist insurgents.

Faced with the civil war, the Head of the SOE Mission Woodhouse reached a state of total frustration. Despite all the obvious issues relating to post-war politics, he still supported EAM/ELAS as the most effective force against the Germans. Yet the SOE leadership in Cairo seemed to be holding him back. Not the least of his worries was that EAM's co-operation was needed for SOE's next major mission, *Operation Noah's Ark* which was designed to harry the German withdrawal whenever it occurred in 1944. With winter setting in, December saw a lull in civil war hostilities, with ELAS desisting from attacks on the other resistance forces. The reason for this is not entirely clear. But, for a time, EAM seemed to think that to gain power they needed the support of and recognition by the British.

In the wake of the internecine warfare, the failure of the *Andarte* mission came home to roost. For that and other reasons mentioned in Chapter 15, the leadership of the SOE Cairo office was under severe pressure. As a result, in September 1943, Glenconner was replaced by Major General Stawell as head of the Cairo Office. By the end of the year, with the establishment of a new SOE base covering the Balkans in Italy, the office in Cairo was downsized, leaving a smaller SOE Force 133 providing the service to Greece.[163] For a

---

[162] This may be found in SOE File HS 5-146.
[163] See *"The Politicization of Intelligence: The British Experience in Greece 1941-44"* by Christina Goulter-Zervoudakis in the Journal Intelligence & National Security Vol 13 Issue 1.

while, air support to the various BLOs and Greek resistance groups continued under the direction of Major Wigginton. However, at the end of the year, his work was passed over to others in Cairo when he was transferred to Italy.

At this point, as Wig transfers to Italy, we leave the story of SOE in Greece. However, the work continued with direction from the Cairo office. Notably, in the next twelve months, there was *Operation Noah's Ark,* the chief aim of which was to delay the German withdrawal bearing in mind the impending launch of *Operation Overlord* in France that was scheduled for April 1944. *Operation Noah's Ark* was deemed to be an outstanding success. In western Macedonia, the SOE teams secured a stranglehold on two of the escape routes and other routes were the subject of repeated attacks from the air with attempts to break out reversed. As part of the operation, SOE teams (with help in Athens from the remnants of the *Apollo* Group) were also involved in "anti scorched earth" missions which led to successful outcomes in terms of protecting the Port of Piraeus, the Olympus Dam, and the St George's Day Power Station.[164]

In December 1944, EDAM/ELAS made one last to take power. But they failed and, by January 1945, the Civil War was finished. With British military assistance, the GGE and King returned, elections were then held, Papandreou was elected as Prime Minister, and the people voted to retain the monarchy. For SOE, the job was now largely completed.[165]

SOE Operations in the Greek Islands

During the war, the Germans and Italians occupied most of the islands in the Aegean Sea. The invaders were not welcomed by the islanders and there was widespread clandestine activity. For the most part, the insurgents were not influenced greatly by the resistance movements on the mainland and did their own thing. They were local bands and leaders pursuing their own missions and, during 1943, Wig was involved in providing supplies by air when SOE resources permitted.

Following the Axis invasion of Crete on 21 May 1941, SOE infiltrated

---

[164] For more about the Apollo Group, see the book by Plato Alexiades *"Target Corinth Canal 1940-44"* (Pen & Sword, Barnsley, 2015).

[165] By the end of the war, 18 months later, a total of 2,064 sorties had been flown to Greece of which 1,714 had been successful. A total of 4,205 tons of materiel had been dropped, 3,000 people had been parachuted into the country, and 600 had been brought out. This information is based on data in SOE File HS 7-11 which is a history of Special Duties operations.

several BLOs to assist in the escape of British troops that had been stranded. In 1942, BLOs made contact with a number of small resistance groups, and laid the foundations for a group capable of assisting in the event of a British invasion.[166] Later, GCHQ initiated a new phase of activity involving hit and run raids on enemy shipping, with back-up from SOE in the form of local agents infiltrated by Wig's team to provide intelligence.

In 1944, an SOE led team kidnapped the commander of the German 22nd Division, Major General Heinrich Kreipe which encouraged the local Crete resistance, off their own bat, to mount significant attacks on German forces with over 120 German dead. Unfortunately, the Germans responded with huge reprisals executing over 1,000 innocent Cretans. After this, the British decided to encourage a more low key approach based on harassment and carefully chosen logistical infrastructure targets, pending German withdrawal. This proceeded without great impact on the local population, and control of the islands was eventually transferred back to the Greek government when the island was liberated in 1945.

During Wig's time, in 1943, progress was made in establishing groups similar to those on Crete, on the islands of Rhodes, Samos, Chios, Mytiline, Scarpanto and Symi. Following the Italian armistice in September, Wig's team organised for Lt Colonel Dolbey to be flown from Cairo to Rhodes to negotiate the surrender of the Italian garrison and there was a similar mission to Corfu. The Italians appeared to be amenable to co-operation with the Allies, but quickly backed off when the Germans moved in to fill the void. However, SOE **were** successful in penetrating Cos, and Leros, and held the territory until back-up from the main military arrived.

For the record, although not contributing greatly to the larger picture, there was a great deal of sea-borne activity between the islands and the mainland. The first sea borne "caique" operation sailed from Smyrna (on the Turkish coast) to Piraeus in September 1941, and this route became so well established for transferring supplies that, in July 1943, SOE eventually established a base on the Chesme peninsula 80 kms west of Smyrna. The following month, a similar base was established on the coast of Thessaly. [167]

Reflection on the War in Greece

---

[166] This account is based on material in William Mackenzie's book *"The Secret History of SOE"* (pages 481 and 482), and SOE Files.
[167] A caique is a small light and fairly flat-bottomed boat.

By most measures, the work of SOE in Greece should be seen as largely successful. In particular, the British BLOs worked tirelessly, supported and sustained by Wig's air operations team in Cairo and a smaller naval team. SOE work involved establishment and encouragement of the resistance, facilitating their work in attacking and holding down significant Axis resources, and undermining Axis supply routes to North Africa. When the time came, the Allies also harried the German withdrawal whilst ensuring relatively little damage to infrastructure. SOE were also instrumental in securing the successful return of the King and government in exile, on the backs of a small British military force. In the process, and in the absence of any significant assistance from the Russians, a communist takeover was averted, and a constitutional monarchy was restored following free elections and a referendum. What had been a pre-war autocratic government was replaced with a liberal democracy.

Although there are few details to tell the story of his personal involvement, there is no doubt that Wig would have been gratified by the outcome and his part in it.

Part Seven: Based in Bari

18: Italian Historical Context

Following his time in Cairo, the next phase of Wig's life took him to Italy where he was head of SOE air operations for southern and eastern Europe. After living with the heat and the dust of North Africa for eighteen months, the prospect of life in southern Europe in winter must have been very welcome. As context for SOE operations based in Italy, and Wig's work there, the following provides a brief history of events in Italy just before his arrival and during his time in the country.

In 1922, after a period of political and economic unrest, Benito Mussolini had come to power. Over the next four years, he eliminated virtually all the structures of democratic government and, harbouring territorial ambitions in the Balkans and North Africa, he eventually allied himself with a resurgent Germany. His first meeting with Hitler was in 1934 and they formed a close working relationship. With fantasies of creating a new Roman Empire, he built up the Italian navy, and in 1935 he invaded Ethiopia. Following condemnation for this aggression, he left the League of Nations. With a new found freedom to act, after Germany annexed Czechoslovakia in March 1939, on 7 April Italy invaded Albania. In May 1939, Germany and Italy formed the so called *Pact of Steel*.[168]

Conscious of poor military preparation, at the beginning of hostilities in September 1939, Italy held back. But they joined the war against the Allies on 10 June 1940, hoping that their alliance with Germany would quickly deliver territory in southern France. Their expectations were almost immediately fulfilled. When Germany signed a treaty with Marshall Petain that took France (Vichy France) out of the war, Italy was ceded French territory. Keen to play his part, in the summer of 1940, Mussolini ordered the invasion of Egypt; but Italian forces were soon driven back by the British and suffered a disastrous defeat at Sidi-Barrani, where 200,000 Italian troops were taken prisoner. In October, Italy invaded Greece and again they were repulsed. However, the Germans made a better fist of it in April and May 1941, when they swept through both Yugoslavia and then Greece.

Despite the success of their German ally, Italy was now faltering in

---

[168] The Pact of Friendship and Alliance was signed by Germany and Italy on 23 May 1939, and provided for co-operation on economic and military policy at the expense of the UK and France. It eventually evolved into the Tripartite Pact with Japan when the Soviet Union also became a target. Italy withdrew from the Pact following the armistice with the Allies in 1943.

various respects. The economy had failed to adapt to the conditions of war, Italian cities were being bombed by the Allies, and Italian troops were disillusioned by their military failures. However, the Germans shared with them the spoils of the invasion of the Balkans, and substantial Italian troops were installed as occupying forces in Yugoslavia and Greece. The Italians also took part in the successful invasion of Crete. Following the failure of the Italian attack on Egypt, in early 1941 Hitler despatched Rommel and his Afrika Korps into North Africa to support the remaining Italian forces. A fierce war ensued in the Western Desert. Eventually, towards the end of 1942, the Allies prevailed and many Italian troops surrendered.

On 14 January 1943, Churchill and Roosevelt met at Casablanca to plan the invasion of Italy which was characterised as *"the soft underbelly of Europe"*. In the following nine months, the country became a major target for both regular armed forces and covert activity. Anticipating this turn of events, the Germans began a steady build-up of defensive forces and positions in central and northern Italy. This suited Allied strategy as it diverted resources from other theatres. On 10 July 1943, in *Operation Husky*, the Allies invaded Sicily from North Africa. This was a major blow to Mussolini and, on 24 July 1943, he was defeated in a vote of confidence at a meeting of the Grand Council of Fascism in Rome. The following day, King Victor Emmanuel III ordered his arrest, and appointed Marshall Pietro Badoglio as head of a new government. Two days later, Badoglio dissolved the Fascist Party. The Allies now put pressure on Italy to pull out of the Tripartite Pact with Germany and Japan and, following lengthy and tortuous negotiations over several weeks, the Italians complied. On 3 September 1943, they signed an armistice with the Allies which removed Italy as a combatant. This threw the country into a civil war, since there were both Mussolini loyalists as well as nascent resistance forces across the whole country. [169]

At this time, the main resistance group was a body called the CLN

---

[169] Of course, the world had not heard the last of Mussolini. After several months of imprisonment, on 12 September 1943 he was rescued from incarceration in a resort hotel high in the Apennine Mountains to the north east of Rome by a daring German paratroop operation *(Operation Oak)* led by the renowned Colonel Otto Skorzeny. After being reunited with his family and visiting Hitler at his headquarters in Austria, Mussolini was then installed as the head of what was called the Italian Social Republic (known as the Republic of Salo) covering most of northern Italy. He ruled there under German direction until the area was over-run by Allied troops in 1945. He was then summarily executed by Italian partisans on 28 April 1945.

("Committee for National Liberation") which was led by Ivanoe Bonomi who would eventually succeed Baglioni as Prime Minister at the end of the war. This grouping, based in Rome, was made up of Communists, Socialists, Liberals, the right wing but non-Fascist Action Party, the Christian Democrats and the Labour Democrats. In the next three years, they were responsible for implementing a loosely co-ordinated and wide range of resistance activity in southern and central Italy which, through SOE, dovetailed with the pursuit of Allied military objectives following the Allied invasion. However, the CLN spawned another grouping in *northern* Italy called the CLNAI (ie the CLN for Upper Italy) who were responsible for co-ordinating activity behind German lines. Based in Milan, this group was led by Alfredo Pizzoni and had strong links to SOE in Berne as well SOE in the south. There were elements in the CLNAI whose objectives were inclined to separation from the rest of the country and even a communist take-over of Italy after the war. But these people never obtained an upper hand.

On the same day in September as the Allies and the King signed the Armistice (3 September 1943), the British 8th Army under Montgomery landed at Reggio Calabria. In the following ten days, there were further landings of the 8th Army along the "toe" including at Taranto. The invasion was met with only light resistance and the troops advanced and consolidated quickly. On 8th/9th September, in *Operation Avalanche*, the American 5th Army under the command of General Mark W Clark landed further north at Salerno together with further British troops. This was met with significant resistance and was the start of a protracted conflict. With an imminent rapid response from the German forces, the King and Badoglio fled to Pescara and Brindisi and thence to a temporary residence in Malta. The Germans occupied Rome on 10 September 1943.

On 11 September 1943, the British forces to the East had reached Brindisi (on the "heel" of Italy) and, significantly for Wig's story, on 14 September they took the major Adriatic port of Bari. Shortly after, Brindisi became the base for the Italian government. Strategically, the taking of Brindisi and Bari in the face of little German resistance was a significant move, as this area provided a relatively secure base for a range of Allied operations. In the next eighteen months, this part of Italy gradually became a major centre for SOE and other covert operations, for missions not only into central and northern Italy, but also to the Balkans, France, and into central and Eastern Europe.

On 23 October 1943, the Badoglio's government-in-exile declared war on Germany and established a fragile pact with leaders of the Italian resistance.

167

And, in the final weeks of 1943, the Allies began a steady but painfully slow progress travelling north, with many lives lost on both sides. The Germans were no pushover, with a succession of defensive lines from the *Gustav Line* across the centre of Italy to the *Gothic Line* further north. And they made frequent counterattacks including a devastating air raid on SOE positions in Bari on 2 December 1943 in which over 1,000 lives were lost.

In mid-January 1944, as Wig was taking up his SOE air operations post in Bari, the Allies commenced an assault on the *Gustav Line* focussing on the hill fortress of Monte Cassino. Over the next four months there were four bloody battles with significant casualties. Finally, the Germans were defeated even as the preparations for the D-Day landings in France were being completed. On 4 June 1944, the Allies entered Rome and the Italian Prime Minister Badoglio was succeeded by CLN leader Ivanoe Bonomi. He moved the provisional government to the capital and led it through the rest of the war.

The Allied advance through central and northern Italy was far from straightforward, and they did not reach Florence until 4 August 1944. As they advanced north, they encountered increasingly difficult terrain, as mountains offered excellent defensive positions for the German forces. The Allies reached the last major German defensive position, the *Gothic Line,* on 15 August. However, victory was hard to complete and the war continued through the autumn and a very difficult winter with territory frequently changing sides. The final Allied offensive was not launched until the spring of 1945, with a ceasefire declared on 29 April. The Germans formally surrendered on 2 May 1945, only a week before the general surrender of all German forces across Europe.

In all, between landing in September 1943 and April 1945 it is estimated that some 60,000 Allied troops were killed in Italy and more than 50,000 Germans, which is not quite what the Allies had expected given Churchill's assertion that Italy would be *'the soft underbelly of the Axis'*. In the aftermath, the Allies worked hard to ensure that the provisional Italian government had effective control to facilitate a return to liberal democracy. Following the cessation of hostilities, in June 1945 Bonomi stepped down as Prime Minister and was succeeded by Ferruccio Parri, who in turn gave way to Alcide de Gasperi on 4 December 1945. On 9 May 1946, King Victor Emanuelle III abdicated, and was succeeded by his son Umberto II. On 2 June 1946, there was a general election and a Constitutional Referendum in which 54% of those voting determined that the monarchy should be abolished. Umberto II reigned for just one month before being required to abdicate in favour of a President. De Gasperi then supervised the transition to a Republic. On 18 June 1946, he briefly became acting Head of State as well as Prime Minister, but ten days later ceded the former role to Provisional President Enrico de Nicola. De Gasperi then continued as Prime Minister, with victory in subsequent elections, until he retired in 1953. In that first post war general election of 1946, a Constituent Assembly of 556 members was elected. Interestingly, given the diverse make-up of the resistance movements, 207 were Christian Democrats, 115 were Socialists and 104 were Communists. This parliament, with government based on a grand coalition, established a new constitution based on a parliamentary democracy. In 1947, under American pressure, the communist were expelled from the government and, in the Italian general election of 1948, the Christian Democrats achieved a landslide victory. They were to remain in power for 40 Years.

19: No. 1 Special Force

One of the main areas of activity that Wig's air operations unit in Bari supported was the work of SOE in Italy itself. The organisation which had responsibility was No 1 Special Force, which was established shortly before Wig moved to Italy.[170] [171]

Following the Allied invasion of southern Italy in September 1943, SOE was keen to expand activity in that country as quickly as possible. By this time, Eisenhower had determined to embrace SOE as a force capable of providing direct support to military campaigns, and envisaged that they would work in co-operation with the American OSS under the direction of Brigadier-General Benjamin Caffey.[172] This view was supported by Eisenhower's British successor in North Africa, General Sir Henry Maitland Wilson (notwithstanding his sometimes frosty relationship with SOE's Cairo office). Accordingly, from this point onwards, SOE in Italy had a special status as a participant in both military and political planning in a way that it had not enjoyed in other theatres. This was to bring both benefits and, for SOE, some frustrating constraints.

In establishing a direct presence in the country, the SOE unit with responsibility for Italy (Massingham in North Africa) implemented a strategy with a number of strands, to meet a variety of objectives. For the first six months, there were two quite separate *operational* missions, with resources split between the east and west of southern Italy. The primary aim of both teams was to establish links with the Italian resistance movements and facilitate their activities. However, there were other aims.

The mission in the west was directed at ensuring the continuation of a close working relationship with AFHQ which, following the invasion, established an advance base at the Italian royal family's palace at Caserta (40 kms north of Naples). There were also significant benefits from having an SOE presence in the east. This second deployment facilitated a close working

---

[170] Previously, SOE activity in Italy was nascent, and a brief summary is provided in Appendix 11.

[171] Much of the material in this chapter is drawn from the definitive book on SOE in Italy by David Stafford entitled *"Mission Accomplished – SOE in Italy 1943-45"*.

[172] The relationship between SOE and OSS was sometimes tense. Efforts were made to address this as recorded in an agreement details of which are provided in Appendix 12.

relationship with the provisional Italian government and political structure which had been established at Brindisi. A base in the east was also a much more logistically convenient location for supporting the resistance movements across the Adriatic Sea than the MO4/Force 133 base in Cairo.

The first SOE operational group to arrive in Italy, was led by Major Malcolm Munthe who arrived by sea from the North Africa on 10 September 1943. They travelled with the Allied invasion force which landed at Salerno to the west. Munthe went on to establish an SOE operation that was eventually named *Operation Vigilant.* A fuller account of Munthe's work is provided in Appendix 11. In the short term, Munthe's specific orders were to establish contact with the resistance, and assist with the harassment of the Axis forces behind enemy lines. Once established, *Operation Vigilant* instigated some 70 missions, although it only persisted as an effective operation for a relatively short period. Despite valiant efforts, Munthe's operations eventually fell foul of the significant shift in SOE strategy towards closer work with the military following the replacement of Lord Selborne by General Gubbins.

While Munthe was setting up *Operation Vigilant* in the west, Massingham proceeded to establish the operational "out-station" on the east coast, and despatched a team who arrived at Brindisi on 28 September 1943 on a ship called the *Mutin.* The SOE chief in Massingham, Dodds-Parker, decided to call this team *No 1 Special Force.* Apart from working with the Italian resistance, it was also given responsibility for working with the Italian government, training agents, and supporting the Italian Navy (based in Brindisi). Initially it also held a remit for operations in Yugoslavia and Albania but, after a couple of months and much wrangling, SOE in Cairo reasserted its control over the Balkans establishing its own team in eastern Italy (of which Wig was a part).

The leader of No 1 Special Force was Commander Gerald Holdsworth, a position that he held for the rest of the war.[173] He had quite a formidable reputation. As Major General William Stawell is reported as saying at the time of his appointment, *"Holdsworth is a most powerful personality. He is an expert in clandestine warfare in all its aspects. He never spares himself. He is somewhat mercurial in temperament, but with careful handling he will*

---

[173] Interestingly, Holdsworth was a relative of Deputy Prime Minister Clement Attlee.

give loyal and conscientious service. "[174][175][176] During the planning stage for this initiative, Dodds-Parker allowed Holdsworth to nominate a code name for his mission and, as confirmed in a cable sent on 19 September 1943, he chose the word "*Maryland*" after his wife. On 29 September, a second ship named *The Gilfredo* arrived from North Africa carrying Richard Hewitt who soon became Holdsworth's second-in-command.

Holdsworth located his headquarters at a place called Monopoli which is a small coastal town about half way between Brindisi and Bari.[177] He chose this location because, with the King and his provisional government having established their base in Brindisi, property in that town was in short supply and there was merit in not being too close to the seat of power. And, it was still only a short distance to the port and airport facilities in Brindisi. The Foreign Office SIS also set up their office there.

Once he was fully operational, and being aware of the existing SOE links with the Italian resistance in the north, Holdsworth quickly saw the potential of the network of contacts and agents run by McCaffery out of Berne in Switzerland and was soon in touch with him. Unfortunately, exploiting this existing team was easier said than done. Around this time, McCaffery had a nervous breakdown which put him out of action for a couple of months. Also, McCaffery and his associates in Switzerland were quite apprehensive about the SOE operation in the south. This was because they saw No 1 Special Force as too closely allied to the royalist government in Brindisi, and the Italian secret service ("SIM") some of whom were suspected of having Fascist leanings. Nevertheless, the British government did take the step of rationalising the command structure. Although the Foreign Office's J Section in London continued to have some dealings with Berne, in November responsibility for Berne operations was transferred to Holdsworth.

---

[174] As the head of Special Operations Mediterranean ("SOM"), Major General Stawell was to become the SOE leader for operations out of Italy directed to other territories including Yugoslavia and Eastern Europe.

[175] This quote and the subsequent account is based on David Stafford's book entitled *"Mission Accomplished SOE and Italy 1943-1945"* pages 46-48.

[176] An extended account of the work of Holdsworth is provided in the book by Charles T. O'Reilly, *Forgotten Battles. Italy's War of Liberation 1943-1945* (Rowman & Littlefield, Maryland, 2001).

[177] Monopoli, which is about 40kms north of Brindisi, was the base for SOE activities in Italy itself. The overarching SOE unit called *Special Operations Mediterranean (SOM),* providing a service to the Balkans and Eastern Europe, was eventually based in Bari.

Hardly had Holdsworth's team arrived in September 1943 than he had his first taste of operational activity. SOE in Cairo conceived a mission to rescue prisoners of war who were held behind enemy lines and who would be available for re-deployment as the Allies advanced through Italy. This project was led by Lt Colonel Tony Simonds and was launched by sea. The project was code named *Operation Simcol.* Despite numerous attempts to round up groups of POWs, the results were disappointing, with fewer than 1,000 men being recovered from the many thousands trapped behind enemy lines. In the meantime, initial sorties from Monopoli to the Italian resistance saw the establishment of several wireless communication units, and the recruitment of over 100 Italians who were prepared to join the resistance and help the Allies. However, operations were severely hampered by a lack of air support. In the period up to Christmas 1943, ahead of the deployment of Wig to Bari, there were virtually no aircraft with which to distribute supplies to resistance fighters anywhere in Italy. Between September and December 1943, there were only 9 air sorties within Italy itself, with most of SOE efforts out of Cairo focussed on the French/Italian border and operations into Greece, Yugoslavia and Albania.

In early 1944, there was a major change of gear. At this time, the over-riding military objective was to get the German commanding General Albert Kesselring to commit as many forces as possible to defending Italy ahead of *Operation Overlord* in Normandy in June. Following a review by Gubbins, SOE established a new command structure for covert operations in which responsibility for No 1 Special Force transferred from Massingham to the over-arching Special Operations Mediterranean ("SOM") in Italy, and SOE air operations capability was expanded rapidly.[178] These changes facilitated a greatly enhanced level of activity on the ground designed to achieve maximum engagement with the Germans.

Implementation of this military objective was heavily dependent on Wig's air operations for insertion and support. The main aim was to provide professional military leadership to a growing army of local CLNAI partisans behind enemy lines with a very diverse set of political allegiances. This ensured that operations undertaken by the resistance were consistent with Allied military objectives, with no particular political forces able to dominate. It was also designed to ensure that they were not diverted into

---

[178] Wig moved across to Caserta in December 1943, and transferred to his air operations role in Bari in early 1944.

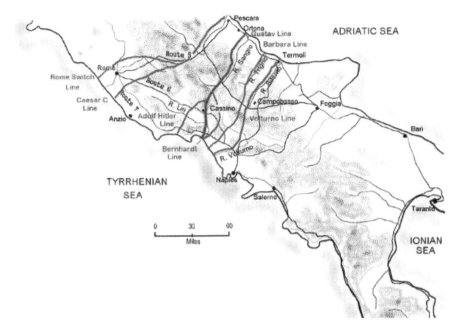

Central Italy 1944 – German Defences - creativecommons

activity that might compromise the Allied political objective of restoring representative democracy. To implement this policy, Holdsworth despatched a sequence of BLOs and air operations provided supplies and equipment. In April, Wig's team dropped some 45 tons of arms, explosives, food, and clothing behind enemy lines in central and Northern Italy, in May there were some 50 drops, and in June Holdsworth despatched another 10 BLOs.[179] Over the period January to July, SOE delivered 20 Wireless/Telephone stations reporting back to Monopoli, 58 training units, 39 sabotage teams and 355 tons of materiel. By now, there were 70,000 partisan fighters in Northern Italy and, together with the Allied armies further south, they were holding down no less than 6 German Divisions

Three weeks before "D" Day, General Alexander implemented *Operation Diadem* which involved destroying as many German units as possible and sabotaging rail and road links in a belt across Italy from La Spezia to Rimini. Despite strenuous German efforts to hold successive defensive lines, US

---

[179] Based on material in Chapter 6 (pages 107-132) of the book entitled *"Mission Accomplished SOE and Italy 1943-1945"* by David Stafford.

174

General Clark's 5th Army eventually took the city of Rome on 4 June 1944. Immediately thereafter, on 9 June, the leader of the CLN, Ivanoe Bonomi, replaced Badoglio as Prime Minister.

In the second half of 1944, Wig's activities within Italy accelerated further. The following are examples of the kind of Italian missions in which his air operations unit was involved. After the fall of Rome, the first BLO to join the partisans in northern Italy was Major Hedley Vincent (calling himself Major Tucker) in what was known as *Operation Coolant*. Vincent parachuted into the Friuli region of north east Italy on the night of 9/10 June 1944, an area which was dominated by the Slovene community loyal to Marshal Tito.[180] From this point he travelled west to find a group called the Garibaldi Natisone Brigade, a formation of about 500 armed partisans. Based just north of the town of Udine which is about 160 kms from the Austrian border, he negotiated with them to accept SOE direction designed to meet the requirements of Allied military strategy, and a dropping zone was quickly established at Monte Joanez 300 metres above Canebola for receipt of supplies. Vincent spelt out his role in his after-action report:

"I was unwilling to assume office (ie take direct overall control). We worked as a force apart, aiming to promote good will, and to direct activities through suggestions and advice which was freely accepted. We lived with the partisans, sharing the ups and downs of their lives and participating in their debates and discussions, and at times we provided direction to ensure the achievement of our military objectives. We proceeded with tact and argument, and this direction was accepted in good humour."[181]

Once in the field, the team maintained regular contact with Monopoli, and arranged the continuing drop of arms, ammunition, explosives, food and clothing. Communications on impending air operations were often dependent on the BBC who included special messages at regular intervals during their broadcasts. A typical code to indicate that a drop was imminent was the message *"The shoes are red"*. Villagers would then light fires around the established Drop Zone, and after the drop, the supplies would be taken to the

---

[180] This material is based on accounts provided on pages 131-157 of Chapter 7 of the book entitled *"Mission Accomplished SOE and Italy 1943-1945"* by David Stafford.

[181] This is a precis of a longer extract from page 135 in Chapter 7 of the book entitled *"Mission Accomplished SOE and Italy 1943-1945"* by David Stafford.

village square for sorting and distribution. By August 1944, the *Coolant* mission encompassed a unit of over 2,000 men, and a small factory had been established to make all manner of munitions. The partisans focussed on attacking rail infrastructure and rolling stock, electricity pylons, and factories. During September, Vincent's group disrupted no less than 40 trains providing supplies to German forces. Eventually, in October, as events overtook the mission, Vincent withdrew to SOE headquarters, being picked up by Wig's team from a place called Otok.

Mind you, not all missions were as successful. On the night of 15/16 June 1944 Major Vivian Johnston parachuted with a team into an area near Monte Albano which is south east of Rome. He linked up with some poorly organised local partisans, and contacted representatives of the newly created Montefiorino Republic, one of several local administrative units formed after the fall of Rome which anticipated an early Allied military victory. Building on this initiative, SOE planned to insert a parachute battalion ('*the Nembo*" group). Over the period 10-25 July 1944, Wig's unit made 38 drops to Johnston in the La Spezia/Modena area. Unfortunately, at this stage, the Germans were far from beaten. In early August, they responded strongly to the creation of the Montefiorino Republic (and several other such local government units) with a huge counterattack. In the so-called *Battle of Montefiorino*, the Germans committed 20,000 German and Fascist troops and overwhelmed the partisans and Allied supporters. The outcome was gruesome. The Germans took no prisoners and implemented a swathe of reprisals on both the partisans and the unarmed civilian population. The *Nembo* initiative was cancelled, and in September Johnston withdrew. The partisans were scattered and the teams established by Johnston were dispersed into three new missions – "Toffee" led by Captain Charles Holland, "Silentia" led by Captain Ernest Wilcockson, and a third grouping led by Captain Jim Davies.

In the months of July, August and September 1944, the Allies made steady progress up the Italian peninsula. By 3 July, they had taken Siena, and the 8th Army now led by General Oliver Leese had taken Ancona. On 4 August, the Allies reached Florence and, by 1 September, they had reached a line stretching from Pisa across to Florence and Rimini.

By this time, Allied forces were advancing rapidly across the whole of Europe, with the entry to Paris on 24 August 1944 and the Russians taking Warsaw around the same time. In Italy, through its air operations, SOE continued to pour in further resources in support of the resistance across the

176

French Italian border and throughout northern Italy. In August 1944, Holdsworth moved the headquarters of No 1 Special Force up to Rome leaving Hewitt in charge of operational activity out of Monopoli. Resources were tightly stretched and SOE was at times torn between the conflicting priorities of supporting partisan forces in Italy, Yugoslavia, Austria and Poland. Within northern Italy, thoughts were turning to the eventual transition to civilian rule. The impact of all the work in Italy is tidily summarised in a No 1 Special Force Report of the time which states:[182]

"Our decision some months ago to commence the despatch of British Liaison Missions to all major organisations in the field is now bearing fruit. Increased control from this headquarters (in Monopoli), improved morale on the organisations concerned, and a general large increase in the effectiveness of patriot activity have resulted. The prospects for the enemy are bleak. Harassed by strong patriot units, and by the mass of the hostile population, their efforts at an organised defence are becoming more and more difficult and we confidently hope will shortly become impossible".

A key operation at this time was *Operation Fairway* and, in anticipation of the mission, Wig's team despatched some 150 tons of supplies to the Apennines in July. The aim of this mission was to optimise the effectiveness of the partisans in the Milan area in impeding the withdrawal of German troops. However, there was concern that, without skilled BLO leadership, this effort might be undermined by local political manoeuvring and interference, with supplies diverted to purposes other than those intended. Accordingly, it was decided to deploy a senior Italian officer who would provide leadership, training and tactics. A number of candidates were considered, and 55 years old General Raffaele Cadorna emerged as the person acceptable to all the political factions within the CLNAI. Once appointed, he went to Monopoli and received extensive briefing and training.

Cadorna was dropped behind enemy lines near Bergamo in mid-August 1944, accompanied by a BLO named Major Oliver Churchill, an Italian liaison officer and a wireless operator who was apparently a mate of Wig's from Cairo days.[183] Because of his black hair and swashbuckling exploits, he

---

[182] This is taken from SOE File HS7-12.

[183] Account provided in Chapter 8 (pp 171-176) *"Mission Accomplished SOE and Italy 1943-1945"* by David Stafford. Churchill's friendship with Wig is according to Wig's wife Eunice.

was known by the name "the Black Prince". In passing, it is worth noting that he was **not** related to the Prime Minister, although at times he played up the possible connection. Whilst based in Cairo in 1943, he trained agents destined for Yugoslavia and Italy and transferred to Monopoli in June 1944. On his personnel file it was said that he *"combined a strong taste for operational work with a sound appreciation of the value of intelligence. He was restless, energetic, but also cautious and shrewd."* For this mission, Cadorna assumed the *nom de guerre* "Valenti" and Churchill called himself "Peters". Whilst he was not given specific instructions, it is clear that Holdsworth hoped that Cadorna would be capable of co-ordinating military resistance and becoming its commander in the push to destroy the German armies in Italy. As recorded in his written instructions to Cadorna, Holdsworth states:[184]

"The organisation of resistance groups in the north along political lines is clumsy and ineffective and should be raised as an issue with CLNAI leaders. Your first task is to achieve the maximum degree of internal organisation and ensure reliable leadership within each resistance group. They should concentrate on receiving and conserving weapons and, while small scale sabotage should be carried out, stores and ammunition should be preserved for the "final effort" against the enemy that would be timed to coincide with wider operations by the Allies. The ultimate objective of all resistance work in Italy must be to harass German lines of communication by sabotage and guerrilla warfare and eventually to impede the withdrawal of German troops so that the Allied armies can attack and destroy them".

Sadly, the launch of the *Fairway Mission* did not entirely go according to plan. The drop was disrupted by an inconveniently timed *rastrellamento* and various supplies went missing.[185] And, within the first few days, a substantial haul of money sent with the mission was stolen. Also, the radio operator proved to be less than competent. Like a number of operations, *Fairway* quickly veered off plan once it encountered the realities in the field. Despite

---

[184] The operational instructions dated 3 August 1944 can be found in SOE File HS 6/862.

[185] Roughly translated *Rastrellamento* means "rounding up" and describes the operations of the Italian Fascist and German troops in rolling back advances by the partisans. Such operations were characterised by ruthless attacks not only on armed forces but also the civilian population.

security concerns, after a few weeks Cadorna became frustrated with communication difficulties and moved from the relative safety of living with the *"Green Flame"* partisans in the mountains adjacent to Milan to liaise with the leaders of the CLNAI based in the city itself.[186] Churchill was left behind in the mountains. Cadorna did establish good working relations with the CLNAI leadership, but they were unwilling to appoint him to an overall leadership role as SOE had intended because of opposition from left wing elements. Instead they confined him to an advisory role. As for Churchill, at great risk, he also moved into Milan in support of Cadorna, and did his best to convey vital information back to Monopoli. However, by early October he was totally frustrated and returned to Monopoli via Berne and London.

Another mission, launched by SOE on 12 August 1944 in central Italy, was *Operation Ruina*. This was led by Major John Wilkinson who adopted the *nom de guerre "Arrow"* or in Italian *Freccia*.[187] He was deployed on what was initially a fact-finding mission, to identify all the local commanders in the area east of Lake Garda, in what is called the western Veneto. This was essential intelligence for the impending push by General Alexander through the Germans' *Gothic Line* and into the Po Valley *("Operation Olive")* scheduled for the autumn of 1944 and before the onset of winter. In particular, the military were looking for a co-ordinated assault by the partisans on road and rail links as well as ambushing convoys, and switching local signs to confuse the enemy as they withdrew! On the ground, Wilkinson was met by an Italian officer named Lt Renato Marini who was well connected with the CLN and had a working knowledge of most of the local partisan groups.[188] Over the next few days, Wilkinson met most of the partisan leaders and discovered a distinct lack of overall leadership capable of delivering a co-ordinated force. Following this initial sortie and reconnaissance, on 31 August two further missions were sent in to support the *Ruina* deployment with the aim of extending the fact finding exercise to Belluno and Monte Grappa. Over time, Wilkinson provided much detail of local operations, but his work was frustrated by frequent *"rastrellamentos"* and the continuing inability of the various partisan groups to accept a unified

---

[186] The "Green Flame" is a reference to a green flashing on the lapels of certain partisan groups originating from the mountains.

[187] It is likely that Wilkinson was a mate of Wig's as they were both recruited into the Cairo office following the conclusion of the war in North Africa.

[188] Again this account is an extract from Chapter 9 (p185) of the book *"Mission Accomplished SOE in Italy 1939-1945"* by David Stafford.

command.

As the war in Italy reached its final stages, in the autumn of 1944, SOE undertook a major review of strategy. The context for this review was a central pre-occupation at all levels of the Allied political and military leadership about how to manage the country immediately after the German withdrawal. There were a number of issues. First of all, there were concerns about the chaos arising from the possible destruction of infrastructure, and the need to direct the partisans to protecting essential services. Secondly, there was discussion about how to achieve a constitutional settlement which would ensure the emergence of a healthy democracy. Thirdly, SOE was concerned about how to best redeploy the very large number of partisans from resistance activity to civilian life once the war was over. Indeed, there was a fear that, in the absence of a unified resistance command structure, the communists would take the opportunity to manipulate this large number of armed men to launch a coup. This fear was not without foundation. In fact, SOE intelligence suggested that the communists were planning to take over government in northern Italy just as soon as the opportunity arose.[189] For SOE, the best hope of staving off this threat was support for the provisional government in Rome under Bonomi, and support to the CLN in the south and the CLNAI in the north which were seen as vehicles for non-party political activity.

To deal with the impact of German withdrawal, taking into account all the above concerns, SOE established what was called the *"Rankin Plan"*, which encompassed a range of "end game" scenarios from total German surrender in Italy to gradual withdrawal. Under the *Rankin Plan*, SOE envisaged a number of roles for partisans as the final stages of the war in Italy unfolded. These included harassment of the Germans' withdrawal, protecting essential infrastructure from German sabotage, preventing reprisals, restoring law and order, and distribution of supplies to the civilian population. The plan also encompassed an employment policy designed to find jobs for redundant partisans, and a communications plan aimed at spreading the message that democracy was the best form of government for Italy after the war.[190] To

---

[189] A fuller account of these events is provided in the book by Tom Behan entitled *The Italian Resistance: Fascists, Guerrillas and the Allies* (Pluto Press, London, 2009).

[190] Interestingly, the British Foreign Office had similar aims, but with somewhat different priorities. Their principal concern was to check communism, and to create a stable pro-British regime. The equally important redeployment of the resistance to ensure the establishment of a harmonious community was a secondary concern.

facilitate the delivery of the potential new roles for the partisans, SOE conceived the establishment of new bases and British Liaison Officers, in Milan, Turin and Genoa. In the meantime, partisans were already taking control of certain parts of the North West including the Dossola valley and Montefiorino.

By 25 September 1944, the *Rankin Plan* was ready to roll. However, there was a delay because, at that very moment, the military advance got bogged down. In fact, far from showing signs of capitulation, the Germans started to fight back. They launched a range of missions in the north, and over-ran Partisan held territories resulting in wholesale *rastrellamentos.* Faced with this dogged German resistance, SOE saw the need to send urgent reinforcements. Despite developments elsewhere, (the Red Army and Tito were arriving in Belgrade, and there was the real prospect of communists taking power in Yugoslavia and even Greece) on 24 October Lord Selborne pleaded with Churchill to switch resources from Yugoslavia to Italy. The tension in Wig's air operations office in Bari must have been palpable. Initially, this request was denied because the Allied Command was concerned to keep faith with Tito, and was anyway anticipating that the war in Northern Italy would be slowed down by the onset of a severe winter. But, with an unexpectedly mild winter Allied Command did eventually approve the redeployment of some resources. As a result, Wig's team escalated the number of drops to the north which grew from a low of 73 tons in October to a peak of 737 tons in December.[191]

Finally, on 23 November 1944, the *Rankin Plan* **was** implemented, with a major effort by BLOs in the field to redeploy resistance forces. Over the next six months, this had the desired effect, in terms of an orderly change to civilian rule. However, the SOE plan did not go without some glitches. In particular, the Allied cause was not helped by a radio broadcast in late 1944 by General Alexander. His message was designed to explain to the partisans that they needed to sit tight during the winter before a final push in the spring of 1945. This was interpreted by many as tantamount to abandonment in the face of the hostile weather not to mention the Germans.[192]

---

[191] According to SOE files, figures during this period were as follows: June 1944 (221 tons), July (281 tons), August (158 tons), September (185 tons), October (73 tons), November (289 tons), December (737 tons), and January 1945 (437 tons).

[192] A more detailed account is given in the book by Charles T. O'Reilly entitled "*Forgotten Battles. Italy's War of Liberation, 1943-1945*".

During the final phase of the War, with Wig still in command of air operations until early February 1945, there were a number of other SOE missions and events of significance. One of the major concerns which the *Rankin Plan* addressed was the fear about the threat to infrastructure. This led to the *Bandon Mission* which was led by Lt Colonel John Stevens. He was sent to impress on the partisans a new strategy which consisted of the following aims: *"To protect the infrastructure that had previously been the subject of attack (such as power plants, utilities, factories, petrol and rail facilities and food stores) and to collect intelligence on German movements so that the Allied forces could move in quickly to fill any vacuum left by departing authorities and obviate communist take-overs."*

The concerns about the political aspects of transition to civilian rule reflected in the aims of this mission were felt right at the top of the Allied cause and, in response, this led to what was called the *"Hyde Park Declaration"*. This was issued in November 1944 by Winston Churchill and President Roosevelt from the latter's home following the end of the second Quebec Conference. This Declaration recognised that Italy was now fighting on the side of the democracies, and it promised full Anglo-American support for the rebirth of Italy as a free and democratic nation. The Declaration went on to say that, from now on, an increasing measure of control would be handed over to the Italian administration providing it could maintain law and order and administer justice.

In late November and early December, SOE put a great deal of effort into tackling the potential post war **political** problem. There were meetings in Monopoli and Caserta at which the CLNAI made undertakings to follow the orders of Allied military command in return for formal recognition. In particular, under what became known as the *Protocols of Rome*, they undertook to protect infrastructure, maintain law and order, and disband once the Germans were expelled in favour of the Bonomi government pending elections. This then led to a formal written agreement between Prime Minister Bonomi and the CLNAI signed in the Grand Hotel in Rome on 26 December 1944.

In the final stages of the war, as Wig was getting ready for a trip back to the UK before being redeployed to the Far East, Holdsworth decided that the time was right to relocate his headquarters further north. In February 1945, he moved No 1 Special Force to Siena. This effectively brought an end to the *Maryland Mission* based in southern Italy. At around the same time, Major General Stawell stood down as the head of SOM and was replaced by

Colonel Louis Franck. As Wig was leaving for the Far East, the enduring SOE pre-occupation was the transition to civilian rule, and the resolution of issues involving the French and Yugoslav borders where partisan groups were in dispute. Missions were sent by SOE to liaise with all the parties. The French border issue were relatively easy to resolve, but the border with Yugoslavia (Slovenia) was more intractable and continued on into 1945 when Tito eventually agreed to withdraw from Trieste which he had occupied in the course of pursuing the Germans through Croatia and Slovenia.

Reflection

For the Allies, the outcome of the war in Italy reflected the best that might have been expected in terms of integrating military, political and covert activities. However, there is far from unanimity amongst historians about the extent to which the Italian campaign was a military success. From the outset, Eisenhower recognised and capitalised on the potential contribution of covert operations to the achievement of military objectives, and there is little doubt that Wig was one of the major contributors to the successful implementation of this strategy. However, it appears that the Allies were genuinely surprised at the strength of German resistance, and the defeat of the German army came at a great cost in terms of the loss of life and took a good deal longer than originally planned. On the other hand, the war in Italy certainly tied down an enormous number of German Divisions which might have been deployed elsewhere. And the resistance forces, led and advised by SOE, contributed hugely to the achievement of specific military targets.

From a political point of view, the work of the SOE BLOs based in Italy (and their OSS counterparts) was pivotal in ensuring that Italians amongst the resistance who had revolutionary intentions were unsuccessful. There was always a significant minority in the resistance who were committed to a left wing coup. And SOE's role, in ensuring that there was due process to deliver elections and constitutional government in the immediate aftermath of German defeat, and redeploying the resistance to peace-time roles, was significant.

As with Greece, I think that Wig would have pleased with the outcome and his part in it.

20: Special Operations Mediterranean

In Chapter 19, we saw the results of SOE's activities in supporting the work of the resistance within Italy. In this chapter we trace the development of the wider SOE organisation based in Italy facilitating covert operations across the rest of southern and Eastern Europe. In particular, this account includes the establishment of the *Special Operations Mediterranean* ("SOM") and then the *Balkan Air Force*, both of which bodies were to have a significant impact on Wig's work in Italy in 1944.

In late November 1943, the Allies held what was called the Sextant Conference in Cairo. [193] At this gathering, it was recognised that the complexity of the structures which had evolved for managing the war in the Mediterranean was undermining operational effectiveness. The problem was that military operations and political matters for the eight countries of southern Europe were being managed in locations that were significantly removed from each other, with consequent communications and logistical issues. Arising from the conference, in early 1944, it was decided to streamline the command structure on the following basis. There would be three *army* groups responsible to AFHQ at Algiers, now led by a Supreme Allied Commander ("SAC") General Maitland Wilson.[194] In Caserta, there was an advanced HQ responsible for the burgeoning Italian theatre.[195] In Cairo there was a somewhat depleted GHQ ME responsible for the Balkans, small military operations in the Aegean, and the now relatively inactive Middle East.[196] The third group in Algiers, which would become the 6th Army was established to plan the invasion of southern France. The *air forces* would be managed through a single line of command under what was known as the MAAF (Mediterranean Allied Air Force) with headquarters at Caserta.[197]

---

[193] The Sextant Conference was held in Cairo between 22 and 26 November 1943. Strangely, it was attended by Churchill, Roosevelt and Chiang Kai Shek, but with Stalin absent because he did not want to offend the Japanese. It was mostly concerned with the conduct of the war in the Far East, but also dealt with Mediterranean matters. Stalin liaised with Churchill and Roosevelt two days later at the Tehran Conference.

[194] General Wilson succeeded General Eisenhower in January 1944 who transferred to the UK ahead of the D Day landings in June.

[195] The Advance HQ was known as AAI, and later became the 15th Army.

[196] The 8th Army had moved on, after the defeat of the Germans in North Africa in late 1942.

[197] The deployment of military resources based in Caserta explains why Wig was sent there in a liaison role before his move to Bari.

The naval command would be unified under a Commander in Chief based at Algiers. For the purposes of *diplomacy*, the lines of command involved a head diplomat at AFHQ in Algiers who was Harold Macmillan, with three subordinates in Cairo (Middle East), Algiers (dealing with the Free French), and Caserta (Italy).[198] There was a separate team of similarly based Americans. Finally, at the same time, it was agreed that the organisation for delivering *covert operations* should be reviewed.

In late 1943, the leadership and deployment of SOE resources was already in a state of flux. In September, General Gubbins had taken over as Chief Executive and, in October, Lord Glenconner had been replaced by Major General William Stawell as head of the Cairo mission. On appointment, Stawell quickly identified the logistical benefits of moving SOE's Cairo based resources to Italy to deliver covert operations into the Balkans. In the face of some resistance from those directly involved, in January 1944 he transferred nearly all the Yugoslav and Albanian sections of SOE from Cairo to Bari.[199] In the meantime, Dodds-Parker in SOE Massingham had not only deployed to Italy the resources that formed the new No 1 Special Force, but also transferred most of the SOE Special Duty squadrons (128 Squadron and most of 624 Squadron) from Blida in North Africa to Brindisi (a total of 24 Halifaxes). Only four aircraft remained at Blida for operations into southern France.

In the final weeks of the year, General Gubbins embarked on a review of all SOE structures in the Mediterranean.[200] Mindful of the changes to military and diplomatic structures mentioned above, he was keen to establish an SOE structure that would streamline the delivery of services across the whole of southern and Eastern Europe and facilitate close co-operation with the military. In conducting this exercise, Gubbins visited a number of missions and was besieged by representations from people with quite conflicting views about how SOE should operate. There was still a significant group who were keen to maintain SOE independence of action but, when he visited Italy in January 1944, he received some very positive feedback about the benefits of SOE working with the military from both the 15th Army and the MAAF.

---

[198] Macmillan was "Resident Minister" at AFHQ. He was a post-war Prime Minister.
[199] Material here is drawn from page 200 of the book entitled *"Baker Street Irregular"* by Bickham Sweet-Escott.
[200] A detailed account of how the new structure came into existence, which was written by Lt Col JG Beevor and Lt Col Pleydell Bouverie, is provided in SOE File HS 7-61.

This confirmed his own preconceptions. On returning to London, he decided to establish a new integrated entity which he called *Special Operations Mediterranean*. The aim was to provide for a unified command structure covering the whole of the Mediterranean theatre with its headquarters in southern Italy.

The structure and role of the new organisation was laid out in a directive from AFHQ. In theory, it was relatively straightforward as follows.[201]

a) SOM HQ was to be a command established to centralise the technical control of SOE units, to co-ordinate SOE and OSS activities, and to manage air sorties and related packing facilities for a range of agencies including PWB (propaganda), A Force (recovery of escaped prisoners of war), and ISLD (intelligence).

b) The head of SOM was to be both the leader of SOE in the Mediterranean, reporting to SOE in London, and an adviser on special operations to the Supreme Allied Commander ("SAC") in Algiers.

c) A special team called G-3 Special Operations was to be established in Algiers under an American Brigadier General Caffey, to interpret and co-ordinate policy.

d) OSS was to function as part of SOM providing a joint Allied unit. (OSS never complied with this and continued to report directly to Washington.)

e) Within SOM, SOE in Cairo (Force 133) would continue to cover Greece and the Middle East.

To be head of this new organisation, in February 1944 Gubbins appointed Major General Stawell, with Colonel Dodds-Parker at Massingham to act as his Liaison Officer with General Maitland Wilson at AFHQ. Stawell was quick off the mark. With staff from the Balkan desks already transferring to Italy, he wanted to move there himself as soon as possible. But his relocation was delayed for two months, because there was resistance from GHQ ME who were most unhappy about the reduction in their own scope of operations arising from the transfer of most SOE resources to Italy. Eventually, though, the impasse with the military was resolved and Stawell moved to Italy. He was replaced in Cairo by Brigadier Karl Barker-Benfield who took up the

---

[201] This is taken from SOE File HS7-61, History of SOM.

position as head of Force 133 on 27 March 1944 with the Cairo Office becoming Rear HQ. In early April, Stawell established the new SOM headquarters in the baroque Castello at Mola di Bari which conveniently sat between Brindisi and Bari.

The scope of SOE organisation and people based in Bari, Monopoli and the surrounding towns and villages during 1944 was immense. Given the relevance to Wig's work, a full listing of all functions, locations, personnel, and country codes is provided in Appendix 13. The key roles, in SOM headquarters, Operations and country section are shown in the tabulation below.

SOE locations in Puglia Italy 1944 - creativecommons

SOE Headquarters	Location	Key Players
Commander's Office and Residence	Mola di Bari	Major General Stawell
Planning and Administration	Torre A Mare/Bari	Lt Colonel Beevor
Finance and Supply	Cairo	Lt Colonel Grove
AFHQ Liaison (until move to Caserta)	Algiers	Colonel Dodds-Parker
Rear HQ	Cairo	Brigadier Benfield-Barker
SOE Operations	**Location**	
Air Operations	Bari	Lt Colonel Wigginton
Main Airfield [202]	Brindisi	
Country Sections	**Location**	**Code Name**
Austria, Germany	Monopoli	No 6 Special Force (Clowder)
Italy	Monopoli [203]	No 1 Special Force
Czechoslovakia, Poland	Monopoli	Force 139
Albania, Hungary	Bari	Force 266
Yugoslavia	Bari	Force 399
Greece, Greek Isles, Bulgaria, Rumania, Mid East	Cairo	Force 133/MO4
South of France	Algiers	ISSU 6 (Signals)
Tito HQ Mission [204]	Drvar	37 Military Division

---

[202] SOE Special Duties aircraft eventually used the airport at Brindisi for flights deployed across the whole of southern and Eastern Europe including Southern France, Italy, the Balkans, Austria, Poland, and Czechoslovakia, with sorties even to Rumania and Bulgaria which were fast coming under Russian control.

[203] Moved to Siena in February 1945.

[204] Maclean also reported to AFHQ and London. When the Partisans became the recognised regular army in Yugoslavia, he transferred to Bari.

188

In addition, there were a range of support functions in neighbouring locations, including signals, training, packing, security and interrogation. There were also holding houses for SOE agents in many of the surrounding towns and villages, and accommodation for a range of SOE support staff, including a group of FANYs who moved over from the Massingham Base in Algiers.

Much has been written about the effectiveness of this new structure and, from the start, some people had considerable reservations. At the very least, the structure presented a number of challenges including the following:

i)   SOE staff were still spread across four separate bases, with attendant communications issues. HQ was at Mola di Bari, AFHQ Liaison was at Algiers, Administration was at Torre A Mare, and Rear HQ was at Cairo.

ii)   SOM was delivering services to agents operating in a very wide range of circumstances, requiring quite different training, equipment, and rules of engagement. In Yugoslavia, Greece, and Albania, BLOs were supporting the Partisans with no direct Allied military involvement. In other theatres, the activity of agents was closely allied to Allied military objectives working in consort with Allied armies in the field.

iii)   SOM was the servant of two masters. It was responsible to SOE in London for all aspects of SOE operations. However, the role of being an advisor to AFHQ in Algiers could lead to conflicting priorities.

iv)   SOM was responsible for facilitating the activities of a number of other agencies which were not accountable to SOE at all. This too was a source of conflicted loyalties.

v)   Communications between SOE and all the other organisations was complex, and signals were controlled by SOE in London.

vi)   In Yugoslavia, Brigadier Maclean continued to represent SOE at Tito's headquarters, with a representative in Bari, Lt Col Vivian Street. But he had a separate line of communication to London with the ability to blind-side SOM.

During the first half of 1944, whilst SOE was consolidating the new SOM structure, AFHQ was giving further thought to the wider question of improving the performance of the various Allied forces being deployed in the "Adriatic" theatre. For one thing, the mix was quite complex. The

189

principal *air forces* unit was No 334 Wing based at Brindisi, which was part of the MAAF. However, there was also a host of smaller air operations, under different commands, and based at other airfields. *Land forces* were co-ordinated by the unit called *Land Forces Adriatic* ("LFA") reporting to AFHQ (Allied Force Headquarters) in Caserta. This included four commando units, and a range of other special units to which was eventually added three squadrons of the Special Boat Service. *Naval forces* were commanded by a Flag Officer (FOTALI) based at the port of Taranto (not far from Brindisi) and responsible to the Admiralty.[205]

In addition to concerns about the efficient deployment of these resources, there was also concern about the effectiveness and integrity of the SOE support provided to resistance movements on the ground. As regards the *effectiveness* of SOE support, there was plenty of evidence that the size of resistance forces was growing, and that this was fulfilling a primary Allied objective which was to hold down Axis troops that might otherwise have been allocated to other theatres. However, with the withdrawal of Italy from hostilities, Allied leaders expected that much more progress should have been made in overcoming the remaining German forces. Instead, it seemed that progress was incredibly slow. This conveniently overlooked the fact that, in January 1944, the Germans actually had no less than 18 Divisions and 50 Battalions (350,000 men) in the Balkans.[206] As regards the *integrity* of SOE support, there was mounting concern that supplies were being used for purposes other than those intended, including internecine warfare and political objectives contrary to those espoused by the Allies.

Given all the above, in May 1944, AFHQ decided to establish a new unified command structure designed to significantly improve the effectiveness of the deployment of all military resources across the Adriatic. The new entity was called the *Balkan Air Force* ("BAF"), and a full account of its history may be found in SOE file HS 7-12. In brief, the BAF was constituted as a body in which there would be three co-equal commanders, one of whom would be charged with the co-ordination of planning and execution of operations. It was agreed that, since the predominant role would be played by the Air Force, the Co-ordinator would be the Air Commander.

---

[205] FOTALI is an acronym for Flag Officer Taranto and Adriatic and Liaison Italy.

[206] The size of these forces enabled them to hold nearly all the Dalmatian coast apart from the island of Vis and Lagosta and, in May 1944, they were able to launch a huge offensive. They drove Tito out of his base at Drvar and he had to take temporary shelter on the island of Vis.

It was also recognised that, given political considerations and the importance of covert operations, the structure would need to provide for regular liaison with the Foreign Office/State Department as well as the local units of SOE and the OSS.

It was agreed that the new unified command structure would be implemented on 7 June 1944, and on 16 June 1944, Air Vice-Marshall Bill Elliott was appointed as the Air Force Commander. At the same time, Brigadier George Davey was appointed as Commander of the LFA, and a Naval Liaison Officer, Captain Ian Black, was selected to represent FOTALI. The BAF established its headquarters in an office in Bari, and several committees were established to provide for effective liaison between all the above mentioned interested parties. Major items of policy were considered at periodic conferences between the three service commanders and their advisers. Air Commodore Sinclair presided over a daily meeting to review current operations. There were also joint political, intelligence, planning, and public relation teams, and a combined signals unit.

On being appointed, it was made clear to Air Vice Marshall Elliott that Tito was a partner of the utmost importance. Fortunately, the sensitive issue with SOE was almost immediately resolved. In July 1944, it was decided to recognise the Yugoslav Partisans as a regular army. As a result, Maclean moved to Bari and his team became 37 Military Division as an operating unit reporting directly to AFHQ in Italy. Stawell also established another Military Division (34 Military Division) to handle redeployment of Yugoslav refugees entering Italy. This involved pick up from Yugoslavia, and training. In the meantime, what was now called SOE Force 399 continued to manage signals and supplies for covert operations in Yugoslavia, Albania and Hungary under the leadership of Lt Colonel (Viscount) Harcourt.

From all accounts, all of these arrangements proved to be highly effective in achieving a co-ordinated approach to the deployment of resources. By December 1944 when Wig was coming to the end of his time in this theatre, its air operations encompassed 18 squadrons and it had become a truly multi-national force.

To give some idea of the scope and kind of activity undertaken following its establishment in June 1944, an analysis of monthly data provided in the *History of the BAF* contained in SOE File HS 7-12 is provided below. The period covered is through to January 1945 which was the last month in which Wig was responsible for air operations. The type of aircraft identified as operating were: Spitfire, Beaufighter, Mustang, Baltimore, Hurricane,

Macchi, and P 39.

	July 1944	Aug 1944	Sep 1944	Oct 1944	Nov 1944	Dec 1944	Jan 1945
Sorties	910	1653	2436	1956	2385	2091	910
Claims – Destroyed	149	232	564	241	324	363	238
Claims – Damaged	579	842	805	426	373	636	445
Lost BAF Aircraft	1	36	37	45	25	19	8

In summary, during this seven month period, the total number of sorties flown was 12,341, for the loss of 171 aircraft. The results of this activity, for the same period, according to the claims made after the missions, was as follows. The numbers reflect the sum of Destroyed and Damaged for the Claims in the first table.

	July	Aug	Sep	Oct	Nov	Dec	Jan
Aircraft	27	2	55	16	1	0	1
Motor Vehicles	140	333	771	362	595	872	36
Locomotives	262	194	107	82	33	30	58
Train Wagons	288	386	328	133	21	90	520
Bridges	6	20	14	1	19	7	1
War Infrastructure	6	36	25	13	25	8	19
Shipping	5	103	69	60	2	2	28

SOM and the BAF continued to be the main basis under which SOE operated in southern and central Europe for the rest of the war. Despite the issues associated with SOM, Stawell and his team managed to make the structure work until it was eventually wound up in May 1945. The final stages of the work of SOM and the BAF operations are not recorded here because in February 1945 Wig moved to another theatre of war, the Far East.

21: The Italian Job

On 15 December 1943 Wig left Cairo for Italy. Initially, he was transferred to an SOE military liaison position at AFHQ in Caserta with a small team including a Major Wooler. His short-term mission was to establish and ensure effective SOE liaison in the Italian theatre of war with AFHQ and the Mediterranean Allied Air Force ("MAAF").[207] In early 1944, he then moved on to a senior position within the newly formed Special Operations Mediterranean ("SOM") based at Bari under the leadership of Major General William Stawell. At this point he was promoted to the rank of Acting Lt Colonel. His new role was to be the head of air operations, with responsibility for facilitating covert activities in Italy, the Balkans (apart from Greece which was still covered from Cairo), Austria, Czechoslovakia, Poland and the south of France. During the next twelve months, he was to be mentioned in despatches on two occasions for his role in SOE air operations (making three in all).

The scope of his job in Bari is described in a telegram sent by SAC General Maitland Wilson sent on 4 February 1944. According to this document, the person in this position would *"Decide from day to day, in conjunction with the military, between the conflicting priority claims of SOE (including Force 133), OSS, SAS, ISLD, and A Force operating in the whole Mediterranean theatre, Balkans, and Central Europe. He would also advise on the operational situation in occupied countries and act as deputy to the Brigadier General in his absence as head of the only staff branch connected with Special Operations."* It was recommended that this role warranted the rank of Colonel.[208]

This new role represented not only an increase in responsibilities but also complexity. In Cairo, Wig deployed air support to resistance movements in Greece and the Balkans, and there were no Allied armies on the ground. Whilst military liaison was important, and there were tensions arising from the sometimes conflicting aims of the Foreign Office, there was a well-defined structure for decision making designed to meet SOE objectives. Towards the end of his time in Cairo, the nature of this work was beginning

---

[207] The records show that, when he moved to Italy, Wig was still employed as a Sherwood Forester. Conveniently for his cover, at the same time, the British 8th Army transferred from North Africa as part of the landings at Taranto to the south of Brindisi.

[208] This material is taken from HS 7/61 – The history of SOM.

to change. Whilst the focus was still on support for resistance movements, the old champions of independent covert strategy loosely linked to political objectives had been replaced by people for whom military and political objectives were paramount. This change in culture certainly transferred to SOE in Italy.

In the newly formed SOM, whilst retaining some independence in the allocation of support to the resistance movements and their BLOs in the Balkans, Wig had to work much more closely with military forces on the ground and be more mindful of political imperatives. And his role extended to providing an air operations service for covert operations across the whole of the European theatres of war apart from those emanating from the UK (which covered north and western Europe), Massingham (which covered the south of France), and Cairo (which continued to provide a residual service to Greece and the Middle East).

It is worth reiterating that the new SOE base at Bari, being on the eastern seaboard of Italy, had significant advantages. Apart from facilitating a degree of physical separation (and independence of action) from the military who were based in Caserta, the Adriatic coast was better from a logistical point of view for supporting resistance forces in the Balkans. It was also handy that the Italian provisional government (the King and Prime Minister Badoglio and his ministers) was just down the road in Brindisi where there was also a well-established airfield and port which served as home base for the Italian Navy.

Initially, Wig took up temporary residence in an office at Torre a Mare with two of his staff, Captain Sheppard and Lt Winser.[209] However, they and other SOE staff including Major General Stawell were soon located at the *Palazzo Alberotanza* in the small Adriatic port of Mola di Bari. This building had previously been Municipal Offices and was selected on the advice Stawell's head of planning, Lt Col JG Beevor.

The Palazzo Alberotanza became a hugely busy centre of SOE activity, accommodating many of the people identified in the listing of SOM staff in the previous chapter. The building also housed the Yugoslavian and Albanian operations (Force 266 and Force 399) under the leadership of Lt Col Harcourt with the related country sections moving from Cairo. Apparently, most of the

---

[209] There is reference to this in SOE File HS 3-171.

staff were boarded in local flats.[210]

Palazzo Alberotanza, SOE HQ in Bari - bellazza@governo.it

There is one photograph from this time which is shown here and was found in my mother's old tin box. It is not certain where and when the picture was taken. Wig is second from the right and, judging by the equipment, there appears to be some sort of film being recorded. The maps in the background suggest an operations centre in Europe in 1944, and the most likely venue is the offices at Palazzo Alberotanza.

Wig's work in 1944 is best considered in two time periods, the six months before the establishment of the Balkan Air Force ("BAF") in June, and the six months after.

Period Prior to BAF

During the first six months of 1944, with SOE slowly building its resources in Bari, the arrangements for providing air support to covert operations involved a multitude of parties competing for relatively scarce resources. During this period, SOE was working alongside Allied military forces, the diplomatic representatives of the British, Americans, Russians, and various governments in exile, and the American OSS. As the months unfolded, other players entered the field with the addition of a number of smaller air forces representing occupied and liberated territories throughout Europe.

To provide an indication of the content of air operations activity during this period, the following are extracts from a Progress Report on missions to

---

[210] This is a based on material on page 118 of the book entitled *"In Obedience to Instructions"* by Margaret Pawley.

195

SOE team filming in Bari

Yugoslavia (Force 266 or B1) in May 1944.[211] [212] May was a significant month given the dramatic rescue of Tito and associated personnel from the Partisan HQ in Drvar, and the withdrawal of support for Mihailović. The Progress Report reads as follows:

"During the month of May, 648 sorties were successfully flown to the Partisans. Two maintenance sorties went to our missions with Mihailović. This doubles the April figure and exceeds any other month by 400. The figure includes 49 pick-up operations to the Partisans and there were 9 pick-ups from Mihailović. The following personnel were infiltrated: 17 Officers and 23 Other Ranks belonging to Force 266, 3 Officers and 3 Other Ranks from the Special Boat Service, and 3 ISLD personnel."

---

[211] B1 is the Code for Yugoslavia, and was also known as Force 399. Other country sections were variously B2, B3 et al.
[212] This is an extract from SOE File HS 5-920.

The Report goes on to indicate that the main infiltrations were designed to facilitate the establishment of new missions, including *Icarus, Cuckold, Homage, Rakeoff, Twilfit, and Bethesda*. On the extraction side, *"these missions facilitated the evacuation of 11 British personnel, 185 US Airmen, 619 Yugoslav wounded, and 9 rescued Prisoners of War."* There is then a brief account of the attack and rescue of the personnel based at Partisan HQ in Drvar which reads as follows: *"The Germans started their offensive on Partisan GHQ on 25 May 1944. Owing to prompt Allied air support, the offensive failed in its main object – the capture of Partisan GHQ ..... All Allied Missions are safe."* The Report concludes with an account of other activity as follows:

a)   A successful sabotage operation on the German occupied Dalmatian coast conducted from the base in Vis.
b)   Build-up of supplies to support the establishment of new Divisions and Brigades.
c)   The removal of all 46 SOE personnel working with Mihailović.
d)   A number of naval operations.

BAF Period

In July 1944, the new operational structure called the Balkan Air Force was implemented. This heralded a more co-ordinated approach to the deployment of resources, and the improved forward planning would have been welcomed by Wig. The SOE Forward Plan for July-September 1944 was issued on 22 June.[213] It commenced with an introductory paragraph which reads as follows, and then specific activities for each of the months:

"In the past, the location of missions in Yugoslavia have depended on the position of the principal Partisan formations. As a result of an increase in operational capability it is now possible to develop areas which have strategic importance, but have been denied supplies because of the weakness of Partisan forces in the field. In particular, we will improve the scale of air support and increase the evacuation of wounded."

---

[213] What follows is a precis of material in SOE File HS 5-920.

197

July 1944

a) Build-up of the existing Mission in the *Istrian Peninsula* to facilitate attacks on German naval installations, sabotage of industrial targets, opening up of sea supplies and support to the Royal Navy in attacks on German shipping.

b) Despatch of a Mission to Kosmaj which will operate as a new base for receipt of supplies and SOE equipment for use in Belgrade.

c) Support of the *Twilfit* Mission and arming of the Partisan 9th Brigade in an area which has previously been dominated by the Chetniks.

d) Consolidation of the *Cuckold, Spike, Brasenose, and Bethesda* Missions in areas where the Partisans are relatively weak, to facilitate attacks on German lines of communication.

e) Maintenance of the previously successful Partisan forces who have been attacking the main Belgrade-Zagreb railway line, and lines of communication between Zagreb and Austria/Italy.

f) Establishment of four new aerodromes, and maintenance of four existing airfields.

g) Development of air support, following the establishment of the Balkan Air Force.

h) Opening of the north Adriatic as British forces advance up through Ancona (Italy).

August 1944

a) Development of support for Colonel Davidson and Partisans in Backa and Banat.

b) Consolidation of new Missions established in July.

c) Maintenance of support to areas where there are already successful Missions.

d) Establishment of a further three new aerodromes, and related pick-ups.

September 1944

In September, the plan was to further consolidate Partisan units in Backa and Banat, maintain existing Missions, and establish a further 3 aerodromes. Preparation for winter was also to be a major focus which included the following:

a) Consolidation of Dropping Zones into areas of liberated territory.
b) Substantial reduction in the number of BLOs.
c) Completion of arrangements to reduce the constraints imposed by the weather, including the establishment of weather stations, and installation of "more modern flying equipment".
d) Provisions of winter clothing and food supplies.
e) Establishment of "reserves" within Yugoslavia of arms, ammunition, equipment, boots, and clothing.

It was envisaged that implementation of this three month plan would translate into over 5,000 sorties. This was a pretty good estimate and, during the *seven* month period that Wig was responsible (July 1944 – January 1945), there were no less than 12,431 sorties. The damage inflicted included the destruction of approximately 100 aircraft, 3,000 vehicles, 1,800 train wagons, 70 bridges, and 270 ships. An acknowledgement of its worth is best shown in the Nomination that Major General Stawell submitted in September 1944 recommending Wig for an OBE (an upgrade on the existing MBE). It reads as follows:

"In November 1942, Lt Col Wigginton assumed the responsibility for the co-ordination of Air Operations, entailing supply, dropping and infiltration of personnel to resistance groups in the Balkans. It is his responsibility to ensure that, with the closest co-operation of the RAF, the detailed and complicated machinery through which air crews are briefed, reception committees in the field are ready, and the correct signals are exchanged, at all times functions smoothly. The sphere of these operations now (in 1944) covers all supplies dropped by the RAF in Northern Italy, Yugoslavia, Albania, Greece, Crete, Poland, Bulgaria, Hungary, Czechoslovakia, Rumania, and Austria. And as many as 60/70 aircraft may be assigned to an equal number of targets in a single night's operations. Due to changing meteorological conditions, or enemy action, or both, difficulties arise which necessitate quick decisions followed by immediate action. This organisation was the first of its type in the Mediterranean theatre, but Lt Col Wigginton has built by his own efforts and ability a system the efficiency of which has earned the admiration of all those whose duty brings them into contact with air operations branch.

*Lt Col Wigginton is untiring in his devotion to duty, which during the period when operations are being flown require him to be available, if not actually on duty, at all times during the night and day and it is largely due to his efforts that the present flow of supplies to resistance movements in the Mediterranean has reached it present volume. Some idea of the extent of this can be obtained from the fact that in July (1944) alone some 1600 sorties were flown of which 75% were successful, this number being over double that for which the organisation was designed. **This officer has flown on many operational missions in order to see for himself what improvements could be made in the organisation.**[214]*

I have no hesitation in recommending that Lt Col Wigginton's outstanding service be recognised by the award of the OBE.[215]

Maj Gen W Stawell
29 September 1944

This nomination clearly reflects the importance of Wig's personal contribution. Indeed, in examining SOE files, his hand was evident in many individual missions. However, the most significant statement in the nomination, as far as insight into the real scope of his work, is the final sentence of the penultimate paragraph which is ***highlighted*** in the above text. On a number of occasions, Eunice talked of Wig's parachuting behind enemy lines. These words by Major General Stawell confirm that what she said was indeed the case. Wig would not have revealed the details to Eunice, but clearly in 1944 he ventured into occupied territory with the most frequent location being Yugoslavia. He was not just a hard working office-bound logistical master-mind. He saw action in the field.

Of course, life in Bari wasn't all work. For twelve months, Wig had the opportunity to "enjoy" a totally new environment. Having got used to life in Cairo, settling in and around Bari must have been quite a culture shock. Despite the heat and dust, Cairo was an international city with restaurants and Clubs. And once the threat of German attack had been removed, life

---

[214] Underlining by author. This is the only evidence I have, apart from anecdotal references from his wife, of Wig's work in the field.

[215] It is worth noting that, in view of SOE's status as a covert organisation which was not part of the military, the honours given to members of SOE were "civilian" (ie such as MBE and OBE rather than honours such as DSO and Military Cross).

outside the office actually provided a degree of peace and quiet. Whilst far from the front line, Bari was a different kettle of fish and, from reading accounts of life there, the Allied staff did not have a very high opinion of the place. Not least this was because, in the absence of fruit and vegetables, health was an issue.

In his book *"Blurred Recollections – 1939-46"* Ian Macpherson states that the town was in the area of Italy that was *"impoverished, backward, and suffering from centuries of neglect."* He says that Bari itself was a *"fairly horrible place"*. Macpherson worked in the same offices as Wig, and he states that for the majority of the staff the working hours were much the same as in Cairo. He would start at around 8.00 am and work through to lunch. There would then be a siesta, with work resuming at around 4.00 pm. At lunch time, people went swimming in the sea off a rocky ledge to the south of the town, or might have a game of volleyball. During the evenings, he would play bridge in the Officers' Mess, and sometimes went to the Opera in Bari. In a recorded interview, Gwendoline Lees, who was a FANY and married another SOE operative Michael Lees in the Bari Cathedral in August 1944, indicates that as a newly married couple she and her husband were lucky enough to live in a villa next to the beach.[216]

In her book, *"In Obedience to Instructions"*, Margaret Pawley also has quite a bit to say about life in Bari and Monopoli. She recounts that the area had a long and rich history extending back to Greek times, with Brindisi an important port and transit point connecting along the Appian Way to Rome. But in 1944, *"Monopoli was a small town of 14,000. There was a small port, with fishing and farming being the main source of income. Brindisi, with its much larger harbour, was 80 kms away and Bari which provided the only source of leisure activity was 40 kms away. There was no public transport, and the state of the roads was unsafe especially after rain leading to several fatal accidents."* However, for those who had the time, apparently there *were* some amusements.[217] She writes that *"a favourite respite was Sunday afternoons, when the naval contingent would take out a motor torpedo boat, ostensibly for "engine trials". There would be tea on board and swimming."*

Pawley also describes the celebration of Christmas 1944, in which Wig

---

[216] This recollection comes from Item 11087 in the archives at the Imperial War Museum.
[217] This material is taken from page 90 of Margaret Pawley's book *"In Obedience to Instructions"*.

must surely have been involved. This began with a church service at Torre a Mare on Christmas Eve. On Christmas Day, the men and the FANYs took part in a football match and then, as was the British army custom, Officers and FANYs served Christmas lunch in the cinema. Later, they listened to the King's Speech. Apparently, celebrations continued through to the New Year.

Meanwhile, down at the airbase, life was very different. The record of Tom Storey's life as a pilot based in Brindisi tells the story.[218] He and his crew moved from Tocra to Brindisi in January 1944. On arrival, the men found that construction of the new extended air base was behind schedule. Accordingly, crews had to sleep in tents and individuals were restricted to one bath a week. The food was limited, and apparently some of the locals were not entirely friendly, with quite a bit of burglary. So the men had to carry a revolver. On the other hand, the weather was milder than North Africa, and the proximity to the city of Brindisi for rest and recreation was a big improvement on Tocra. Air operations commenced on 1 February 1944, with flights to BLOs in Albania. For Tom, subsequent missions involved flights to both Northern Italy, Poland, and other parts of the Balkans. Initially the crews were far from happy about the adequacy of in-flight provisions which were confined to a small packet of often stale biscuits, a bar of chocolate, and a packet of chewing gum for what was sometimes an 8 hour flight. Elkin's account of Storey's life provides insight into the day of a crew. After a day off and ahead of a mission, an average 24 hours would consist of the following:[219]

07.00	Rise and Breakfast
Morning	Crew check the roster of upcoming missions, and undertake domestic and administrative chores
Morning	Engineer and Wireless operator check functionality of plane
12.30	Lunch
16.00	Briefing on mission including flight plan
19.00	Take off for Mission
02.30-04.00	Return
05.00	Debrief
06.00	Breakfast and bed

[218] The following material is based on the book by Jennifer Elkin entitled *"A Special Duty"*, *pages 36 to 67.*

[219] This typical 24 hour routine is based pages 50 and 51 of the book entitled *"A Special Duty"* by Jennifer Elkin.

Finally, during the Italian days, we know that Wig returned from time to time to England. On the shorter visits, he and Eunice would sometimes meet up at the Rembrandt Hotel in Knightsbridge. However, he had a period of three weeks leave from 3 to 24 November 1944 when he would have returned to Nottingham.

22: Other SOE Operations Out of Italy

During his time in Italy, in 1944, Wig was responsible for organising the despatch of aircraft to a number of other theatres of war in Europe that were in reach from airfields in Southern Italy. According to the records, this work included missions to Austria, Czechoslovakia, Poland, and Southern France, as well other parts of the Balkans such as Albania, and Bulgaria. In this chapter, a brief account of those activities is provided.[220] A listing of the code names for European countries is provided in Appendix 2.

Albania

In the 1930s, Albania was a country divided by loyalties to three religious groups, Roman Catholic, Orthodox and Muslim, and by associated deep-rooted tribalism. The British had no particular interest in a country which was seen as having no strategic significance, apart from an oil field and a coast line. When, in March 1939, the Italians annexed the country and established a friendly regime, this act was actually recognised by the British government. King Zog fled the country but, unlike Yugoslavia and Greece, there was no recognised government in exile. Following the Italian occupation, several small resistance groups were established. The royalist Zogists were led by Abas Kupi, and there was a right wing group called the "Balli Kombëtar". Eventually, a left wing group called the National Liberation Front (FNC) was formed, which was connected with the Yugoslav Partisans. The first attempt to assist the resistance was made in April 1941, when SOE despatched a Major Oakley-Hill to liaise with the Zogists. He was captured and the resistance group evaporated into the hills. In May 1942, SOE commenced air operations support, using Liberators deployed from the Cairo office. Initially, the level of supplies was small, not least because the resistance movement was insignificant and difficult to find. However, as the resistance force and activity grew, and with the increase in the number of aircraft available for special duties in 1943, there was a significant boost in supplies.

By this time, Wig was in charge of all air operations out of Cairo, and an Albanian section was established in Rustum Building which submitted

---

[220] Much of the material in this Part of the book is based on *"The Secret History of SOE"* (pages 488-492) by William Mackenzie.

regular requests to his team for supplies. In April, SOE made a further attempt to contact the resistance when a team led by Lt Col NLD Maclean arrived overland from Greece. Maclean's objective was to try and get the various resistance factions to work together, and some progress appeared to have been achieved at a conference at Labinot. In July and August, four further SOE missions were infiltrated with the aim of attacking the oil field. A plan was developed but could not proceed because air support was unavailable, with all available resources allocated to the Allied landings in southern Italy.

In September, Italy signed an Armistice with the Allies. The Albanian resistance was taken off guard, and the Germans were quick to take up Italian positions. Most of the Italians handed over their weapons to the Germans. Around this time, SOE sent in Brigadier E F Davies with a mission to unify the resistance. On arriving, he found himself with little option but to endorse the left wing FNC who, like their counterparts in Yugoslavia and Greece, were engaged in fighting other resistance groups as well as the Germans. As a result, the right wing *Balli Kombetar* were driven into collaboration with the Germans. At the same time, the Germans were very active in pursuit of the left wing guerrillas, pursuing them into the mountains. Davies was soon on the run, and was eventually captured on 8 January 1944. His number two, Colonel Nicholls, died of septicaemia shortly after.

In December 1943, the British made another attempt to unify the resistance. NLD Maclean, now a full Colonel was sent in again and his mission revealed that both *Balli Kombetar* and the Zogists were collaborating with the Germans and actively opposing FNC activity. Given this intelligence, it is clear from correspondence in SOE files that there were now serious reservations amongst some members of the Allied leadership about providing any supplies to any resistance force. This was because Albania was seen as providing little strategic value, apart from engaging a relatively small force of Germans, and there were concerns that the provision of military materiel would just fuel a civil war. However, by late 1943, SOE had determined to focus its efforts in supporting the FNC, mostly in the south where there was greater strategic value given activity in Yugoslavia. Support to other resistance groups, including FNC in the north was confined to specific operations.

As SOE was establishing its new unit in Bari in 1944, the newly appointed head of SOM, Major General Stawell, issued a new remit for supporting the resistance in Albania.[221] The policy framework comprised the following.

a) No declaration will be made in favour of or against any particular party or guerrilla group.
b) Financial and material help will be given to any guerrilla group willing and able to resist the Germans.
c) There will be broadcasts praising those resisting the Germans and attacking those who collaborate.
d) Neither Tito nor any of his staff will be asked to intervene.

To implement this policy, Stawell instructed SOE staff to develop and submit a full plan no later than 1 March 1944, to provide for operational activity designed to address the following:

i)   Maintaining contact with those guerrillas that are actively resisting the Germans.
ii)   Encouraging guerrilla action against German road, rail and signal communications.
iii) Arranging for BLO leadership of guerrilla forces.
iv)   Arranging for sabotage of economic targets.
v)   Subverting dissident elements in occupation forces, and
vi)   Preventing destruction of infrastructure on German withdrawal.

This plan was completed quickly, and encompassed a range of missions many of which were implemented by sea and by air operations that were organised by Wig's Albania Force 266 team at Bari (which had taken over responsibility from Force 133 in Cairo in early 1944). In February, a mission led by Squadron Leader Hands sabotaged the chrome mines at Kam, and in subsequent months several commando groups were despatched to attack German maritime bases. In June, Major Smiley and a small team of Zogists attacked a bridge on the main road at Gjolos and cut a main German transit route for several weeks.

Following the creation of the Balkan Air Force, in July 1944, SOE met with the FNC in Bari to co-ordinate air support operations. During the final months of German occupation, German infrastructure was sabotaged and lines of communication were broken through a number of well targeted

---

[221] This material comes from SOE Files HS 5-18 and HS 5-56 and HS 5-57.

missions. And the FNC performed well in attacking the Germans as they began their withdrawal which was eventually completed by November 1944. Once the Germans had departed, the FNC took over. Whilst this was not the preferred outcome for the Allies, they did little to stop it. Support of the resistance had served its purpose which was to make life difficult for the Germans, and the future for Albania was considered to be of no strategic significance.

According to SOE files, during the period 1942 to late 1944, some 673 sorties were despatched into Albania, of which 572 were successful. 201 people were dropped in and 502 were brought out. To give some indication of the relative importance of this activity, these statistics constitute about one third of the activity level in Greece.

Austria

German troops entered Austria on 12 March 1938. Consistent with its appeasement policy, the immediate response from the British was to accept that Austria was now part of the Third Reich. But, by the time that Churchill had become Prime Minister, Austria was conceived as a potential "Trojan Horse" for undermining Germany through covert operations.[222] SOE designed its policy with two objectives. The first was to encourage and assist political forces opposed to the Third Reich in initiating some form of uprising against German rule. The second was to facilitate the re-establishment of a separate and democratic nation state. The policy was fine in principle, but turned out to be very difficult to implement, not least because Austrian exiles, as reflected in representatives in London, were a diverse group with no cohesion. Meanwhile, inside the country, whilst a deep seated resentment towards the Germans was evident because the benefits of union were not materialising, this did not translate into any form of organised resistance.

The most significant event to impact covert operations at this time was the so called *Moscow Declaration*. This was adopted by Allied leaders on 1 November 1943, and confirmed that, following the defeat of Germany, Austria would gain its independence. This signalled to those within Austria inclined to resist the Germans, that Allied support for their efforts would be

---

[222] Some of this material is based on an article by G Steinacher entitled SOE In Austria 1939-45, published in the "Journal of Intelligence and Counter-Intelligence" (Routledge, London, 2002).

forthcoming. However, there was no support of any significance until SOE had established bases in Southern Italy. With supplies available from Brindisi, it was eventually decided to establish a presence in South East Slovenia, where there was a significant Austrian population, for infiltrating over the border. The main mission to implement this strategy, which Wig's team facilitated, was called *Operation Clowder*. The aim was to establish an *"Advance Base and War Station"* to facilitate contact with resistance groups in central and eastern Europe including Germany and Austria, to undermine German morale, to disseminate "black" propaganda amongst occupying German troops, and to prepare ground for subsequent operations.[223] The mission had the active support of Tito, and was approved in August. It was led by Lt Col Peter Wilkinson and Major Alfgar Hesketh-Prichard who were dropped into Yugoslavia, from where they travelled deep into Slovenia to establish a base at Chirchno some 40 kms from the Austrian border. Wilkinson then returned to London, leaving Hesketh-Prichard in charge. From London, Wilkinson organised a series of drops of men and equipment. The first incursion of an agent took place in late August 1943, but he disappeared. Following this mysterious episode, the main operation did not proceed until 3 December 1943.[224]

In the spring of 1944, significant efforts were made to infiltrate agents. But attempts to cross the border failed. It was not until October 1944 that Hesketh-Prichard with a party of some 80 Slovenes managed to achieve a major incursion and set up a base at Saualpe west of Wolfsberg in the Austrian Alps. But even this mission failed to stir up effective resistance, and Hesketh-Prichard was eventually killed by means unknown. The generally accepted view of all these attempts under *Operation Clowder* is that, whilst there were many in Austria who opposed the Germans, they were not willing to take up arms. Also, there was a real concern that the main people with whom SOE was able to establish a working relationship were Austrian Slovenians who were suspected of being agents of Tito's Partisans with intentions of annexing part of Austria to Yugoslavia after the war.

The other main SOE effort into Austria was directed from the SOE Office in Berne, which was organised by Squadron Leader Mathey who had taken over from John McCaffrey as Head of Mission in September 1944. He liaised with a Catholic resistance group called Patria, through which SOE agents

---

[223] This material is taken from SOE Files and dated 29 November 1943.
[224] Content drawn from the *"Secret History of SOE"* (pages 695-699) by William Mackenzie.

were inserted into the Tyrol area of western Austria. These teams executed some acts of sabotage, infiltrated German police regiments, and successfully defended themselves against German reprisals.

The remainder of SOE operations took place in early 1945, making use of Austrian prisoners of war who were willing to be trained in Italy and return as SOE agents. They undertook a number of missions involving sabotage, harassment of retreating German forces, and securing of the Zeltweg airfield. The star SOE turn was the mission led by Albrecht Gaiswinkler who amongst other things successfully recovered a copy of the Mona Lisa and the Austrian Crown Jewels.

Czechoslovakia

When the Germans annexed and partitioned Czechoslovakia in 1938, all the British SIS agents left and most of the local secret service escaped. However, a few of the locals stayed and their leader Frantisek Moravec joined forces with the head of the Czech Government-in-Exile, Benes. Subsequently, about 20 agents were sent in by parachute to provide intelligence. In late 1941, Benes and Moravec hatched a plot to kill the newly appointed governor Reinhard Heydrich. On 27 May 1942, the agents ambushed Heydrich's car en route to his country residence near Prague. He was severely injured by a grenade and eventually died in hospital on 4 June. In the aftermath, the Gestapo went on a killing spree and the assassins were eventually cornered when betrayed in return for a ransom. They shot themselves. Among their belongings, the address of two villages was found – Lidice and Lezaky. On the orders of Himmler, the Gestapo then obliterated both villages and killed all 5,000 inhabitants. The witch hunt continued, and nearly all the other SOE agents were caught and killed. The impact of these events on Czech resistance was significant. The leaders in London became very cautious and their organisation in the field was broken. They were reluctant to take any action for fear of further reprisals.[225]

In Wig's time, there were a number of other missions involving air operations. In April 1944, four parties consisting of 13 Czechs were safely landed in Czechoslovakia and radio communications were re-established. From this point, there were two major missions with impact on the war, one

---

[225] Based on account by William Mackenzie in pages 527-530 of the book entitled *"The Secret History of SOE"*.

facilitating the Slovak uprising in August 1944 and the second in support of the uprising in Prague in May 1945. The Slovak operation commenced with the dropping of 3 Czechs on 9 June 1944. In early July, and in consultation with the Russians, SOE developed a plan to counter any attempt by the Germans to strengthen its forces in the face of advancing Russian troops. The plan involved an open revolt by a section of the Slovak Army. The expected German attempt to reinforce their position came on 27 August, and on 29 August four Divisions of the Slovak army joined with local partisans. They occupied two airfields in the mountainous centre of the country. On 6 September, the Russians lent their support with 30 transport planes containing armaments. In the meantime, the British and Americans made it clear that they did not have resources to provide major assistance, although the Americans did send some supplies and evacuated Allied airmen. They also dropped SOE's Lt Colonel Threlfall who was head of Force 139 in Bari. He met with the local Slovak commander and explained that he must rely on Russian assistance. He was not well pleased, and eventually, the revolt was crushed by superior German forces.

Towards the end of the year, there was further contact with the Czechs. After much debate, in late December 1944, it was agreed that SOE should provide limited support to the Slovak army in the form of 20 sorties a month from Wig's bases in Italy. This was sufficient to support specific missions, but the Czechs were told that they would have to rely on the Russians for any further help.

During the remaining period of the war, SOE sent in only limited men and supplies, and there were a number of failed missions. One group reached Prague where they maintained a link with London during the general Czech uprising in May 1945, and they organised the reception of supplies to eastern Bohemia. Another established a communications link with the Czechoslovak National Council in Moravia. Subsequent support was minimal, and became redundant when the Russians entered Prague on 9 May. The final contact with the Czechs involved a brief visit by the head of Force 139 Colonel Perkins, but he exited almost immediately. That was the end of SOE involvement and any hope of a Czechoslovakia free of Russian domination.

Poland

Following the German invasion in September 1939, the Poles established a Polish Government in Exile ("PGE") based in London. After the fall of

France, Poland was for a time Britain's only serious ally. General Wladyslaw Sikorski, who was both Prime Minister and Commander-in-Chief of Polish forces, was a close associate of Churchill.[226] However, their influence on war time policy was never really significant, particularly after the entry on the Allied side of the Russians and then the Americans who brought immense manpower and military materiel. Nevertheless, there were plenty of Poles in England who formed a critical resource for the wider Allied war effort.

After German occupation, the principal arm of Polish resistance was the Polish Home Guard (the "AK – Armia Krajowa") which was established in the winter of 1942/43 from supporters of four moderate political groups. The AK had both civil and military commands and was accountable to the PGE. Although dominant, they were not however the only resistance force. In particular, there was a right wing collaborationist group, the National Armed Forces ("NSZ") and the communist led People's Army (the "AL – Armia Ludowa"). As was the case in so many other theatres, these two forces were engaged in what was effectively a civil war but neither had a major military capability. And the AL did not constitute a significant force until the Russian occupation in 1944.

Despite the relatively well organised resistance on the ground, in the early days of the war, SOE in England was able to provide relatively little assistance through lack of resources. However, in the autumn of 1942, the Allies received the first intelligence about the planned *Uprising* and, over the next twelve months, the PGE pressed for the Allies to increase the level of support. During the period September 1942 to April 1943, 62 sorties were despatched from England, 49 of which were successful. Whilst this activity gave the Poles some hope, they were far from satisfied. In particular, they wanted the Allies to deploy a permanent Polish Air Force and eventually land troops to support the planned *Uprising*.

In response to continuing pressure from the Poles and the resistance in other parts of central and Eastern Europe, in March 1943 SOE deployed two British based squadrons. However, these aircraft were not dedicated to Poland, with day to day deployment depending on current Allied military priorities. Over the summer of 1943, there was a lull in operations. When flights to Poland were resumed in September 1943, there was increasing loss of aircraft due to improved German defences. As a result, in that month, flights from England were terminated. For a few months, the Polish No 1586

---

[226] General Sikorski was killed in an air crash over Gibraltar on 4 July 1943.

Flight based in North Africa took up the role. This flight transferred to Brindisi in April 1944.

From this point, No. 1586 Flight became part of the air operations for which Wig was responsible and in June became a unit within the Balkan Air Force. The local Polish and Czech office of SOE Force 139 in Bari at this time was led by Lt Col Henry Threlfall, and Brindisi became a substantial base for supporting the Polish resistance. It had an operations section, a training school, a packing unit for preparing airborne supplies, and a signal station linked to both London and Poland. By July 1944, No 1586 Flight had 11 Halifaxes and 3 Liberators complemented from time to time by additional aircraft from No 334 Wing. During the period of April through July 1944 the supplies were significant, with 318 sorties, 114 men dropped, and 220 tons of supplies dropped for the loss of 8 aircraft.[227] Most of the agents sent in were nominally loyal to SOE, but acted under orders from the Polish government in exile in London. They undertook a wide range of acts of sabotage including the inflicting of damage to some 7,000 railway engines. The influence of all this work on the liberation of Poland was however limited. This was because the Allies eventually agreed a strategy for post-War transition which meant that Poland would be "liberated" by the Russians who were hostile to Polish self-determination.

During this time, the direction of SOE work was severely hampered by lack of intelligence. However, in April 1944, the first high grade report on the state of the resistance was made when Wig's Polish team extracted General Tabor, who was Director of Military Operations of the AK. This operation was followed by two further important missions. In May 1944, a number of important politicians were extracted. Then, in July, SOE was responsible for obtaining some key information about the V2 rocket. Earlier in the year, the Germans had undertaken test launches in rural Poland and a report on the results of these trials was obtained by the AK and smuggled out on 25/26 July 1944. This was probably one of the most important pieces of intelligence to reach London at that time.

In the middle of 1944, there was a major turning point which was to have significant consequences for many decades to come. On 16 July 1944, the Russians opened a major offensive against the Germans near the Polish town of Lvov. By 23 July, they had captured Lublin in central Poland.[228] On the

---

[227] Information taken from *"The Secret History of SOE"* (p. 520) by William Mackenzie.
[228] See *"The Secret History of SOE"* (p. 522) by William Mackenzie.

same day they broadcast a proclamation made by the self-styled Polish Committee of National Liberation. This group was based on senior members of the AL (the People's Army) and other smaller Polish communist groups. The Russians immediately recognised this Committee as the legitimate government of the liberated territory. Not surprisingly, the *Lublin Committee*, as it was called, was denounced by the PGE government in London.

With the Russians advancing on Warsaw, General Tabor met with General Gubbins in London, and it was agreed to proceed with the long planned *Uprising*. The locals were to have full discretion on the exact timing, with both the PGE's AK and the communist AL taking part. By 31 July 1944, a very substantial Russian force was just 15 kms from Warsaw and, in anticipation of their support, the decision was taken locally to commence activity. But then, seemingly by design, the Russian advance halted. On 15 August, they signalled that the *Uprising* was premature and that they could not assist. This put the heat on the British and Americans to take responsibility, and it fell on SOE in particular to do what it could to assist.

SOE had actually became aware that the *Uprising* had started on 2 August, and the provision of assistance was a great challenge for Wig's team. Not least this was because they were sending in supplies to a city in total turmoil, with planes travelling over a flying distance of 1,100 kms from the base in Italy. Initial sorties were cancelled because of bad weather, but on the nights of 8th 9th and 12th August No 334 Wing flew 18 sorties and ten managed to drop their loads without loss. This success led to an increase in the deployment of Liberators which then flew 54 sorties on 13 and 14 August, with 11 aircraft lost. With such losses, SOE redeployed the planes to dropping zones in the Kampinos woods outside the city. These flights continued during September until the *Uprising* concluded on 2 October. In all, SOE flew a total of 161 sorties, of which 79 were successful. In the process, 27 planes were lost. The Poles were deeply disappointed at what they saw as a meagre effort in their time of need. What they did not know was that, given other activities, SOE had a relatively small force available and that the attrition rate was critically high given the limited number of aircraft.

Meanwhile, the Russians who had huge resources adjacent to Warsaw just allowed the Germans to destroy the main forces of resistance. The end of the *Uprising* in early October 1944 effectively meant the end of the Polish resistance, and any chance of avoiding a communist takeover. In London, the

213

failure tore the PGE to pieces. In September, General Sosnkowski was dismissed following criticism he made of the Allies' lack of support. The Prime Minister Mikolajczyk was then replaced by M. Arciszewski who was implacably anti-Russian. On the ground, the field was open to the communist *Lublin Committee* who welcomed the Russians when they eventually entered Warsaw in January 1945.

After this disastrous turn of events, SOE's role was minimal apart from one further mission, called *Operation Freston*. On 26/27 December 1944, during the final period of Wig's time, SOE despatched a fact finding mission from Bari consisting of five men under the leadership of Colonel Marko Hudson of Yugoslavian fame (recently returned from his BLO role with Mihailović). They landed near an AK unit in wooded country not far from Czestochowa in south west Poland and were under immediate threat from the Germans. They managed to escape, and eventually ended up in the hands of the Russians who did not treat them very well. However, during the time they spent with the AK, they were able to obtain important feedback on the reality of events in the field. Hudson, who eventually returned to London by way of Moscow, concluded that had a formal mission been sent to Poland earlier, as had been done in the Balkans, the turn of events at the time of the *Uprising* might have been very different. In particular, with the benefit of direct contact with the leaders of the Polish resistance in the field, the western Allies might well have been persuaded to adopt a much more pro-active role in supporting the AK and other moderate resistance forces, which in turn might have averted the communist take-over. Unfortunately, this knowledge was of little use after the event.

The remainder of the SOE agents left in Poland did not fare as well as Hudson and his team. Many were executed at the hands of the Russian NKVD, or thrown into prison.[229] As Gubbins said of the Russian actions:

> *"And these were the Polish men and women who for years had fought the German enemy, had attacked and sabotaged his communications and transport serving German armies in the East. Perfidy had reached its climax. We are left stunned by this appalling betrayal."*

With the benefit of hindsight, the failure to recognise the strategic importance of Poland in the longer term flow of events is significant. Indeed,

---

[229] The NKVD was the war time equivalent of what became the KGB secret service.

the failure of the *Uprising* in Warsaw in mid-1944 was one of the turning points in recent history and doomed the Polish people to a cruel dictatorship which lasted for over 40 years.[230] One is left to wonder how different things might have been if the western powers had made even one tenth of the effort to assist their Polish allies as that made in supporting the Italians.

Finally, the raw statistics of SOE efforts in support of the Poles are as follows. During the whole war, SOE made a total of 485 successful drops, with the loss of 73 aircraft.[231] 318 members of the armed forces were parachuted in to help the AK, four of whom were British, together with 28 Polish couriers and a total of 600 tons of materiel.

Southern France

Following the German occupation in 1940, SOE was of course a major player in supporting the resistance in France. As Wig was not involved in SOE operations out of the UK, this book is not the place for that story. However, Wig did have a hand in supporting resistance activity in the south of France during 1944, with a number of Special Duty flights from Bari dropping supplies to resistance groups and supporting BLOs in Vichy France, including operations designed to link up with the Italian partisans on the French/Italian border. A key moment in this activity came on 15 August 1944 with the implementation of *Operation Dragoon* which involved Allied landings on the Riviera. This involved the deployment from North Africa of 7 Allied Divisions (four of them Free French) under the command of American General Patch. The landings were mostly successful and this Franco-American army eased its way up to the Rhone Valley and northwards, eventually to join the Allied troops who landed at Normandy.

---

[230] Much of this is based on material in *"The Secret History of the SOE"* by William Mackenzie, including the conclusion on p527.

[231] Extract from pages 191 and 192 of the book entitled *"The Special Operations Executive – 1940-46"* by MRD Foot.

Part Eight: The Yugoslav Imperative

23: Yugoslav Historical Context

I have included this Part of the book, which covers the war in Yugoslavia, for two reasons. First of all, much of Wig's work in 1943/44 involved providing air support to SOE operations in this country. Secondly, there is an interesting counterpoint between SOE work in Yugoslavia and Greece. Whilst in both theatres the war against the Axis forces was conducted in the absence of an allied army in the field, the outcomes in terms of post-war regime and subsequent history were distinctly different. The reasons for this will emerge as the story is told, but much is explained by the different approaches adopted by the respective communist and non-communist resistance leaders.

Before World War Two, Yugoslavia comprised the countries known in the 21st Century as Serbia, Croatia, Slovenia and Montenegro (and some smaller territories now part of Bulgaria and Greece). This entity was established as a constitutional monarchy on 1 December 1918, following the Corfu Declaration in July 1917. This new nation had a strategic position in south east Europe, at the cross roads of what had been for several centuries the Ottoman and Austro-Hungarian empires.

In 1929, there was political unrest, and a Croatian MP was shot by a Serb in the national parliament. Shortly afterwards, King Alexander enacted a new constitution which gave him sweeping autocratic powers. Then, on 9 October 1934, during a visit to France to consolidate an alliance with that country, the King was assassinated by a representative of a Bulgarian separatist organisation. Shortly after, Alexander's first cousin Prince Paul became Regent because the dead king's son Prince Peter was only ten years old.

At the outbreak of the Second World War, it was Yugoslav policy to maintain neutrality but, with neighbouring countries driven into support for the *Axis Pact*, this position gradually became untenable.[232] After much deliberation, and despite opposition from some Serbian politicians, on 25 March 1941 the Yugoslav Prime Minister Dragisa Cvetkovic joined the Pact. Within two days, there was a coup in Belgrade. The Cvetkovic government was deposed, and was replaced by a pro-Allied government led by General Dusan Simovic, with the 17 year old Prince Peter proclaimed King.

These events soon triggered a German response and, even though war had

---

[232] This term refers to the group of countries working together with the Tri-Partite Alliance formed between Germany, Italy and Japan.

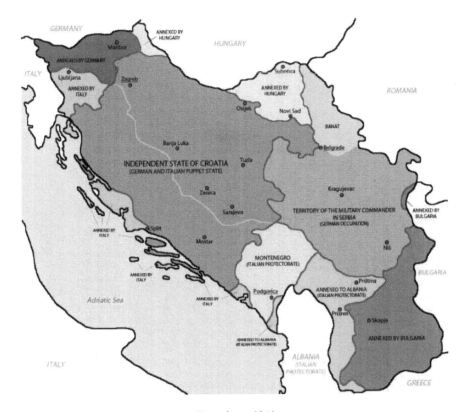

Yugoslavia 1941

not been declared, on 6 April 1941 they bombed Belgrade. This was followed by a full-blooded German invasion which also involved troops from other *Axis Pact* countries. Being attacked from all sides, and with a poorly equipped army consisting mostly of Serbs, the Yugoslavs were quickly overwhelmed and capitulated on 17 April 1941. King Peter and the fledgling Simovic government fled the country, first to Greece, and then to the British haven in Cairo. By June 1941, they had transferred to London where they established a Yugoslav Government in Exile ("YGE"), and were fêted as heroes for resisting Germany and Italy.

By the middle of 1941, and despite their preoccupation with the attack on the Soviet Union in June, the Germans had over-run not only Yugoslavia but also Greece. The Germans then set about dividing up the spoils between their *Axis Pact* partners. Slovenia was partitioned between Germany and Italy,

220

Left: Tito - ww2gravestone.com Right: Mihailovic - kingdom-of-yugoslavia-ww2.com.

Montenegro was passed to the Italians, and Serbia was dismembered. Most of Macedonia went to Bulgaria, the Italians occupied Kosovo which was next to Albania, and Hungary took the Vojvodina region in the north.

Given the ethnic mix within Yugoslavia, the response of the local population to these events varied considerably. In Roman Catholic Croatia, there was a substantial pro-Axis movement called the Ustaše and their leaders established a separate Croatian state called the Nesa Drzava Hrvatska ("NDH"). The NDH government signed the *Axis Pact* on 15 June 1941, and the Ustaše then set about a programme of ethnic cleansing, targeting in particular Orthodox Serbians and Muslims in Bosnia. The enmity to which this gave rise has rippled through subsequent history until recent times. In the rump of Serbia, a similar pro-Axis puppet state was eventually established on 29 August 1941 under a Prime Minister called Nedic who headed what was called a Government of National Salvation. Despite these accommodations, the bulk of the Yugoslav population were opposed to the occupation. And, in the months that followed, there were a number of popular uprisings inspired in particular by two embryonic resistance groups, the Serbian-based *Chetniks* and the more widely dispersed *Partisans*.

The Partisans, who were led by the Croatian Josip Broz known as Tito, had senior staff that were trained by the Russians, and established the first anti-German guerrilla unit called the "Sisak Partisan Detachment". This was

221

based in Croatia and they commenced their formal "military" resistance on 7 July 1941 with an uprising in the village of Bela Crkva. Then, on 28 July 1941 they established the Republic of Uzice which had a population of around 300,000. This was the first of several such independent political units, some of which did not survive for very long.

At the same time, the *Chetnik* movement was established in Serbia and became active with a number of attacks on Axis targets the force of which was tempered by fear of reprisals. In the early days, they comprised Serbian elements of the old Royal Yugoslav army loyal to Colonel Dragoljob Mihailović (Uncle Draža) along with significant numbers of the peasantry, most of whom continued to work on their farms and in their villages until called upon for specific missions.[233] They too established areas which were for a time "liberated".

In response to this organised guerrilla activity, over the next four years the Axis powers launched seven major and a larger number of minor offensives. The Axis forces comprised various combinations of the German and Italian Armies, with contributions from the various satellite states in Croatia, Serbia, Bulgaria, and Hungary.

The first of these battles took place just six months after the initial occupation, when the Axis powers launched an all-out attack on both of the main resistance groups in Serbia, and killed thousands of civilians in the process. As a result, many Partisans fled to the Sandjak mountains and from there to south east Bosnia. And the Chetniks fled to the Serbian mountains. So, by the end of 1941, the Yugoslav resistance was in total disarray. And the same could be said for the Allies in all theatres of war. As a result, despite the best of intentions, the resistance was very much on its own, apart from a small number of BLOs (British Liaison Officers) located with the Chetniks.

In these early days, there was a degree of mutual tolerance between the two resistance forces, but there were already reports of open conflict between them. There were similar tensions between factions within the YGE in London. As a result, on 12 January 1942, Simovic was replaced as Prime Minister by Slobadan Jovanovic. Jovanovic quickly moved to support the Chetniks and, although Mihailović was trapped in the mountains, he was appointed as the YGE Minister of War and promoted to be a General. Despite initial intelligence that the Chetniks were tentative through fear of reprisals, and even collaborating with the Italians and the Nedic regime in Serbia, this

---

[233] This description is taken from SOE File 5-919.

appointment led the British government to treat him as the de facto leader of the resistance movement. In keeping with this recognition, Mihailović was lauded in an edition of *Time* magazine as an anti-Nazi hero. Apparently, he was more than happy to take the credit for leading resistance activity, including some operations which had been undertaken by the Partisans.

In January 1942 the Germans launched significant attacks on the Partisans, with a major offensive in eastern Bosnia. In the spring, this was extended to Montenegro, Sandžak and Herzegovina. Despite suffering casualties, the majority of the Partisans escaped to the hills. There were also limited skirmishes against the Chetniks. However, armed conflict was often averted with the insurgents appearing to retreat in order to avoid bloodshed. And, reportedly, they even offered to assist Axis forces in attacks on the Partisans. During the rest of 1942, hostilities continued, with minimal external support from the Allies. However, BLOs reported that the scope of Partisan activity appeared to be expanding, with the establishment of administrative control over some districts, and even the creation of a rudimentary arms industry. In November 1942, the Partisans formally established what was called the *People's Liberation Army.*[234]

By the end of 1942, the relative performance of the two resistance movements was not lost on the Allies. Many of the telegram messages from BLOs suggested that the Partisans appeared to be more often the target of German military action, that there was a degree of accommodation between Mihailović and the occupying powers, and that there was enmity between the Chetniks and the Partisans although it was never clear at whose instigation.[235]

Concerned by this intelligence, SOE despatched a senior officer to liaise with Mihailović who provided a relatively positive report on Chetnik aims and activities. However, research into military signals revealed that the Germans were spending much more time engaging the Partisans than the Chetniks. This intelligence was passed to Churchill who became convinced of the need to provide support to the Partisans. Based on all the intelligence, the Allies began to canvass four options: exclusive support for Mihailović, exclusive support for Tito, equal support for both parties, and support for

---

[234] This would have been a hot bit of intelligence as Wig joined SOE in Cairo in November 1942.
[235] This account is based on the huge amount of evidence, consisting of cables and reports, in the HS 5 series of SOE files which relate to the Balkans.

neither until they ceased fighting each other.[236] For the time being, it was decided to maintain the current almost exclusive support for Mihailović although, with few aircraft at their disposal, the policy was academic.

As the months of 1943 unfolded, confidence in Mihailović continued to decline. It wasn't just the reports about lack of activity, unreliability, and even collaboration. On 28 February 1943, he made a widely reported speech at a christening in which he attacked *"Perfidious Albion"*, reflecting the view that the British had let him down, and identifying the communist Partisans as a more important adversary than the Germans. This speech infuriated the YGE and Foreign Office in London, with Churchill sending a stiff note of complaint to YGE PM Jovanovic. In response, Mihailović, who was genuinely aggrieved about what he saw as the failure of the Allies to provide material support, defended himself as being mis-reported. But his reputation had been seriously damaged.

Whilst the Allies continued to review their options, the Axis powers launched another major attack on the Partisans in what was called *Operation White*. On 7 January 1943, the Bulgarians had occupied part of Serbia, and this was followed by a campaign which lasted until April during which the Axis powers fought with the Partisans in an area between western Bosnia and northern Herzegovina ("the Battle of Neretva"). This culminated in the Partisan retreat over the Neretva River, and was followed in May and June by the "Battle of the Sutjeska" which involved a complete encirclement of Partisan forces in southeastern Bosnia and northern Montenegro. The Partisans made a narrow escape.[237] At the same time, the Germans tried to capitalise on Mihailović's obvious frustration with lack of Allied support and get him to change sides, but he refused. Subsequently, they also had talks with Tito, seeking to exploit fears about a possible Allied land invasion. However, after six weeks, Hitler pulled out of talks with Tito and the Germans renewed their assault on the Partisans with a second phase of attacks called *Operation Black*.

On 6 May 1943, the Allied Chiefs of Staff had a meeting to review all the current intelligence and formulate future plans. At this meeting, Lord Louis

---

[236] This material is drawn from the book entitled *"The Secret History of SOE"* by William Mackenzie, p428.

[237] A more detailed account of these events may be found in the book entitled *"The Embattled Mountain"* by F W Deakin (OUP, USA, 1971), a number of books by Stevan K Pavlowitch, and the book entitled *"Parachutes, Patriots, and Partisans"* by Heather Williams (C Hurst & Co, London, 2003).

Mountbatten argued for a switch in support from the Chetniks to the Partisans and warned that a failure to support the Partisans might drive them into the arms of the Russians. The Foreign Office were also having doubts about the exclusive support for the Chetniks. As a result, on 7 May 1943, Foreign Minister Anthony Eden invited the YGE Prime Minister to send a message to Mihailović indicating that support would be withdrawn unless he could confirm his willingness to comply with Allied military strategy, discontinue any contact with the Germans and their allies, and cease conflict with the Partisans. The YGE Prime Minister complied on 12 May and eventually, on 1 June 1943, Mihailović replied protesting his loyalty and confirming his future co-operation.

In mid-1943, developments elsewhere came into play. In July, Mussolini was toppled and the new Italian government signed an armistice with the Allies. In September, the Allies invaded Italy. The armistice effectively took Italy out of the war, and 17 Divisions of Italian troops were left stranded in Yugoslavia with loyalties unclear. Many of the soldiers gave themselves up to the Germans, and others made their way back to Italy to join the Italian resistance. According to SOE files, at least six Divisions were disarmed by the Partisans.[238] As a result, the Partisans were substantially reinforced with both men and weaponry. In the absence of a meaningful Italian Army, the Germans took over Albania and Montenegro and assumed control of the Dalmatian coast sharing responsibility with the Croatians. Apart from the reinforcements, the Partisans also sought to exploit the vacuum created by the Italian armistice, with advances into North-East Italy, Zagreb, the Adriatic coast, and Central Croatia. And in Montenegro a number of Chetnik supporters deserted Mihailović to join the Partisans. In frustration with this turn of events, YGE Prime Minister Jovanovic resigned and was replaced on 10 August by Bosidar Puric. The Germans responded strongly to the Partisan advances and, by early October 1943, they had reversed much of their gains.

The longer term consequences of the Italian armistice were significant for all the parties in Yugoslavia. Deprived of the Italian troops, the Germans had to divert substantial forces from the Eastern Front to maintain their position across the Balkans. For the Allies, with a major SOE presence now in southern Italy, it was decided that the time had come to provide a similar level of supplies to both resistance movements, always subject to their commitment to attacking the Germans and not each other. There were of

---

[238] An account is given in SOE File HS 7-271.

course serious reservations about such a change in policy (Mihailović was still the undisputed representative of the YGE and the Partisans were suspected of having revolutionary intentions), but the evidence from the field about which group would engage the Germans with greater force had become compelling. Meanwhile, on 28 September the YGE and King Peter followed the Greeks in removing from London to Cairo.

Reflecting the new policy of supporting both resistance movements, by the end of September, there were 14 SOE missions with the Partisans and 12 missions with the Chetniks. And, from all the intelligence provided by these officers, the picture emerged that there were some 10 German Divisions in Yugoslavia, with the vast majority fighting a body of Partisan forces that had now reached 180,000 men.[239] Reports also suggested that, thanks to the Italian materiel sequestered after the armistice, they had more than enough arms and equipment. However, they were in desperate need of a steady flow of ammunition. This intelligence led Churchill to the view that, whilst it was politic in terms of commitments to the King and YGE to continue support to both resistance forces, the Partisans were the most effective and reliable vehicle for pursuing British military strategy. Consequently, he determined that it was time to have a more direct input to Tito's high command. Having established Tito's acceptance of this idea, in September 1943 Churchill sent Brigadier Fitzroy Maclean to Tito's headquarters near Drvar. His mission was to undertake an assessment of the current position of all resistance forces and eventually to provide a permanent and formal liaison with Tito himself.[240] Maclean's initial report praised the Partisans, confirmed suspicions about the effectiveness of the Chetniks, and even indicated that the Chetniks had allowed the Germans to redeploy troops through the north of the country from Russia.[241] To keep his options open, Churchill also approved the despatch of a senior envoy, Brigadier Charles Armstrong, to liaise with the Mihailović headquarters. But, by now, the Partisans were becoming the main

---

[239] Again, this information is taken from SOE Files HS 7-271/272/273.

[240] As described in Chapter 15, the deployment of Maclean was to have been an SOE operation. But due to personal animosities this was largely of a nominal nature with Maclean taking his orders from MEHQ in Egypt and eventually becoming an independent mission reporting directly to General Wilson and to Churchill himself.

[241] Further information is provided in the book entitled *"Eastern Approaches"* by Fitzroy Maclean as well as SOE Files.

recipients of Allied support.[242]

Between 22 and 26 November 1943, Churchill and Roosevelt met at what was called the Sextant Conference in Cairo. Subsequently, on 28 November, they met with Stalin in Teheran. In these conferences, Churchill strongly embraced the Partisans as the main viable force to counter the Germans and the Americans were brought on side. Interestingly, though, whilst Stalin also supported this policy, he was less enthusiastic than Churchill because he saw the potential for this initiative to detract from his main objective which was an Allied invasion of France.

Having made this decision to switch allegiance, Churchill now turned his mind to bringing about an understanding between the YGE and Tito. This presented some challenges. Firstly, he had to get the YGE to disengage from Mihailović. Secondly, there was a need to redeploy the BLOs based with the Chetnik forces. This was difficult given the loyalties and enmities that had been developed at a personal level. To hasten both these processes, attempts were made to demonstrate Mihailović's ineffectiveness by challenging him to implement a major mission against the Germans. This device proved to be effective when, following an initial positive response from Mihailović and the best efforts of his supporting BLOs, he failed to deliver.

Having prepared the ground, on 22 February 1944, Churchill publicly confirmed the decision to transfer support from Mihailović to Tito in a speech to the House of Commons. Thereafter, following lengthy negotiations with the YGE and the Partisans, the Allies determined to formally recognise a new Yugoslav government with Tito as Prime Minister. However, there was a major unresolved issue. In return for his unequivocal support, Churchill had hoped to obtain an agreement that the 20 year old King Peter should return to Yugoslavia as head of state. However, Tito would not make a commitment, and a decision was postponed until the end of the War.

In the spring of 1944, the Germans made a final attempt to re-establish some form of control within Yugoslavia, with the launch of *Operation Knight's Leap* in Bosnia. However, their campaign was a failure. In particular, this was because the Allies had now established an enhanced air operations unit in Bari, the capability of which was further strengthened by

---

[242] A more detailed account of how the support for the two resistance movements evolved may be found in the book entitled "*Shadows on the Mountains. The Allies, the Resistance and the Rivalries that doomed WWII Yugoslavia*" by Marcia Christoff Kurapovna (John Wiley, New York, 2010).

the establishment in June of the Balkan Air Force. This provided for a systematic co-ordination of military, covert, and political interests and consequently the Allies were able to establish complete air superiority over Yugoslavia.

In late May 1944, the German launched further major attacks on both the Chetnik and Partisan headquarters and SOE implemented operations to rescue both parties. Detailed accounts of both life-saving missions, *Operation Repartee* and *Operation Triumph* in which Wig had a significant hand, are given in Chapter 24. As a result of *Operation Triumph,* Tito escaped to the island of Vis where he set up a temporary headquarters.[243]

At this point, the various Partisan groupings in Serbia, Macedonia and Slovenia began to coalesce into serious armed forces. In the spring, the Macedonian and Serbian groups came under a joint command, and later the Slovene Partisans joined them to form a single army. By mid-1944, the Yugoslav Partisan movement had grown to become the largest resistance force in occupied Europe, and was reported as having as many as 800,000 men, organised into four separate field armies. On 16 June 1944, representatives of the Partisans and the YGE met at Tito's headquarters on Vis. To facilitate negotiations, the Allies insisted that Prime Minister Puric be replaced by Ivan Šubašić who took office on 9 July. After lengthy talks, the YGE signed the Tito-Šubašić Agreement designed to unify the two potential rivals for future government of what was called Democratic Federal Yugoslavia. In particular, it was agreed that, at the end of the war, the YGE's Šubašić would become the foreign minister in a coalition government led by Tito. And the Allies recognised the Partisan's *National Liberation Army* as Yugoslavia's official army, transforming it from its "resistance" status. The Agreement also called on all Slovenes, Croats, and Serbs to join the Partisans, a call which of course fell on deaf ears as far as many Chetniks were concerned.

In August 1944, there was an anti-German coup in Rumania, and the Rumanian army joined forces with the Red Army to assist in an attack on Prague. Bulgaria was quick to follow suit, and Bulgarian forces were permitted by the Partisans to enter Yugoslavia with the aim of blocking the German retreat from Greece through the east and centre of the country.

---

[243] It is interesting to note that, over the previous 100 years, this island had changed hands between Italy and Yugoslavia on several occasions. Fortuitously, in October 1943, the island was occupied by the Allies.

Macedonia and eastern Serbia were then liberated. On 10 September, Bulgaria declared war on Germany, with the German retreat confined to the western side of the country. The Partisans and the Red Army then attacked Belgrade, and took the city on 20 October 1944. By the onset of winter in 1944, the Partisans now controlled the entire eastern half of Yugoslavia—Serbia, Macedonia, Montenegro—as well as much of the Dalmatian coast. The Axis powers still controlled Croatia, and they held their position in what was effectively a western corridor through the winter of 1944–45 in order to aid the continuing evacuation of German troops from Greece. By prior agreement, the Red Army was redeployed back into the heart of Europe as part of the final push on Germany. They never returned.

On 1 November 1944, Tito and Šubašić signed the *Belgrade Agreement*, consolidating the earlier agreement. This new pact had provisions for the establishment of an interim government in March 1945, pending democratic elections. Despite this Agreement, the real power in the emerging government sat with the Communist-led Anti-Fascist Liberation Council of Yugoslavia ("AVNOJ").

In early 1945, the Germans continued their retreat through the western corridor, relatively unharmed. They even scored some tactical successes against elements of the Yugoslav army not all of whom, after years of guerrilla war, were experienced in "conventional" military encounters. On 22 February, the Germans evacuated Mostar in southern Bosnia but maintained their position in Sarajevo as a withdrawal route to Croatia and beyond. On 8 March 1945, a new coalition government was formed in Belgrade with Tito as Premier and Ivan Šubašić as Foreign Minister. King Peter agreed not to return until after an election and plebiscite on the future of the monarchy.

On 20 March, the Yugoslav army launched a general offensive against the Germans and their remaining allies. Between 30 March and 8 April 1945, the Chetniks mounted a final attempt to establish themselves as a credible force, and suffered a major defeat at the hands of the Croatian Army. But this was the last gasp of both forces. With the Chetniks in disarray, the Croatians retreated into Austria to surrender to the Allies. Finally, on 15 April 1945, the Germans capitulated at Sarajevo and, by 20 April, a Yugoslav army had reached the western border of Yugoslavia. They crossed the border and captured the Italian city of Trieste. In the meantime, another Yugoslav army had taken the Croatian capital of Zagreb, and then proceeded to Slovenia.

On 8 May 1945, the German leadership surrendered unconditionally and the war in Europe officially ended. Despite the German capitulation, the Yugoslav Partisans continued to face resistance from Croatian and other anti-Partisan forces and, on 14/15 May 1945, the last battle of World War II in Europe took place at Poljana, near Prevalje in Slovenia. It was the final exchange between the Partisans and a mixed column of 30,000 Germans, Croatian Ustaše, Croatian Home Guard, Slovenian Home Guard, and others who were attempting to escape to Austria. Most of them made it to the Austrian border town of Bleiburg, and tried to negotiate a surrender to the British. But their representations were ignored. The majority were turned over to the Yugoslav government as part of what is sometimes referred to as *Operation Keelhaul*. Although they had strayed into Austria, on 20 May Yugoslav troops started to withdraw. On 8 June, the United States, the United Kingdom, and Yugoslavia agreed on a new Yugoslav-Italian Border and on the control of Trieste which would eventually return to Italian jurisdiction.

In November 1945, Tito held elections and won a significant majority in a newly created National Assembly. On 29 November, this parliament voted to establish the Federal People's Republic of Yugoslavia as a socialist state, with Tito appointed as Prime Minister. On 13 March 1946, after many months on the run, Mihailović was captured by agents of the new government. During a trial which lasted for five days, he faced charges of high treason and war crimes. On 15 July, he was found guilty of collaboration and sentenced to death by firing squad. A clemency appeal was rejected by the Presidium of the National Assembly and, during the early hours of 18 July, Mihailović, together with nine other Chetnik officers and military leaders of the Serbian Nedić government, was executed in Lisičiji Potok.

24: SOE Operations in Yugoslavia

The principal force deployed by the Allies to support the resistance in Yugoslavia was SOE. The purpose of this chapter is to present an account of SOE's activity during the time in 1943/44 that Wig was responsible for the related air operations.[244] During 1943, operations were mostly deployed from Cairo but, in early 1944, responsibility was transferred to Bari in Italy.

When Wig joined the Cairo office in November 1942, the main SOE involvement in Yugoslavia consisted of a small number of BLOs in the field, and virtually all of its air operations were being deployed to support General Mihailović and the Chetniks. Tito was an unknown quantity, although the office was already receiving intelligence that the Partisans were more active in fighting the Germans than their Chetnik counterparts. With evidence that there was an undeclared civil war, attempts had already been made by SOE to get the two resistance groups to reach some form of accommodation, but to no avail. In any event, SOE's ability to assist either side was limited due to lack of aircraft. Whilst there were advocates for extending support to the Partisans, the prevailing position at this time was to provide exclusive support to Mihailović, and this is recorded in an SOE policy paper which was the template during the first six months of Wig's time in the Cairo office. It reads as follows.[245]

a) *We would rather back a known quantity* (the Serbian Chetniks), *than the Croats and Slovenes who are an unknown quantity* (the Partisans).

b) *If the resistance in Yugoslavia is made up of elements which are hostile to each other, we are unlikely to reconcile them by supporting all of them. That would fan the flames. It would be better to support just one of them.*

c) *With limited aircraft, it is better to concentrate rather than disperse our efforts. Moreover, Serbia is within easier reach from Cairo.*[246]

---

[244] Wig was responsible for air operations to Yugoslavia from early 1943 until SOE terminated support towards the end of 1944.

[245] This material is taken from SOE File 5-919 and is dated 19 January 1943.

[246] There were only a few Special Duties fleet available from Cairo, and the Partisans were mostly located further to the north with aircraft requiring more fuel to reach them.

d)   *General Mihailović is War Minister of the YGE which is recognised by and in alliance with Britain.*

e)   *There is a case for establishing contact with the Partisans, and keeping options open particularly bearing in mind Russian support for them.*

This policy left no doubt about the content of Wig's job as head of the small Air Operations Unit based in Cairo. However, Wig's boss, Brigadier Keble, was very conscious of the need to expand capability whoever the recipients were to be. Accordingly, he prepared a submission requesting 8 more long range Liberators and, as recounted in earlier chapters, this found its way to Churchill who was supportive. However, additional planes were a long time coming.

Meanwhile, conscious of the need to find out more about the Partisans, SOE proceeded with the *Typical Mission* designed to make direct contact with Tito. In April 1943, Wig's unit deployed two exploratory missions, *Operation Fungus* in which a team parachuted into Croatia and *Operation Hoathley 1* in which a second team parachuted into Bosnia. They were well received, and subsequently Keble sent a more formal mission involving both SOE (Bill Deakin) and SIS (William Stuart). This team reached Tito's headquarters in Bihac on 28 May 1943. Deakin's remit is contained in SOE Files, a precis of which follows:[247]

"a)   *You are appointed Liaison Officer with Partisan HQ. Unless specifically advised otherwise, you will not take orders from Col Bailey (who was the existing senior BLO based with Mihailović).*

b)   *Your duties are to explain to Partisan HQ that an Allied offensive in Yugoslavia is now imminent and synchronisation with Partisan activities is therefore desirable. You will seek to arrange for the Partisans to attack specific targets with Allied assistance. You will report on the military situation in Yugoslavia and provide advice on targets, and you will act as an intermediary in communications between GHQ Middle East and the Partisans.*

c)   *You are to explain that it is not until recently that the British government has become aware that some Mihailović forces have "compounded" with the enemy. On our hearing of these liaisons,*

---

[247] This is a precis of a much longer document in SOE Files.

> *we have requested Mihailović to disown those forces. In the*
> *meantime, other Mihailović forces are seen as having the*
> *potential to assist the Allies.*
>
> d) *GHQ Middle East wishes to work with all elements in Yugoslavia*
> *who offer resistance to the Germans."*

Deakin arrived just as the Germans were intensifying their attack on the Partisans in the *Battle of Sujetska* in Montenegro. Undeterred, on 30 May, he met with Tito who indicated that he was willing to work with the Allies. In particular, this would include the deployment of a senior British officer to join his HQ, and Partisan co-operation with attacks on specific sabotage targets as nominated by the Allies.[248] This response was relayed back to Allied command and, in the meantime, attempts were made to reconcile the two resistance forces. In particular, it was suggested to Mihailović that he should restrict the geographical scope of his operations, but he refused.

In June 1943, in response to Keble's earlier plea for more resources, and with the invasion of Italy pending, Churchill authorised the redeployment of additional aircraft to operations into Yugoslavia with the number increased from a handful to 36. Foreign Secretary Sir Anthony Eden also promulgated the new British policy that both sides would now receive supplies on the condition that they did not attack each other. This change of policy had a huge impact on Wig's job. Although many of the additional aircraft (Halifaxes rather than the Liberators requested) were not suitable for longer flights, for the first time SOE had the capability to make regular sorties to both the Chetniks and the Partisans, although the number of aircraft was still insufficient to keep all missions fully operational.

Following the Italian Armistice in early September, SOE upgraded the missions to both Mihailović and Tito. The new head of mission with Mihailović was Brigadier Charles Armstrong, who was inserted by Wig's team under what was called *Operation Seizure*. Unfortunately for Mihailović, whilst Armstrong did his best to provide the latest information on Chetnik activity, he was not a particularly effective advocate.[249] The person appointed to liaise with Tito was the newly promoted Brigadier

---

[248] This account is based on pages 138 and 139 of Heather Williams' book *"Parachutes, Patriots and Partisans."*

[249] This statement reflects the view held by Heather Williams as expressed in her book *Parachutes, Patriots and Partisans* on pages 179 and 249.

Fitzroy Maclean who had a direct line to both Churchill and the Military and had a remit which read as follows:

"1.   You are appointed as Head of Mission attached to Tito. Whilst a member of SOE you should also consider yourself a member of the Foreign Office and/or responsible to the British Ambassador if he transfers to Cairo.

2.   You should report to the Foreign Office on a range of matters relating to the political aspects of Partisan activities.

3.   You have complete freedom of movement and should liaise regularly with the SOE mission at Mihailović HQ.

4.   Support to Mihailović and Tito is conditional on their not fighting each other, and not collaborating with Axis forces. Supplies from the Allies are linked to the achievement of Allied military objectives."[250]

Wig's team delivered Maclean to Yugoslavia in September 1943 in what was called *Operation Pikestaff*. Maclean quickly established a rapport with Tito, and soon became convinced that he was an effective force against the Germans (a view that was supported by Churchill's son Randolph who joined Maclean's team). After only a few weeks in Yugoslavia, he returned to Cairo where he met with Anthony Eden and presented a report in which he asserted that the Partisans were *"more numerous, infinitely better organised, better equipped and better disciplined"* than the Chetniks, and better placed to reconstitute the state as a federal entity once the Germans were expelled.[251] Although he had not met Mihailović, he suggested that the Chetniks were occasional collaborators, and that the YGE would establish the old regime under Serbian dominance.[252] He concluded that the withdrawal of support for the Chetniks would produce immediate military benefits, reduce Soviet influence, and end the civil war because without British support Mihailović

---

[250] This is a precis based on a longer document in the SOE Balkan Diaries.

[251] This is a reference from William McKenzie's book, *"The Secret History of SOE"* where file FO371/37615 is cited.

[252] According to Heather Williams, on pages 183-87 of her book *"Parachutes, Patriots and Partisans SOE & Yugoslavia 1941/45"*, Maclean's Report was highly biased in favour of the Partisans, not least in terms of wildly over-estimating the size of Partisan forces, and failing to account for the grass roots support for the Chetniks in Serbia. However, it should be said that SOE had well established BLOs with Mihailović, some of whom presented much the same picture of the Chetniks as that provided by Maclean.

would collapse.

At the same time as Maclean was reporting to Eden, Armstrong also produced a status report, suggesting that support for the Chetniks was still worthwhile if appropriately directed.[253] Unfortunately, the delivery of this report via the SOE office in Cairo was delayed by several weeks, and it never reached Churchill or Eden ahead of important international conferences on the future of the war which would determine the future direction of SOE support to the Yugoslav resistance.

Bearing in mind all this intelligence, during the last three months of 1943, SOE increased the total number of BLOs deployed in Yugoslavia but began to switch support from the Chetniks to the Partisans. By December, whilst the total number of agents had increased by 20%, the proportion with the Chetniks had fallen from 40% to 35%.[254] Perhaps more telling is the data on the number of air sorties despatched by Wig's team, details of which are provided in Appendix 14. In July 1943 Mihailović received 56% of sorties but, by October, this figure had fallen to 36%. By now, the Partisans were in the ascendant.

In the final weeks of 1943, the Allied leadership met in Teheran and it was agreed that the Partisans should now be the main recipient of support. This must have come as a great relief for Wig for whom the resolution of priorities was a constant source of worry. When the Allied decision became apparent to Mihailović, he did try to save his position by suggesting a further attempt at a reconciliation with Tito. However, his proposal fell on deaf ears, and any hope of saving his position was lost when, on 22 February 1944, Churchill made public his decision to transfer support from Mihailović to Tito. The BLOs with the Chetniks now had no choice but to withdraw, and Wig's team were soon very busy in arranging their extraction including Deakin who transferred to Cairo.

With the removal of support for Mihailović, 1944 saw a wholly different approach to SOE's work in Yugoslavia. At the same time, SOE established its new SOM command structure. The Yugoslav country section was moved to Italy, and Wig established his new air operations unit in Bari. This change in logistics substantially improved effectiveness, although there was something of a hiatus during the winter months as the redeployment was implemented. However, in the spring, Wig's team gradually increased the

---

[253] Armstrong Report dated 23/11/43 may be found in file FO371/37617.
[254] This is taken from SOE Balkans Diaries, Oct-Dec 1943 as found in SOE File HS7/271.

number of sorties.

In June 1944, the Balkan Air Force was established under Air Vice-Marshall William Elliot, and planning for the deployment of SOE resources into Yugoslavia became the responsibility of the Special Operations Committee (of which Wig was a member) chaired by Major General Stawell. Deakin moved from Cairo to Bari as head of the Yugoslav desk and, at the same time, a whole new team of agents were deployed. They were met with varying degrees of welcome by the Partisans, given that many had previously been with the Chetniks.

The impact of all these changes is shown in the following figures on supplies sent to Yugoslavia.[255]

	By Air (tonnes)	By Sea (tonnes)	Personnel Evacuated
1943 (Oct-Dec)	114	1,857	
1944 (Jan-Mar)	321	6,398	
1944 (Apr-Jun)	3,023	5,679	3,390
1944 (Jul-Sep)	3,380	7,072	8,915
1944 (Oct-Dec)	2,406	15,005	1,124
1945 (Jan-Mar)	3,264	15,748	

Despite the switch of support from the Chetniks to the Partisans, SOE still sent some support to Mihailović, and the Chetniks continued to assist the Allied cause in selected missions. Of particular note were a number of operations to rescue Allied airmen shot down in combat over enemy territory. In the field, the Germans had taken up the slack created by the defection of the Italians, and Tito moved his headquarters from Jajce to Drvar in western Bosnia.

In mid-1944, both resistance movements were under heavy pressure from the Germans, and both headquarters had to be evacuated in two missions in which Wig had a major hand. The first was called *Operation Repartee*.[256] Interestingly, in a reference to Wig in his book *"Flights of the Forgotten"*, Ken Merrick writes: *"Originally planned as a series of No. 148 Squadron*

---

[255] This data is taken from SOE Balkans History files.
[256] This is a reference from page 193 of the book by Ken Merrick entitled *"Flights of the Forgotten"* (Arms and Armour Press, London, 1989).

Lysander sorties, Wing Commander Francombe and Squadron Leader Noon from No 267 Squadron learned of the operation from Colonel Wigginton on 18 May 1944."

Opération Repartee involved a plan to evacuate 120 personnel of the Mihailović mission using Dakotas. In his book, Merrick provides a full account of the mission, including the careful preparation beforehand involving test runs of the length of the runway to effect a safe landing and take-off. The operation commenced on 28 May, with Francombe landing successfully and meeting up with the heads of the British and American missions, and the Chetnik leaders. It was a close run thing as regards the length of the runway, but they just managed to take off carrying 20 passengers. Francombe signalled Wig's office at Bari to indicate that a smaller number of passengers would be a safer bet. The second Dakota captained by Flight Lieutenant Rice followed this advice and again only just managed to escape with a wheel sinking into the mud which took an hour to get it free. In true British understatement Rice later described the effects of the soft patches as "interesting". With further flights, the operation was completed on 30 May and the evacuees included 44 Allied airmen and army officers who had been taken prisoner in Greece and who had been in Yugoslavia for three years.

The second evacuation mission, which in some ways was more significant, occurred in early June. *Operation Triumph* is one of the few missions for which we have direct evidence of Wig's role.[257] On 25 May 1944, following heavy bombing, the Germans launched an airborne attack by glider and paratroop forces on Tito's headquarters at Drvar, which was a centre for both Tito's staff and the Maclean and Russian Missions. There had been some prior intelligence regarding this attack, including reports of reconnaissance flights by German aircraft, as a result of which staff had been removed from the main encampment. However, the landing of paratroopers was a surprise. Urgent messages for help were sent to the Allied headquarters in Italy, and Wig had responsibility for leading and coordinating evacuation. Although initially surrounded, the personnel evaded immediate capture and were then on the run in the adjacent forests for about ten days. On 29 May, they managed to pass through German lines at a place near Poljice. On the night of 3/4 June, during the space of just 12 hours, all these staff were

---

[257] Details of this operation are drawn from accounts provided in SOE File H5 5-934, HS 7-232 and HS 7-233.

evacuated from the area called Zlosela by a combination of Russian, American and RAF aircraft and brought to Bari. Meanwhile, the British launched a diversionary attack on the adjacent island of Brac which involved nearly 3,000 partisans and 1,000 British commandos.

The scope of this operation was significant. In all, there were over 150 people within Tito's headquarters including a number of key people in the British and Russian missions. The details of this operation involved a complex set of arrangements. Wig liaised with local contacts to prepare an appropriate airfield and supporting facilities, Tito's high command, and representatives of the Allied forces who were to be evacuated, the RAF, USAAF, and Russian air force and a range of insurgents who were acting in support to provide cover and diversionary efforts. It was a mammoth task organised at very short notice. The mission was totally successful. All 150 people and their equipment and materials were safely removed and flown to Bari.[258] After a brief stay, on the evening of 6/7 June, Tito and the British Mission were taken by British destroyers to the island of Vis.

The extent to which these and other missions in 1944 were valued is reflected in a message to air crews sent by the Deputy Air Commander-in-Chief MAAF, Air Marshal Sir John Slessor which reads as follows:[259]

"I must congratulate you on the great job of work you are doing. Please tell all air crews and ground personnel employed on special operations how very greatly their efforts are appreciated. They are doing an immensely valuable job at a critically important time and doing it very well. They should also know that General Korniev, the head of the Russian mission with Tito, has just expressed his appreciation of their help to the Partisans, which he has reported to the Soviet Government."

Although *Operation Triumph* must stand as the peak of Wig's performance in 1944, in the citations relating to his work there is also reference in the previously mentioned letter of thanks from the American General Twining of the 15th USAAF, and his OBE citation, of his help in rescuing American air crews. Recent American versions of the story do not make very flattering reference to SOE involvement, but this does seems to

---

[258] An interesting account of the extraction is provided in SOE File HS 5-934 in a memo from DH to CD in London. A copy is provided in Appendix 15.
[259] This is taken from the SOE Balkans history files.

be the most obvious candidate for his being "Mentioned in Despatches" at this time. *Operation Halyard* was designed to rescue American airman that had been downed in air raids on the Ploesti industrial area in the summer of 1943 and who were in the hands of Mihailović. In early 1944, he contacted the Allies and suggested a rescue. By this time, the Chetniks had lost favour, but SOE did co-operate and, although there were several aborted attempts, a rescue team was inserted on 2 August 1944. In the days ahead, a landing strip was prepared near Pranjani, and on 9 August four C47s arrived to commence an extended evacuation exercise. In only the first two days, *Operation Halyard* successfully retrieved 241 American airmen. Events now took an interesting turn, as Tito's forces arrived in the area and the Chetniks withdrew. However, *Operation Halyard* continued on and off for several months until December 1944 when Wig completed his time at Bari. In all, a total of 417 Allied airmen were airlifted during *Operation Halyard*, of which 343 were Americans.

By mid 1944, there was a major change in the character of Allied support for the Partisans. With Tito established in Vis, the Allies took the opportunity to convene a meeting with the YGE. In July, Tito met with the newly appointed YGE Prime Minister Šubašić and they formed an Agreement to work together. Consequently, Tito was recognised by the YGE as the head of "internal affairs" and, henceforth, Allied missions to Tito's forces were seen as support for a recognised government and regular army rather than a resistance movement. At the same time, Brigadier Maclean now became the Supreme Allied Commander's representative in Yugoslavia with a rear HQ in Bari. In practice, this meant that all requests for support would go through the BAF system to be assessed with other military plans. SOE did however retain a small team for continuing covert operations.

The transition did not go smoothly. Following several attempts to co-ordinate forward plans, on 12 August 1944, there was a top level conference between the Allied leaders and Tito at the AFHQ offices in Caserta, Italy. [260] At the conference, Tito requested an urgent increase in the level of SOE air operations. In response, Air Marshall Slessor indicated that this was not feasible given that Yugoslavia was already receiving 65% of all sorties available from the deployment of 100 aircraft with 2,000 tons delivered in July alone. Tito reluctantly accepted the constraints but indicated that there was a need for improved effectiveness in terms of delivering the right

---

[260] Based on material in SOE File HS 5-869 – Caserta Conference.

supplies to the right place. He offered to nominate a representative who would liaise with No 334 Wing of the BAF, and this was welcomed by the Allies. At this time, Tito also met with Churchill and assured him that he was not going to establish a communist state and would make every effort to keep up the attacks on the Germans.

On 1 September 1944, the Allies launched what was called *Operation Ratweek,* an attempt to hinder the withdrawal of German troops from Serbia. The air attacks organised by Wig were focussed on bridges across the Danube, the Athens-Belgrade railway, and other transport infrastructure. The Russians then entered Yugoslavia. On 14 October 1944, they assisted Tito in liberating Belgrade. With this event, the work of SOE in Yugoslavia effectively came to an end. At this point, Wig's energies were switched to other theatres of war in Italy, and central and Eastern Europe. And, within three months, he would be redeployed to the Far East.

25: A Reflection on Yugoslavia

The history of Allied efforts in Yugoslavia, and the role of SOE, has been the subject of some quite diverse accounts by historians. Given the significant role played by SOE, and Wig's part in it, a comment on the performance of the various parties and the ultimate outcome is warranted.

Until Russian forces assisted the Partisans with their final push to Belgrade in 1944, there were no Allied military forces on the ground. As in Greece, Allied policy and strategy was implemented through the work of SOE working with the resistance. The over-riding Allied objective was to inflict on the Axis powers the maximum penalty for occupying the country, in terms of the resources required to maintain control and the casualties involved. Whilst the British government also had a political agenda of restoring a constitutional monarchy, it would seem that this objective was secondary. Much has been written about other agendas, such as the idea that SOE was used to manipulate a communist takeover. Whilst the staff of SOE included people of all political persuasions, the actual evidence for this in SOE files is slight. Of course, if such a communist plot existed, the perpetrators may have covered their tracks.

Before Wig's involvement in early 1943, the quantum of resources committed to achieving the Allied military objective was modest apart from the insertion of a small number of BLOs. And it wasn't until 1944 that SOE capability became a significant factor. However, by the end of the war, some 215 personnel had been sent to Yugoslavia (compared with 80 in Greece), of whom about 25 were killed. And, back at the bases in Cairo and then Italy, there was a smaller number of dedicated officers who were responsible for providing direction and support through the delivery of huge quantities of military and other supplies by air and by sea over an extended period. There is little doubt that this support was a significant factor in enabling the Allies to meet their military objective, which in turn made a major contribution to the wider defeat of the Germans.

In pursuit of its military objectives, the beneficiaries of SOE support on the ground gradually evolved. Whatever interpretation commentators may wish to place on the turn of events and motives of all the parties, by pursuing a pragmatic approach, SOE were largely successful in achieving their main military objectives. And the eventual decision to side with the Partisans eventually brought to an end what was a damaging civil war. In the view of

Churchill at least, the consequence of this decision, in terms of the form of government established in Yugoslavia after the War, was the price that had to be paid for defeat of the Germans.

And the relationship that was forged with Tito did bring some benefit as regards British foreign policy. Attempts to restore the constitutional monarchy were unsuccessful. But, more importantly, despite their best efforts at the end of the war, Tito resisted Russians attempts to bring Yugoslavia within the Soviet bloc. Even though Russian troops accompanied him in the final act of liberation, he insisted on their withdrawal and they never returned. Thereafter, whilst he established a communist state, he pursued an independent foreign policy and non-aligned status which enabled dealings with the west.

The big loser in all of this was Mihailović. As William Mackenzie has put it "At best, he was a non-belligerent ally rather than a neutral." From all the evidence I have obtained, the contribution of the Chetniks in defeating the Germans was relatively small. They undertook minor sabotage missions, and they did assist with the evacuation of a substantial number of Allied escapees. But, for all sorts of reasons (Mihailović variously blamed lack of SOE support and the hostility of the Partisans) the Chetniks often they failed to deliver. As the representative of the YGE, Mihailović did have an opportunity to become a national leader. However, there is significant evidence that he remained confined to his Serbian roots, that his efforts to attack the Germans were often compromised by his fear of reprisals, that he was even willing to assist the Germans in attacking the Partisans, and that he failed to establish an effective command structure to deliver on implementation of agreed plans.

In making this assessment, there is an obvious comparison between Mihailović and the leader of the moderate resistance group called EDES in Greece. Despite the existence of a similar British supported communist resistance movement, Napoleon Zervas continued to play a part in attacking the Germans in Greece and sustained a loyalty to the Allied cause through to the bitter end. Also, although his forces were relatively small in number, he maintained effective control of the missions to which he was deployed and delivered on his commitments.

In contrast to Mihailović, Tito played a major part in achieving British aims. The Partisans contained and pinned down a significant number of Axis divisions for an extended period, excluding them from deployment to other fronts. Following the Italian armistice, in December 1943, there were no less

242

than 18 German divisions in Yugoslavia. They may not have been crack troops, and casualty rates compared with other fronts were relatively low. But nevertheless this was a major positive outcome for which the Partisans can take most of the credit. Also, during the critical weeks in 1944, the Partisans inflicted considerable disruption to German communications, transport, and infrastructure as their forces withdrew. Finally, the Partisans co-operated with the Allies and the YGE in facilitating the re-establishment of a legitimate government, although the outcome of subsequent elections might not have been exactly what the Foreign Office would have wanted.

From Wig's perspective, as he winged his way to the Far East, he must have had much to reflect upon. Like all the SOE people involved in Yugoslavia over 1943 and 1944, he must have felt conflicted by the many and diverse demands placed upon his team. But he must surely have taken some pride in the part he played in saving Tito and ensuring an Allied victory.

Part Nine: A Test of Character

26: The War in the Far East and Burma

In the final stage of his life, in 1945, Wig lived in Calcutta with responsibility for SOE air operations in Burma. An account of SOE activity in this critical phase of the war in the Far East, and Wig's life and work in Calcutta, are provided in Chapter 27. However, as context, we begin with an account of the origins and content of war in the Far East and Burma.

Prior to 1914, Japan was an ally of Britain and deployed its naval forces against the Germans in support of the Allied cause in World War One. In the post-war settlement, it acquired a variety of German territories in the Pacific such as the Marshall Islands. It also joined the League of Nations as an apparently good international citizen. However, in the 1930s, it pursued an expansionist policy and aggressive action against China. Consequently, it fell foul of the international community, left the League of Nations, and became locked into a trade war with the west. After fruitless negotiations to avoid conflict, on 7 December 1941 Japanese forces attacked Pearl Harbor and a range of other British and American targets. The following day, both Britain and the US declared war on Japan.

With the Allies unprepared for hostilities, in the months that followed, the Japanese armies quickly captured Hong Kong, Indo-China, the Philippines, the Dutch East Indies, parts of Papua New Guinea, and the entire Malay Peninsular culminating in the occupation of Singapore on 15 February 1942. Following the British surrender, the Japanese then advanced towards Burma and Borneo with their eyes on India to the west and Australia to the south.

Given the target of attacking India, and its presence in China, the best route into Burma would have been from the north east. But the Chinese Nationalist army was well entrenched in that part of China and bordering territories. Accordingly, even before they had taken Singapore, on 21 December 1941 a military alliance was formed with the Thai government. The Japanese Fifteenth Army then moved into northern Thailand and, in January 1942, they launched an attack over the jungle-clad mountain ranges into the southern Burmese province of Tenasserim (now known as Tanintharyi) with the aim of taking Rangoon before the onset of the monsoon in May. Thailand was quick to join the Axis Pact on 15 February 1942, even as Singapore was surrendering.[261]

---

[261] Siam changed its name to Thailand on 23 June 1939, but reverted to Siam for four years after World War Two. Thailand was again adopted as the name from 11 May 1949.

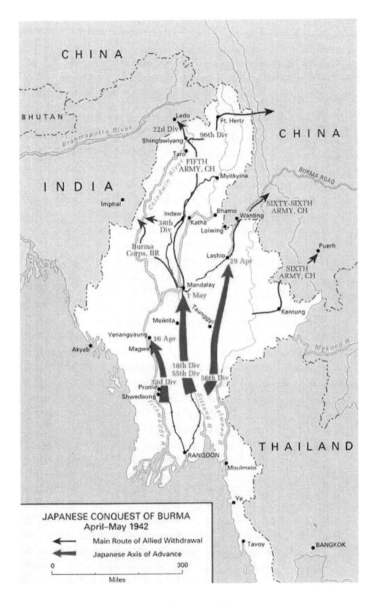

Japanese Conquest of Burma 1942 - wikipedia

248

By March 1942, and before the onset of the monsoon, the Japanese had advanced up the south east leg of Burma through the Mon and Kayin States to take Rangoon, with General Sir Harold Alexander's Burma Army in full retreat to the west where an extended period of hostilities then continued through 1943 and 1944. On 21 March, the Thai and Japanese agreed that the north eastern part of Burma, consisting of the Kayah and Shan States, were to be under Thai control, with the Japanese controlling the rest. On 10 May 1942, the leading elements of the Thai Army crossed the border into the Shan State to engage with the Chinese and, by July, the Chinese had been expelled from the province with many captured or killed. Further south, the Japanese advance had outrun its logistical support and, with the onset of the monsoon, there was a lull in hostilities. The Japanese did not immediately renew their offensive until after the monsoon had ended in late 1942.

Although there was resistance, the Japanese invasion of Burma had some local support from a population living under a relatively unenlightened colonial system.[262] [263] In the early 20th Century, the country had been an outpost (and a backwater) of the British Empire and treated as part of India with only basic infrastructure and services sufficient to enable the exploitation of resources and rudimentary communications. [264] During the 1930s, there had been student riots in support of greater self-rule and, after an extended period of agitation by the Burman population, the Thakin movement had emerged.[265] [266] In response, the British had granted a degree of self-rule. But many Burmans were not satisfied with this limited level of autonomy and some viewed the potential Japanese invasion as a form of liberation. However, the response of the hill peoples to the east of the country

---

[262] This view reflects the account and views of George Orwell in his book entitled *"Burmese Days"* (Harper & Bros, New York, 1934).

[263] At the time of the invasion, the population of Burma was around 17 million, of whom 12 million were ethnic Burmans. The balance was made up of 1.5 million Karens, 1.25 million Shans, 1 million other local ethnic groups including Kachins, 1 million Indians, and 250,000 Chinese.

[264] The staple of the economy was rice, and the main resources included Forestry (especially teak), oil, lead, zinc, silver and wolfram (a compound of iron and manganese otherwise known as tungsten with a variety of uses including lamp filaments).

[265] The name "Thakin" translates as 'master'. It was a term used for the British, but was appropriated by the movement to reflect the aim of Burmese people to become the masters of their own destiny.

[266] This material is based on the Article by Dinyer Godrej entitled "A Short History of Burma" published in New International Magazine issue 410 on 18 April 2008.

(in particular the Karen, Shan, and Kachin) was at best apathetic and mostly hostile. With their own agenda for autonomy, they remained aloof from the Burman moves to "independence", and a significant number were loyal to the British in whom they placed their trust. Their reaction to invasion was therefore to withdraw to the mountains. The response of other ethnic minorities was to escape, with many of the Indians and Chinese fleeing to India.

To ease the challenges of occupation, the invading Japanese army brought with them a force which later became known as the Burma Independence Army ('BIA"). The nucleus of this group were the so-called "30 Comrades" who had been trained by the Japanese in Formosa and Hainin Island and included both U Nu and Aung San who were later to become leaders of the post-war independence movement. Following the invasion, the BIA set up committees to handle local administration whilst, in Rangoon, the Japanese engaged with representatives of the Thakin movement to develop a new constitution for the country. In August 1942 a new national administration was established under the leadership of the Burman leader named Ba Maw, and the BIA was transformed into what became the Burma Defence Army eventually led by Aung San.[267] [268] Although this change to local governance appeared to reflect a degree of autonomy, in reality Burma was now a client state. This involved Japanese control of all resources, and the forced deployment of local labour to building new roads, railways and airfields in support of their war effort. Included was the construction of the Thai-Burma railway during which some 90,000 Burmese as well as many Allied prisoners of war died.

As the dry season returned, the Japanese resumed hostilities and surged north. By the end of 1942, they had occupied most of Burma. For them, 1943 then became a period of consolidation ahead of the attack on India. In response, with limited resources, all the British could do was retreat and prepare to fight another day. Nevertheless, there were some concerted efforts to undermine Japanese control.[269] In early 1943, there was a military (as

---

[267] Initially, Aung Sun co-operated with the Japanese before switching loyalty to the Allied cause. After the war, he became the leader of the country, and negotiated independence. He was eventually assassinated. He is father of the leader of Aung San Suu Kyi, whose National League for Democracy won power in Myanmar in 2015.

[268] Less than a year later, Burma was quite erroneously declared to be an independent country.

[269] A full account may be found in the book entitled *"Burma: The Longest War"* by Louis Allen, (Dent, London, 1984).

opposed to covert) initiative under the command of Brigadier (later Major General) Orde Wingate. In February, he obtained permission to lead a long-range penetration unit known as the *Chindits*.[270] In a campaign codenamed *Operation Longcloth*, some 3,000 uniformed troops were infiltrated through Japanese lines, and they marched deep into northern Burma towards the Chinese border. As a result of this campaign, working with Chinese troops and local Kachin Hill Tribes, they were successful in cutting the railway line for at least two weeks. But they suffered heavy casualties, and by late April 1943 most of them had trickled back to India.[271] [272]

In August 1943, the Allies reinvigorated their command structure in the Far East. In particular they created South East Asia Command ("SEAC"), a combined military structure responsible for the whole South-East Asian Theatre, and in November Admiral Lord Louis Mountbatten was appointed as Supreme Allied Commander. The organisation and competence of Allied forces in the Far East were also significantly upgraded. In particular, under the leadership of Lieutenant General William Slim, the training, equipment, health and morale of Allied troops under the British XIVth Army based in India steadily improved, as did the reliability and capacity of the communication system in North-Eastern India.[273] In the following twelve months, this army was to become a formidable force, capable of both withstanding the anticipated Japanese onslaught, and eventually launching a massive counter attack.

In the meantime, during 1943, the Allied cause amongst the local Burmese population was not entirely lost. In addition to the significant covert operations behind enemy lines in the north of the country involving the

---

[270] Chindit is a corrupted form of the Burmese mythical beast called *Chinthay*, statues of which guard some Buddhist temples.

[271] In March 1944, Wingate undertook a second campaign in which a group was inserted to work closely with the American General Joseph Stilwell whose Chinese army was advancing out of China into the north east of Burma. This time, they established fortified bases behind enemy lines, out of which they conducted offensive patrols and blocking operations to counter the Japanese advance northwards. However, this mission was slowly wound up after the death of Wingate in a USAAF plane crash on 24 March 1944. A more extensive review of the Wingate experience, in a contemporaneous assessment, is available in SOE File HS 1-46.

[272] There is a recent biography of Wingate, entitled *"Orde Wingate: Unconventional Warrior from the 1920s to 21st Century"* by Simon Anglim, (Pen and Sword, London, 2015).

[273] See the biography entitled *"Slim – The Standard-bearer"* by Ronald Lewin (Leo Cooper, London, 1976), and Slim's memoirs, *"Defeat into Victory: Battling Japan in Burma and India 1942-45"* (Cooper Square Press, London, 2000).

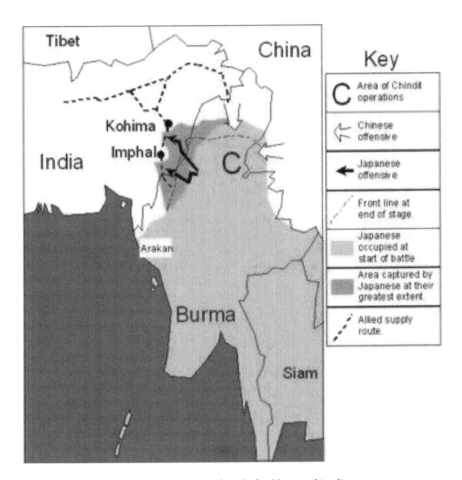

Japanese Attack on India 1944 - wikipedia

Kachin Hill Tribes, there were also sporadic attacks by BLO led teams of Karen and Shan levies.[274] SOE provided support to all this resistance activity, with a range of airborne missions.[275] Also, after the experience of forced labour and failure to achieve independence, the majority Burman population were beginning to re-assess their support for the Japanese. In particular, the Burmese leader of the BDA, Aung San, had become disillusioned and was

---

[274] The words "levy" and "levies" refer to the military formations of native citizens, usually under British officers.

[275] More details are provided in Chapter 27 which covers Force 136 operations.

considering the possibility of changing sides.

After many months of preparation, in early 1944, the Japanese made their ill-fated attack on India, crossing the border on 22 March. After two months of brutal fighting, their expansion plans were finally halted on the battlefields at Imphal and Kohima in the north east of India. On 31 May, they retreated back across the border, on 20 June the siege of Imphal was lifted, and on 22 June the Battle of Kohima ended with an overwhelming British victory. The battle at Kohima gave rise to the famous epitaph which appears on so many memorials of the time, and which remains the wording used to close all meetings of branches of the Royal British Legion:

"When you go home
Tell them of us, and say,
For their tomorrow
We gave our today"

While the Japanese had been pursuing this ill-fated attack on India, they were also engaged on a second front in the north east of Burma. In a series of attacks by Chinese troops, supported by British led local Kachin insurgents, the Allies had seized the airfield at Myitkyina which provided an "air-bridge" from India to Chungking in China. In other operations, Japanese military infrastructure and communications systems in the north of the country were severely damaged. Having achieved the aim of establishing a line of support for their battle with communist forces, the Chinese resisted British requests to pursue the Japanese and slowly withdrew, but their intervention had significantly assisted the wider Allied cause.

With the Allied offensives in Europe in full flow, the Allies now contemplated the liberation of Burma with an attack from India. From experience in the European theatres, they knew that the most effective strategy was to integrate the efforts of military campaigning with clandestine resistance. As regards the military, the army mostly consisted of Indians, Ghurkas from Nepal, and more than 100,000 troops posted from colonial Africa. On the covert side, SOE staff were now becoming available from Italy and the Balkans to support the resistance. However, the deployment of guerrillas was quite complex because the range of players was diverse. In the north east, the Allied led Kachins had already been active. To the south-east, in the Karen Hills, there was a huge potential ready to be activated, but this would require the deployment of many BLOs to provide leadership. To a lesser extent there was also the potential for similar work involving Hill Tribes in the Shan States to the east. Then there was the main body of Burmans consisting of several groups. The Burmese Defence Army ("BDA"), which was based in the central area of Burma, were ready to change sides. They had already been joined by a number of BLOs, and their leader Aung Sung began asking for arms and supplies. The other Burman resistance force was the Anti-Fascist Organisation (AFO) in Rangoon which had strong communist leanings. For some time, they had maintained contact with SOE through an officer called Eric Battersby and they also requested the supply of military materiel. Finally, there was also a Burmese government in exile based at Simla in India.

Taking into account all these factors, by late 1944 Mountbatten had developed an invasion plan. However, to proceed, he needed the approval of the British Cabinet and military in London, not only for the advance of Allied armies from India but also for a range of SOE operations designed to activate the resistance. This did not go smoothly. When the Burmese government in exile heard of the plans to arm the locals, they were concerned about the long-term political implications and sent representatives from Simla to SEAC HQ in Kandy to argue their case for caution. But Mountbatten got his way and, in February 1945, London approved the full-scale invasion of Burma with permission to support all resistance groups. This was subject to certain protocols which provided that the resistance should act in accordance with military objectives. The British also reserved the right to prosecute anyone found to have been guilty of war crimes whilst previously supporting the Japanese.

In the final phase of the war, the British strategy was to take Rangoon before the start of the monsoon season which traditionally commenced on 15 May. The role to be played by the BDA and the Karens proved to be vital in the eventual success of the military campaign.[276] [277] In early 1945, a series of pre-emptive attacks were launched. On 3 January, the Allied force occupied

---

[276] As we will see in Chapter 27, much of this activity was dependent on the air operations managed by Wig.

[277] After the war, the role of the SOE led Karens was significantly under-rated and quickly forgotten by the Allied leadership. More than anything, this was because the leaders of the Burmese ethnic majority BDA, who were responsible for negotiating independence, got to write the history of the time! As Churchill told Roosevelt and Stalin at the Tehran Conference in 1943: *"History will judge us kindly"*. When asked how he could be so sure, he responded: *"Because I shall write the history"*. And he did.

Akyab Island off the west coast, and on 21 January, British troops landed on the adjacent Ramree Island. These targets were essential because they would provide airfields for Allied planes in support of the impending attack on central Burma. In the meantime, as an initial defensive move, the Japanese retreated across to the east side of the Irrawaddy River. The scene was now set for the invasion. The main Allied military group was Slim's 14th Army, which entered Burma from India to the north-west in early February. By 20 March 1945, they had re-taken Mandalay in central Burma, and embarked on the 650 kms journey to take Rangoon. It was at this critical point that SOE's enhanced air operations capability came into play and, to appreciate subsequent events, it's important to understand the physical landscape. There are two major river systems in Burma which run north south and are separated by the Pegu Yomas Mountains. These are the Irrawaddy to the west and the Sittang to the east.[278] On 22 March 1945, the Allies began their advance down the Irrawaddy River valley experiencing stiff resistance from the Japanese at Pyawbwe. The attackers were initially halted by a strong defensive position, but a flanking move by tanks and mechanised infantry struck the Japanese from the rear and shattered them.

The Allies then advanced into the Sittang Valley, moving towards Toungoo and its strategically placed airfield which was another 200 kms away and only 240 kms from Rangoon. It was at this point that covert operations were to play a major part in the fortunes of the 14th Army. On 28 March, following extensive support from SOE, the BDA rose in revolt against the Japanese transforming itself in the process into the Burma National Army ("BNA"). Within a short period, they killed over 700 Japanese and prevented them from attacking the 14th Army from the west. At around the same time, again with huge SOE input, the Karen guerrillas launched a full scale uprising in the east, preventing troops from the reorganised Japanese Fifteenth Army reaching the strategic facilities and airfield at Toungoo before the Allies captured it.[279] These major assaults enabled the 14th Army to advance down the main road to Rangoon with relatively little organised military opposition.

On 25 April, the leading Allied troops engaged with Japanese rear guards north of Pegu (now called Bago), 70 kms north of Rangoon. In defence of

---

[278] Sittang is now spelt Sittaung.
[279] See pages 186-88 in the book entitled *"SOE in the Far East"* by Charles Cruickshank, OUP, Oxford, 1983.

Rangoon, General Kimura had formed a scratch formation consisting of regular troops, naval personnel and even Japanese civilians into what was known as the 105th Independent Mixed Brigade. This group managed to delay the British advance until 30 April whilst the Japanese evacuated the Rangoon area. However, on 1 May 1945, in *Operations Dracula and Castle*, the Allies launched a sea-borne and air attack on Rangoon, with a Gurkha battalion being dropped by parachute at Elephant Point to the west.[280] They quickly cleared the Japanese rear guard forces from the mouth of the Rangoon River and, on the next day, the 26th Indian Infantry Division landed by ship.

When the Allies arrived in Rangoon, they discovered that the Japanese had indeed evacuated in the previous week, leaving the place in quite a mess.[281] Ahead of schedule, on the afternoon of 2 May 1945, the monsoon rains began in full force, but the door was now open for the arrival of the 14th Army. On 6 May, the leading troops of the 17th and 26th Indian divisions met at Hlegu, 45 kms north of Rangoon.

The end of the war in Burma came with the Battle of the Sittang Bend and the so-called Japanese "Breakout". Between early July and early August, surviving elements of the Japanese Army attempted to escape eastwards across the Pegu Yomas Mountains to join other Japanese troops retreating from British forces. As a preliminary, the Japanese Thirty-Third Army attacked Allied positions in the Sittang Bend, near the mouth of the river, to distract the Allies.[282] However, the British had been alerted to the break-out attempt and the Japanese were almost completely routed, with heavy losses and some formations being totally wiped out. In total the Japanese suffered around 14,000 casualties, with well over half being killed, while British forces suffered only 95 killed and 322 wounded. The attempt to escape, and the ensuing battle, became the last significant land battle of the Western powers in the Second World War.

Subsequently, Japanese troops began a slow and painful retreat to the east, harried by the efforts of the Allied *Operation Character* of which more in the next chapter. The main Japanese army were finally expelled from Burma by the end of July, and on 6 August 1945, the atomic bomb was dropped on

---

[280] A full account of both these operations is provided in SOE File HS 1-46.

[281] Again, an account of the chaos left by the Japanese is provided in SOE File HS 1-46.

[282] See the book entitled *"Sittang: The Last Battle"*, by Louis Allen (The Book Service, London, 1973).

Hiroshima. This was quickly followed by a second bomb dropped on Nagasaki on 9 August. Six days later, Emperor Hirohito announced Japan's surrender and the war in the Far East was over, with 15th August 1945 declared as VJ Day. However, this did not necessarily mean the end of hostilities on the ground as subsequent events, including the crash of Dakota KN584 carrying Wig, will reveal. Japanese troops were still present in the jungle, and the remnants did not surrender until 13 September.

At the end of this victorious campaign, staff of the 14th Army generously acknowledged that Force 136, in their support to the BNA and Karen resistance movement, had made a major contribution towards their success.[283] Wig's role as the officer in command of air operations was also specifically acknowledged. The respect for the contribution of the Karen levies to these events is reflected in a tribute made by General Slim in mid-1945. He said that:

> "In the Karenni Hills we also had levies that played their part. We left an officer there in 1942, but unfortunately this initial party were all either killed or captured by the Japanese.[284] In spite of that, the gallant people kept in touch with us and later we were able to put back a very considerable number of British officers – somewhere in the number of 100 – who organised a very large force which was armed and fed from the air by us. The Karen then made a really great contribution, because I gave them the task of delaying the 15th Japanese Division which was trying to get into Toungoo before we did. They delayed the Japanese by 7 days and thus enabled us to get to Toungoo first. The levies have rendered us a good and faithful service and have done a considerable amount towards the restoration of Burma."[285]

Finally, following the surrender of the Japanese, the Allies engaged in a number of post-war activities. Of particular interest to our story is the RAPWI (Relief of Allied Prisoners of War and Internees) project. The operation was approved on 28 August 1945, and Wig was personally involved in implementation immediately thereafter. Indeed, it was this

---

[283] This reflects the comments of Bickham Sweet-Escott on pages 247-249 of his book entitled "*Baker Street Irregular*".
[284] A reference to Hugh Seagrim of which more in the next chapter.
[285] This is taken from SOE Burma History files.

project which led to him to make his final trip to Burma which led to his untimely death. Further information on this activity is covered in the next chapter.

27: Calcutta Days

In his book "Baker Street Irregular", Bickham Sweet-Escott noted that *"it is an elementary principle of warfare that guerrillas work best when working in unison with regular troops."* This dictum would come to its fruition for the Allies in the Far East.

British covert operations commenced in 1940, with the establishment of what was called the *India Mission*. The headquarters were at Meerut near Delhi, and initially its activities were largely confined to India and neighbouring Burma, with a separate mission in Singapore.[286] Given the events in Europe, the Far East was not a priority for the Allies and the organisation was starved of resources. From early 1941, the head of the India Mission was a civilian named Colin Mackenzie (later to become Sir Colin Mackenzie). From all accounts, Mackenzie was an exceptional character. He was a classical scholar, obtained a First in English at Cambridge, and was immensely well read. He had lost a leg in World War One, but he was widely travelled, and he combined the unusual gifts of imagination, and good judgement with a personality of great charm.[287]

In 1942, and following the Japanese invasion of Burma, the scope of operations was expanded, with SOE bases established in Calcutta and Colombo. And on 8 August, Mackenzie received a Directive expanding his remit which read as follows.[288]

> *"On your arrival in India in 1941, you were attached to the Viceroy of India, in order to assist the government of India. You are now called upon to do work of a nature, and in territories beyond the sphere of the Viceroy, in which you must assist and be controlled by the Commander in Chief ("C-in-C")."*

The Directive went on to indicate that, because of the remoteness from London, the India Mission would need to work within broad policy rather than receive operating instructions, and that the nature of the work was to undertake activities which were *"outside the scope or capacity of any overt*

---

[286] The Singapore staff transferred to India in February 1942.

[287] This characterisation is provided by Bickham Sweet-Escott on page 228 of his book *"Baker Street Irregular"*.

[288] The source of the information in this section is SOE Files HS 7-111 to 114.

organisation" subject to two limitations:

a)   Tasks must either be initiated by the Viceroy or the C-in-C, or (if initiated by the Mission) receive the approval of the Viceroy and/or the C-in-C as appropriate.

b)   Mackenzie was to be mindful of the physical limitation imposed by time, space, people and equipment. He must not undermine his effectiveness by taking on more than he could manage.

The upshot of these guidelines was that SOE would be the servant of two masters, political and military, an arrangement all too common for the organisation. The Directive then identified the scope of operations within the Far East as follows:

Country	Type of Activity					
Afghanistan, Tibet, Eastern Persia	Subversive Political Activity	Sabotage	Subversive Propaganda			Support to military in the event of war
India (In event of invasion)		Sabotage	Counter subversive Propaganda	Organisation of guerrillas	Establishment of secret communications	
Burma		Sabotage		Assistance to anti-Japanese elements	Establishment of secret communications and signals	
Thailand, Indo-China, Malaya, Indonesia, Pacific Islands and Australia	**US mandate from Chungking in China and Australia. SOE to stay clear.**					

In the period that followed, SOE became active in each of these theatres. However, in the account which follows, the focus will be on Burma because from February 1945 this is where Wig was engaged.

Covert operations in Burma began in earnest with the establishment of a group called GSI (Z) with their base in Calcutta. Z Force as they eventually became known consisted of a number of agents who were planted in parts of Burma where they could live without being noticed with the aim of establishing good working relations with the locals.[289] Most of them were ordered to go north from where they then fed back intelligence on Japanese movements and other relevant information.

As the Japanese advanced through Burma in 1942, SOE authorised one person to stay on as a British Liaison Officer in the south of the country. Major Hugh Seagrim, two other British officers, a Karen officer, and a group of Karen forces were left behind to live in the Karen Hills. In many respects, Seagrim operated like Orde Wingate in the north, mounting guerrilla attacks using "hit and run" tactics, albeit with virtually no support from Calcutta. However, whilst Wingate undertook what might be regarded as regular army work, Seagrim worked under cover. In the course of his activity, he laid the ground work for later SOE success in terms of organising the local resistance forces, and he became a much loved and revered person amongst Karen people despite a series of brutal Japanese reprisal attacks on Karen villages.[290]

In 1943, SOE sought to supplement the unit led by Seagrim. In February, in *Operation Harlington*, a reconnaissance party led by Major James Nimmo was dropped into the Karenni Hills. The party was well received and progress was soon made in establishing a number of embryonic operational units who would be able to contribute once the Allies returned to Burma. In the meantime, Seagrim and his Karen forces continued a concerted campaign of sabotage against the Japanese occupation, supported by SOE air operations. Whilst developing contacts with the Karen, SOE also inserted BLOs to link up with the Kachins in the north who became active in gathering intelligence and sabotage operations. As mentioned in Chapter 26, this included co-operation with Wingate and the Chinese.

By the end of 1943, the resistance was on an advanced footing and the position is summarised in a report in SOE Files, from which the following is a modified extract.[291]

> "*SOE's role is to activate latent anti-Japanese potential and, by propaganda, personal leadership and individual example, turn it into a*

---

[289] GSI stands for General Staff Intelligence.

[290] He is revered to this day. In my visits to World War Two veterans in 2014, I met several octogenarians who mentioned and praised this man.

[291] This material, prepared in December 1943, was prepared by BLOs and is taken from SOE Files HS 1-310 and HS 1–320.

military weapon of significant proportions. The people that inhabit the hill tracts which form the eastern boundary of Burma, the Kachins and the Karens, have for the most part remained loyal and, even where loyalty has wavered, they will rise up in support when the Allies return. The areas inhabited by these people have not been greatly infiltrated by the Japanese or the Burmans. Little is known of the Shan. The Burmans have started to feel the effects of Japanese imperialism, but have not yet reached the stage where they are willing to actively participate in assisting the return of the British. It is expected that the Chinese and Indian communities will welcome an opportunity to assist in the ousting of the Japanese."

The report then goes on to outline the future strategy for SOE in Burma as follows:

a)   *To establish a line of friendly territory throughout the hills bordering the east of Burma from which armed irregulars can harass the rear and flank of the Japanese and disrupt their lines of communication, and to prepare for reception of airborne formations for similar operations.*

b)   *To re-arm the Delta ex-Army Karens and police, and to win back such of them as have been coerced into supporting the BIA, with a view to harassing the Japanese in the Delta at the time of the main Allied advance.[292]*

c)   *To contact the Burman population in the plains with a view to turning them against the Japanese and harassing their lines of communication.*

d)   *To sabotage lines of communications in the main centres of population using agents placed in such centres.*

e)   *To slow down Japanese communications, by interference with Indian dock and railway labour around the main centres of communication.*

f)   *In performance of these tasks to inspire throughout the country confidence in the ultimate return of the government in exile.*

g)   *To report such intelligence of a military, political or economic*

---

[292] The "Delta" refers to the area around Rangoon where the Irrawaddy and Sittang enter the Indian Ocean.

nature as may be gathered in the performance of these tasks."

Finally, the document provides a status report on the following current operations all of which were receiving SOE support:

a)   The *Task Mission* encompassing *Operation Dilwyn*, and *Operation Spiers* working with the Kachin and *Operation Harlington* working with the Karen.[293]

b)   The *Capable Mission* also working with the Karen.

c)   The *Mahout Mission* aimed to engage Indians working in the Rangoon docks.

d)   The mission to maintain regular contact with anti-Japanese elements in the Burman community, through the work of a Lt Col Edgar Peacock.

Despite these plans, and before much progress could be made with the Karen, in early 1944 the Japanese mounted a major sweep through the hills to liquidate the SOE teams. As a result, the Seagrim units were eliminated and, to prevent further bloodshed, on 15 March 1944, he surrendered himself to the Japanese forces. He and eight of his Karen companions were then executed by the Japanese on 22 September 1944 in Rangoon.[294] After a period of recuperation, the remnant force of Lt Col Peacock and others were redeployed to *Operation Character* which was launched at the end of the year.

In late 1944, the Supreme Allied Commander Mountbatten persuaded Mackenzie to transfer SOE headquarters to Kandy in Ceylon so that it was adjacent to the new headquarters of the South East Asia Command ("SEAC").[295] At this point the SOE operation became known as Force 136

---

[293] Sadly, both Major James Nimmo, and Captain Eric McCrindle who joined *Operation Harlington* in December 1944, were captured and executed by the Japanese.

[294] He was posthumously awarded the George Cross in 1946 for gallantry in captivity. In late 1944, the remnants of Seagrim's force, which at this stage included Peacock, were withdrawn.

[295] The SOE facilities, consisting of "basha" huts, were located on the far side of Kandy from Mountbatten's headquarters in the King's Pavilion of the Peradiniya botanical gardens. The SOE staff lived in a variety of residences, including the Riversdale Bungalow, which was home for Mackenzie, John Anstey and Bickham Sweet-Escott. The Riversdale Bungalow has been made famous through its use in the film *"The Bridge over the River Kwai"*. The bungalow was used for the scene where the British agent is interviewed before insertion.

or GS I (K) *(General Staff Intelligence – Kandy)* and it was quickly organised into two main operational units.

The first of these units, which was called *Group A,* had its headquarters in Calcutta, and covered Burma, Thailand, China, and French Indo-China. The head of Group A was Lt Colonel Gavin Stewart who was also Sir Colin Mackenzie's deputy.[296] Initially, the head of operations was Lt Colonel R A Critchley who later had command of one of the *Operation Character* sectors, called *Mongoose,* which is the area where Wig met his death. *Group B,* which was headed by Colonel Chris Hudson, was based in Colombo, and covered Malaya, Anglo-Dutch Territories including Indonesia, PNG, and other island territories in the Indian Ocean. As well as supporting Allied military operations, Group B undertook a number of joint operations with SOA (Special Operations Australia) who were based in Melbourne.[297]

In early 1945, these groups were supported by a wide range of resources. There were a number of related country sections collecting intelligence and processing requests for assistance, and there were Special Duties aircraft based at airfields at Jessore (near Calcutta) at Chittagong in India, and at Sigrye and Mineriya in Ceylon. There were bases for naval operations in Madras and Trincamalee (Ceylon), and storage facilities in Bombay, Poona, and Jubbulpore. Parachute training was undertaken at Rawalpindi, and there was a jungle training facility at Horana near Colombo named ME 25. The main military forces with which Force 136 worked at this time were the 14th Army which was under the control of Allied Land Forces South East Asia ("ALFSEA") based at Calcutta, the RAF deployed through SEAC in Kandy, the Royal Navy controlled by the Admiralty in London, and supplies and transport controlled were from GHQ in Delhi.

In January 1945, the Force 136 leadership were keen to recruit the best people available from Europe where SOE activity was winding down. In particular, they sought military staff with experience in covert operations. In the case of Group A, Lt Colonel Stewart identified Wig as one such expert.[298] The offer to take up the position of "Head of Air Operations" in Calcutta

---

[296] Gavin Stewart is the person after whom the author is named, vis Gavin Sydney Stewart Wigginton.

[297] One of their most famous missions, *Operation Jaywick*, which involved a successful attack on Japanese shipping in Singapore in 1943, was made into a Mini Series on Australian Channel 10 called *"Heroes"*.

[298] According to Sweet-Escott, on page 240 of his book *"Baker Street Irregular"*, Wig's appointment was vital and his expertise was indispensable.

came to Wig when he was still in Italy.[299] According to material in his SOE Personnel File, the War Office did not handle this transfer very well. For some reason, before taking up the position, he was temporarily deployed to a "holding" unit with the prospect of demotion! As correspondence in the personnel file in his own fair own hand indicates, he was not happy with this bureaucratic manoeuvre, and eventually received a fairly grudging acknowledgement that he was still a Lt Colonel from a man named Major Mackenzie. In any event, he formally left SOE in Italy on 7 February 1945 and, after three weeks in England during which time the author was conceived (!), joined SOE Force 136 in Calcutta on 28 February 1945.

The move to Calcutta (now called Kolkata) would have been quite a shock to the system. After three weeks in the depth of an English winter, Wig arrived in a climate which is typically "tropical wet and dry". In late February, daily maximums are around 30C with 60% humidity. However, although the climate was uncomfortable, the city offered decent living conditions for Europeans. It had previously been the capital of the Indian empire and was still a major centre.[300]

Wig lived in a suburb called Chowringhee.[301] The exact address is not known, but this was a well-heeled part of the city which included some notable mansions, department stores, St Paul's Anglican Cathedral, a number of clubs at which serving officers were welcome subject to certain conditions, and some famous restaurants. In my research for this book, I came across the menu for an Italian restaurant in Chowringhee Road called Firpo's as shown in the picture which Wig may well have frequented. I was intrigued by the very British nature of the food on offer in 1945 - steak and kidney pudding, Melton Mowbray pie, and roast lamb, new potatoes, and green peas!

Life in Wig's office was very different from his experience in Italy. In particular, management of office relationships was complicated by the multicultural nature of the staff. There were people from Hindu, Muslim, Christian, and Buddhist faiths, all with different customs and requiring

---

[299] Material on Group A activities in the chapter has been drawn from a number of SOE Files, including File HS 1-310 which contains a brief history.

[300] New Delhi became the capital on 13 February 1931.

[301] SOE records show that Wig had an account at the branch of Lloyds Bank in that suburb, as well as the Market Square in Nottingham where all members of the Wigginton clan have had accounts from time to time since the 1930s. The Lloyds Bank in Calcutta was located in Virginia House which used to be owned by the Imperial Tobacco (India) Ltd and was in the main thoroughfare alongside the New Club (founded 1884).

265

Chowringhee Square, Calcutta 1945 - oldkolkatablogspot.com

separate eating and living arrangements. However, from all accounts, it was an amenable environment which Wig would probably have enjoyed. Having said that, after three years overseas he may well have had enough of everything foreign. Indeed, in his correspondence with Eunice at the time, he was certainly contemplating life after the war back in England home and beauty.

Wig's new boss, Lt Colonel Gavin Stewart, had been in India since 1942 and, in the early days, he had surrounded himself with a range of largely non-military assistants recruited from the management of local British businesses who were referred to as "Quai-Hais".[302] Despite the pressures of war time work, this team maintained a civilised existence and, according to Sweet-Escott, Stewart in particular was famous for entertaining people with his

---

[302] This is a Hindi term which translates to "Who's there". It was used to describe the ruling Anglo-Indians, and derives from their propensity to call for a servant.

266

curries including a famous spicy Duck and peas. The original SOE office was located in an area of Calcutta called Ballygunge, and in a house which was previously a place of "ill repute". The main airfield used by Wig for his air operations was at Jessore (some 100kms distant). From examining his SOE personnel file, it is clear that Wig spent much of his time in the Calcutta office. However, his responsibilities took him to Kandy in Ceylon where SOE worked closely with staff from the SEAC headquarters, and included numerous field trips to the airfields at Akyab and Ramree Island on the west coast of Burma, Rangoon, and Toungoo airfield in central Burma. As his direct superior officer Colonel Stephen Cumming said at the time of his death:[303]

LUNCHEON served from 12 noon to 2-30 p.m.

STEAK & KIDNEY PUDDING, Rs. 1/8
HAMBURG STEAK & ONIONS, Rs. 1/8

Luncheon, Rs. 2/12

(3 Course with Coffee)

1 Consomme Frappe Or 2 SCOTCH BROTH
3 FILETS DE POMFRET FRITS SAUCE TARTARE
Or 4 Prawn Mayonnaise
5 ROAST LAMB, NEW POTATOES & GREEN PEAS
Or 6 SAUSAGES & MASHED POTATOES
(7) COLD MEATS, 7 Roast Fowl & Ham or Roast Duck
8 Roast Sirloin of Beef 9 Roast Pork
10 Roast Lamb 11 Roast Saddle of Mutton
12 Pressed Beef 13 Spiced Ham
14 Melton Mowbray Pie 15 Steak & Kidney Pie
16 Chicken & Ham Pie
17 GATEAU MILLEFEUILLES
18 COFFEE 19 FRUITS

A. FIRPO LTD, Caterers
Calcutta, Friday, the 30th, March, 1945.

Menu from Firpo's Restaurant, Calcutta, 1945 - oldkolkatablogspot.com

"Wig arrived in the Far East at a time when we were very heavily involved in the campaign in Burma. His knowledge and experience were of the greatest possible assistance to us. In fact, much of our ultimate success as a force in that campaign must be credited to the excellence of his work. Later, when the war against Japan ended (August 1945), we were given many tasks in connection with bringing aid to the Allied Prisoners of War and Internees in Japanese hands, and much of the responsibility for arrangements in this connection fell on him. He tackled the many problems involved with his usual keenness."[304]

Similarly, in his comments on Force 136, SOE officer J G Beevor who knew Wig through the office in Italy as well as Kandy, wrote:

"SOE in South East Asia had the benefit of several favourable factors

---

[303] This is taken from a letter to Wig's wife in late 1945.
[304] A reference to the RAPWI Project.

including the availability of several senior SOE officers redeployed from Europe, conspicuously Brigadier John Anstey, Colonel Bickham Sweet-Escott, and the Air Operations expert Lt Colonel Sydney Wigginton.[305] [306]

The other favourable factors in the South East Asia theatre of war cited by Beevor were the supreme commander, Mountbatten, the continuity of SOE leadership (the organisation had retained the same commander, Sir Colin Mackenzie, from start to finish), and the pro-Allied anti-Japanese attitude of some but not all the indigenous populations. In particular, this was a reference to the Hill Tribesmen in Burma, the Karens in the south and the Kachins in the north. It should also be noted that, just ahead of Wig's arrival in Calcutta, the fleet of 357 Squadron was upgraded, with the old Mk III Liberators being replaced by the Mark VI, the Mark III Dakotas being replaced by the Mark IV, and the last of the Hudsons being retired.

From the above comments, the contribution of Wig to the great success in Burma cannot be underestimated. As the senior officer responsible for air operations during the critical months between February and May 1945, his work was a major factor in the successful advance of the 14th Army from the north to Rangoon. During this period, Wig was responsible for implementing countless operations to supply BLOs, weapons and other materiel to the Karen resistance movement as part of *Operation Character*. This work sustained their resistance to Japanese occupation and their eventual rebellion. At the same time, Wig's team provided air operations support to the BDA in the west and central area of Burma and the AFO around Rangoon.

To handle the planning of Group A operations at this time, SOE established the *Clandestine Operations Committee*.[307] During this critical period of the war, and until the Japanese were defeated in August, this committee met weekly at Advance HQ ALFSEA in Calcutta.[308] Chaired by Brigadier Graham Scott, meetings were attended by staff officers of

---

[305] This quote is taken from page 224 of the book by J G Beevor's entitled *Recollections and Reflections 1940-45"*, The Bodley Head (London, 1981).

[306] Bickham Sweet-Escott provides a range of insights throughout his book entitled *"Baker Street Irregular.*

[307] This account, including the Terms of Reference drafted by Major General CP Walsh, is based on material in SOE File HS 1-298.

[308] ALFSEA stands for Allied Land Forces South East Asia.

ALFSEA HQ, SOE, OSS, E Force, Z Force, and ISLD.[309] The SOE representatives were Gavin Stewart, Wig, and Wig's two team leaders who were Majors Hodgart and Jones.[310] The committee had oversight of all covert operations in Burma, reviewing current missions and issues, and making decisions about the future deployment of people and supplies. The terms of reference for the Committee make interesting reading, and reflect the complexity of co-ordinating a variety of clandestine groups whose requirements were quite different and at times even conflicting. The bodies for whose activities they had responsibility were as follows.

Force 136/American OSS
a)   Provision of "medium range" intelligence
b)   Sabotage
c)   Organisation of resistance movements
d)   D Division operations designed to deceive the Japanese.

ISLD (Inter-Service Liaison Department – Foreign Office Secret Intelligence Service)
a)   Provision of "long range" strategic intelligence, requiring the dropping of intelligence agents and supplies
b)   *Once an area is declared as a battle field*, maintenance of existing intelligence operations with information to be supplied to Commander in Chief ALFSEA.

Z Force
a)   Provision of "short range" intelligence for specific purposes
b)   Insertion of "pathfinder" patrols, ahead of major military missions
c)   Assistance to Force 136 and OSS in rapid transmission of intelligence.

E Force
Planning the support and rescue of prisoners.

---

[309] E Force was a unit set up in the Far East to organise the rescue of prisoners and evaders, similar to MI19.
[310] Family members would especially enjoy the eventual correction of Wig's name in the Minutes of these weekly meetings which is initially spelt Wiggington with a correction using a primitive form of "white-out" to exclude the extra "g".

In co-ordinating the work of these bodies, the rules of engagement included some important constraints such as the following:

1. P Division (a managing unit within SEAC) was responsible for co-ordinating civil, military and clandestine operations.

2. *Outside a battle area*, command and control was exercised by Supreme Allied Commander (SAC) through P Division.

3. *Within a battle area*, clandestine operations were to be designed to assist military operations and could not proceed without military approval. SOE/OSS were permitted to suggest operations or mount them in response to military requests.

4. Operations involving points of major policy which have repercussions beyond the immediate control of one military commander were be referred to ALFSEA HQ.

5. Operations involving points of major policy which have political implications were to be referred to the SAC.

As can been seen, these provisions were built on all the learning acquired in the European theatres regarding the effective management of operations with military, diplomatic and covert dimensions.

The details of Wig's achievements during this period are probably best told through the work of the various missions in the field to which his team provided logistical support. As related in some detail in a number of books, there were a large number of SOE operations during the period (February to September 1945) all of which would have received men and supplies provided through Wig's unit.[311] A full listing of the main operations and related activities are provided in the Appendix 2, and it should be noted that missions were sometimes used for more than one purpose, with the main task supplemented with other activities such as propaganda through the dropping of leaflets, and replenishment of basic operational supplies.

The operations fall into four main mission categories, all of which were active during Wig's time:

---

[311] *"The Moonlight War- The Story of Clandestine Operations in SE Asia, 1944-45"* by Terence O'Brien, and *"Tigers Burning Bright"* by Alan Ogden are two notable sources.

a)   Diversionary Action Mission
    • *Operation Cloak*

b)   Guerrilla Support Missions
    • *Operation Character* – eastern Karen Hills - Karen
    • *Operation Nation* – central Pegu Yomas Hills – Burmese National Army
    • *Operation Dilwyn* – northern hills - Kachin
    • *Operation Hainton* – east of Mandalay – Shan
    • *Operation Nutshell* – south of Moulmein during Japanese withdrawal

c)   Reconnaissance and Surveillance Missions
    • *Operations Bison, and Ramrose*

d)   Debriefing POWs - The RAPWI Project Mission
    • *Operations Birdcage, and Mastiff*

One of the first missions in which Wig was involved, in March 1945, was *Operation Cloak* which fell into the "Diversionary" category. The aim was to facilitate the XIVth Army crossing of the Irrawaddy River so that they could secure Mandalay and the neighbouring airfields. Achievement of this objective was vital because, without taking that major logistical hub, the Army would be stranded at the end of a supply line stretching over 1,000 kms to the north. Meanwhile, the Japanese would be sitting comfortably, with the port of Rangoon to their rear supplying their every need. The greatest obstacle to Slim's advance from the north was the physical barrier presented by the Irrawaddy River with the Japanese having established a defensive position on the eastern side. To block Slim, Japanese General Kamura assembled an army of 100,000 men in the Mandalay area.

Slim's plan was to convince the Japanese that the main crossing of the Irrawaddy would be some distance north of Mandalay, drawing the enemy forces to that point. In the meantime, the main body of the XIVth Army would sweep around in a wide arc to cross the river a hundred and sixty kms to the south. Once over the river, Slim would move east to cut the Japanese supply lines to the south, and also take the strategically placed airfields at Meiktila. This position was the key to the corridor that led down to Rangoon.

To implement the plan, SOE provided air operations to support D Division whose job was to convince the Japanese that the XIVth Army were to cross the river to the north of Mandalay whilst they were actually crossing to the south. D Division employed a range of deceptions. A small airfield was established on the west side of the Irrawaddy River and 357 Squadron with American help mounted what appeared to be a major airlift in preparation for a crossing. They sent all sorts of false radio messages, there were men marching up and down the river banks all night with lights, whilst others were felling trees with chain saws. Jeeps were driving up and down all day, and a tank was lumbering back and forth. They also planned a series of incidents which would suggest a crossing to the north, including a fake air crash, and a major drop on the west bank of 8 tons of supplies which would appear to be in support of the crossing of the main army. The materiel had all sorts of explosives designed to give the impression of a major attack, with timers to go off 24 hours later. The strategy was a great success. The Japanese were duped and the XIVth Army made a successful crossing to the south, trapping the Japanese in a pincer movement in the process.

Amongst the "Guerrilla Support" category of missions, *Operation Character* takes pride of place in this book as the archetypal SOE activity, demonstrating the true value of integrated military and covert activity. It was also the largest mission in which Wig was involved. It was conceived in late 1944, with the aim of developing a co-ordinated resistance capability behind Japanese lines across central and south east Burma. The strategy was to draw Japanese resources away from the path of the Slim's 14th Army which was heading south through the Sittang Valley to Rangoon, and then to harry the retreat of the whole Japanese army as they sought refuge back across the Thai border. The remit also included the provision of intelligence to Slim on Japanese positions and movements, undermining Japanese morale, and surveillance of the north-south road and rail links between Pyinmana and Pegu, and the east-west roads from Toungoo to Bawlake and Loikaw.

Initially, it was planned to have three operating zones with a centralised command and control system. However, by the time it was fully implemented in early 1945, it was recognised that there were considerable complexities in co-ordinating the deployment of BLO levies in the jungle environment, with wireless operations frequently failing, and communications often relying on fit young runners carrying messages between groups.

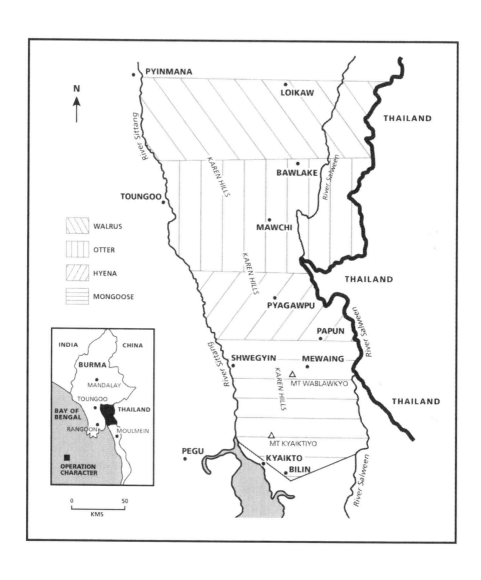

Burma 1944/45 – Operation Character Sectors

273

As a result, the operation was divided into four regional areas, configured as shown in the map below, with a number of semi-independent sectors within each area.[312]

The first to be established was the *Otter* zone, commanded by Lt Col Edgar Peacock who was deployed on 20 February 1945. [313] His team was responsible for both sides of the Mawchi Road, from the foothills near Toungoo to the Thai border. The *Hyena* zone, initially commanded by Major Rupert Turrall who arrived in late February, and then by Lt Colonel H W

Howell, operated around Pyagawpu. The northernmost zone, concentrating their efforts on the area between Bawlake and Loikaw, was named *Walrus,* and was commanded by Lt Col John Cromarty-Tulloch. He and a team of 19 were deployed by parachute on 24 March 1945. Finally, in the south, the *Mongoose* zone operated in an area bounded by Shwegyin to the west, Papun to the north and Bilin to the south, and was commanded by Lt Colonel R A Critchley a protégé of Wingate. Of particular interest for this book is that the headquarters of a section of *Mongoose* was at Mewaing of which a description is given later.

The scale of *Operation Character* is demonstrated by the fact that in the early days more than 80 British officers and 30 NCOs (mostly wireless operators), and more than 200 Karens, were inserted by parachute. By the end of the war, more than 12,000 Karens had been armed and were active across all sectors. The main function of the British officers and NCOs was to plan operations, train the Karen tribesmen, and lead them into their first action. Thereafter, local Karen or Ghurka officers often took on a leadership role. The nature of the local guerrillas, who eventually came to be highly regarded by their British leaders, is worth noting. One of the BLOs wrote in the SOE Burma Diaries (SOE Files HS1/44-46):

"The Karens are not by nature militarily aggressive, and do not love war for its own sake. On the whole, the villagers in my area were timid and taken to panic when first taken into action. But, once successful under competent officers, once they had been shown how easy it was for well-armed parties to

---

[312] This section is based on material in from the book entitled "*Memoirs of the Four Foot Colonel*", a biography by General Smith Dun (Cornel University, USA, 1980).
[313] This material in based on the SOE Burma diaries, but also relies on an article by Harry Fecitt (kaiserscross.com, 2016). The contribution of Harry's Sideshows is acknowledged.

ambush the Japanese, their fighting spirit rose high. Soon, they produced their own leaders, and displayed initiative and a spirit of attack. They also took rapidly to explosives and used them a lot without damage to themselves."

In the early stages of *Operation Character, Walrus* and *Otter* saw most of the action, because they were sitting astride the busy east-west Toungoo-Mawchi Road. On 13 April 1945, all sectors were sent word by the Slim's XIVth Army that the Japanese were beginning to send their XVth Division south from the Shan state

Karen Levy Soldier, 1945 – National Archives

to reinforce resistance to the British advance. The XIVth Army were then in Pyinmana in central Burma, so the odds of being first to reach Toungoo looked fairly even. But the Japanese were delayed for at least seven days thanks to the attacks from Cromarty-Tulloch's and Peacock's levies. Operations included ambushes, road blocks, and demolitions as well as sniping. By the time that the forward battalions of the Japanese XVth Division had emerged from the hills into the plain, Slim's XIVth Army had taken Toungoo and its vital airfield.

Having lost the opportunity of stalling the Allied advance, the Japanese were confronted with a rapidly deteriorating position. With the benefit of Toungoo airfield, Slim's XIVth army was racing south and would take Rangoon on 2 May 1945. This left the Japanese with at least 20,000 men to the west of the Rangoon-Mandalay road and about 50,000 men to the east in the Shan State and north Kayin. All these Japanese troops now tried to travel east in order to escape into Thailand, and had to pass through the Karen country dominated by the *Operation Character* forces. From May onwards, the Karens were sitting on all the main Japanese escape routes, and all four zones – *Walrus, Otter, Hyena* and *Mongoose* - were involved in heavy and continuous action drawing on huge aerial support from Wig's team.

275

Although the *Operation Character* forces concentrated on guerrilla tactics, they also engaged the Japanese using military formations. One of their biggest concerted offensive actions was an attack on the headquarters of the hated Kempeitai in Kyaukkyi a town about 100 kms north of Kyaikto in the southern *Mongoose* sector.[314] This took place on 15 April and was led by Turrall, who got injured in the process. The Karens captured the town, killed 41 Japanese, and rescued some Karens who were being held captive by the Kempeitai. The levies then withdrew and left the town to be defended by the Burmese National Army which had recently changed sides and were now working with the Allies. Sadly, the levies' work was wasted. On the night of 19 April, whilst the BNA troops were sleeping, the Japanese recaptured the town catching them unawares and killing many of them.

Apart from this relatively rare formal action, most of the attacks on the retreating Japanese involved setting ambushes, and sniping at the troops as they proceeded along mountain tracks. As recorded in the SOE Burma Diaries, one of the most effective type of ambush involved the installation of a length of cordex up to 200 yards long with charges and grenades at 10 metre intervals.[315] On either side of the track, the levies would plant sharpened bamboo stakes. Once the Japanese were in the ambush zone, the charges would be detonated and they would then impale themselves on the stakes as they dashed into the undergrowth.

In the final days of the war, a large body of Japanese troops moving east had to cross the Sittang River next to Shwegyin which is about 60 kms north of Kyaikto. At this time, there was no bridge and there were no obvious crossing points. Anticipating this challenge, the *Mongoose* commander (Critchley) deployed a number of gun posts which lined 30 kms of the east bank of the river. To cross the river, the Japanese either seized native craft or made rafts of bamboo. Once they had embarked, they were inevitably swept down-stream by the strong current and thus had to pass at least one of the machine gun teams. In one week, the levies claimed at least 900 Japanese exposed in this way.

---

[314] The Kempeitai were the much-hated military police of the Japanese Imperial Army, who had a lot on common with the German Gestapo. They ran extensive criminal and collaborationist networks, extorting money from businesses and civilians wherever they operated. They also ran the Allied prisoner of war system which treated captives with extreme brutality. Their other activities included sexual slave labour, and they also carried out biological and chemical experiments on live subjects.
[315] This description is taken from SOE Files HS1/44-46.

The impact of all this Karen guerrilla activity is best told in a Japanese document which came into Allied hands after the Japanese surrender in September 1945 and is recorded in SOE files.[316] The document, a precis of which follows, gives an interesting insight into the effect that *Operation Character* had on the Japanese troops. It is a report to his divisional commander prepared by a Colonel Tsukada commanding the 215th Infantry regiment of the Japanese 33rd Division.

"*1.*   *In our retreat, we have had to pass through the country between Mawchi (north) and Papun (south).*

2.   *This took us through territory occupied by guerrillas whose work proved very effective in delaying or halting the movement of small parties, rear units, walking wounded and sick.*

3.   *The guerrillas spread great alarm, and reports of their activity caused great uneasiness to our men. Our access to supplies was also hampered.*

4.   *The guerrillas were well trained, and our lines of communication were cut. As their activities increased, we had to keep guards posted day and night which gave the men no time for rest.*"

From all accounts, *Operation Character* exceeded all Allied expectations. At the start of the operation, SOE thought that it might be possible to raise between 3,000 and 5,000 levies, but eventually the Allies were successful in arming 12,000. Apart from the delay imposed on the Japanese 15th Division, which had a decisive bearing on the advance of Slim's XIVth Army to Rangoon, the operation was responsible for the death of at least 12,500 retreating Japanese troops and indirectly responsible for the deaths of thousands more through SOE deployed air attacks directed by levy officers. In all, less than 100 levies were killed and only half a dozen British officers and men lost their lives.[317]

At the end, in August and September 1945, *Operation Character* experienced a hiatus which was to have a very personal impact on Wig. After the Japanese surrender on 7 August 1945, it took a long time for the word to

---

[316] This report can be found in SOE HS 7/114.

[317] This figure comes from the book entitled *Grandfather Longlegs* pp 156-65, by Ian Morrison (Faber and Faber, London, 1947). Grandfather Longlegs is a reference to Major Hugh Seagrim.

Lysander at Mewaing Airfield 1945 – British National Archives

get out to Japanese in the field who were reluctant to accept defeat. They were bewildered, and no-one came to tell them what to do. All of this was not cleared up until a comprehensive surrender was implemented on 13 September. As a result, during the critical period in early September when Wig undertook his final mission, there were renegade troops in the jungle engaging with the Allies on a spasmodic basis. Such a group within the *Mongoose* Zone may well have been a factor in Wig's fatal air crash on 7 September. As will be seen later, Wig's plane crashed bang in the middle of this zone and it was a *Mongoose* team that ultimately had the responsibility for finding the crash and burying the casualties.

This leads me to one final word regarding the *Mongoose* Zone which is of significance for the final parts of this book. One of their sections had a base at the village of Mewaing about which there are numerous operational reports in the SOE Burmese diaries.[318] Apparently, every able bodied Karen of the 7,000 people living in this area joined the levies, and the wider population of the district could be relied upon to provide local intelligence on the movement of the Japanese. The local levies also included a small group of Shan who acted as the Home Guard, and provided a resource for maintenance of the airfield and porterage. The British leader, Lt Colonel Critchley, established very good relations with the local headman whose name was Saw Mya Shwe. Mya Shwe was a retired major from the Burma Rifles and played an important role in maintaining good working relations between the Karen and the Shan. The Burma diaries also refer to the head

---

[318] A full account of the SOE base at Mewaing is provided in SOE File 7-106.

monk at Mewaing monastery who was said to be co-operative, supplying fruit and vegetables. Significant for our story, he also provided ground for the burial of the dead.

The base had a fully functional airfield with an all-weather landing strip which was constructed using no less than 28,000 bamboo poles, and drained with side channels. It remained operational throughout the monsoon season. The runway, which was 590 yards long, was constructed with two layers of uncut bamboos with sand in between, on top of which was then laid a further section of tightly bound split bamboos. And there was a wind sock made from a parachute. The base was under attack from the Japanese on more than occasion.

According to the diaries, the main aircraft to use the airfield were a fleet of 5 Lysanders, although a Dakota could probably have landed if pressed. There were some 88 sorties during the *Mongoose* Zone's existence in 1945. A typical mission involved the supply of food and materials, and/or the removal of personnel including the sick, and the transport of new personnel to join the *Mongoose* team. In passing, it is interesting to note that, in making contact with the villagers nearly seventy years later, there were still people alive able to talk about the war years in this district. However, no-one mentioned the airfield or the base.

The second arm of the SOE "Guerrilla Support" category of missions was *Operation Nation*. This project was designed on the same principles as *Operation Character*, and involved insertion of BLOs into the area of Burma to the west of the Sittang River in the central Pegu Yomas mountains where Burmans were the main local force. Following the success of *Operation Cloak* in mid-March 1945, the XIVth Army had entrapped some ten thousand or so Japanese, and the aim of *Operation Nation* was to observe and harass this force. [319] Unlike *Operation Character*, the initial insertion involved just a few dozen men. However, they very rapidly managed to develop a guerrilla force almost as large as that across the valley in the Karen Hills. This is because the *Operation Nation* BLOs had the advantage of working with existing organised resistance groups. However, arguably, the effectiveness of the *Operation Nation* teams did not match to those of *Operation Character*. Led by commanders appointed by the recently defected Burmese National Army, the *Operation Nation* teams operated as small independent

---

[319] Material drawn from page 236 of the book by Terence O'Brien entitled *"The Moonlight War - The Story of Clandestine Operations in SE Asia, 1944-45"*.

units, and they lacked the co-ordination, discipline and expertise of the British led and trained Karens of *Operation Character*. According to Terence O'Brien, writing from a pilot's perspective, you could even tell the difference between the two guerrilla groups from the air.

> *"On arrival at a Character drop zone, you would see figures waving and even elephants running about the site, and the actual zone would be lit up by fires. At a Nation drop zone there would be few signs of life; if you looked down closely you might discern one or two figures skulking about the bordering trees, and the parachutes would all be dragged back out of sight into the jungle within minutes of landing. Their fires were often nothing more than glowing sticks, fanned to give flame when you were actually over the site."*

According to O'Brien, another difference between the two operations was the response to air crashes. When an aircraft crashed in the Karen Hills, SOE would learn about it at once. Apparently, *"Everyone was so involved with the struggle against the Japanese that, even in the most remote Karen villages, people would hurry to a crash site to try and help. Even if the crew had been killed, SOE did at least get details back from the field."* But if an aircraft crashed in the Pegu Yomas area, the RAF would have to search for the wreckage themselves. Apparently, the local Burmese were not interested in Allied casualties except perhaps to loot the crash, and of course they would never admit to knowing the location.

Another mission operating during Wig's time was *Operation Dilwyn*. This had commenced in early 1943, and was an early and smaller scale version of SOE's *Operation Character*, working in the far north to the east of Bhamo next to the Chinese border. The local Kachin levies led by British officers, gathered information about local Japanese activities. Although happy to use their intelligence, their direct involvement in hostilities was not always welcomed by American General Stilwell who doubted their ability to work in unison with the military. Also, the agents worked in the same area as the Chindits who were resistant to any co-operation with what Orde Wingate saw as ill-disciplined insurgents. Nevertheless, a number of small groups continued to operate very successfully and performed an important intelligence role during Wig's time in early 1945.

Yet another mission supported by Wig's team in 1945 was *Operation Hainton,* which was a guerrilla force operating in the mountainous border country to the far east of Mandalay. It was approved by Chiang Kai-shek's Chief of Staff on 17 March 1944 and initially consisted of three teams. The objective was to obstruct Japanese reinforcements which might try to move through the mountains on the Thai border, and to collect related intelligence. This was to be achieved by attacking lines of communication. They were also to make contact with Thai soldiers who were disaffected from the formal alliance of the Japanese and Thai armies. By September 1944, the mission's activities had been split into two groups called *Operation Heavy* and *Operation Wolf.* Their HQ was at Loi Awng Lawng. On 20 February 1945, Lt Colonel Dennis Herring and others were dropped in to lead the recruitment and training of additional guerrillas. By April, the operation had been successful in driving back the Japanese. But then serious issues arose between the British and Chinese regarding what appeared to be a Chinese takeover of that part of Burma. In the end, *Operation Hainton* become a vital force to hold back not the Japanese but the Chinese. As noted by Alan Ogden, this left Lt Col Herring, who was eventually extracted on 2 July, somewhat frustrated. Ogden's view of the operation was as follows.[320]

> *"The Hainton mission epitomises the complexity of many SOE operations in the Far East. At a political level, there was underlying friction with the Kuomintang, relationships with the US came under strain for so-called boundary transgressions, local politics threw up ethnic hatreds, and the Japanese enemy proved to be elusive and devious when attacked. And then there was the awful weather."*

Having said that, the local knowledge of the people involved in *Operation Hainton* was of particular help towards the end of the war when the Allies were seeking to establish contact with the many thousands of POWs in camps on the Thai border.

In April and May 1945, Wig's team facilitated the implementation of *Operation Nutshell.* The aim of this mission was to establish positions to observe the Japanese as they were escaping into Thailand from the Moulmein and Kawkareik areas in southern Burma. There was a secondary aim to recruit and train levies to take aggressive action against the Japanese troops as they fled. Also, the Foreign Office's SIS were interested in using this mission to make contact with POW groups. In its final stages, *Operation*

---

[320] This is based on pages 279-85 of Allen Ogden's book entitled *Tigers Burning Bright.*

Nutshell experienced the same problems as *Operation Character*. The local Japanese were confused and it took several weeks before they all surrendered.

It is difficult to give an indication of the casualties inflicted in all the "hit and run" attacks mounted by SOE led resistance teams under the "Guerrilla Support" category of missions. During Wig's time in the Far East, from February to August 1945, an estimate of the casualties inflicted by the main hill tribe resistance forces (taken from SOE files) is as follows:

Force	Japanese Killed	Japanese Wounded	Japanese POWs
Karen	12,474	644	119
Kachin	239	59	0
Shan	526	74	4
Total	13,239	777	123

The figures for the Kachins provide a false picture of their overall contribution because, by 1945, most of their activity in the north had been completed. They inflicted casualties into the thousands in 1944.

The third category of operations in which Wig was involved was "Reconnaissance and Surveillance". This was a key part of SOE work in all theatres, and always required air support with supplies and equipment. In Burma, there many such missions of which the following are just a couple that occurred during Wig's time.

a)   In March 1945, *Operation Bison* involved an SOE hideout overlooking the road to the north of Mandalay. The agents reported the movements of all Japanese traffic. The Drop Zone was in a valley a few kms back from the road.

b)   *Operation Ramrose* was established to check local sympathies near Ramree Island on the west coast where a landing was planned.

The final category of mission during Wig's time was the "Debriefing of POWs". The *RAPWI* project, which involved all the security services, was implemented on 28 August 1945. The target was the prison camps in Thailand and French Indo-China ("FIC"). On arrival, the teams, which included a doctor, started immediate medical care and listed not only the names of survivors but also those known to have perished. There were also significant drops of medical supplies, food and clothing. At the time of Wig's death, the lift out of the survivors was just beginning, and that is what took him to Rangoon in early September (an account is given in Chapter 29). He was organising transport, debriefing a number of the survivors, and monitoring progress. Thankfully, none of them made it onto the flight of KN584 on 7 September. All the 35,000 survivors of the camps in Thailand were removed in a matter of weeks.[321].

There were several other operations closely associated with the *RAPWI* Project, called *Operation Birdcage, Operation Mastiff, and Operation Swansong. Operation Birdcage* involved dropping leaflets with information about survival and rescue arrangements. *Operation Mastiff* involved delivering medical teams and supplies to the 64 POW camps. *Operation Swansong*, involved a bold move, led by Colonel Douglas Clague, to convince the Japanese to allow access for prompt medical and nutritional aid to the POWs.

There is direct evidence of Wig's leading role in organising air support for these final operations. On Sunday 19 August 1945 at Group A Headquarters in Calcutta, Wig chaired what would have been one of the last of the meetings to review the status of current operations. At this particular meeting, Wig is recorded as proposing that Lt Colonel Driscoll lead a multi-section team to implement *Operation Mastiff*.[322]. The Minutes also record a report from a Colonel Clague on his operation in Thailand and French Indo China, and confirmation of the medical and food supplies to be dropped.

Finally, and not fitting into the above categories, one of the key actions during the advance of the XIVth Army on Rangoon, was *Operation Dracula.* The officer in charge of this operation, Squadron Leader T S Tull, prepared a full report for Wig dated 14 May 1945 which is in SOE files. Given the personal connection, it is included here to provide some insight into the co-operation between Force 136, the air force and the army. The following is an extract from his report.

The report from Tull begins with comments on preparation. He then

---

[321] According to Terence O'Brien on page 340 of his book "*The Moonlight War- The Story of Clandestine Operations in SE Asia, 1944-45*".

[322] This record, in SOE Burma Diaries also records that in the coming Moon period, which runs through his last and fatal trip, there would be 30 Dakota and 25 Liberator sorties.

recounts how the whole team led by a Major Headley is transferred by air to Akyab on the western coast, with the operation proceeding as planned on the night of 30 April/1 May. He goes on to explain how the deployment of the men and then the packages were guided by Force 136 personnel on the ground including Captain Planell and 40 levies who had checked out the Dropping Zone near the village of Tawkai beforehand (just 40 kms south of Rangoon). Finally, he provides an account of the successful battle to take Elephant Point to the east of Rangoon. At the end of his report he provides some comments on learning as follows:

> *"The link up with Force 136 agents proved extremely useful and this should be done in all future airborne operations. It would be useful to drop an initial team to link up with Force 136 personnel ahead of the main drop. The liaison between Major Headley and my team worked particularly well, and was largely instrumental in saving three villages from annihilation; quite apart from the saving of civilian life and property, this meant that our lines of communication from the main DZ was clear and that men and bullock carts could be procured."*

A great summary of the contribution of all these missions during Wig's time was provided by the then Commanding Officer of Special Duties Squadron 357, Wing Commander Lewis M Hodges DSO DFC (later to become Air Chief Marshall Sir Lewis Hodges) in an address he made to all ground personnel on 5 May 1945 as the XIVth Army was reaching Rangoon.[323] [324] The following is an extract.

> *"We have all been working very hard for the past few weeks, and I thought you should know that this Squadron has greatly assisted the speedy capture of Rangoon with comparatively light losses. You can see the disposition of our forces in Burma on this map. Whilst there still remains a considerable area under Japanese control, it is held mainly by isolated garrisons whose fighting efficiency has been greatly reduced by Allied attacks. We have secured all the main roads and railways, and our*

---

[323] Sir Lewis Hodges became a pilot in the early part of the war and was known as Bob, and worked with Wig. He took command of Squadron 357 in December 1944 and served until July 1945 when he was succeeded by Peter Gaskell.

[324] This address is a shortened version of material in SOE File HS 7-111.

forces are astride the road at Pegu, which is the main Japanese escape route to Thailand.

As regards recent events, after the capture of Mandalay, the main route of advance for the 14th Army was obviously going to be down the road and railway to Toungoo, and then direct to Rangoon. In order to make the drive as quickly as possible, ahead the monsoon, it was essential to protect the flanks to left and right of the valley. Without this protection, the Japanese would have had little difficulty in ambushing our armoured vehicles and transport columns as they moved south. To provide the necessary protection, the Army asked for airborne troops to be landed in strategic positions to harry the Japanese forces and prevent them from interfering with the advance of the main army. On the map you will see the areas into which those airborne troops were parachuted. The country is very wild and mountainous, and it was a difficult job to put the men down in the right places without injury, and unfortunately casualties did occur. The teams inserted consisted of British Officers commanding small parties of 10 to 15 Burmese, and their job was to organise the local Burmese living in the villages into guerrilla parties of considerable size. The parties were then supplied with weapons and food dropped by Liberators.

All this started in February, and as soon as the Japanese discovered what was happening, they despatched troops to the hills to try and destroy the parachutists. Unfortunately for the Japanese, they underestimated the capability of the burgeoning force of guerrillas in the hills with whom they became heavily engaged. In the meantime, the 14th army were able to advance rapidly down the road to Rangoon.

The entire responsibility for keeping the guerrillas supplied and reinforced has been ours, together with 358 Squadron and 200 Squadron as well. General William Slim, the Commander of the 14th Army, has said that, but for the work of the guerrillas, the capture of Rangoon before the monsoon would not have been possible."

Finally, I would like to make a special mention of one man who worked closely with Wig during 1945, Terence O'Brien who was a Squadron Leader of 357 Squadron with responsibility for the Dakota fleet. In three books published after the war, he provides an extensive detailed account of all the

Burmese air operations activity.[325]

We leave this account with a quaint anecdote which is indicative of the times. The period immediately following VE Day in June 1945 was a difficult period for all the staff in the Far East. They were happy for their comrades in Europe, but were far from certain as to when their own battles would end. Mountbatten was very conscious of this issue and made great efforts to maintain morale. Indeed, he made a point of touring SOE and military units in India, Ceylon and Burma to meet local staff and give them a pep talk. He is said to have finished each speech with the words *"Now come on chaps, pull up your pants, and let's get cracking."*[326] And so they did, for several months to come. Sadly, even at this late stage, some would not see the end.

---

[325] Terence O'Brien worked closely with Wig. His exploits are recorded in great entitled *"The Moonlight War – The story of Clandestine Operations in SE Asia 1944-45"*, Collins (London, 1987). He died in 2007 aged 97.

[326] This material, including the quote, is based on the account provided by Bickham Sweet-Escott on page 255 of his book *"Baker Street Irregular"*.

28: A Reflection on Myanmar

Given that it is Wig's final resting place, I have come to feel a special bond with what used to be called Burma. Because of this, and the knowledge acquired through my research into the war years, I have formed certain views about the history and current status of the country. First of all, it is clear to me that the war in Burma has received relatively little attention compared with events in other theatres during World War Two. This is probably because, before the war, Burma did not rank highly in British interests. And, after the war, British commitments were relinquished very quickly because of the other priorities of a newly elected and anti-imperialist Labour government. For the other external players, the same was true. With the benefit of hind-sight, the lack of attention and commitment by the British was and still is a significant oversight.

British Perspective

Before and during the war the British recognised the port at Rangoon as a significant maritime staging post, and the largely unexploited natural resources represented a significant future asset worthy of defence. But, when confronted by superior Japanese forces in 1942, the British had very little choice but to retreat and live to fight another day. The over-riding strategy was to defend from invasion the more important sub-continent of India, and geography dictated that the key part of Burma was in the north-west where the entry into what is now Bangladesh is a relatively narrow land corridor north of the Bay of Bengal. This is where the British determined to make their stand. Working in their favour, were the ever lengthening lines of supply and increasingly difficult lines of communications for the Japanese, and the eventual release of Allied resources from other theatres of war. Also, the Japanese were fighting on two fronts. They were confronted with Chinese forces in the north east. The American led Kuomintang armies eventually deployed significant resources to establish a "land-bridge" connecting China with India.

Whilst the Japanese were preparing for the attack on India in 1944, the British took the opportunity to greatly enhance their fighting capability. Accordingly, they were able to make a stand at Imphal and Kohima, and mount a successful campaign to repel the Japanese. In subsequently prosecuting the advance back into Burma, the Allies applied the very best of their learning from Europe theatres in co-ordinating military and covert operations. This combination, relying heavily on Wig's air operations, proved to be a highly potent force in the first half of 1945. Clearly the main reason for Japanese surrender in August 1945 was the dropping of atomic bombs, but the Allied victory in Burma was a major contributing factor in their defeat.

Japanese Perspective

The Japanese invaded Burma in 1942 to consolidate their rapid advances across China and Indo-China, and to enable delivery of the ultimate prize – a successful invasion of India and all the wealth that this sub-continent presented. Ideally, they would have wished to launch an attack across the north of Burma, but they were blocked by the Chinese Kuomintang. As a result, they had to proceed from the south east and, in the end, the ease with which they were able to advance was their own undoing. Their lines of supply and communication became excessively extended, and they launched their attack on India at the very time when the Allies were able to access forces released from other theatres.

The failure of the Japanese attack on India left them highly vulnerable. In 1944, they fought hard to retain the territory they had so easily annexed two years before, and retreated to what they saw as defensible positions to the east of the Irrawaddy River. But they underestimated the impact of strengthening Allied military forces and widespread covert operations. In particular, they underrated the effectiveness of the Hill Tribes, and they miscalculated the loyalty of the Burmans whose hospitality they had abused. Their retreat was long and bloody, driven by their belief in their own invincibility. But their defeat was inevitable given the superiority and potent combination of Allied resources.

The Locals

The majority Burmans welcomed the Japanese as liberators from British colonial rule. But, following the regime of forced labour and other indignities, and the introduction of a constitution which left the Japanese with effective control, they began to realise that the Japanese might even be worse than their British predecessors. In 1944/45, it also became apparent that the British with their US and Chinese Allies would return, and so they changed sides. The resistance within Burma consisted of several quite distinct forces, with strategies which at times were seriously conflicted but, when the time came, they all played a part in ousting the Japanese. Mind you, some would say that they left it quite late. When General Slim arrived in Rangoon in May 1945, the Burmans were still wearing Japanese military uniform! As has been related anecdotally, Slim made it very clear to the Commanding Officer of the Burmese Defence Army, Aung San that, if he wanted to negotiate the future of his country, he'd better get into civilian clothing "pretty damn quick".

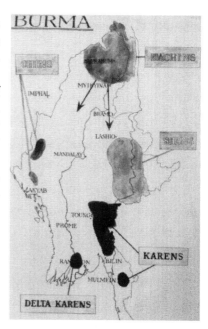

Location of Burmese Hill Tribes 1945 - National Archives

The position of the main Hill Tribes, the Karen, the Shan, and the Kachins, was always quite different from the majority Burman population. To some extent, the Japanese invasion was seen as an obstacle to implementing their autonomy or even independence from the Burmans. The spread of the resistance groups that formed in the hills is shown on the map. In varying degrees these groups were either apathetic or hostile to the Japanese, there was little or no allegiance to the Burmans, and there were significant elements who were totally loyal to the British. The response of the Hill Tribes to the Japanese invasion was to melt into the jungle and the mountains. When the time came, they then played a vital role in defeating the Japanese and, in so doing, they had an expectation that, in a post war settlement, the British would honour a commitment to facilitate autonomy. Of all the Hill Tribes, the Karen were probably the most important group. They were also important players in the final year of Wig's life, and in the treatment of his remains following his death.

Post War Legacy
The aftermath of the war in what became Myanmar is in many ways a sorry

289

tale, and I suspect that people like Wig would have been disappointed with what happened. Once the Japanese had been expelled, the leadership of the Burman majority under Aung San were single-minded in the pursuit of complete independence and separation from British influence. They had not forgotten the neglect and lack of interest of their colonial masters before the war, and were pleased to seize on British willingness to relinquish all responsibility. At the time, whilst many British people were keen to acknowledge the contribution of the Hill Tribes in the war, they were powerless to honour commitments to protect their rights and aspirations. When the Allies failed to involve them in discussions about the post-war political settlement, they must have felt sorely let down. Thereafter, following an initial period of fragile democracy, the history of Myanmar has been dominated until recently by a fairly ruthless military regime controlled by the Burman majority which has paid scant regard for Hill Tribe interests. As a result, to this day, the country is confronted by Hill Tribe led insurgencies.

It is the author's view that Britain's interest in Burma prior to the war, and the efforts of many Burmese citizens to assist the Allied cause during the war, warranted a greater contribution to post-war reconstruction. In the period after the war, there was also a moral responsibility to honour commitments that had been made to many sectors of the Burmese community. Even from the point of view of British self-interest, the potential of the country, in terms of its resources and culture, should not have been so easily relinquished.

Latterly, it would seem that western countries are beginning to wake up to the strategic importance of modern day Myanmar. During his period in office, President Obama certainly understood the strategic importance of this country in the Euro-Asian geopolitical landmass and, consequently, he made strenuous efforts to encourage the development of liberal democracy. And it is not too late for British leaders to reflect on how the hill people were left in the lurch. Belatedly, they could act in supporting their cause for autonomous political units within a federation. Indeed, it could be argued that the aspirations of the Karen and other minority groups are just as valid as other campaigns for self-governance nearer to home.[327]

---

[327] This is a reference to the campaigns of minority groups in the UK, Spain, Turkey and other countries in the West.

Part Ten: World Without War

29: Just One Last Mission

With the end of hostilities in Europe in May, and the surrender of the Japanese in August, life after the war was uppermost in the minds of most combatants who were about to return to Britain in the late summer of 1945. According to my mother, this was certainly the case for Wig not least because something special was also on the way. Following his visit to England in February, another child was due in November. And the authorities had indicated that he would be demobbed in September, after tidying up a few loose ends in the Far East. He would be there for the birth.

At this time, Wig's plans for a return to civilian life were certainly well advanced. As early as May, this had included the preparation of a resumé. A copy written in his own fair hand sits within the family archives. A typed up version, together with a covering letter dated 24 May 1945, was sent to a Mr Morley who was the General Manager at the Nottingham City Transport Department where he had worked before the war. In this letter Wig indicated that he would definitely be returning to his previous place of work although, given his personal development during the war, it remained to be seen in what position this might be. In this context, it is interesting to note that Wig's annual salary for the last job he held with the Department of Transport in 1939 was £195! In the early months of 1945, records show that as a Lt Colonel he was being paid an annual salary of £2,028 which wasn't too bad for a 31 year old.[328] However, one doubts whether he would have stayed with the Nottingham City Council for very long. There is evidence that, through the many and various contacts he had made during the war, there were several offers pending. Indeed, in family files, there are a number of letters suggesting to him that he might like to take up a variety of other careers in a wide range of private businesses. In her comments on the period just before his death, my mother indicated that he was seriously looking at jobs both in the UK, in Canada, and in South Africa and had lined up interviews. Having lived there herself in the 1920s, Eunice had good things to say about Canada, and I do wonder sometimes what it might have been like to be a Canadian. Brrrr!

And so, for all the family, the early days of autumn were full of anticipation that the dreadful nightmare would soon be over. And there was

---

[328] The figure of £2,028 is equivalent to £60,000 in 2017 money.

so much to live for. But, for Wig, it was not to be. Following the Japanese surrender on 13 August, the war in the Far East was petering out with only spasmodic resistance in remote areas. However, there was a lot of business to wind up, including the pressing demands of local independence movements in India and Burma and the repatriation of thousands of Allied troops.

For a few weeks after VJ Day, Wig continued working from his office in Calcutta. One of his final jobs, before returning to England and safety, was to organise the debriefing of personnel being released from Japanese Prisoner of War camps (part of the previously described *RAPWI* project) and this involved travelling to a range of locations in Thailand and Burma. He was due to return to England on 14 September.[329] With repatriation plans well advanced, he made one last trip to Rangoon to personally supervise arrangements being made for the processing of Prisoners of War released from camps in Burma/Thailand. He left the airfield at Jessore on the morning of 4 September 1945, and arrived later that day at Rangoon's Mingaladon airport. In the next couple of days, he proceeded with his business, including a visit to British headquarters in Rangoon which was in a building that is now the main office of the City Council in the centre of modern day Yangon. The work included interviews and debriefing of several key people. Having finished his schedule, on the morning of 7 September, he returned to Mingaladon Airport, and boarded the Dakota Mark IV plane number KN584 of 357 Squadron. The plane took off at 8.43 am for the return journey to Jessore. En route, the flight was scheduled to make a supply drop over the Karen Hills to members of an *Operation Character* unit, to refuel at Toungoo, and to make a stop at Akyab on the west coast.[330] The pilot for this flight was Canadian Warrant Officer Harold Smith. Poignantly, according to research of flight records for that period, Smith's previous flight had been a mission out of Jessore and via Mingaladon to drop supplies to the *Otter* team of *Operation Character* in late August. The Flight Record of W/O Smith's penultimate mission is shown in Appendix 16. Flying over the Mewaing area was not new to him.[331]

---

[329] In his book, *Baker Street Irregular*, p 171, Bickham Sweet-Escott with whom Wig worked records "*A week before he was due to fly home for demobilisation after VJ Day his aircraft crashed into a mountain in Burma and he was killed.*"

[330] The source for the departure time and stop at Akyab is a letter between two relatives of the casualties in SOE File HS9-1395-7.

[331] SOE File HS 1-22 provides all the Flight Records for that period.

As far as the authorities and SOE were concerned, the first news that something was awry was when the plane failed to arrive at Toungoo airfield. At that point, the staff at the airfield would have posted the plane as delayed for reasons as yet unknown, and they would not necessarily have feared the worst because communications were often interrupted on account of poor weather. However, the matter was reported to Colonel Stephen Cumming at Group A Headquarters in Calcutta. Then some news filtered through from SOE staff in the field. The plane had been spotted by some local people in the area to the west of the SOE *Operation Character* base at Mewaing who said that they had seen and heard a crash with reports of smoke. The local account suggested that the plane was flying over the relatively low hills to the north west of Bilin, had been hit by lightning during a squall, with a wing tip then catching a rock face. In the absence of corroborative evidence, all 16 people were deemed to be missing in action which included not only Wig but his friend and colleague Lt Colonel Edgar Kennedy.

As with any missing plane, after a short period, the wheels were quickly turning to discover what had happened. Flight Commander Terence O'Brien, an Australian who was a flight commander with SOE 357 Squadron, now takes up the story immediately following the crash. As recorded in his definitive book on war time air operations in the Far East, it was he who led the initial search for the lost plane.[332]

"In September 1945, we had one post surrender crash. The relief of prisoners was of such priority for all squadrons (ie ferrying them back home) that no aircraft could be spared for normal transport duties, and any air aircraft going back to India for maintenance was ordered to be fully loaded. So, one of our Dakotas (KN584) going back to Jessore finished up loaded with some urgent supplies for Operation Character personnel as well as ten Indian Army passengers.[333][334] It never reached

---

[332] This account comes from pages 342 and 343 of the book written by Terence O'Brien entitled *"Moonlight War- The Story of Clandestine Operations in SE Asia, 1944-45"*. O'Brien was placed in command of 357 Squadron in September 1945.

[333] The Flight Code in parenthesis has been added by the author.

[334] There is no official documentary evidence of O'Brien's assertion that there were also some Indian Army passengers, and a subsequent Court of Inquiry makes no mention of them. However, some anecdotal evidence from local people who eventually collected the bodies suggests that there may have been at least one Indian on board the plane. It is not clear how they would have known that.

India. We learned from the field that the aircraft had circled the Drop Zone ("DZ") but it had begun to rain just as it was turning into position for the drop and they never saw it again.[335]

The next day, I took off on a search just after day break, certain in my mind that all "fourteen" aboard were now dead.[336] To my surprise, we were able to reach the actual site of the DZ, but visibility during our search was only intermittent. As we flew low along the ridge a strong wind funnelled through the valley, the trees were flailing wildly, and shreds of clouds were swirling and wreathing up the mountain side like flurries of smoke from a bushfire. We found no sign of a crash nearby, but we could see so little between the flitting clouds that we may have missed it from only fifty feet above the trees. We searched the hills for another nine hours without a single instant of hope.

It was a week before the crash was discovered in reconnaissance some fifteen kms away. The aircraft had flown into a hillside about a thousand feet above the level of the DZ and everyone on board had almost certainly been killed on impact."

The results of this reconnaissance were soon reported back to the authorities in the SOE Calcutta headquarters. However, pending a visit to the crash site, the people on board were still designated as "missing in action". Thus began a period of nearly four months before the full story including subsequent actions could be confirmed.

---

[335] According to a witness on the ground (see next chapter) the actual circumstances were a little more melodramatic, with the possibility that a renegade Japanese unit fired on the plane, and that the crash arose from evasive action with a wing clipping the trees on top of the mountain.

[336] This number of 14 is definitely incorrect and certainly at odds with the official record (from the Court of Inquiry into the crash) of 16 named casualties consisting of British and Canadian military personnel who boarded the plane.

30: Immediate Aftermath

Following his failure to return to England as planned, Wig's wife Eunice got to hear the news of his crash in a communication dated 18 September. The words in the telegram, which was signed by the Under Secretary of State for War, read:

> *"Notification received from India that Lt Colonel Wigginton Sherwood Foresters was reported missing on 7 September 1945 on an aircraft flight. The Army Council express sympathy. Letter follows shortly."*

The contents of the telegram were of course Eunice's worst nightmare. One can only imagine that terrible sinking feeling. The reference to "missing" could have meant anything, but the fact that there was apparently no material evidence of a crash was a slim source of cruel hope.[337] The reality was that, at this stage and given the route of the flight over dense jungle of the Karen Hills, no-one was able to say exactly what had happened. So a period of waiting then commenced during which the Wigginton family lived through great and mounting stress. In the weeks that followed, Eunice corresponded with Colonel Cumming who kept his intelligence very close to the chest. Although the crash site had in fact been identified in mid-September, nothing was confirmed because of the remote location, lack of on-site inspection, and uncertainty regarding survivors. Accordingly, in a letter to Eunice in early October which was perhaps designed to soften the blow, Cumming wrote about the *possibility* of the plane having crashed in the Karen Hills:

> *"If the plane did crash there, it was in a friendly country and among people who remained loyal to us throughout the war, and with whom the most important of our operations which he controlled were connected. I am sure that, if he had known it had to be, it would have been in Karenni and among the Karens that he would have chosen to give his life."*

At this point, Eunice was eight months pregnant. She also had an ailing

---

[337] By this time, the crashed plane had already been spotted on the ground but this information was withheld.

mother who suffered from angina. Eunice was living in Nottingham and she very much hoped that the news about Wig's disappearance would be kept from her mother living in London. But the news was gazetted and, in early November, Eunice's mother read the story in a newspaper. Shortly afterwards, she had a heart attack. Because the birth of her second child was imminent, Eunice was unable to travel and see her mother in hospital. On the fateful night of 7 November 1945, her second son Gavin was born in a Nursing Home in Nottingham and her mother died in London without the comfort of her daughter.

Following the birth of her son and the funeral of her mother, Eunice continued to correspond with Colonel Cumming, and there are copies of the correspondence in Wig's SOE personnel file. Weeks passed with nothing confirmed. However, in late November, SOE officers in the field actually made it to the crash site on Mount War Plar Lay (Wablawkyo). The long delay was because the incident happened in a remote place, during the monsoon season, with no access tracks, and in territory frequented by tigers and bears. It was only now that the identity of the casualties was confirmed, and the bodies removed to their final burial place. A detailed account is provided in Chapter 31.

Information about this field trip was not transmitted to the families of the casualties and, fearing the worst, Eunice continued to press for an indication of what had happened. Christmas 1945 must have been the most miserable "celebration" of her whole life. Eventually, however, after official due process and more than four months of waiting, on 22 January 1946 Colonel Cumming wrote to Eunice as follows:

"I am afraid that by now the sad confirmation of your husband's death will have reached you. As I predicted in my last letter, the aircraft did crash in the Karen Hills. I have not been able to visit the scene, but I have received reports from some of my officers who were sent to visit it. From their reports, I am glad to be able to tell you that none of those who were killed can have suffered, as in all cases death must have been instantaneous. It has been possible to have the grave of those who died in the crash photographed, and I am sending the results (three photos) with this letter. It is a lovely country and among the Karens who are a lovable and very Christian people. It (Mewaing) is also a village which was outstanding for its loyalty during the war. You may therefore feel assured that they rest among friends."

Mewaing Monastery – burial site 1945

The letter from Colonel Cumming reported on the outcome, but didn't tell the full story as will be evident in Chapter 31. Once the crash site had been identified from the air, SOE organised a field trip led by a Major Bourne and involving some of those who had originally sighted the crash. The bodies, or at least all of remains that could be recovered after two months in the jungle, were collected and carried to the grounds of the monastery in nearby Mewaing, and Major Bourne then prepared a report which was eventually submitted to a Court of Inquiry established to investigate the circumstances of the crash. However, SOE activities being secret, these details were not released to the public or the relatives.

Back in Britain, Eunice was doing her best to cope with the dreadful news. The aftermath of any military death is quite poignant as regards the due administrative processes. In Wig's SOE Personnel File, I found a Certified Inventory of his personal effects which I reproduce as Appendix 17. This tells much about the content of his everyday life and, amongst other things, the inventory indicates that he smoked a pipe! All these items would have been returned to the family. My brother and I were too young to remember the day, but strangely I do have a memory of that pipe which surfaced and lingered on at our home in Nottingham for several years.

In any event, 1946 was a tough year for Wig's surviving family. Settling down with two small children was very difficult for Eunice. In early 1946, the sister with whom she had been living at Orston Drive in Wollaton Park Nottingham got remarried after the death during the war of her first husband. Edie and her new husband planned to move to a new house in Dalby Square which was also in Wollaton Park. So Eunice had to find a new place to live. She was fortunate in that her sister proved to be enormously supportive. Edie had no children of her own and undertook to look after Eunice's young children while she went out to work.

In those days, houses were obviously in short supply. There were waiting lists and no mortgages. Eunice qualified ahead of others because, as a War Widow, she had lots of points qualifying her for priority treatment under a system introduced by the new Labour government. She had a bit of luck in finding a builder who was constructing a row of new detached houses on farming land adjacent to Nottingham. The road was called Ranelagh Grove, and she was allocated no 64. In those days, the Grove was next to fields that stretched from the ancient village of Wollaton to the outskirts of the city.

The new house at Ranclagh Grove was furnished by the usual combination of family heirlooms and whatever Eunice could pick up in post war austerity. The only pieces of furniture which have survived from those days are the china cabinet in my study at Callignee, and Wig's desk from school days which rests lonely but cared for in my shed. 64 Ranelagh Grove was a detached three bedroomed house and there were fireplaces in four rooms including two of the bedrooms. As was common in such houses, there was an oak panelled hallway leading from the entrance. There was a big larder, and the laundry equipment was in the kitchen consisting of a big copper pot and a mangle. Heating was by coal and there was a coal shed built into the side of the house. There was a substantial garden at the rear.

As a War Widow, Eunice was helped by many people. For example, an associate of her friend Lily Kirk was a plumber and he obtained pre-war plumbing items including what was then a very fashionable pale green coloured bath (white was the war time norm). And the builder allowed her to share his telephone on a party line - although this was far from ideal. The telephone always seemed to be engaged, with the builder running his business from home, and Eunice was inundated by neighbours who did not have a telephone so soon after the war.

As soon as she was able, Eunice's commenced a part time job working with Sir Julian Kahn who was helping refugees. But, in 1946, she got an administrative post at the University of Nottingham where she eventually worked for over 35 years. It was a part time role and she also did various other part time work from time to time, including typing theses for students and academics. And so some form of normal life, without Wig, established itself. But it must have been a lonely and miserable time.

The one redeeming feature was that, once Wig's body had been found, she was entitled to some financial support from the government. Indeed, as long as she did not re-marry, she received a War Widow's pension and was provided with substantial financial assistance towards the education of her sons. Because she never did re-marry, both children were able to attend a fee paying school, and this continued until her younger son left school in 1964.

As final words, all one can say is that, in great adversity, Eunice took responsibility and did the right thing. She brought up two children both of whom thrived and went on to have successful lives of their own. Her eldest son Michael became a Professor of Architecture, and her younger son held senior management positions in both the private and public sectors. I would say this, but I think that Wig would have been proud of her and what was achieved. And in 1986 her younger son, the author of this tome, migrated to Australia. In 1995, Eunice joined him in Australia where she spent the last 15 years of her life living independently in a leafy suburb of Melbourne until the last nine months. She died peacefully in her bed in 2009.

Part Eleven: Vale

31: Unearthing the Story of Dakota KN584

And so to the 21st Century. I started the research which led to this book through an initial enquiry submitted to the British Ministry of Defence ("MOD") in 2003. This initiative was triggered during an interview with my mother, which I undertook shortly after she was diagnosed with cancer and there was a possibility that she might not have long to live. At this point, I was particularly interested in how Wig died, and I knew nothing of the history described above. In response to the enquiry, the authorities simply indicated that he had been killed in a plane crash on 7 September 1945, and that his remains were interred in the grounds of "Pongyichaung" at a place called Mewaing with a map reference, QG 854668. Mystifyingly, they then went on to say that he had no known grave, but was commemorated at a memorial in Yangon in a manner that reflected that he was "Missing in Action". On approaching the Commonwealth War Graves Commission, I was able to establish that Wig was indeed commemorated on Face 15 of the Memorial for Allied Troops which is located at the Taukkyan War Cemetery in what is now the city of Yangon.

With a busy life, and my mother not keen to pursue the matter any further, we let matters lie and I did not resume my investigations until well after my mother's death in 2009. That was a tough year for me, with fire destroying my home in the country, and recovery from the trauma took several years. When I eventually got around to going through my mother's effects in 2013, the discovery of letters, pictures and other memorabilia instigated a new investigation. On resuming my research, I initially traced further information about the plane crash through the apocryphal records provided by the "RAF Commands" web site which read as follows.

> *"The crash of the Dakota Mark IV number KN584 of 357 Squadron, Burma 16, was on 7th September 1945. The plane left Rangoon en route for Kandy. The aircraft was recorded as missing on a day sortie, but the cause of its loss was not established. There were sixteen crew and passengers, including Lieutenant Colonel Sydney Isaac Wigginton, 31, OBE, Sherwood Foresters Regiment."*

In following up a trail of messages from relatives of people killed in the crash, it appeared, anecdotally, that the reason for the crash was that the aircraft was *"knocked out of the sky by a sudden gust of wind"* whilst flying through mountains. This seemed a bit far-fetched but, at this stage, I knew nothing of the Myanmar weather conditions in September except to say that it would have been the monsoon season.

In addition to investigating information about the crash, I also tried to find the site mentioned by the MOD. I searched in vain on modern maps of Myanmar for the place called Mewaing, and the map reference provided by the authorities was of no help. The search was not assisted by the fact that the local names with which I was working had all been changed since the Second World War by a Myanmar regime keen to extinguish all vestiges of the British presence. However, I eventually located the town of Mewaing through what were quite serendipitous circumstances. In the summer of 2013, I was visiting the UK and met up with an old friend of mine, Dick Gupwell, who I had not seen for over 40 years. Our meeting was arranged through a mutual friend, Roger Mallion, and we got together at Roger's home in Canterbury Kent in July. I told Dick about my research and he put me in touch with a retired University of London military historian Colonel Sam Pope, and an associate of his Sally Maclean, who worked with Karen war veterans. He knew both of them from when he had worked at the European Commission in Brussels. After several exchanges about my research, Sam located Mewaing using Google Earth. He also identified that the word "Pongyichaung" actually meant monastery. When I followed up with my own search on Google Earth, I found what seemed to be an existing village by a river and an area that looked very much like a temple complex. Other information on the internet showed hills around 1500 to 2000 metres above sea level to the west.

In the meantime, about a month later back in Australia, and again quite by chance, I was telling a friend of mine Robert Agnew about my research. He told me that his son Toby played Australian Rules footy with a chap called Tom Kean who had married a Burmese woman, and who was now working as a journalist in Yangon. I contacted Tom and he put me in touch with a Burmese lady called Khaing Tun (known as Khine) who amongst other things had undertaken investigations into World War Two crash sites. Khine offered to make some initial enquiries about Mewaing on my behalf, and she learnt from the Head Monk at a monastery in Bilin (about 200kms to the north-east of Yangon) that the village of Mewaing certainly still existed, but was off limits for foreigners because local Karen insurgents had until very recently been engaged in hostilities with the Burmese army. This left me very

306

Mewaing Monastery Entrance Gate (left) and burial site (right), 2014

much in a quandary, and I started a discussion with Khine about her going to Mewaing on my behalf.

Then, in early 2014, I was contacted again by Sam Pope indicating that his colleague Sally Maclean was about to visit Burma as a part of her work with veterans and refugees. In the course of her visit in early February, she was planning to meet with a Karen lady called Naw Jercy who worked with the Royal Commonwealth Ex Services League.[338] After some email exchanges ahead of her trip, I negotiated through Sally for Naw Jercy and her son Ephraim to make a field trip to Mewaing to reconnoitre the village and monastery, and undertake a search for the plane and the burial site. This was scheduled for early March.

Naw Jercy and Ephraim left Yangon on 17 March 2014. They travelled east by bus to Hpa-an where they stayed overnight with friends. On 18 March, they headed north to Bilin, and then up to Papun where they hired a motor bike and joined up with a support team of three other people including a Baptist minister who provided a pastoral service to Christians living in Mewaing. The following day, the whole group then travelled to Mewaing along an unsealed road through thick vegetation.[339] It took about four hours to get to their destination, and their journey included a crossing of the main Bilin River and a local tributary close by the village.[340]

---

[338] "Naw" being the Karen word for "Mrs/Ms/Miss".

[339] I have subsequently been told that this was a track established by the British and Karen during World War Two.

[340] The location of Mewaing can be seen on the Operation Character map in Chapter 27.

According to Naw Jercy's investigations, Mewaing turned out to be a village of around 700 people and 100 houses which sits in a cleared area, with fields cultivated for rice production. The surrounding hills are rich in minerals, and the village depends in part on gold prospecting. On arrival, she met with village elders and began to explain the purpose of her visit. At first, she was viewed with some suspicion. But she gained acceptance with the assistance of the Baptist minister who quickly contrived a story that she wanted to visit the burial site of her grand-father. She was then shown around. As expected, on the edge of the village there was a monastery complex, including communal buildings some of which were currently being used by the Myanmar military. The monastery was still operating and had an elaborate entrance gate and a small stupa, together with living quarters for a number of monks. It also had a burial ground. In the monastery, Naw Jercy met and talked with the Head Monk, U Tun Lin. He took Ephraim to the burial site which is now covered by banana trees.

Mewaing Monastery – Naw Jercy meets Saw Thone Khin

Naw Jercy and Ephraim stayed at the village of Mewaing for about a week. During their visit, they ventured along a walking track towards the location of the crash site and visited the adjacent village of Lerwahkho which is about four hours walk from Mewaing. There, Naw Jercy was introduced to a man who claimed to be 96 years old and who was able to recall the air crash in 1945. His name was Saw Thone Khin *("Saw" meaning "Mr")*. Saw Thone was an ex-serviceman who had served in the Home Guard during the Second World War and had clear memories of the British. He told the following story.

"In September 1945, the villagers witnessed the crash and, later, a local British Officer named Eric and a red head organised a party of 20 villagers

308

to go to the site.[341] [342] We travelled for a couple of days through thick jungle and located the plane. As requested by Eric, we removed the bodies, and brought them back to Mewaing where the monks buried them in a grave in the grounds of the monastery with a cross and name plate as advised by the British officers."

It is almost certainly the case that the Eric to which Saw Thone Khin referred was Eric Battersby and that he or a colleague took the photographs of the burial site which were then returned to the authorities in Calcutta and London.[343] Copies were then sent to the relatives in the UK. The Wigginton copies remain in family archives.

Oxygen Bottle from KN584

Saw Thone went on to tell Naw Jercy that, in the weeks following the crash, the villagers removed parts of the plane and carried these items back to the village where they were utilised for various purposes. Remnants included several oxygen bottles, an item frequently carried by the Dakota aircraft, which have subsequently been used as a water tank and a still by the villagers of Mewaing and other adjacent settlements. There is evidence from local villagers that much of the plane was eventually removed for its scrap metal value.

During the visit, Naw Jercy's son Ephraim and a friend attempted to follow a path up to the location of the crash site in the mountains which the local Karen people call War Plar Lay (Wablawkyo in 1945 and now Baik Kyi Ma in Burmese). It was anticipated that the round trip would take two to four days, and might involve some danger as the area was frequented by tigers and bears. However, after walking for about two hours, Ephraim was stopped by the commander of the local KNU (Karen National Union) insurgents and prevented from completing the journey. Ephraim believed

---

[341] The officer in charge of this team was in fact Major Harold Bourne, who gave evidence to the subsequent Court of Inquiry.

[342] I have subsequently identified the red head as a Dennis Ford, otherwise known as Haggis. He died in 2009.

[343] Initially, Battersby was a liaison officer with the AFO in Rangoon and was later with the Mongoose team of *Operation Character,* placing him at Mewaing.

that they suspected him of looking for some items of value to remove. He was not therefore able to confirm the location of the crash site, or determine whether there was anything left of the plane on location.

A few days later, Naw Jercy passed news of the success of her trip back to our team in England and Australia. I received an email from her with great excitement. Later, she returned to Yangon with photographic and video evidence which was sent to me. In turn, this material was passed to the newly appointed British Defence Attaché in Yangon Colonel Tony Stern, the Commonwealth War Graves Commission ("CWGC"), and the MOD who deal with the relatives of casualties. Following Naw Jercy's intrepid journey, the CWGC acknowledged that the site at Mewaing might warrant recognition as a war grave, as did the MOD. However, amongst other things, they indicated that formal recognition would require the despatch of an investigating team to confirm the existence of the remains of the 16 casualties.

After the success of Naw Jercy's trip, in May 2014, I made a decision in principle to visit Myanmar in person in order to check out for myself all the information about the crash and burial sites that had been obtained on the first reconnoitre. I say "in principle" because, without some form of official support including special travel permits, I knew that any such trip might be restricted in value through denial of full access to the sites. To improve the chance of success, I did my best to secure some sort of formal commitment from the CWGC to recognise the burial site, as I judged that this might have some influence with the Myanmar government in granting a special visa to visit Mewaing.

At this point, the CWGC were non-committal. Their recognition of a burial site is not given lightly, and is based on due process involving their independent verification of all the facts. In particular, they will not recognise a burial site unless they have satisfied themselves beyond reasonable doubt that it contains genuine remains. However, they have limited resources, and are loath to commit themselves unless they think there is a good chance of finding sound evidence. At least in this case, SOE had confirmed the original site in 1946, with photographic evidence and correspondence to my mother (and the relatives of other casualties). And when I had made enquiries in 2003, the MOD had confirmed the location as a monastery at Mewaing.

Some months passed, during which time I became increasingly frustrated. Then, on 16 June 2014, I received confirmation from Sue Raftree of the

MOD that the CWGC were indeed sending a team to investigate the site. In an email she said:

> *"I have highlighted this case with the CWGC who have asked for their outer area representative to visit the area. I do not know how long this will take. If it is decided that the grave contains the crew and passengers of Dakota KN584 they will inform us and our work begins."*

On receiving this news, I immediately wrote to the CWGC seeking written confirmation. I received a positive response from them on 24 June 2014, indicating that *"the Commission is now looking into this matter, and our Commemorations Policy Manager will be in touch with further details in due course"*. Around the same time, it was suggested to me by Sam Pope that I should approach Viscount Slim for his support in achieving recognition of the site, and the contribution of my father to the war effort in Burma. Viscount John Slim is the son of General William Slim who commanded the 14th Army that recaptured Rangoon in May 1945 (and was later to become Governor General of Australia). At the time of writing this book, Viscount Slim was both the President of the Burma Star Association, and the Britain-Australia Society.[344] [345] I wrote to Viscount Slim in June 2014 and, in a letter to me dated 3 July 2014, I received heartening support which spurred me on to make a personal visit to Myanmar. I scheduled this for late October 2014 and then focussed on trying to get a permit to visit Mewaing. Whilst, at this point, I was in no doubt that my trip would be worthwhile, I had no illusions about the challenges of reaching the burial site not to mention the crash site. After the difficulties encountered by Naw Jercy, it was very clear that the sites were in an area which was off limits, and that any trip to the crash site would be especially challenging given the terrain and wild life.

From the period commencing June, I made strenuous efforts to obtain from the Burmese government a permit to travel to Mewaing. I pursued various avenues, including in particular the Burmese Embassy in Canberra, and the British Embassy in Yangon. I never received a response to any of the enquiries at the Burmese Embassy. However, the Defence Attaché in Yangon

---

[344] The Burma Star Association is an organisation which provides for communication between the members of allied forces who were engaged in the war in Burma during World War Two.
[345] The Britain-Australia Society is an organisation which fosters relations between Australians and British people with Australian connections.

continued to make efforts on my behalf. Matters were not made any easier by the rising tensions between the Burmese Army and local KNU insurgents with at least one fatality during this period.

In August, I was fortunate to have an opportunity to have a conversation with the aforementioned Burmese journalist Tom Kean who was on a visit to Melbourne and interviewed me about the case. Subsequently, he wrote an article on Wig which was published in the Myanmar Times on 13 October 2014. Tom did a great job of telling Wig's story and linking it to my personal journey, and it put Wig's exploits on the public record for which our family should be for ever grateful to him. Apart from that, and with more immediate concerns in mind, after publication it must surely have been the case that none of the authorities in Yangon could now be ignorant of either my intended visit or the need for a permit!

I now concluded arrangements for my visit, which include both a tourist trip to regional Myanmar, as well as an extended period in the Yangon area with the hope of being able to visit the burial and crash sites. For me, this was quite a challenging prospect. During my life I have done a fair amount of overseas travel, but I have not ventured to relatively remote places on my own for quite a while. That's because, at 70 years of age, whilst I am still relatively fearless I am not quite as physically resilient as I once was. In the case of the trip to Myanmar, I perceived a number of risks. These included not only the problems with the local insurgency, but the physical challenge of trekking through a jungle supposedly inhabited by bears and tigers, not to mention the health risks from malaria and Dengue Fever. Then there was the risk of kidnapping! He was only half joking when my son Andrew asked me, as he took me to the airport for the start of my journey, how much I wanted him to pay for the ransom!

I left for Melbourne in late October and arrived in Myanmar on the morning of Wednesday 29 October. It was a hot and sticky day, and it remained that way for the entire trip. From the first moment in Yangon, I sensed that this was a friendly and reasonably well ordered place, at last on the surface. It was quaint that the passport control area of the airport had lines for Myanmar Nationals, Foreigners, Diplomats and Seamen. There didn't appear to be any seamen, and somehow I doubted whether the folk in the Diplomat queue were diplomats. In fact the place was swarming with foreign aid and development workers speaking Russian, German, French, and several other languages.

The first thing that strikes you when you get onto the roads in Yangon is

312

the volume of traffic, which frequently grinds to a halt that in 2014 could then last for quite a long time. Compared with other Asian cities I know, in

Yangon there were very few motor bikes and scooters – they're apparently banned except for certain government employees of the under-cover variety. And of course, there was the curiosity of having the mostly right-hand vehicles driving on the right hand side of the road. It made alighting from a bus

Plate from KN584 fuselage

especially dangerous. My hotel was well appointed and a good base for what lay ahead. It was opposite the People's Park, close to the Shwedagon Pagoda which dominates the Yangon skyline, and just a $2 taxi trip from down town. In the first few days, I got in touch with Colonel Tony Stern at the British Embassy, Tom Kean at the Myanmar Times, and Naw Jercy. I arranged to see them all before setting off on a tourist trip.

I met Colonel Stern at my hotel. He was a friendly but very proper British Army kind of a guy, and he had some bad news for me. On the very day of my arrival he had received an email from the Office of Military Security Affairs ("OCMSA") saying that a permit for me to visit the burial and crash sites was most definitely refused "on security grounds". Colonel Stern's advice to me was to abandon the field trip. The risk of being caught was significant and, given the official edict, my insurance cover would be invalidated. He also told me what he knew of the crash of KN584. It was his information that there were more than 16 bodies, and that only part of the bodies had been removed from the crash site to the monastery in Mewaing, the femur bone. The upshot of this was that most of the remains were still up on the mountain side where they'd probably been buried near the crash.

I also met with Naw Jercy at my hotel. She and her son Ephraim came together with a friend named Ada Htwe who helped with translation and transport. Our conversation was a deeply moving experience. For the first time, I was talking to people who had actually stood within feet of Wig's remains. Naw Jercy was keen to give me a full account of their trip to Mewaing, and Ephraim pulled out of a paper bag the first bit of concrete evidence of the crash, two pieces of metal plate from the plane, which he

313

gave to me.[346] In turn, I shared with them the disappointment of being banned from visiting Mewaing.

A couple of days later, I had a second meeting with Naw Jercy at her home, in a suburb of Yangon called Insein (pronounced "insane") which is the home of a major settlement of Karen people. She lived in quite a big house with a second storey given over to accommodating Bible Students. At Naw Jercy's suggestion we began my visit by driving over to see one of the Karen "comrades", a man called Tancy McDonald. Now deceased, when I met him he was aged 91 and living with his daughter and extended family. He spoke excellent English and talked about his ancestors (he had a Scottish grandfather), his life, his family, his work in the timber industry and a bank, and his time as an agent for the British during the 1940s. He also spoke in particular about *Operation Character* and the role of the Karen resistance movement in undermining the Japanese in the months before and during the advance on Rangoon in May 1945 of General Slim's 14th Army. He told me that the Japanese were just as well organised with their intelligence services as were the British, and that there were frequent close escapes from capture. We also talked about the grave site in Mewaing and he suggested that we should move the remains to Yangon. This was for two reasons. He thought that they would be more accessible to relatives, and he believed that the Buddhists in Mewaing would not want a new and Christian memorial in their cemetery. He did not hold out much hope about the political situation, telling me that the Karens were going through a difficult time, with a split between those who were willing to accept federalism and those who wanted an independent Karen state. After leaving Tancy, we went to visit another old combatant, a lady now deceased who called herself Major Godwiler's No 1 wife, he having married a second younger lady late in life. The Major was now deceased. She told me of her time as a nurse during the war, related her husband's exploits for the British in the Karen Hills, and showed me some wonderful wartime photographs.

After these memorable visits, we returned to Naw Jercy's home. Sitting in her lounge room, cooled by a fan which intermittently stopped working as there were frequent power cuts, we then got down to the serious business of re-living her trip to Mewaing in March. This included anecdotes from the

---

[346] He had been given these by Saw Thone Khin. Experts on Dakota aircraft to whom I have had access through a friend of mine Stuart Strachan, have indicated that this plate is probably the door of a small compartment from inside the plane.

Left: Taukkyan War Cemetery. Right: Wig's name on colonnade at Taukkyan

journey as well as pictures and videos. The experience was totally overwhelming for me, and the information provided was like gold dust. We then considered the news that I was not allowed to visit the burial or crash sites, and entertained a plan which would involve Ephraim visiting Saw Thone Khin in the remote village near the crash site and inviting him to meet me in Bilin in mid-November. At the end of our meeting, I went away to think about this plan.

Before setting off on my tourist trip which started on the evening of Sunday 2 November, I had one other excursion which I undertook on that morning. I took a taxi out to the Commonwealth War Graves Cemetery at Taukkyan which is about 20 kms to the north of Yangon. It was another hot and sweaty day. Although there were initially a few local people taking a walk in the grounds, I soon had the place to myself apart from the sounds of some Buddhist music in the distance. Perhaps not surprisingly, on walking down the main pathway, I found myself overcome with grief. This place was the first real connection with Wig, even if only by association. I had seen pictures before, but it was very moving to actually be there.

The main building in the cemetery grounds is a classical structure, with columns that commemorate all those lost souls for whom there is no marked grave (the Missing in Action). And, laid out before the building, are lines of the graves of those whose bodies actually lie in the cemetery. Quite a number of the head-stones carry the poignant messages of loved ones. High up on the 15th column of the main structure I found the memorial to Wig as shown in the picture. The sight of this brought tears to my eyes. As I stood reflecting on what it all meant, I was approached by a kindly and somewhat official

315

City Hall, Yangon

looking local man. He asked me where I came from, and he listened carefully as I explained the reason for my visit to the memorial. He then told me about the cemetery and the two other similar sites for Commonwealth soldiers in Myanmar, in central Yangon for people who died in the city gaol, and down south for the British, Australian, and Dutch soldiers who died during the construction of the Thai-Burma railway. Afterwards, he offered me a trip back to Yangon in his 4WD with his wife. During the journey he proceeded to inform me that he was in fact Thet Mon, the CWGC Regional Manager with responsibility for all CWGC sites in Myanmar. He knew Colonel Stern, and was acquainted with Viscount Slim. We talked about Wig and the burial site in Mewaing, and I alerted him to the commitment by the CWGC in London to investigate. He showed great interest and support and, not for the first time, I felt that I was being blessed with good fortune in meeting someone whose knowledge and experience was so relevant to my mission.

On the drive back to Yangon, we also discussed the options for dealing with the bodies of the casualties. Thet Mon indicated that he was sympathetic to the idea that the remains should be brought to Taukkyan and he suggested that, at the very least, a special memorial might be established in the grounds of the cemetery. There was certainly room in the grounds for a new monument. He was interested in seeing any evidence of the burial site in Mewaing and I agreed to provide the pictures taken in 1946, together with a map of the monastery grounds. We also considered the problem that might arise if it was confirmed that parts of the bodies were up on the mountain, and we agreed that dealing with this might be quite a challenge. In our discussion, Thet Mon gave me his take on the political situation, and explained that little could be done about the access issues until there was a political and associated military settlement between the Burmese government and Karen independence movement. He said that such a settlement might be some way off, but that things in Myanmar sometimes changed quite quickly. Finally, he told me that 2015 was a big year for the

316

CWGC in Myanmar because it was the 70th anniversary of the end of the war. The way in which this would be commemorated was the subject of much discussion by all those involved, because the Japanese were now friends and trading partners of Myanmar and the form of any ceremony would need to be respectful of their sensitivities. We noted that it was quite likely that Lord Slim would visit for this event and we held out some hope that the KN584 issue would be resolved by then.

That Sunday evening, back in my hotel, I joined up with the charming group of English, New Zealand and Australian folk with whom I would spend the next ten days visiting a number of places including Mandalay, Bagan, and Inle Lake. On the first day, this tour took in highlights of Yangon, including the Town Hall which was the British Headquarters in colonial times and during the war. It's a building with a strange mixture of British colonial and oriental architecture and was the place frequented by Wig just before he died in September 1945. I was conscious of that strange feeling of *deja vu* as I looked upon it, envisaging Wig as he walked up the steps.

During the next ten days of tourist travel, I gave a lot of thought as to whether we should proceed with the plan to bring Saw Thone Khin to a meeting in Bilin. After consulting with my nephew Alex, I decided that it was too much to ask of a 96 year old man to undertake a ten hour trip with a return trip to follow. So I thought through some other options and came up with a Plan B, which would involve Ephraim undertaking another mission to visit Mewaing and Saw Thone Khin with the object of checking out some unresolved details of what happened in 1945. I documented the aims of this plan as the following:

a)   To give a letter to Saw Thone Khin to thank him for his part in the burial of Wig, and the support he gave to the British cause in the War. Knowing the problem with language, I determined to have this letter translated into Burmese.

b)   To make a gift to Saw Thone Khin as a token of appreciation.

c)   In conversation with Saw Thone Khin, to obtain the answers to some questions which were designed to clarify a number of points about the crash and the burial.

d)   To prepare a detailed map of the monastery in Mewaing, including an indication of the burial site in the banana grove, for use by the CWGC.

e)   To speak with representatives of the local school to find out what help they might like through some form of gift in kind.

I emailed this plan to Naw Jercy and, on my return to Yangon, she called me to confirm that Ephraim would undertake the mission. The following day, we met and confirmed the details of the plan and the terms. With our negotiations completed, Naw Jercy then took me to visit another retired Karen soldier, Saw Berny, who was a radio operator in the *Otter* zone of *Operation Character* in 1945. He was a frail and blind man, but his mental capacity was excellent. He said that he remembered my father's name, and he introduced me to a great deal of interesting information, including material taken from a book on the work of Lt Colonel Edgar Peacock.[347] He said that he had recently been visited by Peacock's grand-son, Duncan Gilmour and gave me contact details. He also told me that he prayed for the British royal family every night! After this further wonderful experience with a nonagenarian, I returned to my hotel utterly astounded by the continuing good luck in connecting with anecdotal war time history. That evening, I contacted Duncan Gilmour by email and he responded immediately. Amongst other things, he was able to provide me with a great reference to the crash of KN584 in the book on SOE in the Far East by Terence O'Brien which is the source of material in this book.[348]

The following day, Ephraim set forth on a mission that turned out to be far from straightforward. For this trip, and travelling with his uncle, he took a more direct route to Mewaing from Bilin in the south and, after some hours, he was stopped by the KNU who told him that he could go no further. He returned to Bilin but, not one to be easily deterred, he then travelled alone up to Papun, to seek out the Baptist Pastor who had helped him and his mother on the trip to Mewaing in March. Once in Papun he consulted with his mother, who contacted me. We discussed whether he should make another attempt to reach Mewaing, and Ephraim seemed keen to try and complete the mission, so I agreed that he should go. And go he did on Sunday 16 November.

Whilst Ephraim was undertaking his mission, I decided that, since I was barred from going to Mewaing, I would at least make an attempt to get as close as I could to the Karen Hills where the crash and burial took place. I

---

[347] Some elements of Edgar Peacock's work are recorded in Chapter 26.
[348] See the book by Terence O'Brien entitled *"The Moonlight War- The Story of Clandestine Operations in SE Asia, 1944-45"*.

arranged a trip to the pagoda that sits on top of Mount Kyaiktiyo which is 30 kms north of Bilin and about 30 kms south as the crow flies from the crash site. The journey from the town of Kyaikto up the mountain to the Golden Rock pagoda on the top is quite an experience, involving an hour's drive up a steep and circuitous road in the back of a lorry jammed close with the locals including monks and a scattering of tourists. The pagoda, sitting on top of the finely balanced golden rock, is a spectacular spot, as are the 360° views from the adjacent plaza. From this place, I looked north, to the fold of hills stretching to Mount War Plar Lay in the distance. It was the closest I would get to Wig's final resting place on this trip, and I couldn't help thinking that this golden rock may well have been one of the last things that the servicemen on KN584 saw before they died.

In the meantime, Ephraim travelled to Mewaing with the same Baptist Pastor who had accompanied him earlier in the year. They travelled without incident and, over the next few days, Ephraim was able to undertake all the elements of his mission. On his way back, on Wednesday 19 November, he stayed the night in Mewaing. Late in the evening, he was woken by a troop of Burmese Army soldiers, who took him away to their barracks in the village and interrogated him about why he was in Mewaing. He explained what he was doing and they were sceptical, suspecting him of being up to no good. They took his camera and telephone, returned him to his house, and left him with the clear impression that he might be hearing more. He retired, in a state of shock. Then, as he was lying in bed, he was visited by soldiers of the KNU who also wanted to know why he had persisted in visiting Mewaing, despite the fact that they had turned him back on the previous journey from the south. He again explained what he was doing and they seemed to accept his explanation. To his relief they let him go, but by now even the cool headed Ephraim was quite shaken.

The next day, Ephraim returned to Papun from where he telephoned his mother. It was late morning, and I was visiting her to discuss progress. He provided a full account of all that had happened and also, true to his mission, provided me with answers to the questions I had asked him to put to Saw Thone. He reported on other aspects of his trip and indicated that he would send a map of the monastery when he returned. However, he explained that it had been difficult to talk with the school and this would have to wait for another day. We were all relieved that he had survived the ordeal.

319

Mount Kyaiktiyo Monastery (above) and Karen Hills north of Mt Kyaiktiyo (below), 2014

The following day, whilst he was recuperating in Papun, Ephraim was again visited by the Burmese Army. Thankfully, having checked out his story, and with the evidence of my mission available through the Myanmar Times article by Tom Kean, they returned his telephone and told him that if he wanted his camera he'd have to report to their local headquarters. He let that pass and, with much relief, he returned to Yangon. At this point, it appeared that on this SOE type mission all was well that ended well. But I had some misgivings that this was not the end of the story.

32: An Appropriate Memorial

As I returned from Myanmar on 21 November 2014, my mind was totally overwhelmed with the detail and insight obtained during the visit. Although I had not been able to personally access either the burial site or the crash site, there was now enough first hand and corroborative evidence to sustain my submission to the CWGC for a formal recognition that the casualties of KN584 were buried in Mewaing and that a change in the nature of the commemoration in Yangon was warranted. Once the hostilities between the Burmese government and Karen insurgents was settled, a personal visit to the sites was also plausible, although I would certainly be taking note of advice from Ephraim and others that any search party for the plane would require a hunter given the tigers and bears in them there hills!

While waiting for the political settlement which would open up the area to foreign visitors, the next stage was to brief the CWGC with all the information on the crash and burial sites now to hand, including the evidence of Saw Thone Khin and the map of the Mewaing monastery.[349] I decided that this briefing would need to include reference to the options for managing the remains, and achieving an appropriate commemoration. As regards the remains, they could either be left where they were or moved to Taukkyan Cemetery in Yangon. And, at the very least, there would need to be a new form of commemoration at Taukkyan as the casualties were most definitely not "Missing in Action".[350] The briefing was sent to the CWGC in England and Myanmar in December.

In the meantime, following the trip to Myanmar, the time had come to initiate a systematic attempt to contact the surviving relatives of the 15 other casualties from the crash. They were certainly entitled to know the full story, and to have a say in what happened to the remains. To set the ball rolling, in January 2015, my nephew Alex and I commenced a project to track down as many of the parties as we could. We did this by using the RAF Web site designed to connect old war time colleagues and their relatives. We did

---

[349] At the time of writing, a peace settlement has been agreed between the Myanmar government and the KNU, and there has also been a General Election in which a non-military government has come to power. The parties are now set in earnest to negotiate a settlement within some federal framework.

[350] It is important to note that the existing commemoration at Taukkyan reflects the view that the persons named are "Missing in Action" with no known burial site.

immediately manage to identify and contact the relatives of three of the other casualties. They were supportive of our efforts, and were able to provide considerable intelligence from their own efforts over several years. At a later stage, this list was extended via the veteran network to include the relatives and friends of five further casualties making nine of us in all.

The CWGC replied to my submission regarding a change to commemoration arrangements on 23 January 2015. Whilst sympathetic to my representations, they indicated that the current arrangements at Taukkyan Cemetery continued to be an appropriate commemoration of the casualties of Flight KN584. They noted that the current commemoration had been established because the "grave investigation unit" working in Myanmar after the war had indicated that the burials at Mewaing were "unrecoverable and unmaintainable". They stated that this assessment had now been the subject of review, and that the previous decision to commemorate the casualties as "missing" continued to be appropriate. This was because it was not safe to go to Mewaing, and because the condition of the *possible* grave site had deteriorated over time to the point where it was not a suitable location for the commemoration of Commonwealth war casualties.

I was obviously most disappointed with this response and, in a letter dated 17 February 2015, I indicated that I did not accept the decision to take no further action. The reason for my reaction was that the burial site for the casualties of the crash of KN584 were in fact known and corroborated. The casualties were **not** missing, and therefore the commemoration was inappropriate. In my letter, I then went on to propose a number of options for an appropriate commemoration, including a memorial at Mewaing when circumstances permitted, and acknowledgement of the casualties at Taukkyan through a new memorial indicating the names of the deceased, the location of the remains, and the date and place of the crash.

There the matter lay until I made another visit to England in May 2015. In mid-June of that year, I made a major break-through. As part of my research for this biography at the British National Archives, I obtained access to Wig's SOE personnel file.[351] To my astonishment, contained in this file was the record of the *"Proceedings of a Court of Inquiry"* conducted at Meerut (SOE Headquarters in India) on 29 January 1946 and presided over by a Major D C McCoull. The Inquiry had been convened by Lt Colonel O H Brown (Officer Commanding ME 25 – the Jungle Warfare School) and

---

[351] See SOE File HS 9/1589/8.

was a relatively routine matter to provide clarity that the deceased did not in any way contribute to their own demise.[352] During proceedings, evidence was taken from two officers, Lt Colonel Robert de Lisle King and Major Harold Bourne and their testimony was recorded for posterity. Lt Colonel King confirmed that Wig and five other SOE staff (three officers and two other ranks) were on the plane KN584 travelling on 9 September 1945 from Rangoon to Calcutta, and that the plane was scheduled to make a drop to Allied forces stationed near Papun. Major Bourne provided a detailed account of how he visited the crash site and arranged for the casualties to be removed to Mewaing monastery where the bodies were interred. The full transcript of his evidence is provided below as the authoritative account.

"On 23 November 1945 (11 weeks after the crash), *Wing Commander Gane and I proceeded to the scene of the wrecked aircraft, map reference QG 726604. The aircraft had flown into the mountain about 200 feet from the top, where it had burst into flames immediately. It had then turned and slid down the face of the rock and settled on a ledge about 50 feet below leaving its starboard engine above where it first struck the mountain. The plane then appears to have exploded as I found pieces of metal quite some distance from the plane. I am sure that no one would have been able, had they been injured, to have escaped from the wreck because as the aircraft slid down the rock the whole of the cargo would have pinned them down. I found nothing amongst the wreckage by which I could identify any individual person.[353] I had all the remains brought back to Mewaing; there, I tried to piece them together but only by the femur bones could I make anything out at all. The number of femur bones found were thirty, making fourteen pairs and two of which did not match. The remains have been interred at Mewaing in the grounds of Pongyichaung, map reference QG 854668."*

In response to questioning, Major Bourne went onto confirm that the tailpiece of the plane was intact and bore the registration number KN584. The record concludes with a summary by the officer who convened the Inquiry, Lt Colonel Brown, in which he states that:

---

[352] ME 25 was the code names for the SOE Jungle Training School in the Far East at that time.
[353] There is anecdotal evidence that a log book or diary was found, but this is not recorded by Major Bourne or corroborated by any other source.

324

"I am of the opinion that the personnel under enquiry were killed in the aircraft found by Major H E Bourne. In my opinion, it has been clearly proved that they were on duty and there appears to be no evidence that they were in any way to blame for the accident."

This was of course the most conclusive evidence one could encounter to verify the fact of the flight, the crash site, and the burial site. It was also of interest that, as mentioned earlier in this book, in 1945/46 Mewaing was not some remote village in the middle of nowhere. It was in fact an established SOE base within the *Mongoose* zone of *Operation Character*, with a runway, control tower and accommodation for SOE operatives and Karen levies. In finding this transcript, I felt that the end of the journey to obtain appropriate recognition was in sight. Needless to say, I passed a copy of the documentation to the CWGC and, when I met the Commemorations Policy Manager, Nic Andrews, on 16 July 2015 I received an encouraging response. It was agreed that I should make a fresh submission for what is called an *"Alternative Commemoration"* of the casualties at Taukkyan cemetery.

On 22 July 2015, I returned to Australia and immediately made a fresh submission to the CWGC for a new form of recognition for the casualties of the crash of Dakota KN584, including a full and final account of the crash and burial which is shown in Appendix 20. The gist of this submission was that, when the security situation permitted, there should be a memorial at the village of Mewaing commemorating the crash and the burial of the casualties. In the meantime, since the current memorial at Taukkyan was not appropriate (commemorating as it does casualties who are "missing in action"), a new form of memorial should be established. Under the CWGC policy for Alternative Commemorations, this was likely to consist of a memorial providing details of the crash and burial site, together with individual commemorations for the 16 casualties each with an inscription provided by the surviving relatives where possible.

After quite a wait, on 26 April 2016, the CWGC approved the proposal for an Alternative Commemoration. They determined that there would indeed be a new memorial at the Cemetery which would indicate the date and place of the crash of KN584 and the place where the casualties were buried in Mewaing. There would also be an individual head stone for each of the casualties. The issue of a memorial at Mewaing would be addressed at a later stage when the security situation allowed. An official commemoration service for the new memorial was scheduled for November 2016. In the meantime, the Regional Manager of the CWGC made contact with both the Head Monk at Mewaing Monastery and the local Baptist Minister. They reached an agreement that the burial site would be respected and preserved within the grounds of the monastery.

In early November 2016, I again travelled to Yangon for the ceremony which took place on 13 November at Taukkyan Cemetery. It was attended by relatives of four of the casualties. The Commonwealth War Graves Commission did an excellent job, with both the central memorial and individual headstones.

New Memorial 2016

New Memorial 2016

Author with Naw Jercy and Ephraim 2016

327

Apart from the relatives, the ceremony was also attended by Naw Jercy and Ephraim, the British Ambassador, James Patrick, and a number of other dignitaries. And, afterwards, we were all invited back to the Ambassador's residence for a reception. Over brunch, the relatives scoped one final mission for Ephraim, which he undertook in the following week to check out a number of further details about the crash and burial sites with surviving veterans in Mewaing. A few days later he returned, and confirmed that in 1945 the recovery team had indeed removed all the body parts that they could find to the burial site at the Mewaing Monastery, with bones enclosed within metal boxes. The locals were in some doubt about the number of casualties, leaving the official body count of 16 as the most likely number.

The following week, I met with Thet Mon, the CWGC Regional Manager and thanked him for all his efforts. He confirmed that the engravings for both Wig and Lt Col Kennedy would now be removed from the columns of Taukkyan because they were no longer "Missing in Action". And he held out hope for a local memorial in Mewaing, one day when the security situation is resolved. For now, this was an end to the matter.

33: Wig's Citations

To provide an overview of Wig's war time achievements, the most authoritative source is the "secret" citation which led to his posthumous OBE on 20 September 1945, and the other tributes made in the previous three years. (A copy of the Commemorative Scroll for the OBE is provided in Appendix 18.) The citation reads as follows:

"Lt Colonel Wigginton was given responsibility for Air Operations of SOE in November 1942, when mounting air supplies to Allied and partisan formations and missions in enemy occupied territory was in its infancy. His work was one of the major factors which raised the percentage of success of clandestine air sorties to a level which encouraged the military and air force to allot the aircraft and other resources necessary for a large scale expansion of Special Operations.

In 1944, as GSO 1 Air of HQ SOM (top ranking General Staff Officer of Special Operations Military), he was responsible for the mounting of air sorties for a range of special agencies in the MTO (Military Transport Operations) including ISLD, PWB, OSS and IS9. [354] [355] [356] [357]

During 1944, the results achieved by SO (M) Air Operations were far in excess of anything which had been envisaged. 15,000 sorties were flown of which over 10,000 were successful, a total of 20,000 tons of stores were supplied to over 200 missions or supply zones in the Balkans, Italy, Austria, Czechoslovakia, Poland, and Southern France. For this, Lt Colonel Wigginton was responsible for mounting air operations to be carried out by over 200 aircraft of 5 different nationalities (British, American, Russian, Polish, and Italian) from 7 different airfields to pinpoints in 11 different countries.

The organisation and control of these operations was more than a

---

[354] The ISLD Inter Service Liaison Department, a euphemism for SIS (Foreign Office).

[355] The PWB is the Political Warfare Bureau.

[356] The OSS is the Office of Strategic Services of the United States which was a predecessor of the CIA. Further information is contained in Appendix 12.

[357] Intelligence School 9 was established in January 1942 as the executive branch of MI9. Its job was to assist British and Commonwealth service personnel to evade capture when behind enemy lines and to assist Prisoners of War to escape. Arguably IS9's most important work was to gather intelligence from and boost the morale of Allied POWs.

remarkable achievement having regard to the difficulties of clandestine W/T (Wireless/Telegraphy) *communications, the number of pinpoints and countries involved, the need for organising ground reception with all the problems of light signals and security considerations, and the variety of the requirements of different agencies.*

During this period, Lt Colonel Wigginton was also responsible for initiating the organisation for the emergency landing grounds for pick up operations in enemy occupied Yugoslavia. Of particular note is one example when, at 12 hours' notice, Marshal Titos's HQ was successfully evacuated to Italy together with his staff and attached British and American Missions consisting of a total of 150 officers and men.

The Commanding General 15 USAAF (General Twining) also wrote to commend Lt Colonel Wigginton for his work in organising the evacuation by air of large numbers of American aircrews from enemy occupied territory.

For the remarkable success that this officer has achieved by his outstanding qualities of far sightedness, initiative, and clear thinking, I have the honour to recommend he be awarded the OBE. Should this award be approved, it is requested that no details of this commendation be made public or communicated to the press."

The above mentioned letter from General N F Twining to Major General Stawell, dated 22 July 1944, reads as follows:

"It has come to my attention that Lieutenant Colonel S I Wigginton of your command has rendered extremely valuable services to the Fifteenth Air Force. Colonel Wigginton established contact with the Fifteenth Air Force Escape Intelligence Section in early April 1944 and since that time has maintained close liaison with this Headquarters. He has been personally responsible for developing and maintaining the excellent relationships that exist between this Headquarters and Air Operations SO (M). He has exerted himself to see that this Air Force is at all times posted on the latest information pertaining to air evacuation of USAAF personnel from the Balkans.

With the assistance of Colonel Wigginton, valuable contacts were established with other Special Operations sections, resulting in considerable improvement of Fifteenth Air Force escape intelligence technique and the successful evacuation from the Balkans of several hundred valuable airmen. I wish to commend Lieutenant Colonel Wigginton, and to express my appreciation for the services he has rendered to the Fifteenth Air Force. His achievements are a credit to himself and to the armed forces of the United Nations."

Needless to say, Major General Stawell passed on the commendation from General Twining at the time, and there is correspondence on the matter involving Lt Col J G Beevor who logged away the material for future reference in terms of an award.

In addition to receiving the OBE, Wig was "mentioned in despatches" on several occasions as mentioned elsewhere in this book. He was also awarded the following more routine military honours: Africa Star with 8th Army clasp, Italy star, Defence Medal, 1939-45 Star, and War Medal 1939-45. These honours bring us back to where we started this journey. This story had to be told, for all the Wiggintons that follow. Now it is done.

Part Twelve: Postscript

34: A Final Reflection

When I began this book, I did not know where the research would take me. At first, I was just inquisitive about how my father met his end. But, as I uncovered something about his life and the world in which he lived, I became enthralled. And, looking back over the last three years, I can surely say that there was a need for this story to be told. And, in the process, there has been much learning.

First, it is self-evident that people who suffer untimely deaths do not live to tell the tale. I am pleased to have shed light on a life which, without this project, would probably have been left in obscurity for ever. Secondly, I think that my father's short life demonstrates the possibility for the triumph of character in the face of adversity. Wig's story should be an inspiration for all who experience a tough start in life.

Next, I have some reflections on the role and conduct of Irregular Warfare. This takes me back to my visit to Sandhurst College. The reader may recall the words in the *1939 Officer Training Handbook* which read as follows (this is a re-wording):

> *"A Nation must protect the interests vital to its security, and uphold the international covenants to which it is a party. When either of these imperatives is endangered, we endeavour to persuade our would-be opponent to abandon his policy, by all the means in our power – i.e. by imposing our will on him. The means employed are: Diplomacy, Economic Influence, and War. The armed forces are only one means of overcoming the will of the opposing nation. Diplomacy and economic warfare also play an important part in the struggle for supremacy, by assisting our Allies and embarrassing our opponents."*

It would seem that, for the British military in 1940, the concept of generating a *covert* war from within an occupied country was novel because there is no recognition in the *Training Handbook* of the role it might play. And yet, within five brief years, a whole system of conducting unconventional warfare was established which played a major role in World War Two. The key condition for success is that, within every society which fails to meet certain standards of governance and accountability, there will be a residual group who have the potential to resist the brutal and sometimes petty use of authority. Therein lies the seed of destruction for those who would have authoritarian and sociopathic power over others. The brilliance of those who created SOE was the insight to recognise the opportunity for deployment of resources within an occupied land that would encourage that resistance. And, in the implementation, it soon became apparent that this was not only a weapon for developing and sustaining internal resistance but a powerful tool in optimising the conduct of military and political activity.

Although SOE was closed down in 1946, the learning obtained in World War Two was not lost. Many of the people and ideas were transferred to the Foreign Office and what became the Ministry of Defence. Given his reputation, I do wonder whether Wig might have been drawn into continuing his covert activities after the war. We will never know. But, the learning from his ilk lives on in the work of MI6, the SAS, and all the related agencies around the world.

Much has been said about the performance of SOE. There are some who have written histories of this organisation that present a picture of ambition, intrigue, adventure seekers, and even bumbling incompetence. My father's contribution bears witness to the fact that there were people in SOE, I would say a majority, whose main or only concern was to do the right thing and to serve their country with bravery, hard work, and determination. And together, by many measures, they were successful in defending the values in which they believed. I have no hesitation in saying that Wig, and others like him, made a difference.

As regards the more general conduct of the Second World War, the examination of source material on SOE activities has led me to take a mostly positive view about the execution and outcome of the conflicts in Italy, Greece and Yugoslavia. This may be at odds with the views expressed by some other authors who did not have access to the material only released in recent years. The papers I have read indicate that there was no shortage of strategy in all theatres. But the complex and fragmented organisational structure which the British established for the conduct of the war, with the Foreign Office, Military HQ, and SOE each pursuing in good faith separate policy at various times, was bound to produce internal conflict. Add to this, the hugely different local history, political positions, and personalities in the field in those three countries and you have a recipe for outcomes which may not have always been predictable or met expectations. It is also not difficult to conclude that the seeds of subsequent post-war history in those three countries were being sown in full measure. In a different way, much the same

336

is true of the conflict in Burma although it is a special case given the pre-war status as a British colony.

My research has also led me to reflect on the war time strategies of the various combatants. For both the Germans and the Japanese, it was always about a small group of men indulging their sociopathic passion to "dominate" peoples that were considered to be inherently weak and/or inferior. And, with the benefit of hindsight, one cannot fail to be struck by the obsessive/compulsive nature of their strategies, which underestimated the potential for significant resistance, aided and abetted of course by the Allies and organisations like SOE.

For the Allies, it has to be said that, whilst their strategy secured eventual victory in all theatres of war, there was for ever a tension between long term political aims and short term military expediency, with SOE sometimes stuck in the middle. And, whilst the western democracies won the war, as with the Great War, their leaders did not secure an entirely just peace. The quote from Churchill during the Yugoslav campaign, to which I have referred previously, has in particular stuck with me. When presented with the consequences for Yugoslavia after the war, of Allied backing for the communist partisans (to meet short term military objectives of tying down German troops), he is reported as saying *"Well, we won't have to live there after the war, will we."*

The research for the book has led me to modify my view of 20th Century history in a wider sense. In particular, I had not appreciated the extent to which Fascism had infested the governance of what we regard today as the western democracies. Far from being confined to the high profile regimes in Germany, Italy and Spain, by the 1930s various kinds of fascist and/or authoritarian government had extended to virtually every corner of Europe. The pre-war regimes in Greece, Yugoslavia, and Portugal bear witness to this. And there were strong voices and sympathies for Fascism elsewhere, even in Britain, France and the USA. Amongst other things, this right wing extremism was of course a reaction to the fear of Bolshevism. But it also reflected a deeper commitment amongst ordinary people, when faced with economic and social adversity, to embrace a form of populist tribalism which lingers on to this day in so many parts of the world. It also reflects the power of, and danger presented by, vested interests which, if given free rein, can consume a nation.

This learning has resonance in today's global society. In the 21st Century, we in the West tend to take for granted, and indeed take pride in, the accountability provided by our democratic institutions which we naively believe will protect us from the excesses of unbridled power wielded by a few. However, in many respects, nation states have now been replaced by global companies for whom systems of accountability arc few and weak, and the recent rise in anti-establishment populism demonstrates that democracy is potentially fragile and still open to exploitation by demagogues who play loose with the truth.

As regards the Wigginton family, I have reflected on the life that might have been, had Wig survived the War. By all accounts, the match between Wig and Eunice was a happy one. They had a lot in common but also brought to their union complimentary talents. Together, I think they would have achieved a great deal. And I am also sure that they would have had more children. This leaves me with a sadness. One cannot fail to think about the Wiggintons that might have been, and we should cherish the small Wiggintons that we have. Above all, what happened to Wig is such a shocking waste. But that is the consequence of war, which should never be entertained or entered into lightly.

On a more positive note, as I come to the end of the adventure, I have a sense of personal discovery. For 67 years of my life I lived without a father. Long before the start of this journey, I had convinced myself that I did not miss what I had not had. But now I think differently. Children inherit from their parents not only physical characteristics but also something deeper and more difficult to fathom. I am not religious, but I do have a sense of spirit. And I think that this is something that passes between generations. It manifests itself in our sense of belonging, who we think we are, the things for which we feel a passion, and what we think we might achieve in life. Without all of this, our lives have less meaning. Knowing my father as I now do, I have a better sense of who I am and why I am here.

In a wider sense, we are also defined by the people with whom we live and chose to call our friends. In the case of my father, the war time years brought him into contact with some remarkable people, many of whom would go on to make significant contributions to British society. In Appendix 19, I provide a snapshot of these people many of whom would have figured in Wig's life for many years after the war had he survived. Through them, we also know him.

Finally, as I write, the western world is facing a new threat to its existence, the unbridled fanaticism of a new brand of Fascists who describe themselves as Jihadists, and the back-lash into nationalistic tribalism which has

338

manifested itself in various parts of the western world. The insidious forces of terrorism will not be defeated by military means alone. If ever there was a need for a new and improved version of SOE, it is now. I suspect that, in the form of MI6 and the SAS, it already exists. But, as in the 1940s, we the public do not know about their aims or deeds. I sense that, even now, there are people like Wig defending what we have. We should be grateful.

Appendix 1: Eunice's Story

The following is a brief biography of Wig's wife Eunice, which provides some context for the current book. Eunice Piper was born on 14 January 1917 in Clapton, London. She was one of five children of her mother Edith who had been married twice. Edith's first husband, John Doyle with whom she had three children, died of consumption before the First World War. Her second husband, Charles Piper, died in 1921 from wounds received in the First World War. Edith (maiden name Carlisle) was a book-binder, and Charles was an engineer. They both had Scottish ancestors.

Between 1917 and 1922, Eunice lived in London. However, in 1922, following the death of her husband, her mother decided to migrate to Canada. She and the children moved to the industrial town of Oshawa in Ontario Province. Her elder sister (known as Edie to the family) became an Office Manager for Chevrolet and her younger brother Bill became a logger. After a short while, her elder brother Ernie who was a chef left for Australia where he settled for the rest of his life. In later years, her other younger sister Rene would marry an Australian and settle in NSW.

In 1924, the main family returned to London because they did not like the cold, and were home sick. From 1924 to 1935, Eunice lived in a flat near Old Street Tube Station with her mother, her brother Bill, and her younger sister Rene. Eunice was enrolled at and attended Catherine Street Primary School. She then got a scholarship to St Anne's School (a private day school) which she attended between 1928 and 1933. She was a good student and stayed on to matriculate in 1933 when she was 16. She was good at sport and played hockey, tennis, and cricket where her main claim to fame was her fielding. Like Wig, she was a good runner.

Eunice Wigginton, with sister Rene in 1937

In 1933, Eunice enrolled at Goldsmith College where she did courses in English and Social Administration. She graduated aged 18 in 1935 and then obtained a job as a secretary with John Player and Son at their offices in Lenton Boulevard, Nottingham. Her brother-in-law Harry (sister Edie's husband) worked in the marketing department of the parent company, Imperial Tobacco. Moving from London, Eunice lived with Edie and Harry at 9 Orston Drive in Wollaton Park. She was soon promoted to be Junior Secretary and worked for the three Player family members in the business, John, William, and Ashley (the handsome one, according to Eunice). She cycled to work, but sometimes went by trolley tram. It was on a tram in 1936, at the age of 19, that she met her "husband to be" Wig. At the time, he was living in Lenton not far from the John Player site.

Eunice and Wig courted for three years before being married on 10 October 1939. Her first child, Michael was born on 26 March 1941. She and Wig lived at Orston Drive for most of the War, between 1935 and 1945. However, in 1941/42 the immediate family had a spell living at Brockham near Dorking just before Wig set sail for North Africa.

Life in Nottingham in the war was not easy. There were food shortages, and bombing of Nottingham started in early 1941. They had a shelter in the garden. Apart from work, Eunice drove an ARP vehicle in the evenings and was a blood donor.

342

Over the next three to four years, Wig returned after various missions to receive orders for the next. The returns always involved a reunion with Eunice and Michael. Sometimes, he didn't make it back to Nottingham. Eunice would just get a message from the authorities that he would soon be back in England, and she would go to stay with her mother in London until he arrived. As described earlier in this book, she would then get a further communication from Wig, and they would meet up and stay at the Rembrandt Hotel in Knightsbridge.

When the war finished, Wig was expected home in mid-September. As Eunice waited for his return, she received a telegram saying that he was missing. This was a very worrying time, but Eunice didn't tell her mother because she suffered from angina. However, the news got into the newspaper in November. Eunice's mother read about it and had a heart attack. She died on 7 November, a few hours before Eunice's second son Gavin was born. Wig's plane was found in November 1945, and he was buried in the grounds of the monastery at a village called Mewaing. The death and burial were not confirmed until January 1946.

Settling down after the end of the war with two small children was very difficult. After Wig's death, she decided to move into a place of her own. She bought her first house in 1946, at 64 Ranelagh Grove in Wollaton. In those days, the Grove only had a few houses and the property was adjacent to fields which stretched from the village to the outskirts of Nottingham.

Immediately after the war, Eunice did some work for Sir Julian Kahn helping refugees. However, although she received significant financial assistance from the government as a War Widow, she needed an additional source of income. So, in 1946, she got a job at the University of Nottingham where she worked for over 35 years, retiring in 1981. It was a part time job and she also did various other part time work from time to time, including typing theses for students and academics. She couldn't have done this without the help of her sister Edie who looked after the children while she was at work. Eunice loved the work at the University. She was responsible for establishing

343

and running the Convocation department looking after Past Students and her work brought her into contact with family friend and SOE stalwart Sir John Anstey. She had a great little office at one end of the Great Hall, with a view from her window across lawns and chestnut trees. Today, there is a memorial seat opposite this window with a plaque commemorating her time there which was organised by Gavin and nephew Alexander. Initially, Eunice cycled to work, a distance of 8 kms from Ranelagh Grove initially carrying Gavin in a basket set on the handlebars. Later, when the family got their first car in 1962, she drove to work.

Eunice received a substantial war pension, providing she did not re-marry. She never did. And she received financial assistance for the education of Michael and Gavin until both had gone to university. As she often said, despite the tragedy of losing Wig, she thought of herself as a very fortunate person. Yet in rare moments, I sensed in her a deep and enduring sadness which never completely left her.

Eunice's health was generally very good. It was just as well, since there was only one bread-winner and parent. However, in 1967 when she was 50, and with her children living independent lives, she suffered a prolapsed disc which incapacitated her for a while. She tried all sorts of treatment, and did recover a reasonable quality of life. But this injury put paid to her golf. Instead she learnt to play bridge, initially at the golf club.

With the children gone, Eunice sold the family home and moved to a three bed-roomed town house in Nottingham Park where she lived for 25 years. She became quite a globe-trotter including visits to East Africa, France and Spain (painting holidays) Egypt, Israel, Turkey, Norway and the Arctic Circle, Oberammergau, a trip down the Rhine, Dubrovnic, Switzerland, Bruges, Paris, Florence, Canada, and the United States.

In 1974/75, following the death of her sister Edie, Eunice suffered a significant mental breakdown. To make matters worse, she had a car accident. She had electro therapy which seemed to cure her condition but resulted in some memory loss.

After retiring in 1981, Eunice worked for 11 years in a voluntary job at the Queen's Medical Centre. She was Secretary to the Chaplain and, after training, became a post-operative health visitor, a role she undertook for several years.

Following Gavin's move to Australia in 1985/86, Eunice frequently visited Australia and, in 1995, she decided to migrate to Australia to spend her latter years near Gavin who undertook to look out for her in her twilight years. In Melbourne, she bought a two bedroomed bungalow and lived there until 2008.

Eunice settled down well in Melbourne. She made the odd side trip to New Zealand and inter-State, but never left the Southern Hemisphere again. She made some good friends through the Church at Holy Trinity in Kew, and the Bridge Club. She loved her house and garden, and was pleased for her air conditioning on those

Eunice Wigginton, with son Gavin in 2007

hot summer days. She kept physically active through walking every day, and swimming until she was in her nineties.

In 2002, Eunice developed cancer, a lymphoma of the intestine. She had treatment, which turned out to be very successful. So, she had another wonderful five years of quality life and, on 14 January 2007, she celebrated her 90th birthday in the garden at 10 Edgevale Road, Kew, in Melbourne. It was a warm summer's day and there were over 50 people present including grand-daughter Julia and her partner Mark from England, and Andrew who flew back from holiday on Kangaroo Island for the occasion.

Sadly, in late 2007, the cancer returned. She lived independently for another 18 months until she became frail after further cancer treatment. She spent the last nine months in a nursing home called Broughton Hall and died there peacefully on 20 May 2009 aged 92.

Appendix 2: SOE Operational, Unit and Country Codes

NORTH AFRICA OPERATIONS

Code Name	Nature of Operation	Commencement
Lightfoot	Air attack on Germans at El Alamein	Oct 1942
Supercharge	Attack on Germans near El Alamein	Nov 1942
Torch	Anglo American invasion of Algeria	Nov 1942
Yak	Attempts to recruit Italian POWs	April 1941

YUGOSLAVIAN OPERATIONS

Code Name	Nature of Operation	Commencement
Black	German attack on Partisans	Mar 1943
Disclaim	Fact finding mission in Yugoslavia	Feb 1942
Fungus	Exploratory mission to Croatia	Apr 1943
Halyard	Evacuation of US airman from Balkans	Aug 1944
Henne	Fact finding mission in Yugoslavia	Jan 1942
Hoathley	Exploratory mission to Bosnia	Apr 1943
Huggate	Mission to Chetniks	Mar 1943
Hydra	Fact finding mission in Yugoslavia	Feb 1942
Keelhaul	Transfer of defeated Axis troops to Tito	May 1945
Knight's Leap	German attack on Tito	Apr 1944
Monkeywrench	Liaison with Yugoslav Partisans	Sep 1943
Pikestaff	Maclean's insertion to join Tito	Sep 1943
Ratweek	Harassing German exit from Serbia	Sep 1944
Repartee	Evacuation of Mihailović	May 1944
Seizure	Insertion of Armstrong to Chetniks	Sep 1943
Typical	Insertion of Croat ex-pats to liaise with Tito	Aug 1943
Triumph	Extraction of Tito and supporters to Vis	July 1944
White	German attack on Partisans	Jan 1943

GREEK OPERATIONS

Code Name	Nature of Operation	Commencement
Animals	Diversion operations in Greece	June 1943
Harling	Insertion of Myers/Woodhouse into Greece	Sep 1942
Mercury	German invasion of Crete	May 1941
Noah's Ark	Harassment of German evacuation of Greece	October 1944

ITALIAN OPERATIONS

Code Name	Nature of Operation	Commencement
Avalanche	American landing at Salerno Italy	Sep 1943
Balaclava	Seaborne operations out of Bastia, SW Italy	Dec 1943
Bandon	Protection of infrastructure	Nov 1944
Coolant	SOE contact with Partisans in Northern Italy	June 1944
Diadem	Attacks on infrastructure at La Spezia/Rimini	June 1944
Fairway	Deployment of team to lead Partisans in Northern Italy	July 1944
Husky	Invasion of Sicily	July 1943
Rankin	Allied Action Plan in event of sudden collapse of Germany	1944
Shingle	Landings at Anzio Italy	Jan 1944
Simcol	Rescue of POWS from behind enemy lines	Sep 1943
Vigilant	Initial SOE mission to Salerno	Sep 1943

REST OF EUROPE OPERATIONS

Code Name	Nature of Operation	Commencement
Barbarossa	German attack on Soviet Union	June 1941
Carpetbagger	US code for supplies to France, Norway, Denmark, & Low Countries	Jan 1944
Clowder	Liaison with resistance in Germany/Austria	Dec 1943
Dragoon	Allied landings in Riviera, France	Aug 1944
Felix	German plan to occupy Portugal	1940
Freston	Mission in Poland	Dec 1944
Husky	Invasion of Sicily	July 1943
Overlord	Invasion of France	June 1944
Periwig	Deception re Overlord Plans	May 1944
Ploesti	US attack on Rumanian oil fields	Aug 1943

BURMA OPERATIONS

Code Name	Nature of Operation	Commencement
Birdcage	Part of RAPWI Project to assist POWs	Aug 1945
Bison	Observing Japanese movements along the Mandalay Rd	Feb 1945
Blast	Observing opposing nationalist groups north of Bilin	July 1945
Bloodhound	Observing Chinese communist movements in the north	April 1945
Carpenter	Surveillance of Japanese shipping movements	April 1945
Character	Support and leadership of Karen in Karen Hills	1944/45
Cloak	Diversionary tactics to facilitate XIVth Army crossing of Irrawaddy	March 1945
Conclave	Diversionary tactics	March 1945
Corpse	Drop of dead body to fool Japanese re death of Seagrim	Early 1944
Dilwyn	Support and leadership of Kachin guerrillas in northern Burma	1944/45
Dracula	Seaborne Assault on Rangoon	May 1945
Elephant	Drop to Shwebo to provide intelligence for XIVth Army	Jan 1945
Hainton	Recruiting/training guerrillas to east of Mandalay	1944/45
Harlington	Initial operations with Karen	Dec 1943
Heavy	Recruiting/training guerrillas to east of Mandalay	Feb 1945
Longcloth	Wingate operation to cut Burma North/South railway	Feb 1943
Lynx	Guerrilla ops at Burma/Thailand/Laos border	1944/45
Mastiff	Part of RAPWI Project to assist POWs	Aug 1945
Mint	Surveillance of Japanese movements	Jan 1945
Mouse	Surveillance of Japanese at Arakan	Dec 1944
Nation	Support of BNA in Pegu Yomas Hills	1944/45
Nutshell	Surveillance/harassment of Japanese retreat through Moulmein	Apr/May 1945
Ramrose	Reconnaissance at Ramtree Island	Feb 1945
Spiers	Guerrilla training on Chinese border	1944
Swansong	Part of RAPWI Project to assist POWs	Aug 1945
Thursday	Chinese incursion into Burma	Feb 1944
Wolf	Recruiting/training guerrillas to east of Mandalay	Feb 1945

OTHER FAR EAST OPERATIONS

Code Name	Nature of Operation	Date Of Operation
Evidence	Malaya	1945
Gustavus	Malaya	1945
Jaywick	SOA attack on Japanese shipping in Singapore	1943
Multiple	Malaya	1945
Oatmeal	Reconnaissance in Malaya	1945
Panicle	Thailand	1945
Phukeo	Thailand	1945
Zipper	Seaborne Assault on Malaya	Sept 1945

SOE UNITS

Code Name	Base	Field of Operation
Force 133/MO 4	Cairo	North Africa, Balkans, Italy
Force 136	Meerut/Kandy	Burma, Thailand, Malaya, Australia, PNG, Singapore
Force 139	Monopoli	Poland and Czechoslovakia
Force 266	Bari	Albania
Force 399	Bari	Yugoslavia
ISSU 6	Algiers	France (Massingham)
No 1 Special Force	Monopoli/Siena	Italian resistance
No 6 Special Force	Monopoli	Austria
Forces, F, RF, DF	London	France
Force EU/P	London	Poland

SOE COUNTRY CODES (Used for Signals)

Country	Code Name
Albania	Barking
Bulgaria	Brentford
Czechoslovakia	Not stated
France	Piccadilly
Greece	Greenwich
Hungary	Aldgate
Italy	Tooting
Poland	Kensal
Yugoslavia	Surbiton

Appendix 3: SIW Chronology

Date	Location	Activity
Early Years		
10/12/13	Toton, Notts	Born. Lives in Toton
1920	Nottingham	"Adopted" and starts living at 6 Kennington Road, Lenton, Nottingham
1920-1924	Nottingham	Attends Radford Boulevard Primary School
1925-29	Nottingham	Attends High Pavement School
1929	Nottingham	Matriculates at High Pavement School
1929	Nottingham	Joins Nottingham City Council Transport Department
1930s		
1930-39	Lenton	Continues to live at 6 Kennington Road, Lenton, Nottingham
1935	Nottingham	Wins Berrey Cup for Rowing
02/09/39	Nottingham	Resigns from Transport Department and volunteers to join Army
06/09/39	Nottingham	Appointed as Gunner at Unit 276 of 68th AA Regiment (Royal Artillery ("RA") of Territorial Army)
21/10/39	Nottingham	Marries Eunice
Nov 1939	Scunthorpe	Territorial Army Training
1940		
1939/40	Nottingham	Training at Alfreton Road Nottingham
22/03/40	Nottingham	Appointed Lance Bombardier
14/06/40	Nottingham	Appointed Bombardier
June 1940	Nottingham	Michael conceived
10/07/40	Sandhurst	Admitted to Officer Cadet Training Unit
01/11/40	Sandhurst	Appointed to a Commission with rank of 2nd Lieutenant. Leaves RA
08/11/40	Nottingham	Deployed to Sherwood Foresters Regiment. Training at Infantry Training Centre in Derby
04/12/40	Keighley	Joins 14th Batallion Sherwood Foresters. Training

Date	Location	Activity
1941		
01/02/41	Chippenham	Attached to HQ 8th Armoured Division (14th Foresters in nearby Lambourn)
26/03/41	Nottingham	Michael born
01/04/41	Dorking	Acting Captain and appointed Divisional HQ Liaison Officer 8th Armoured Division
June 1941	Dorking	Family lives at Brockham Hall for nine months
21/10/41	Dorking	Wedding Anniversary telegram
1942		
08/05/42	UK	Captain and L/O 8th Armoured Division HQ. Left UK
08/06/42	UK	8th Armoured Division leaves Scotland UK for North Africa
June 1942	Portugal	Card sent to Eunice
01/07/42	In transit	Full Captain
05/07/42	Cyrenaica	Arrives in Cairo, and moved out to Cyrenaica.
Aug-Nov 42	Cyrenaica	North Africa war, including El Alamein in Egypt
29/11/42	Cyrenaica	Posted to MO Operations 4 in GHQ Remains XI
01/12/42	Cairo	Joins SOE Force 133 (Balkans and Greece). Air Liaison Officer (Liberators). Qualified as parachutist
1943		
01/03/43	Cairo	General Staff Officer 3 (Air)
12/05/43	Cairo	Acting Major with SOE Force 133 – General Staff Officer 2 (Air). Mentioned in Despatches/DAQME
12/08/43	Cairo	Full Major
04/09/43	Cairo	MBE
11/11/43	UK	Two weeks leave in the UK
26/11/43	Cairo	Returns from leave in UK
15/12/43	Italy	Moves to AFHQ Caserta, and then to Bari. Acting Lt Colonel, SOM – General Staff Officer 1 (Air). 2nd Mention in Despatches

1944		
1944	Italy	Letter from Barbara Sampson, his Secretary for six months in 1944
15/03/44	Italy	Full Lt Colonel
12/04/44	Italy	Posted to ME 61
29/06/44	Italy	Letter confirming he was based in Italy
14/07/44		Letter of Commendation from General Twining, C/O 15th USAAF
01/10/44	Italy	SOS MEF to Bin 7 in ME 61
03/11/44	UK	Three weeks leave in UK
24/11/44	Italy	Returns to Bari
1945		
05/02/45	Italy	Terminated with ME 61. Left Bari for UK
07/02/45	UK	Three weeks leave in UK. Appointed to ME 81 Far East
Feb 1945	UK	Gavin conceived
22/02/45		3rd Mentioned in Despatches by Supreme Allied Commander in Chief, Mediterranean Fleet (ME 126)
28/02/45	Calcutta	Arrives in Calcutta to start work with Force 136
28/02/45	Calcutta	Joined SOE Force 136
25/05/45	Calcutta	Letter sent from PO Box 10207
24/06/45	Colombo	Letter sent
27/08/45	Colombo	Letter sent
07/09/45	Mewaing	Plane crashes and he dies
20/09/45		Posthumous OBE
07/11/45	Nottingham	Gavin born

Appendix 4: Finding the Ancestors

The reader will appreciate that the science of tracing genealogy is imprecise. However, from all the evidence, I believe that I have found the true line of descent. The origins of the Wigginton line trace back to the village of North Luffenham in the County of Rutland.[358] This statement is founded on an investigation into Wig's parents, an account of which is provided in Chapter 2. The main source documents for my detective work were the ten yearly Census Records covering the period 1841 to 1911, and the records of Births, Deaths and Marriages covering the period since 1837 which are available at the British National Archives. [359] [360] The source of earlier information on the family was the Parish Records of St John the Baptist church at North Luffenham which, going back to the early 16th Century, are available on microfiche at the Leicestershire County Archives.[361]

Based on this material, I was able to create a family tree for the Wigginton family commencing in the early 18th Century. This can be found in Appendix 5. I would have liked to go back further, and earlier documents are available. But the writing and spelling was almost indecipherable without expert advice. And that's not to mention the bits nibbled away by the mice!

North Luffenham is an ancient centre of population whose history stretches back to Saxon times.[362] Before the Norman Conquest, in 1066, this land had been owned by Queen Edith, the wife of King Edward the Confessor. Following the Norman Conquest in 1066, the land was allotted to Hugh de Port, who later became a monk

---

[358] The village of North Luffenham has been identified by tracing backwards through records of births, deaths, and marriages, from more recent generations of the family who lived in Nottinghamshire and left their roots in the mid-19th Century.

[359] The British National Archives are located in Kew, London, UK.

[360] All are available electronically. Hard copies may be obtained for a small fee from the General Register Office.

[361] The Leicestershire Archives are located in Wigston Magna which is a small town on the outskirts of Leicester, UK.

[362] Excavations in 1900 revealed a Saxon Cemetery to the north of the village, and artefacts dated back to the 5th Century.

whereupon the property reverted to the Crown. So, by the time of the Doomsday survey in 1086 the Luffenhams, as the local settlements were called, were part of the royal lands. And, in the 12th Century, they were considered to be part of Nottinghamshire.[363]

During medieval times, North Luffenham was an independent manor, with a series of owners, and had its own priest. However, in the 16th Century, Queen Elizabeth I gave the manor to William Cecil of Burleigh.[364] The Archdeacon of those days, Robert Johnson, is of special note, as he founded both the Oakham and Uppingham public schools. During the Civil War, in 1642, the royalist Noel family was besieged in North Luffenham Hall by the Parliamentary army and, after quite a battle, surrendered. Subsequently, the village was sacked. In the 17th Century, ownership of the manor passed through several hands.

In the 18th Century (when the last Stuart monarch Queen Anne was on the throne, and the family ancestor John Wigginton is known to have been living in the village), the population was around 500, and local activity was dominated by farming. By now, the village and surrounding land was owned by the Ancaster family. In the annals of 1813, the parish was described as consisting mostly of open fields, except for a few old enclosures. The geological formation reflected the fact that, to a considerable extent, water once covered the valley containing the village.[365]

Today, North Luffenham is a village of 2,034 acres with a population of 700 people, including the farming community, workers in the neighbouring water industry (the adjacent Rutland Water is a major wetland feature) and commuters travelling to neighbouring

---

[363] The history which follows is in part based on material published by the St John the Baptist Church.
[364] Lord Cecil was chief adviser to the Queen for most of her reign, and was variously Chancellor (1551), Secretary, and Treasurer.
[365] In a Deed of 1237 a description of the land makes reference to "magna acqua".

industrial centres.[366] The number of houses has not changed greatly, although some new construction is under way. As of old, the current landscape consists of rolling hills dominated by arable farming. A third is grassland and there are a few spinneys of woodland. The parish of North Luffenham is separated from South Luffenham by the River Chater from which the land rises to around 100m above sea level.

North Luffenham Village Sign

These days, there are relatively few 18th Century buildings still standing. Of particular note are the parish church of St John the Baptist (dating from the 12th Century), the adjacent vicarage, the local Fox Inn (the interior of which has been completely modernised), an ancient barn, and a handful of other buildings in Church Street. The church has many interesting features, including a special connection with the Royal Canadian Air Force who were based at an airfield adjacent to the village in World War Two. There is a memorial to them in the church, and several airmen are buried in the cemetery. There is a potential link with Wig, as the Canadian pilot of the plane in which he crashed in September 1945 (Harold Smith) may have been trained at

---

[366] The estimate of 2,034 acres and other data comes from "British History On-line".

St John the Baptist Church, North Luffenham

North Luffenham.

Apart from the buildings, some of the ancient names of the village survive. For example, there is still a lane called the *"Jetties"*, which refers to the row of cottages running off the main road where farm workers lived.[367] According to records in the Leicestershire Archives, some members of the Wigginton family lived in one of those houses in the early 19th Century.

I have a final word about this village. Without knowing why, throughout my young adult life in England, I remember feeling a strange affinity with the County of Rutland. Interestingly, when I was a teenager, the school which I attended (Nottingham High School) used to play sports against Uppingham School and, in the 1960s, I quite probably ran across the fields adjacent to North Luffenham in cross country competition. For some peculiar reason, in later years, I

---

[367] The term "jetty" derives from the physical "projection" off a main road.

visited the towns of Oakham and Uppingham on numerous occasions. Walking the streets of North Luffenham in the summer of 2015, perhaps I now understand why I was drawn to the place. It is not fanciful to say that, having found the graves of my ancestors in the graveyard of the church, I could sense their presence and my connection going back more than 300 years. This is, I think, how you define belonging. As I have found, for people of European descent who have migrated to Australia, it is something strangely missing from life in the Antipodes.

Returning to the ancestors, the earliest member of the family that I was able to trace during my research was a John Wigginton who was born in North Luffenham around 1710. (*The exact date is difficult to fix, not least because of the change from the Julian to the Gregorian calendar in 1752.*) John Wigginton, and the next two generations (son William was born in 1745, and grandson James was born in 1780) lived in the village during the period before the Industrial Revolution, and were all farm workers.[368] [369]

The earliest member of the family born in the 19th Century, James Wigginton (the son of the above mentioned James and born in January 1813), was also a farm worker. His gravestone sits leaning against a wall in the graveyard of St John the Baptist church. He died aged 75 on 16 August 1888. James was married to Elizabeth Beale (named as Betsy on his gravestone) who came from the neighbouring village of Edith Weston.

The gravestone of James is one of 12 for Wigginton family members which are located in the cemetery, from a James born in the 18th Century to a Jonathan who was buried in 1922.[370] Most are not identifiable because the carving on stone has weathered away. James and Elizabeth had a son called Isaac (note that this was Wig's middle name), who was born on 17 March 1847. Isaac lived his early years in

---

[368] John Wigginton was married to Elizabeth.

[369] William's date of birth, 29 May 1745, and his parentage were recorded in the North Luffenham Register.

[370] This statement is based on records available through a Web Site called *"findagrave.com"*.

North Luffenham and married a local girl with the same name as his mother, Elizabeth.

In the 1870s, no doubt in search of work and a better life, this family moved to Toton in Nottinghamshire which was a booming centre of the railway industry. The Census of 1881 shows that Isaac was a Rail Guard. The records of the local Parish Council also show that, in his later years from 1895 until 1907, he was a Parish Constable for which he was paid 10 shillings per annum.[371][372] This was a respected position in the community with some status and administrative power. Isaac died at the age of 69 in 1916, and his wife Elizabeth died in 1917. Isaac and Elizabeth had at least ten children including a girl called Annie born in 1879.

The village of Toton, to which the Wigginton family moved around 1865-70, is in the county of Nottinghamshire, not far from the town of Long Eaton which lies in the county of Derbyshire. The village dates back until at least Norman times, with an entry in the Doomsday Book. For most of its history, it was dominated by agriculture, with irrigation from the River Erewash. However, in the mid-19th Century, the village expanded because of the establishment of Toton Sidings, a huge marshalling yard of the Midland Railway, where coal from the Nottinghamshire coal field was sorted before being sent to the rest of the United Kingdom.

During the time that the Wigginton family were resident, the area's population grew substantially when most of the adjacent area of level ground was occupied by a facility of the Shell Oil Company. One of the main access roads to this works became a gated military roadway, known as Chetwynd Road, and the site is now the home of the Chetwynd Barracks. By a remarkable coincidence, this military installation includes buildings which currently contain the Mercian

---

[371] From 1894, Toton was administered by Stapleford District Council. In 1935, this Council was merged with Beeston Urban District Council to form Beeston and Stapleford Urban District Council and, on 1 April 1974, this Council became Broxtowe District Council, currently known as Broxtowe Borough Council within the City of Nottingham.

[372] Isaac's pay is recorded in the Minutes of the Toton Parish Council held in the vestry of the Church on 21 February 1895. The Minute Book is held in the Nottinghamshire Archives.

Regiment Archives. These archives include the records of the Sherwood Foresters Regiment which were the source of significant material about Wig's time in the regular army.[373]

Today, Toton is practically an outer suburb of Nottingham, with a population of around 1,000. There are virtually no buildings of any age or character going back to Wig's time in the early 20th Century. The only trace of the Wigginton family that I was able to find is in the Census records. These show that members of the Wigginton family lived in a house (now demolished) in Nottingham Road, Toton during the first two decades of the 20th -Century. But that's where the trail disappears. On checking the local electoral register I could find no record of any Wiggintons living in this area in current times and this is as far as we need go in the search for Wig since, as described in Chapter 3, at an early age he finds himself transferred to Lenton in Nottingham itself.

---

[373] As will be indicated in a later chapter, the Sherwood Foresters were amalgamated with the Worcestershire Regiment to form the Mercian Regiment following the Second World War.

Appendix 5: Wigginton Family Tree

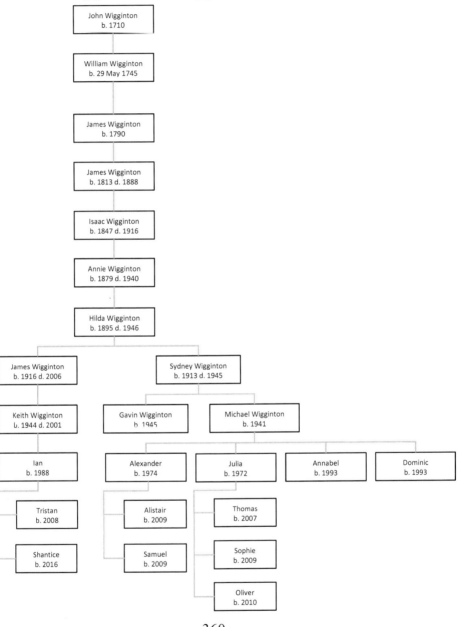

John Wigginton
b. 1710

William Wigginton
b. 29 May 1745

James Wigginton
b. 1790

James Wigginton
b. 1813 d. 1888

Isaac Wigginton
b. 1847 d. 1916

Annie Wigginton
b. 1879 d. 1940

Hilda Wigginton
b. 1895 d. 1946

James Wigginton
b. 1916 d. 2006

Sydney Wigginton
b. 1913 d. 1945

Keith Wigginton
b. 1944 d. 2001

Gavin Wigginton
b. 1945

Michael Wigginton
b. 1941

Ian
b. 1988

Alexander
b. 1974

Julia
b. 1972

Annabel
b. 1993

Dominic
b. 1993

Tristan
b. 2008

Alistair
b. 2009

Thomas
b. 2007

Shantice
b. 2016

Samuel
b. 2009

Sophie
b. 2009

Oliver
b. 2010

Appendix 6: Wig's Brother James

Wig's younger brother, James Edward, was born in December 1916. When I discovered my uncle's existence in late 2013, I was totally amazed because no-one in our part of the family had ever mentioned him to either my brother Michael or me. As mentioned earlier in this book, I came across his name quite by chance when I found my parents' wedding certificate. James Edward Wigginton was identified as a witness. And his identity as a brother was confirmed when in 2014 I obtained Wig's official MOD record. This included a form he had completed when joining up in September 1939, just before he got married. In this document, he stated that his next of kin was his brother James Edward.

For about 12 months after making this discovery, I pursued a number of paths to investigate and confirm the existence of this family member. As a last resort, before searching Births Deaths and Marriages at the National Archives, I did a Google search of obituaries published in the local Nottingham press.[374] Up popped a Notice which made reference to the death of a James Edward Wigginton on 11 January 2006. The Notice also made reference to a deceased son Keith, and another living descendant who was a grandson named Ian.[375] In March 2014, I attempted to track down Ian Wigginton by sending an email "on spec" to a variety of possible accounts, including a couple of gmail versions. I sent a simple message which read *"Was your grandfather James Edward Wigginton?"* I obtained no reply, and the trail went cold.

On 22 January 2015, an email arrived in the name of Ian Wigginton which read *"Yes he was."* My heart leapt, and I immediately sent another more informative message, identifying who I was and why I was making the enquiry. Again, there was no immediate response, and

---

[374] The Nottingham Evening Post.

[375] This death notice also referred to James' deceased wife Nell, and the wife of the son Keith whose name is Patricia.

I was beginning to wonder whether I had found a random false trail. I also started to think about why there had been a break between the families of the two brothers, and wondered if I was about to discover some long-lived, deeply-held secret which I might regret uncovering.

A week later, all my speculations came to an astounding conclusion. On 26 January 2015, I received a second email from Ian Wigginton indicating that the means by which I had found him was a gmail address of which he made little use. He had now stumbled upon my later email and was delighted to confirm that he was who I thought he was. In the following weeks, Ian and I exchanged family information and the following story emerged. Wig did indeed have a younger brother James Edward or Jim as he was known by his immediate family, and they certainly lived together with guardians at the address I had for them in Lenton, a suburb of Nottingham. Interestingly, Ian indicated that his father (Uncle Jim's son) was unaware or at least never divulged that the people with whom Wig and James were living were guardians, and he had no knowledge about the existence or identity of the real parents.

My uncle Jim was married to his wife Ellen Buck ("Nell") on 23 December 1939, a few months after Wig married Eunice. During the war, Jim served with the RAF. Little is known about his wartime service, but thankfully he survived. After the war, he joined Boots the pharmaceutical company where he was employed for his entire working life. Uncle Jim and Nell had one son, Keith, who was born on 29 January 1944 and he married his wife Patricia in 1966. He died of cancer on 15 January 2001, but Patricia is still alive.

Keith and Particia had one son, Ian, who was born on 4 December 1968. He is married to Karen, and has a son named Tristan and a daughter named Shanice. Ian is a consultant with a nuclear energy company and the family live in Hampshire. Jim's wife Nell predeceased him by one year in 2005. They had been married for over 60 years.

There is evidence that, during the war, there was amicable contact between Wig and his brother. To what extent there was a wider relationship involving all the parties, including the guardians and/or natural parents, is unclear. However, after Wig's death, contact seems to have been terminated by one or both parts of the direct family. Ian and I have speculated as to why the two branches of the family parted company. Sadly, since all the people on my side of the family are deceased, we only have one side of the story. According to Ian, whilst he believes that James was proud of his brother and his achievements, he thinks that there was an animosity perhaps between the female members of the family. He also remembers mention that Wig and his batman visited James during the war and that there was some discomfort between some of those present because of the relative social status of the two brother[376]. Knowing my mother as I do, I find it hard to believe that any break in relations between the parties was of her doing. However, I do know that my Aunt Edith took issue with quite a few folk, including the wives of her brothers. As a result, we had no contact with those family members until after her death in the 1970s. I can only surmise that something similar happened between Eddie and Jim's wife Ellen with perhaps my mother the "meat in the sandwich". In any event, 70 years has passed before contact has been resumed and the fact that Ian and I were even able to find each other is a minor miracle.

Wig's story belongs to Ian and his family as much as it does to the rest of the Wigginton clan. In June 2015, I visited Ian and his family at their home in Hampshire, where I was warmly welcomed. I shared with him all the information that I had about the family and he was able to give me a number of photos and stories of his immediate family. We speculated about the circumstances of the two brothers and came to a similar view about their parentage including the likelihood of having different fathers. However, at this stage, we do not know and perhaps never will.

---

[376] The term "batman" refers to a soldier assigned to a commissioned officer who acts as his servant. The position was phased out after the war and replaced by what are now called "orderlies".

Appendix 7: SOE Leadership

Head Office in London

Date	Minister of Economic Warfare	Executive Chairman (CD)	CEO
19 July 1940	Hugh Dalton	Sir Frank Nelson	Gladwyn Jebb
19 Feb 1942	Lord Selborne	Sir Frank Nelson	
5 May 1942	Lord Selborne	Sir Charles Hambro	
Sep 1943	Lord Selborne	Sir Colin Gubbins	

Cairo Office

January 1941	Lt Col George Pollock
May 1941	Brigadier George Taverner
July 1941	Terence Maxwell
July 1942	Lord Glenconner
October 1943	Major General Stawell
April 1944	Brigadier Barker-Benfield

Appendix 8: Far East Air Operations Activity - 1945

The personnel who flew and manned 357 and 358 Squadron came from four countries. The vast majority (around 90%) were from the UK. However, there were also pilots and other air crew from Canada, Australia, and New Zealand.

During the final stage of the war, the Squadrons had just over 20 Planes, including 11 Liberators, 11 Dakotas, 1 Harvard, and 1 Auster. The following statistics from the first eight months of 1945, when Wig was involved in planning SOE missions for Group A (Burma) in the Far East, are drawn from Squadron records maintained at the National Archives in Kew. Wig actually took up his responsibilities on 28 February 1945.

Month	Number of Operations	Success	Flying Hours	People Deployed
Jan	105	74%	1,061	656
Feb	124	53%	1,250	700 estimate
Mar	149	73%	1,474	735
Apr	144	74%	1,500	732
May	138	82%	1,500 est	784
Jun	116	70% est	1,100	368
Jul	168	64%	1,800	809
Aug	61	85%	600	330
Total	**1,008**	**66%**	**10,285**	**5,114**

Appendix 9: Balkans Personnel – Country Analysis, 14 September 1943

Theatre	BLOs	Other Ranks	Local Officers	Local Other Ranks	OSS	Canadian Croats	Total
Yugoslavia	33	37	5	8	2	21	106
Greece & Islands	62	42	32	38			174
Albania	9	15					24
Rumania	1	1					2
Total	**105**	**95**	**37**	**46**	**2**	**21**	**306**

This report was sent to CD in London by SOE in Cairo.

Appendix 10: Cairo Air Operations in Mid-1943

It is interesting to note the following analysis of air sorties during the months of June, July and August 1943 which appear in the SOE history files and demonstrate both the change in focus and level of success. [377]

Sorties	June	July	August
Successful	102	108	145
Failures due to signal issues	19		
Failures due to weather	12		
Mechanical Failure	3		
Total	136	138	183
Percentage Success	75%	78%	79%
Deployment			
Greece	75%	55.5%	N/A
Yugoslavia	17%	38%	N/A
Albania	3%	4.5%	N/A
ISLD Missions	5%	2%	N/A

---

[377] This data is taken from SOE File HS 7-12

Appendix 11: SOE Activity in Italy Prior to No.1 Special Force

Shortly after its formation in 1940, SOE established a desk at Baker Street with specific responsibility for covert activity in Italy. It was called J Section. From October 1941, the head of this section was Lt Colonel Cecil Roseberry. In the early days, the main task of this team was to prepare and distribute propaganda designed to undermine Italian morale. They also attempted to establish contact with Italians who were opposed to Mussolini and were thought to be sympathetic to the Allied cause which included the chief of the Italian armed forces general staff, Marshal Pietro Badoglio. In the autumn of 1943, following the overthrow of Mussolini, Badoglio became Prime Minister in exile.[378] J Section in London was to have responsibility for SOE operations in Italy right through to the time in 1943 when new SOE missions were being established on the mainland of Italy following the Allied invasion of the country in the autumn of 1943.

As we have seen in Chapter 12, in the early days of its existence, SOE also established a station in Berne, in neutral Switzerland. In the early years of the war, this team reported to J Section and was responsible for significant activity in northern Italy. The mission was led by a John (Jock) McCaffery who was a Catholic of Irish descent and an ardent anti-communist. In the early days, he organised operations over the Italian border, to establish contact with a range of sympathetic parties in the north.

In due course this led him to providing financial assistance to insurgents and recruiting agents, and Italian Counter-Intelligence duped him into supporting a number of bogus covert networks including two groups of resistance fighters called "the Tigers" and "the

---

[378] Some of the material in this chapter is based on Chapter XXIII in the book by William Mackenzie entitled *"The Secret History of SOE"*. Other sources include Roderick Bailey, "Target Italy; the Secret War against Mussolini 1940-43" (Faber & Faber, London, 2014), MacGregor Knox, *Hitler's Italian Allies. Royal Armed Forces, Fascist Regime and the War of 1940-43* (CUP, Cambridge, 2000); and Pietro Badoglio, *Italy in the Second World War. Memories and Documents* (Greenwood Press, New York, 1976); Piero Pieri, *"Pietro Badoglio, Maresciallo d'Italia"* (UTET, Torino, 2002)

Wolves".

In his work, McCaffery liaised closely with both the Foreign Office SIS, SOE in London, and, eventually, the American OSS. McCaffery continued to be an important player during the whole of the war, forming strong links with what became the northern CLNAI. When the SOE leadership in Bari took over responsibility for Italian operations in late 1943, McCaffery continued his work maintaining a reasonable working relationship with the SOE leader, Commander Gerald Holdsworth RNVR.

During the period before the Italian armistice in September 1943, there were several relatively unsuccessful missions. Probably the most notable example of collaboration between SOE and the Italian resistance was a project to facilitate an antifascist uprising in the Italian territory of Sardinia, which failed. Another mission of note was *Operation Yak*. Following the unsuccessful Italian campaign in the Western Desert of North Africa, the Allies took many thousands of Italian prisoners. In April 1941, SOE despatched Peter Fleming to try and recruit agents from amongst the incarcerated. [379] Unfortunately, he met with little response. SOE attempts to search among Italian immigrants in the United States, Britain and Canada for agents to be sent to Italy, had similarly poor results.

Despite these setbacks, conditions in Italy deteriorated significantly, and Mussolini's popularity went into decline. Militarily, although Italian forces gained access to Yugoslavia and Greece on the backs of the Germans, they experienced a number of heavy defeats in North Africa, particularly at Sidi Barrani where 200,000 troops surrendered to the British. And the Italian economy was in dire straits, with food shortages and industrial unrest. As a result, the forces of resistance within Italy began to blossom, not only amongst communist and trade unions, but also amongst the wider population. The territory was now ripe for SOE activity.

---

[379] Peter Fleming was the elder brother of Ian Fleming the creator of James Bond.

Political Liaison and Intelligence

In August 1943, a radio operator Lt Cecil (Dick) Mallaby had been deployed to the Como area with the aim of establishing an effective link between SOE and the resistance. [380] Unfortunately he fell into the hands of SIM and was imprisoned. But, fortuitously, this was just before the secret talks on the armistice were getting under way, and SIM decided to use him for coding many essential messages between Badoglio and Eisenhower which turned out to be a major contribution to the achievement of the agreement on 8 September. Mallaby was subsequently released and eventually accompanied the Italian government force which arrived in Brindisi in September. A few days later, Captain Edward de Haan was also deployed from Massingham to Brindisi with the aim of establishing a unit to conduct intelligence operations. He and Mallaby soon joined forces and started to consolidate links to those elements of SIM that had transferred their loyalty to the Badoglio government at the time when Mussolini was deposed. De Haan and Mallaby continued to be important players through the rest of the war, focussing on intelligence matters.

Operation Vigilant (Western Italy)

The first SOE operational group to arrive in Italy, was led by Major Malcolm Munthe who arrived by sea from the North African base at Massingham on 10 September 1943. They travelled with the Allied invasion force which landed at Salerno to the west. Munthe went on to establish an SOE operation that was initially called the *'Brow'* Mission, but was eventually renamed *Operation Vigilant.* In the short term, Munthe's specific orders were to establish contact with the resistance, and assist with the harassment of the Germans and Fascist forces behind enemy lines. His team included the indomitable Massimo Salvadori who was known as Captain Max Sylvester, and

---

[380] This account comes from the book by David Stafford entitled "Mission Accomplished"

370

who came to play a huge role in all manner of SOE activity in Italy right through to the end of the war.

Once established, *Operation Vigilant* was very active, although it only persisted as an effective operation for a relatively short period. In the early days, one of its most notable exploits was the extraction to Capri (just off the coast from Naples) of Italian intellectual Benedetto Croce. Amongst other things, Croce was seen as a potential leader of a National Liberation Front and was potentially helpful in a number of other ways. However, in the event, he did not assume a leadership role, not least because he was not well regarded by the newly appointed Prime Minister Badoglio. In the next few months, Munthe instigated some 70 missions in support of local partisans, operating in a relatively freelance way which was consistent with how SOE had operated in the past. However, despite valiant efforts, his operations eventually fell foul of the significant shift in SOE strategy towards closer work with the military.

In particular, in the autumn of 1943, following a number of incidents where SOE operations had been seen to confound other Allied objectives (see Chapter 15), there was serious talk of SOE activities being totally run by the military. Although this idea was eventually scotched, in September, there was a major shake-up in SOE leadership, with General Colin Gubbins taking over from Sir Charles Hambro as CEO (CD) and significant changes in the Cairo Office. Gubbins was a great supporter of closer co-operation between military and covert operations, and he instigated a wholesale review of all SOE activities. As a result, in December he decided to close down *Operation Vigilant.* By January 1944, all of its missions had been terminated, with responsibility transferred to the SOE bases in the east. However, a small sea borne mission did continue to operate out of the Corsican port of Bastia, called *Operation Balaclava*, under the leadership of a Major Croft. During December 1943 to July 1944, over 50 operations were despatched by this team, after which it was also wound up.

Consistent with his aim of consolidating SOE operations, Gubbins

371

also attempted (unsuccessfully) to get the intelligence and propaganda sections of SOE based in Brindisi to move to the No 1 Special Force base at Monopoli. They resisted because they wanted to be close to the SIS who were based in Brindisi.

In any event, to follow through on his commitment to a more co-ordinated military-covert approach, in December 1943, Gubbins directed that several SOE Cairo staff including Wig should be deployed to Caserta to ensure effective liaison with the military. This was a prelude to what became a major operational centre for air and sea borne operations in the whole Mediterranean (Italy and beyond) based at Bari in the east.

Appendix 12: SOE and the OSS in the Balkans[381]

It is clear from Wig's OBE citation, and correspondence involving the American military, that Wig had considerable dealings with the OSS. SOE's relationship with its American counterpart was at times uncomfortable, but they managed to work in unison most of the time. In 1943 and 1944, there is evidence in the SOE files of various attempts to establish a "modus vivendi". The British position, as expressed by SOE's Executive Director "CD" was fairly clear. *"We may not trust them, but if we don't work with them it will poison the rest of the relationship."*

On 26 July 1943, CD met with his American opposite number G.50,000, Brigadier William Donovan, at which the following was noted regarding OSS work in the Balkans: [382]

a)   SOE welcomed the involvement of OSS

b)   Suitable OSS officers might join SOE operations

c)   Independent OSS missions were not precluded

d)   OSS would use the British cipher and war station in Cairo

e)   By agreement, OSS operations may be extended into Albania and Greece.

f)   With SOE help, OSS would establish operations in Rumania and Bulgaria, and possibly in Hungary

g)   OSS would provide demolition squads/explosives for use throughout the Balkans

h)   OSS would endeavour to secure the deployment of additional aircraft to assist covert operations in the Balkans

This agreement was subsequently endorsed by Brigadier General Deane in Washington, with the additional note that support to resistance movements should be provided on the basis that resources

---

[381] Based on material in SOE File HS 5-150

[382] This is the same Bill Donovan that Roosevelt sent to Britain in 1940 to advise on the ability of Britain to resist the Germans.

were committed to defeating the Axis powers, and without regard to ideological issues.

As reflected in an internal Memo of December 1943, despite this agreement, there was continuing concern on the British side that the Americans might go off and do their own thing, and that they were a creature of the military operating without regard for the political consequences.

To address this issue, it was thought advisable to establish a joint committee to ensure effective liaison on operational matters. There was also a wish that management of all operational matters would continue to be in the hands of the Commander in Chief ME.

In June 1944, CD, drafted a proposal to address this issue for discussion with colleagues. In this document, a basis for working together was proposed as follows. SOE would respect the American chain of command, in which OSS reported to the military without reference to the State Department, but both parties would agree to comply with what was called the *London Agreement* (subject of a Memorandum between the parties on 28 July 1943). This provided that no initiatives would proceed until the British Minister agreed and all operations were to be under joint control.

Appendix 13: Special Operations Mediterranean (SOM)

Headquarters and Support	Location	Personnel
Commander's Office and Residence	Mola di Bari	Major General Stawell
Administration	Torre A Mare	Lt Cols Ashton/Penman, and Major Butler
Administration	Bari	Cols Franck/Seddon, Lt Col Clements,
Planning	Bari	Lt Col Beevor
Finance	Cairo	Major Pedder
Supply	Cairo	Lt Colonel Grove
AFHQ Liaison (until move to Caserta)	Algiers	Brigadiers Dodds-Parker/Anstey
Training	Carovigno	Lt Colonel McClenaghan
Parachute Jump Training	San Vito di Normandi	
Parachute Packing [383]	Torre A Mare	Brigadier Miles
Paramilitary Battle Training	Santo Stefono	
Wireless Training Centre (Hill Side)	La Selva	
Main Stores	Monopoli	Major Lewis
Air Packing	Brindisi	Major Wooler
Sea Packing	Monopoli	Captain Dolphin
Camouflage Equipment	Monopoli	Major Williams
Signals Stores	Monopoli	Lieutenant Thorp
Field Security/Interrogation (300FSS)	Bari	Major Peter Lee
Operations	**Location**	**Personnel**
Air Operations	Bari	Lt Colonel Wigginton
Quartermaster	Bari	Lt Colonel Byng
Main Airfield [384]	Brindisi	

[383] This unit was called ME 54 and employed hundreds of people. It was organised on the same basis as the unit at Saffron Walden.

[384] Special Duties aircraft eventually used the airport at Brindisi for flights deployed across the whole of southern and Eastern Europe including Southern France, Italy, the Balkans, Austria, Poland, and Czechoslovakia, with sorties even to Rumania and Bulgaria.

Country Sections	Unit	Location	Personnel
Italy	No 1 Special Force +	Monopoli	Commander Holdsworth
Poland and Czechoslovakia	Force 139	Monopoli	Lt Col Threlfall
Austria and Germany	No 6 Special Force (Clowder)	Monopoli	Lt Col Wilkinson
Albania Hungary & Yugoslavia	Force 266 Force 399	Bari	Lt Col Harcourt
Greece, Crete, Aegean, Middle East	Force 133/MO4	Cairo	Brigadier Benfield
Bulgaria and Rumania	Force 133/MO4	Cairo	Brig Benfield
South of France	ISSU 6 (Signals)	Algiers	Lt Col Nichols
Tito HQ Mission [385]		Drvar	Brig Maclean

+ Moved to Siena in early 1945

---

[385] Maclean also reported to AFHQ and London

Appendix 14: Air Sorties to Chetniks and Partisans in Mid-1943

	July		August		September		October	
	Chet	Part	Chet	Part	Chet	Part	Chet	Part
No of Sorties	35	27	41	34	40	36	15	26
Successful	22	19	30	24	26	18	12	11
Unsuccessful	13	8	11	10	14	18	12	11
Personnel Dropped	7	11	6	14	13	17	1	9
Tonnage	30	25	30	32	38	25	5	28

Appendix 15: Operation Triumph – First Hand Account

(Letter dated 5 June 1944)

TO: CD

I think you will be interested to hear some of the details behind the story of Tito's evacuation last night reported in our signal of 4 June 1944.

1. Tito's GHQ with the British and Russian Missions were kept on the run practically day and night from the 25th May to 3 June. One BLO, King, said that he had lost all count of days as it had been a non-stop affair. A small Russian officer of an intellectual and un-athletic type, said that it had been all right for the British as they had been more accustomed to sport, but he personally had found it hard to keep up. They might well have kept going for many days longer but Tito found it impossible to control operations.

2. During that period we got practically no news from them, and there was very little that we could report to anybody.

3. The first suggestion for evacuation came from the Russian Mission who quite clearly began to make their plans in advance of the others and get in touch with their aircraft at Bari which keeps W/T contact with them. So far as we were concerned the first request for evacuation was not received until after 1400 hrs on 3 June, and I think it reflects credit on all concerned, particularly the air force, our air Ops section (Wig) and B.1., that the evacuation of over 100 men from an untried landing ground was successfully completed within little more than 12 hours after the request was first received.

4. The Russian aircraft, which had obviously been summoned separately and received earlier warning, picked up Tito, Korniev, Vivian Street, and other members of Tito's staff and was back at Bari airfield by 0300 hrs. It landed down and taxied immediately to the far side of the airfield from the Control Tower to the usual parking

place of this aircraft. A Russian staff car was waiting at this point and Tito and some others were rushed off in this car before even General Velebit could see them, and without any reference to the Security Control Authorities in the airfield. The party then appears to have split up and Tito spent the night at the Partisan Delegation's flat. The Russians presumably were put up by their own delegation in Bari.

5.   I am told that Tito came out on the Russian plane merely because it was the first to arrive and because he did not know what others were coming.

6.   The Russian aircraft immediately refuelled and flew a second sortie bringing back a total of about 30 bodies in the two sorties.

7.   The three American planes which brought out 51 Partisans, 14 Russians, 4 British Mission personnel, and 5 RAF personnel came into Bari between 0200 and 0330 hrs. The first to arrive brought General Gorthchacov and his Russian interpreter to whom I had a talk. I asked the Russian interpreter "How far were the Germans from the landing ground?" His knowledge of English being somewhat imperfect he thought I had said "How far were the Germans from Leningrad?" and appeared surprised at my lack of interest in his personal movements, but we sorted that one out!

8.   There are 30 more Partisans and about 100 wounded whom we hope to get out tonight. Last night, in addition to the Tito party, over 100 were evacuated from Berane.

9.   When you remember that the Mihailović Missions were brought out last week and that Wildhorn II has also been achieved in the same period, it is clear that No 334 Wing and Air Operations section (Wig) have done a wonderful job and deserve the highest credit.

10. It looks as though the original attack at dawn on 25 May would have caught the party completely napping had it not been for Street's good sense in insisting that they should move a short way from their original HQ because of suspicious aerial recces which had been

taking place over that area.

11.   Tito had expressed a wish to see non-one outside his immediate staff until he has got back to Partisan territory on Vis, after which he will be glad to see any Allied authorities who wish to see him. It is tiresome and might, at first sight, be considered narrow-minded, but he is naturally exhausted and probably feeling somewhat humiliated at having to come out at all, so it is understandable and probably right.

12.   I attach copies of the signals from the Field and the 3 June requesting evacuation.

13.   It is unfortunate that we have not been able to get Randolph Churchill out but we are making every effort and hope in may be possible in a day or two when he has reached a suitable area.

Yours

DH

Appendix 16: Last Trip to Otter

An important feature of every airborne mission, whatever the theatre of war, was the Operations or Flight Report. This was completed by the leader of the mission, usually the Pilot, immediately after returning. It was then sent to the Commander of the Special Duties Squadron and other parties including in particular SOE (eg Wig). As part of the research for this book, I went through an enormous number of these Operations Reports including the records for the Far East in 1945, right up to when KN584 took off on 7 September. Not surprisingly, there is no document in the files for that flight since it never returned. However, I was able to trace the flights previously undertaken by the Canadian pilot of KN584, Warrant Officer Harold Smith. Interestingly, after the end of hostilities, he didn't do a lot of flights, and the last one that I was able to discover was on 26 August 1945. This was probably the final sortie prior to the fatal flight on 7 September. I have reproduced this Flight Report below, both to provide the reader with the level of information available to SOE, and because it has some poignancy given the events two weeks later.

The Flight Report consists of 13 sections which provide space for information about every aspect of the flight, including date, time, pilot, people and materials to be dropped, flying conditions including weather, efficacy of reception party, issues arising and comments of responsible officer. Interestingly, for this sortie, the flight is to the Otter Section of *Operation Character*, and the mission was to drop a range of supplies to keep the team going. As often happened, the Reception Party did not successfully establish the Primary DZ, and so a Secondary DZ was used. There were no less than 12 passes over the DZ before all the packages had been despatched. Also, under the General Report section, Harold Smith reports that this was **not** a good DZ due to high hills!

AIRBORNE OPERATIONS REPORT

1.   **CODE NAME**   CH/Otter   **DATE**   26/08/45   **REMARKS**   Completed

2.   **DROP ZONE**   3.   **RECEPTION BRIEFED**

         1 ary DZ No   677   Ref   Panels   T

         2 ary DZ No   721   Ref   Fires

         3 ary DZ No   779   Ref   Letters (a) W   (b) B   (c) W

4.   **A/C** Dakota **LETTER** J584   **SQUADRON** 357   **CAPTAIN**   W/O Smith

5.   **LOAD**   **MEN**   **CONTAINERS**   **PACKAGES**   **WEIGHT OF STORES**

                                                     70   5593

6.

TIMES	**TIME**	**PLACE**		**TIME**	**PLACE**
T.O.	05.35	Base	LANDED	12.20	Ming
T.O	14.40	Ming	LANDED	19.25	Base
T.O			LANDED		

7.   **ROUTE**

8.   **WEATHER**   7/10 – 8/10

         En Route

         DZ Zone

9.   **GENERAL REPORT BY CREW**

         REACHED DZ   10.20   hrs   LEFT DZ 10.48   hrs

         Saw a DZ 3-4 miles S of Peak. 8000' by area and letter N. Definitely not W. Went onto

         Secondary where we found correct reception

10.   **REBECCA RESULTS**

         Successful

         Unsuccessful

11.   **DETAILS OF DROP**   1.   2.   3.   4.   5.   6.   7.   8.

         TIME

         HEIGHT   ASL

                            GSL

         SPEED

         COURSE

         MEN

         CONTAINERS

         PACKAGES

12.   **LEAFLETS/MATCHES**

         Signature

13.   **A.L.O'S REMARKS**

         Date

Appendix 17: Wig's Kit

HQ GROUP A
FORCE 136

CERTIFIED TRUE COPY OF INVENTORY OF KIT OF LATE LT COLONEL WIGGINTON

Trousers – Service Dress	2 pairs		Slippers	1 pair
Trousers – Corduroy	3 pairs		Stockings – Khaki	12 pairs
Trousers – Khaki Drill	2 pairs		Puttees *– Large	1 pair
Trousers – Grey Flannel	1 pair		Puttees – Small	1 pair
Shorts – Khaki Drill	3 pairs		Garters	1 pair
Shorts – Rugger	1 pair		Sun Glasses	1 pair
Dressing Gown	1		Mirror	1
Underpants	6 pair		Cigar Case	1
Under vests – white cotton	3 only		Pipe	1
Under vests – flannelette	3 only		Photograph Holder	1
Shirts – Civilian	3		Tobacco Pouches	2
Shirts – Service	4		Medal Ribbons	8 sets
Table Cloth – Small	1		Cigarette Lighter	1
Pyjamas	2 sets		Watch Straps	3
Bedspread	2		Collars – Khaki	4
Towels	3		Ties	6
Blankets	2		Assorted Handkerchiefs	9
Battledress Jacket	1		Regimental Insignia	
Service Dress Jacket	1		Buttons Various	
Suede Waistcoat	1		Dressing Case – with toothbrush	
Khaki Jackets	2		and shaving brush	
Sam Browne (belt/strap on shoulder)		1	Bathing Trunks	1
Raincoat	1		Pullover	1
Shoes	2 pairs		Khaki neck bands	3
Chapplies (a type of Indian sandal)		1 pair	Braces	2 pairs
Writing Case containing letters		1	Gloves	2 pairs

* A puttee is a cloth binding for the lower leg

15 September 1945

383

Appendix 18: Commemorative Scroll

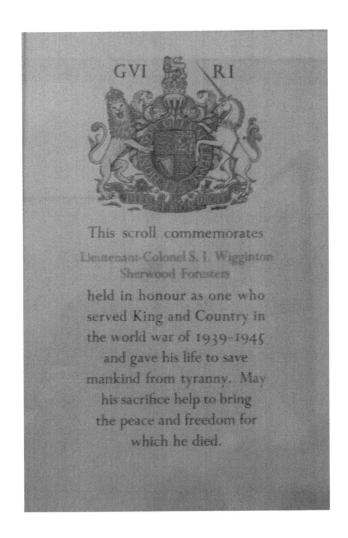

This scroll commemorates

Lieutenant-Colonel S. J. Wigginton
Sherwood Foresters

held in honour as one who
served King and Country in
the world war of 1939-1945
and gave his life to save
mankind from tyranny. May
his sacrifice help to bring
the peace and freedom for
which he died.

Appendix 19: Friends and Contemporaries

To some extent a person is defined by the people with whom he or she chooses to associate. During his life, and especially during his time in SOE, Wig made many friends. The purpose of this Appendix is to share with the reader what we know about both his friends and his contemporaries who would no doubt have figured in a post-war life had it made it that far. The brief descriptions which follow are of interest from both a family and a historical point of view.

i) Sir John Anstey

Brigadier Sir John Anstey was a friend of both Wig and Eunice. He was born in Tiverton in Devon in 1907, and was educated at Clifton College in Bristol and Trinity College Oxford where he read Economics. He was a tall man amongst his contemporaries, at 6ft 2in. In his SOE file he listed his leisure interests as "all country pursuits". Between 1927 and 1939, he worked at Mardon's, a printing company, which was a subsidiary of Imperial Tobacco Ltd.

After initial posting in the regular army, Sir John joined SOE as a Major in December 1942 around the same time as Wig. Initially, he was based at Massingham in Algiers, reporting to the head of mission Dodds-Parker who thought very highly of him. In 1944, he transferred to a senior position in Bari, where he first got to know Wig. Then, in November 1944, he joined Force 136 in Kandy as Sir Colin Mackenzie's Deputy, and Wig moved to the Far East shortly thereafter.

After the war, Sir John was appointed to run John Player and Son in Nottingham. In 1948, he also became a member of the Council of the University of Nottingham, a body on which he served for 45 years during which time he was both Treasurer and Pro-Chancellor. During this period, he had frequent dealings with Eunice when she was running the Convocation Department of the University. He retired from Imperial in 1967, and during that year was High Sheriff of

Nottingham. He subsequently became a leader in the National Savings movement and was knighted in 1975.

From the late 1940s, Sir John lived in Newark, Notts, and was a dear friend to Eunice. In those difficult years after the war, he visited the family frequently, and I have memories of him. He died in 2000 aged 93.

ii) Malcolm Campbell

I am not sure how Wig came to know the Campbell family, but this association was recorded in conversations with Eunice. Sir Malcolm Campbell raced cars and was a motoring journalist. He held the world speed record on land and on water at various times during the 1920s and 1930s using vehicles called *Blue Bird*. He died in 1948.

iii) William Oliver Churchill

Major Oliver Churchill DSO MC was born in 1914 in Sweden. He was not a relative of the Prime Minister, although he didn't disavow people who thought that he was. He was the son of a British Consul who served in Mozambique, Amsterdam, Brazil, Sweden, Italy, and Algiers. The family got about, and in the 1920s Oliver was a boarder at Stowe School. He went on to study architecture at Cambridge.

At the beginning of the war, Oliver joined the Worcestershire regiment, and he and his brother Peter both joined SOE in 1941. In December 1941 he was posted to Malta to train Italian partisans. Later, he was involved in clandestine operations in Italy and Greece. He was well known to and spent time with Wig. After the war, Oliver practised as an architect and he died in Cambridge in 1997 aged 82.

iv) Stephen Cumming MBE

Wig worked closely with Stephen Cumming and, earlier in this book, there are extracts from his letters to my mother written in 1945 and

1946 after the crash. Born in 1911, Colonel Mount Stephen Cumming came from Dufftown in Scotland. He was educated at Fettes College in Edinburgh and studied Classics and Law at Cambridge. He was a bachelor, and he identified as his hobbies sailing and mountaineering. Before the war he worked as a Shipping Agent in China. At the outbreak of war, he joined the army in Malaya, and was with the troops that withdrew from Burma into India in July 1942. He joined Force 136 in August 1942, and eventually became the Commander of Wig's Group A unit. He was based in Kandy, and reported to Gavin Stewart who in turn reported to the boss, Sir Colin Mackenzie.

v) Alan Goldsmith

In 1945, Alan Goldsmith spent a lot of time with Wig in Calcutta, and he was killed in the crash of Flight KN584 in September 1945. Alan Leslie Goldsmith was born in 1916 and came from Suffolk. He went to Ipswich School and obtained qualifications as a Chartered Surveyor. Immediately prior to the war, he was a Surveyor and Valuer with Westminster City Council. He joined the army as an engineer, and joined Force 136 in Calcutta in May 1945.

vi) Basil Irwin

Captain Basil William Seymour Irwin worked with Wig in the SOE Cairo office, and was a friend. Basil came from Tonbridge in Kent, but was born in Dublin in 1919. Before the war he worked in a bank, and he was a sportsman playing rugby, hockey, and squash. Like Wig, he also boxed. According to his SOE file, Bill was a quiet and reserved fellow, and he was assessed as being reliable, thorough and intelligent – all qualities which made him an ideal person to work in the difficult SOE Cairo office environment. He stayed with SOE until the end of the war, and his activities included a period in March 1945 with the *Clover* mission in Northern Italy working with the resistance.

vii) Mervyn Keble

Given the kind of person he was, I couldn't say whether Brigadier Keble was a friend of Wig's. But he had a huge influence on Wig's life in Cairo for a very important twelve months during 1943. Brigadier Cleveland Mervyn Keble was born in Kent in 1904. He was educated at Cheltenham College and was admitted to Sandhurst as a regular in 1924. Before the war, he saw service with the Wiltshire Regiment in Egypt, Singapore, Bangalore and Palestine. From the beginning of the war, he spent most of his time in Egypt, as Deputy Assistant Adjutant and Quartermaster General at MEHQ. Latterly, before joining SOE, he had responsibility for intelligence.

Keble joined SOE as Chief of Staff in the Cairo Office on 25 September 1942 and recruited Wig to his first job in SOE in November 1942. Thereafter he was Wig's boss until December 1943 when, after a number of incidents with various British authorities, he was moved back into a regular army job. After the war, he became Commanding Officer of the 2nd Battalion Wiltshire Regiment.

As recorded earlier in this book, Keble was a colourful character, who spent much of his time in a T shirt and shorts. "Bolo" as he was known, was an energetic man with a head for detail. He was aggressive and had a bullying tone that did not make him popular. He was also ambitious, and this eventually led to him over-reaching himself. He died at the early age of 43 in 1948.

viii) Edgar Kennedy OBE

Edgar Kennedy was a colleague and friend of Wig's in Cairo, Bari and the Far East. He died with Wig on Flight KN 584. Lt Colonel Edgar James Kennedy was born in 1901 and came from Colchester in Essex. Both his parents were born in Ireland. In the First World War, he had seen service as a lad in the Royal Navy, and he joined the Royal Signals in 1920. For a couple of years he had been in the Royal Ulster Constabulary, and then for 5 years he was in the Merchant Navy. In the 1930s, he had a civilian job and acquired a qualification in electrical engineering. According to his SOE file, in peace time, Edgar was keen on riding, sailing, shooting and driving.

Following Sandhurst, in October 1939, Edgar joined the Royal Signals. Like Wig, he was recruited into the SOE in 1942. For 18 months he was based in London, and he was then sent to Cairo. He joined the team in Bari in May 1944, and was posted to the Far East in October 1944. In Calcutta, he was responsible for all Force 136 W/T communications involving Burma, Thailand, and French Indo-China.

ix) Dugald Macphail MBE

Dugald Macphail was a good friend of Wig's. They were the same age, and they first met when both were stationed in the SOE Cairo offices. Subsequently, they were both in Bari and then the Far East. Lt Commander Dugald Stewart Macphail RNVR was born on 5 September 1913. He was a surgeon and was frequently parachuted into the field to undertake medical work. Latterly, he was for a time responsible for Group B operations into Malaya, and was sent into the field in June 1945. He was eventually awarded an MBE for his services to SOE.

x) Gavin Stewart

Gavin Stewart was a friend of Wig's in the Far East. He came from a family who controlled an engineering business with a branch in India. He was six foot three inches tall and, from all accounts, he was an ebullient character with a great sense of adventure. He joined SOE in Meerut, and was then responsible for establishing the base at Calcutta where he spent three years working closely with Colin Mackenzie.

In the early part of the war, Gavin took part on a number of daring escapades including *Operation Creek* which has been the subject of a film *Sea Wolves* made in 1980. He was responsible for a wide range of operations including propaganda, co-ordination of signals, guerrilla training and operations, intelligence, and boring old administration.

xi) Bickham Sweet-Escott

Bickham Sweet-Escott was well known to Wig and their paths crossed frequently. Bickham Aldred Cowan Sweet-Escott was born on 6 June 1907 in Newport Monmouthshire. He was the son of a senior diplomat who had held several senior posts including Governor of Fiji. He was educated at Winchester College and Balliol College Oxford. Before the war he was personal assistant to the Chairman of Courtaulds, and he joined the SIS of the Foreign Office in 1939.

Bickham transferred to SOE when it was established in 1940. He was regional director of the Balkans and the Middle East mission in 1941 before being appointed as personal assistant to the SOE CEO Sir Frank Nelson. In July 1942 he had a spell with the SOE mission in Washington, and during 1943 was a senior policy officer in the SOE Cairo office.

From January to December 1945, he was Chief of Staff of Force 136 SEAC in Kandy. After the War, Bickham became a banker in the City of London, and a businessman. He died in 12 November 1981, aged 74.

xii) Robert Wade

Robert Wade was a good friend of Wig's and worked with him in the North Africa campaign and then in the SOE Cairo office. Captain Robert Pollack Wade came from Kenilworth in Warwickshire but was born in New Zealand in December 1913. He had also lived for several years in Canada. Before the war, he was a game farmer and horse breeder. Very much a country guy, he listed hunting and shooting as his hobbies as well as being a boxer. In his SOE file, he was assessed as being intelligent, shrewd and practical. Interestingly, he spoke French and Serbo-Croat.

Between March 1943 and March 1944, he was an agent with the *Huggate* and then the *Rhodium* Missions in Serbia and spent time in Bari, no doubt catching up with Wig. In 1944, he also went on sabotage missions with SOE in France. SOE Files contain a report from Captain Wade on his time in Yugoslavia, during which he moved from the Chetnik to the Partisan camps. Interestingly, some of his report has been redacted until 2028 for security reasons.

In his remarks about the Chetniks, he leaves no doubt that Mihailović's main objective was to defeat the Partisans, with the Bulgars and Germans running second and third in that order.

His view about the Partisans was that they were well organised and good fighters, although he did not enjoy the persistent communist propaganda to which everyone in the Partisan camps was apparently exposed day and night.

xiii) Leonard Ward

Leonard Ward was one of Wig's closest friends before the war. He and Wig were both Schedule Clerks with the Nottingham City Transport Department, and they both rowed for the Nottingham Britannia Rowing Club. Leonard was a god-father to my brother Michael. After the war, I believe that Leonard kept in touch with the family, and was a dutiful god-father. But I have no anecdotal information. From newspaper cuttings, I believe that he died on 10 April 2008 around the age of 95.

xiv) Digby Willoughby

When he was at Sandhurst, Wig met a number of people who became good friends. One such individual, with whom he rowed, was a young man named Digby Willoughby. Digby Michael Godfrey John Willoughby also happened to be the 12th Lord Middleton, a peerage created in 1711. Until 1925, the Middleton family owned Wollaton Hall which figured strongly in the post-war lives of all the Wiggintons.

Perhaps it is no coincidence that my brother was named Michael John.

Digby was born on 1 May 1921, and died aged 90 on 27 May 2011. Through his great-grandmother, Julia Louisa Bosville (1824-1901), he was a direct descendant of Frederick, Prince of Wales, via his illegitimate daughter Maria Louisa. Raised at the family estate at Birdsall House in Malton North Yorkshire, he received his early education at Eton. At the age of 18, he was admitted to Sandhurst and, like Wig, received his commission in November 1940. Rising to the rank of Major in the Coldstream Guards, he went on to receive the Military Cross and Croix de Guerre for bravery in saving his men during the invasion of Normandy. He was a Conservative member of the House of Lords.

Appendix 20: Definitive Account of Crash and Burial

KN584 Crash Site in Karen Hills

At 8.43 am on the morning of 7 September 1945, Dakota Mark IV plane KN 584 took off from Mingaladon Airport in Rangoon, in heavy rain, on course to the main SOE base at Jessore, with a fuel stop scheduled for the SOE airfield at Toungoo. On board were 16 British and Canadian servicemen (at least five of whom were with SOE). The plane was full because air transport at this time was in short supply with so many people returning to base after the end of the war a few weeks' previously.

On the way to Toungoo, the plane took a planned diversion to the east, passing over Mount Kyaiktiyo towards the Karen Hills, to drop supplies to Operation Character staff in the field (Mongoose zone) who had a base with a fully operational airfield and Dropping Zone at

Mewaing. It was late morning, but the crew of KN584 had difficulty finding the Dropping Zone because of the heavy rain and low cloud.

There is speculation that, as the plane approached the Dropping Zone, it was fired on by a renegade Japanese troop unaware of the surrender on 15 August (the final surrender by local Japanese was not concluded until 13 September) and the pilot took evasive action. Whether or not this is the case, in the appalling weather, the starboard wing caught a rock and/or the trees about 200 feet from the top of Mount War Plar Lay (Wablawkyo) at an elevation of 1500-2000 metres.

The plane burst into flames, and then slid down the face of the rock and settled on a ledge about 50 feet below leaving its starboard engine above where it first struck the mountain. The plane then exploded and all on board were killed. The plane and the bodies were scattered over a stretch of open rock several hundred yards in length, and into a ravine. According to an eye witness in the local village, a couple of days' walk from the site, they heard the crash and saw smoke.

The next day, and on successive days, Flight Commander O'Brien of SOE 357 Squadron went looking for the plane, but visibility continued to be poor and they could not find the crash site. It was not found through aerial surveillance, until at least a week later. Two months later, and once the weather had improved, an SOE team led by Major Harold Bourne, and accompanied by Wing Commander Gane and 23 members of the local Karen Home Guard, walked for two days from Mewaing to the crash site to investigate what had happened and deal with the casualties. On 23 November 1945, they located the crash site, finding the plane and the bodies which by now were badly decomposed. It was not possible to identify the bodies. The team did their best to gather all body parts for burial.

The remains of the casualties were carried from the crash site and taken to the SOE base in Mewaing (about 13 kms from the crash site as the crow flies). Major Bourne examined the bodies and counted the femurs, being the only part of the bodies which were fully intact. He counted 14 pairs of femurs with two odd femur bones to spare. From this he concluded that there were 16 bodies. In Mewaing, the body parts were placed in metal boxes and interred in the grounds of the monastery in a communal grave six to eight feet deep with a wooden fence built around it and topped with stones. A cross was installed with the names of the 16 Canadian and British casualties on the vertical stem. Photographs were taken to send to the relatives.

Subsequently, the plane has never been fully excavated, but parts have been brought from the site, including oxygen bottles used by local people as a still and several other minor parts. There is reason to believe that most parts of the plane have been removed for trading in the scrap value. Two metal items are in our possession thanks to Ephraim who obtained them from a Saw Thone Khin who had helped remove the bodies in 1945 and still lives in an adjacent village.

Bibliography and Sources

British National Archives, Kew – SOE Papers

HS1/19	Burma Air Operations 1945
HS1/22/23	Far East Missions 1945
HS1/44-46	Burma Diaries 1943-45
HS1/298	Far East Clandestine Operations 1945
HS1/310	Far East Group A Activity (Burma) 1943-45
HS1/320	Far East Security Reports 1945
HS3/123	Policy in SOE Cairo and Evacuation Plans 1942
HS3/171	SOE Cairo Organisation 1944
HS4/22	Czech Air Operations 1944
HS5/18	Albania Air Operations 1943/44
HS5/56-57	Albanian Operational Directives 1944
HS5/145-149	Balkans Planning and Operations 1943/44
HS5/150	SOE and OSS in Balkans 1943
HS5/157-160	Balkans Activity Reports 1943/44
HS5/425-27	Greek Operations 1943/44
HS5/868/870	Yugoslav Operations 1943/44
HS5/869	Caserta Conference August 1944
HS5/904	Yugoslav Operational Activity 1941/42
HS5/920	Yugoslav Air Operations 1943/44
HS5/934	Yugoslav Operational Reports 1944 with Op. Triumph
HS6/862	Fairway Mission 1944
HS7/11	History of Special Duties Operations, Med 1942-45
HS7/12	History of Balkan Air Force (Prepared July 1945)
HS7/13	Clandestine Air Operations South East Asia 1942-45
HS7/14	History of Air Liaison Section 1941-45
HS7/61	History of Special Operations Mediterranean 1944/45
HS7/105/106	Burma Country Notes 1945, including Mewaing Airfield
HS7/111-114	Far East History 1944/45
HS7/158	Greek Activity History 1941-44
HS7/199	Berne Mission History, 1944
HS7/232-233	Balkans Diaries and Operations 1944
HS7/238	North Africa Operations 1943
HS7/268-273	Middle East War Diaries 1943/44

HS9/41/5	John Anstey Personnel File
HS9/719/2	Basil Irwin Personnel File
HS9/830/7	Edgar Kennedy Personnel File
HS9/971/5	Dugald Macphail Personnel File
HS9/1543/4	Robert Wade Personnel File
HS9/1589/8	Sydney Wigginton Personnel File

Other Public Archives

Historical Disclosures, Army Personnel Centre, Glasgow
Imperial War Museum, London
Leicestershire County Archives, Long Street, Wigston Magna,
Leicester
MOD Medal Office, Gloucester
Nottinghamshire County Council Archives, Nottingham
The Mercian Regimental Museum, Chetwynd Barracks, Chilwell,
Nottingham
The Sandhurst Collection, Sandhurst Royal Military College,
Sandhurst

Private and Personal Archives

Correspondence from Col Stephen Cumming, George Cunningham,
Sir Colin Mackenzie, Dugald Macphail, Geoffrey Meredith, G H
Parker, Barbara Sampson and others.
High Pavement Society Archives, Nottingham
Janet Whittaker, Church Warden of St John the Baptist Church,
North Luffenham
Nottingham Britannia Rowing Club
Robert Bartlett MA, Surrey Historian

Published Works

Author	Title	Publisher	Place	Date
Alanbrooke, Lord	The Alanbrooke War Diaries 1939-45	Weidenfield & Nicolson	London	2001
Alexiades, Plato	Target, Corinth Canal 1940-44	Pen & Sword	Barnsley	2015
Allen, Louis	Burma: The Longest War	Dent	London	1984
Allen Louis	Sittang: The Last Battle	The Book Service	London	1973
Anglim, Simon	Orde Wingate: Unconventional Warrior from the 1920s to 21st Century"	Pen & Sword	Barnsley	2015
Bailey, Roderick	The Wildest Province	Vintage Books	New York	2009
Bailey, Roderick	Forgotten Voices of the Second World War	Ebury Press	London	2008
Bailey, Roderick	Target Italy; the Secret War against Mussolini 1940-43	Faber & Faber	London	2014
Bailey, Roderick	Communist in SOE: Explaining James Klugmann's Recruitment and Retention: Intelligence and National Security, 20:1, 72-97.	Routledge	London	2005
Badoglio, Pietro	Italy in the Second World War, Memories and documents	Greenwood Press	Connecticut	1976
Beevor, J G	SOE – Recollections and Reflections 1940-45	Bodley Head	London	1981
Behan, Tom	The Italian Resistance: Fascists, Guerrillas and the Allies	Pluto Press	London	2009
Bosworth, RJB	Mussolini	Arnold	London	2002
Bowen, John	Undercover in the Jungle	William Kimber	London	1978
Clark, Alan	Fall of Crete	Cassell	London	2000
Clogg, Richard	A Concise History of Greece	CUP	Cambridge	2002
Clutton-Brock, Oliver	Trusty to the End – The History of 148 (Special Duties) Squadron, 1918-1945	Mention the War	Leeds	2017
Cooper, Artemis	Cairo in the War: 1939-1945	H Hamilton	London	1989

Cruickshank, Charles	SOE in the Far East	OUP	Oxford	1983
Deakin, W D	The Embattled Mountain	OUP	Oxford	1971
Deakin FW	The Brutal Friendship: Mussolini, Hitler, and the Fall of Italian Fascism	Weidenfield and Nicolson	London	1962
Dodds-Parker D	Setting Europe Ablaze: Some Account of Ungentlemanly Warfare	Springwood	Windlesham, Surrey	1983
Dun, Smith	Memoirs of the Four Foot Colonel	Cornell University	USA	1980
Elkin, Jennifer	A Special Duty	Mention the War	Leeds	2015
Fecitt, Harry	Article on SOE in Burma	Kaiserscross.com		2016
Foot, M R D	SOE An Outline History of the SOE 1940/46	BBC	London	1984
Godfrey, Dinyer	A Short History of Burma in New Internationalist magazine Issue 410	New Internationalist Publications	Oxford	2008
Gooch, John	Mussolini and His Generals the Armed Forces and Fascist Foreign Policy 1922-42	CUP	Cambridge	2007
Goulter-Zervoudakis	"The Politicization of Intelligence: The British Experience in Greece 1941-44"	Intelligence & National Security Journal	Abingdon	1990
Hamilton, Nigel	Monty the Making of a General 1887-1942	McGraw-Hill	New York	1981
Horrocks, Brian	Corps Commander	Charles Scribner's	New York	1977
Horrocks, Brian	A Full Life	Collins	London	1960
Jeffrey, Keith	The Secret History of MI6	Penguin	London	2010
Kennedy, J F	Why England Slept	Wilfred Funk	New York	1940
Knox, MacGregor	Common Destiny	CUP	Cambridge	2000
Knox, MacGregor	Hitler's Italian Allies, Royal Armed Forces< Fascist Regime and the War of 1940-43	CUP	Cambridge	2000

Kurapovna, Marcia	Shadows on the Mountains. The Allies, the Resistance and the rivalries that doomed Yugoslavia in World War Two	John Wiley &Sons	New York	2010
Latimer, John	Burma, The Forgotten War	John Murray	London	2004
Lees, Michael	Special Operations Executed in Serbia and Italy	William Kimber & Co	London	1986
Lewin, Ronald	Slim – The Standard-bearer	Leo Cooper	London	1976
Mackenzie, W J M	The Secret History of SOE	St Ermin's Press	London	2000
Maclean, Fitzroy	Eastern Approaches	Penguin	London	1949
Macmillan, Harold	War Diaries: Politics and War in the Mediterranean January 1943-May 45	Macmillan	London	1984
Merrick, K A	Flights of the Forgotten	Arms and Armour Press	London	1989
Morris, Dickson G	Beyond the Irrawaddy and the Salween	Garden Vale	Victoria	1996
Morrison, Ian	Grandfather Longlegs	Faber and Faber	London	1947
Muller, Klaus-Jurgen	Deception and Military Operations, ed M Handel	Frank Cass	London	1987
Munthe, Malcolm	Sweet is War	Duckworth	London	1954
Nicolson, Nigel	Alex: The Life of Field Marshal Earl Alexander of Tunis	Weidenfield and Nicholson	London	1973
O'Brien, Terence	The Moonlight War – The story of Clandestine Operations in SE Asia, 1944-45	Collins	London	1987
O'Reilly, Charles T	Forgotten Battles: Italy's War of Liberation 1943-45	Lexington Books	Oxford	2001
Ogden, Alan	Tigers Burning Bright: SOE Heroes in the Far East	Bene Factum	London	2013
Orwell, George	Burmese Days	Harper & Bros	New York	1934
Pavlowitch, Stevan K	Tito	OSU	Ohio	1990
Pattinson, Juliette	Secret War – A Pictorial Record of SOE	Caxton	London	2001

Pawley, Margaret	In Obedience to Instructions	Leo Cooper	Barnsley	1999
Phillips, Lucas	Alamein	William Heinemann	London	1962
Pieri, Piero	Pietro Badoglio Maresciallo d'Italia	Utet	Torino	1974
Seaman, Mark	SOE – A new Instrument of War	Routledge	London	2006
Slim, William	Defeat into Victory: Battling Japan and India 1942-45	Cooper Square Press	London	2000
Smiley, David	Irregular Regular	Michael Russell	Norwich	1994
Smith, Dennis Mack	Mussolini a Biography	Knopf	New York	1982
Spencer, William	Air Force Records	Cromwell Press	Trowbridge	2008
Stafford, David	Mission Accomplished – SOE and Italy 1943-45	Vintage	London	2011
Stafford, David	Secret Agent – The True Story of SOE	BBC	London	2000
Stafford, David	*Camp X: Canada's School for Secret Agents*	Lester&Orpen Dennys	London	1986
Steinacher, G	Article on SOE in Austria, 1939-45, in Journal of Intelligence and Counter-Intelligence No 15	Routledge	Abingdon	2002
Sweet-Escott, Bickham	Baker Street Irregular	Methuen	London	1965
Sweet-Escott, Bickham	SOE in the Balkans	Barnes and Noble	London	1975
Tudor, M E	Special Force: SOE and the Italian Resistance 1943-45	Emilia	Newtown	2004
Turner, Des	Aston House Station 12 – SOE's Secret Centre	History Press	Stroud	2006
Walker, Godfrey	A Family of Fighting Men	Mercian Regiment Archive		1980
Williams, Heather	Parachutes, Patriots and Partisans – SOE & Yugoslavia 1941-45	C Hurst & Co	London	2003
Wylie, Neville	The Politics and Strategy of Clandestine War – SOE 1940-46	Routledge	London	2007

Glossary

"A" Force	Mediterranean deception unit
AA	Anti-Aircraft
ABWEHR	Military Intelligence of German General Staff
ACC	Allied Control Commission
ACSEA	Air Command South East Asia
AD	Armoured Division
ADC	Aide de Camp
AFHQ	Allied Forces Headquarters (Mediterranean – Algiers and later Caserta)
AFL	Australian Rules Football
AFO	Anti-Fascist Organisation (Burma)
AK	Armia Krajowa (Home Guard in Poland)
AL	Armia Ludowa (Peoples Army in Poland)
AL	Air Liaison section of SOE
ALFSEA	Allied Land Forces South East Asia
AMF	SOE operations operating into France from Algiers (Massingham)
ARP	Air Raid Precautions
AVNOJ	Antifasisticko Vijece Narodog Oslobodenja (Anti-Fascist Council for National Liberation of Yugoslavia)
BACSA	British Association for Cemeteries in South Asia
BAF	Balkan Air Force
BBC	British Broadcasting Corporation
BDA	Burma Defence Army
BLO	British Liaison Officer (SOE leader in the field)
C	Symbol to refer to Head of Secret Intelligence Service/MI6
CD	Symbol used to refer to Executive Director (ie not Chairman) of SOE
CGE	Czechoslovakian Government in Exile
CIGS	Chief of the Imperial General Staff
C-in-C	Commander-in-Chief

403

CLN	Committee of National Liberation (Resistance in mostly southern Italy)
CLNAI	Committee of National Liberation (Resistance in northern Italy)
CWGC	Commonwealth War Graves Commission
CMF	Central Mediterranean Force
D	"Deception". A sabotage unit within the SIS (MI6) and forerunner to SOE
E Force	A Far East unit whose role was to rescue escaped prisoners
EAM	Ethnikos Apeleftherotikos Metop (The Greek "National Liberation Front")
EDES	Ethnikos Dimokratikes Ellinikos Syndesmos (National Republican Greek League)
EKKA	Ethniki Kai Koinoniki Apeleftherotikos (The Greek "National and Social Liberation")
ELAS	Ellinikos Laikos Apeleftherotikos Stratos (Greek People's Liberation Army)
FANY	Field Ambulance Nursing Yeomanry or First Aid Nursing Yeomanry
FIC	French Indo China
FO	Foreign Office
GGE	Greek Government in Exile
GHQ	General Head Quarters
GSO	General Staff Officer
G(R)	MIR in Cairo
IS9	Intelligence School 9 (MI9 - Escapers)
ISLD	Inter-Service Liaison Department (cover name for SIS in Cairo)
ISRB	Inter Service Research Bureau (cover name for SOE)
ISSU	Inter-Service Signals Unit (cover name for SOE)
J	J was the Italian Section of SOE at Baker Street
KNU	Karen National Union, a political organisation representing Karen people
Levy	A military formation of local citizens in Burma, led by British officers
M	Head of SOE operations in London
MAAF	Mediterranean Allied Air Force

MEDC	Middle East Defence Committee
MEW	Ministry of Economic Warfare
ME 25	Jungle Warfare School in Ceylon
MiD	Mentioned in Despatches
MI(R)	Military Intelligence Research/Guerrilla Warfare unit of War Office
MI5	Military Intelligence section 5 (The British Security Service)
MI6	Military Intelligence section 6 (cover name for SIS/Secret Intelligence Service)
MI9	Military Intelligence section 9 (SIS escapers and evaders unit)
MOD	Ministry of Defence
MO4	Name for Section D to become SOE in Cairo/Force 133
MIA	Missing in Action
NDH	Nezavisna Drzava Hrvatska (Independent State of Croatia)
NID(Q)	Royal Navy code name for SOE
NKVD	Narodny Komissariat Vnutrennikh Del (People's Commissariat for Internal Affairs)
NSZ	Narodowe Siły Zbrojne (Anti-Fascist and Anti-Communist National Armed Forces in Poland)
OBE	Order of British Empire
OSS	Office of Strategic Services (of the United States of America)
P Division	Department of SACSEA co-ordinating secret organisations
PGE	Polish Government in Exile
PWB	Psychological Warfare Bureau/Branch
PWE	Political Warfare Executive
RAF	Royal Air Force (UK)
RAPWI	Relief of Allied Prisoners of War and Internees
RF	Name for SOE in France
RHN	Royal Hellenic Navy (Greece)
RSS	Radio Security Service
SAC	Supreme Allied Commander

SACSEA	Supreme Allied Command South-East Asia
SAS	Special Air Service (UK)
SEAC	South East Asia Command
SF	Sherwood Foresters (Nottinghamshire and Derbyshire)
SHAEF	Supreme Headquarters Allied Expeditionary Force (NW Europe)
SIM	Servizio Informazioni Militare – the Italian secret service
SIMCOL	Operations launched by Col Simonds to rescue escapees in Italy
SIS	Secret Intelligence Service (see also ISLD)
Sit Rep	Situation Report
SOA	Special Operations Australia
SOE	Special Operations Executive
SOM	Special Operations Mediterranean (also known as SO(M))
SO 1	Propaganda branch of SOE
SO 2	Operations branch of SOE
SO 3	Planning branch of SOE
STS	Special Training School (run by SOE)
TA	Territorial Army
US(A)	United States(of America)
USAAF	United States Army Air Force
V	Unit of SIS working on counter intelligence
WO	War Office
WOK	Work Out Key
W/T	Wireless Telegraphy
YGE	Yugoslav Government in Exile
Z	Symbol used by Sweet-Escott for C the head of MI6

Index

407

409

410

Printed in Great Britain
by Amazon